Improving Comprehension Instruction

Rethinking Research, Theory, and Classroom Practice

Cathy Collins Block

Linda B. Gambrell

Michael Pressley

Editors

JOSSEY-BASS
A Wiley Imprint
www.josseybass.com

KH

Published by Jossey-Bass
A Wiley Imprint
989 Market Street, San Francisco, CA 94103-1741   www.josseybass.com

INTERNATIONAL
Reading Association
800 BARKSDALE ROAD, PO BOX 8139
NEWARK, DE 19714-8139, USA
www.reading.org

When ordering through IRA, refer to this ISBN: 0-87207-458-7.

Jossey-Bass books and products are available through most bookstores. To contact Jossey-Bass directly call our Customer Care Department within the U.S. at 800-956-7739, outside the U.S. at 317-572-3993 or fax 317-572-4002.

Jossey-Bass also publishes its books in a variety of electronic formats. Some content that appears in print may not be available in electronic books.

Library of Congress Cataloging-in-Publication Data
Improving comprehension instruction : rethinking research, theory, and classroom practice /
Cathy Collins Block, Linda B. Gambrell, Michael Pressley, editors.
     p. cm.— (Jossey-Bass education series)
Includes bibliographical references and index.
   ISBN 0-7879-6309-7 (alk. paper)
   1. Reading comprehension. I. Block, Cathy Collins. II. Gambrell, Linda B.
III. Pressley, Michael, 1951– IV. Series.
   LB1050.45 .I47 2002
   372.47—dc21   2002011040

Printed in the United States of America

FIRST EDITION

HB Printing 10 9 8 7 6 5 4 3 2

11/22/04

Contents

Tables, Figures, and Exhibits

Chapter Five

Chapter Six

Chapter Seven

Chapter Eight

Foreword

Old-timers like to reminisce about the good old days. Their message always seems to be that things are worse today than they have ever been before. The current national debate about the state of reading instruction is much like that. There seems to be a belief that everything would be OK if we could just go back to the good old days.

Well, I'm an old-timer in reading. I've been teaching kids and teachers for almost fifty years. But take it from me—we do not want to go back to reading's so-called good old days. The usual old-timer's credo notwithstanding, we teach reading better today than ever before. This book is proof. Consider that the subtitle of this book indicates a rethinking of comprehension. But when I started teaching, we didn't think about comprehension, much less rethink it. In those days comprehension was a desirable outcome, but we had no real understanding of how it worked or how you taught it. We assumed comprehension was primarily a matter of intelligence: if your students were smart and could decode, they would comprehend. But you didn't teach it.

But four major movements have pushed us well beyond that point. First, starting in the 1960s, Ken Goodman, together with Yetta Goodman and their colleagues, established the primacy of meaning and the holistic nature of literacy. Then, in 1975 and subsequently, P. David Pearson and Richard Anderson and their colleagues at the Center for the Study of Reading at the University of Illinois used schema theory to bring instructional substance to what had formerly been an intangible notion of comprehension. In the 1980s Lee Shulman and Judith Lanier, with their research on teaching colleagues at Michigan State University and elsewhere, began unpeeling the classroom teaching onion, revealing that instruction involves layer after layer of complexity with multiple elements woven together in a variety of ways. Most recently, studies of exemplary teachers by Dick Allington, Mike Pressley, Barbara Taylor, and others have reaffirmed that classroom teaching of literacy is a multifaceted endeavor.

These movements resulted in both good news and bad news. On the one hand, we learned lots, which is good news. But on the other hand, we encountered the harsh reality that it is a giant step from raw knowledge to effective implementation in classrooms. We had lots of studies, lots of findings, and some exemplars. But translating all this into practice requires a resource that not only pulls together the available knowledge but does so in a way that guides teaching.

This book fills that void. Under a single cover, the threads from all four major influences have been woven together into a single resource emphasizing the teaching of comprehension. We are provided with coherent synopses of important research and theory, principles essential for understanding the nature and teaching of comprehension, numerous practical examples of how to teach comprehension in various instructional situations, suggestions for applying what we know to technology, and recommendations for continued professional growth. The editors, who are three of the best-known comprehension scholars in the world, orchestrated all this by assembling a cast of chapter authors who are themselves leaders representing various specialties ranging from research, to policy, to program development, to teacher education, to classroom practice.

The result is an important compendium of first-class information. It is a valuable instructional guide at a time when classroom teachers are under unprecedented pressure from the nationwide move to standard-based reform and high stakes testing. Rather than continuing the myth of the good old days of reading instruction, this book ensures that comprehension will become an integral part of the nation's literacy agenda.

In sum, this book is a comprehensive, coherent source of knowledge about teaching comprehension. Scholars, teacher educators, and classroom teachers alike will find it to be a fundamental reference as we continue improving reading instruction in the years ahead.

Gerald G. Duffy
Professor Emeritus, Michigan State University

Preface

For some people, comprehending seems to develop automatically. As many other adults and children are painfully aware, however, learning how to comprehend involves negotiating so many cognitive, metacognitive, and affective processes that they simply avoid complicated texts and contexts. These readers do not understand due to ineffective prior instruction, limited background knowledge, weak decoding skills, and negative self-concepts. The purpose of this book is to enable all students, from preschool to adulthood, to fully comprehend the information they read, hear, and view. No book could address a more crucial ability for the advancement of humanity. To date, few books have focused as directly on research-based instruction of complex comprehension processes.

Why is comprehension such an important issue today? In 1974 many educators argued that students should not be taught comprehension lessons. Even as recently as 1998, many students left primary and secondary schools having experienced very little training in cognition and metacognition and very little teaching of how to process text independently. Most so-called comprehension lessons consisted merely of a teacher's direct questions about material that students were supposed to have comprehended. Educators did not explain, model, or demonstrate how to understand.

What are the reasons for this absence? Learning to teach comprehension is one of an educator's greatest challenges. Building students' comprehension abilities also requires much instruction before students demonstrate independence in understanding. Moreover, some practitioners do not feel comfortable responding to the varied interpretations that students often express during highly effective comprehension lessons. Because classes of the past spent only a few minutes a week in true comprehension process instruction, past generations received little or no training in how to improve their comprehension. As a result, many of today's educators plan comprehension lessons with limited pedagogical knowledge. Many students possess false assumptions about what it means to comprehend. They were not taught with the lessons in this book. They were not taught how to unite complex cognitions and metacognitions. Fortunately, this book addresses these deficits.

Since 1990, we have learned more about the teaching of comprehension than at any point in history. Numerous research investigations reported herein have engaged diverse populations in innovative methods that build highly advanced levels of independent comprehension. They have yielded positive and consistent results relative to the efficacy of teaching. Although a few teachers, researchers, and teacher preparation programs are discovering some of the research and pedagogical practices contained in *Improving Comprehension Instruction,* no book has combined all of these recent innovations in a single volume.

What is new in this book? The rethinking of research, theory, and classroom practices portrayed here demonstrates the gains in knowledge that have occurred since the early 1970s. Because of today's standards-driven climate, with its special attention on closing the achievement gap, we are experiencing an ever-increasing plea for improved research-based techniques to teach comprehension. The innovative practices and advancements in this book respond to these demands. For example, chapters report numerous improvements taken within the last five years to ensure that all readers can

- Connect relevant prior knowledge to what they read
- Select valid thinking processes
- Construct mental images
- Question
- Infer
- Summarize
- Monitor whether or not they are understanding
- Eliminate confusions

One of this book's objectives is to address the challenges to comprehension instruction that the Department of Education's Office of Educational Research and Improvement, RAND Reading Study Group, and the National Reading Panel identified. These groups set a framework of research in reading comprehension and stimulated major conversations about increasing understanding in language arts, content disciplines, struggling readers, and technologically based texts. This book is the first to test the newest research in the classroom, work environment, and clinical settings. At the same time, chapters identify immediate actions that educators can take to move us further still.

This book is the first to provide practitioners and academicians with specific and highly effective approaches to teaching comprehension, rather than just testing or interrogating students to determine their comprehension. The chapters demonstrate methods and research applications that deepen the pleasures and profits that readers—from preschoolers to adults—gain from understanding. It explores additional issues that scholars have not heretofore discussed in a scientific context. Chapter authors address (1) approaches to teaching networked cognitive processes, (2) schoolwide initiatives that significantly advance comprehension, and (3) methods of assisting students to understand the multiple temporal, personal, social, cultural, motivational, cognitive, and metacognitive strengths that they can bring to any comprehension task. In addition, the majority of chapters in this book include lesson adaptations that significantly increase the comprehension of students who come from less advantaged literate backgrounds or limited English language environments.

Why did we assemble this book? Reading comprehension is an urgent national priority whose time has come! No other body of knowledge is the foundation for all content knowledge. Researchers in this book recommend daily interventions that empower students to enjoy and fully engage in a wide variety of text and hypertext content. This book consists of an introduction, seventeen chapters, and a concluding discussion. For the reader's convenience, we have divided these discussions into four parts:

Part One   New Directions in Comprehension Instruction
Part Two   New Comprehension Lessons Across
              the Curriculum
Part Three   Integrating Technology and Innovative
              Instruction
Part Four   Overcoming Comprehension Challenges

Each chapter analyzes in depth one facet of comprehension instruction, how it occurs in a specific content area, context, or population of readers. Chapters introduce a segment of reading comprehension, briefly chronicle the research that led to an instructional innovation, and conclude with specific lessons in how to teach students to understand what they read. Our readers will discover the ever-mounting body of knowledge that supports the highly effective teaching of comprehension. Researchers, classroom teachers, reading specialists, and central administrators should find this volume a valuable resource in their professional libraries.

This body of knowledge includes the following themes:

Highly effective comprehension instruction includes ample reading and rich experiences with fiction, nonfiction, and technologically centered texts.

Teachers can effectively teach their students more than thirty cognitive and metacognitive processes that build comprehension power.

At least fourteen published programs are available to teach comprehension.

Highly effective instruction must include modeling, scaffolding, opportunities to practice comprehension independently, and a time for students to tell teachers what they need and want to learn to comprehend better.

Highly effective assessment should include an evaluation of students' internalized self-regulation of comprehension processes.

Students can more quickly apply what they understand when teacher-student interactions include collaborative talk, teacher-reader groups (in which students teach comprehension processes), and student-led "think alouds."

Students cannot easily transfer processes to new content without direct instruction.

Who should read this book? In addition to practitioners and academicians, literacy and media specialists, content educators and researchers, educators in many pedagogical disciplines will gain from the information in *Improving Comprehension Instruction.* Its content contains multiple applications to broader issues of teaching and learning and to contemporary literacy concerns. It addresses the differences between comprehending, or taking in, and deeply understanding the applications and significance of bodies of knowledge. Teachers can teach students to engage more thinking processes as they read. It will enable educators and researchers to describe the comprehension process.

This book differs from other scholarly texts on several counts. First, it includes innovative research-based instructional lessons that reconfigure traditional approaches. Second, it provides an extensive presentation of alternative methods for addressing the needs of less advanced students and multicultural populations. Third, it truly shows how to teach comprehension as processes that contain many interrelated components. Fourth, it helps students use comprehension processes automatically and habitually, and it portrays adaptations that address the needs of special students. Fifth, it demonstrates how we can provide more time during class periods for comprehension instruction across content domains.

This book was truly a collaborative venture. When planning it, we discussed its content with numerous colleagues throughout the country. These individuals included researchers within and outside of the literacy community as well as educators from elementary schools, secondary schools, and universities. Many people assisted in the development of this book, and to each we extend our heartfelt thanks.

We extend our deepest appreciation to the chapter authors for the significant portion of time that they took from their busy lives to contribute to this collection.

Finally, we close with a personal message to the reader. The editing of this volume was truly a labor of love. Sharing in the contributions that authors have made to our body of knowledge was a real joy. Although some chapters may at first glance hold more interest for you than others, we would urge you to read all of them. The content of the entire book can provide you with a gestalt of the wide-ranging and complex courses of action that compose highly effective comprehension instruction.

It was our pleasure to serve as volume editors. Our goal will be realized when your abilities increase so that you can implement the highest-quality instruction. We hope you will gain as much enjoyment from reading this book as we experienced while editing it.

Cathy Collins Block, Texas Christian University
Linda B. Gambrell, Clemson University
Michael Pressley, University of Notre Dame
July 2002

The Editors

CATHY COLLINS BLOCK has served on the graduate faculty of Texas Christian University since 1977. A member of the national faculty of the University of Notre Dame, she has taught at Southern Illinois University–Carbondale, served as research assistant at the Wisconsin Research and Development Center for Cognitive Development, and taught kindergarten through high school in private and public schools. Dr. Block has directed and served as principal investigator of six nationally funded research projects and has served or is serving on the board of directors for organizations including the International Reading Association, the National Center for Research and Training for Learning Disabilities, and the National Reading Conference.

LINDA B. GAMBRELL is the director of the Division of Education at Clemson University. She has coauthored books on reading instruction and written numerous articles published in journals such as *Educational Psychologist, Journal of Educational Research, Reading Research Quarterly,* and *Reading Teacher.* As a principal investigator at the national Reading Research Center, Dr. Gambrell directed the Literacy Motivation Project. She has served on the board of directors of the International Reading Association and the National Reading Conference. In 1998 she received the International Reading Association's Outstanding Teacher Educator in Reading Award. She has also served as the president of the National Reading Conference and the College Reading Association.

MICHAEL PRESSLEY is the Notre Dame chair in Catholic education and professor of psychology at the University of Notre Dame. He is an expert in comprehension processing and in primary-level reading education, which is related to his career-long research on children's learning. He has published about 250 articles, chapters, and books. His most recent research involves exploration of how to motivate literacy in classrooms.

The Contributors

Janice F. Almasi, Associate Professor of Education, Department of Curriculum and Instruction, The State University of New York, Buffalo

Thomas W. Bean, Professor of Reading/Literacy, University of Nevada, Las Vegas, NV

Kay Camperell, Associate Professor of Secondary and Elementary Education, Utah State University, Logan, UT

Cheryl A. Cress, Teacher, Benchmark School, Media, PA

Bridget Dalton, Director of CAST, Peabody, MA

Pamela J. Dunston, Professor, Department of Curriculum & Instruction, College of Health, Education and Human Development, Clemson University, Clemson, SC

Douglas Fisher, Associate Professor, School of Teacher Education, San Diego State University, San Diego, CA

James Flood, Professor, School of Teacher Education, San Diego State University, San Diego, CA

Irene W. Gaskins, Director of Benchmark School, Media, PA

Douglas K. Hartman, Associate Professor, Department of Language and Literature, University of Pittsburgh, Pittsburgh, PA

Kathy N. Headley, Professor and Coordinator, Reading Education, Clemson University, Clemson, SC

Bena R. Hefflin, Professor, Department of Instruction and Learning, University of Pittsburgh, Pittsburgh, PA

Rebecca B. Johnson, Elementary Teacher, Fort Worth, TX

Jean Keeler, Reading Specialist, Mountain View Elementary, Pendelton, SC

Ellin Oliver Keene, Adjunct Professor, Pennsylvania State University, School of Education at University Park, CA

Linda D. Labbo, Professor of Reading, Department of Reading, University of Georgia, Athens, GA

Sally R. Laird, Teacher, Benchmark School, Media, PA

Diane Lapp, Professor of Education, San Diego State University, San Diego, CA

Colleen O'Hara, Teacher, Benchmark School, Media, PA

Chris L. Peters, Associate Professor of Education, Clemson University, Clemson, SC

Gay Su Pinnell, Professor, School of Teaching and Learning, Ohio State University, Columbus

D. Ray Reutzel, Professor and Director of Eccles Jones Center for Early Childhood Education, Utah State University, Logan, UT

Victoria Gentry Ridgeway, Professor, School of Education, Clemson University, Clemson, SC

Lynn Romeo, Associate Professor, School of Education, Monmouth University, NJ

David Rose, Professor of Education, Harvard University, and Co-Executive Director of CAST, Peabody, MA

Theresa Scott, Teacher, Benchmark School, Media, PA

John A. Smith, Associate Professor, School of Education, Utah State University, Logan, UT

Catherine Snow, Professor, Harvard Graduate School of Education, Cambridge, MA

Lisa Patel Stevens, Assistant Professor of Language and Literacy, School of Education, University of Hawaii, Honolulu

Anne P. Sweet, Scholar-in-Residence at RAND, and Senior Researcher, U.S. Department of Education

Terrell Seawell Tracy, Professor of Education, Governor's Institute of Reading, South Carolina Department of Education

Karen D. Wood, Professor of Education, University of North Carolina, Charlotte, NC

Part One

New Directions in Comprehension Instruction

Introduction

Improving Comprehension Instruction: An Urgent Priority

Linda B. Gambrell,
Cathy Collins Block,
and Michael Pressley

The message is clear—the most important thing about reading is comprehension. We also know much more about how to prevent reading comprehension failure. We introduce this book by defining reading comprehension, briefly chronicling the development of the knowledge base related to comprehension development, describing recent theoretical and research findings relevant to effective reading comprehension instruction, and making suggestions for the future of reading comprehension instruction. In doing so, we hope that classroom teachers, reading specialists, and reading researchers will gain a comprehensive picture of meaning-enhanced literacy instruction for preschool, elementary, middle, and high school students so that all children fulfill their potential to become good readers.

What is a good reader? We can draw some insights about what constitutes a good reader from the work of the National Assessment of Educational Progress (NAEP). NAEP is a large-scale assessment and survey of fourth, eighth, and twelfth grades from across the United States. For over three decades, NAEP has provided educators and policymakers with information about the status of student reading performance and the factors associated with achievement. The NAEP results include not only students' scores on the reading assessment but also information regarding the background and instructional experience of students.

The publication *Reading Framework for the National Assessment of Educational Progress: 1992–1998* (1998) and the report of the RAND Reading Study Group (2001) identified several important characteristics that distinguish good readers from less proficient readers.

1. Good readers have positive habits and attitudes about reading.
2. Good readers are fluent enough to focus on the meaning of what they read.
3. Good readers use what they know to understand what they read.
4. Good readers form an understanding of what they read by extending, elaborating, and critically evaluating the meaning of the text.
5. Good readers use a variety of effective strategies to enhance and monitor their understanding of text.
6. Good readers can read a variety of texts and can read for a variety of purposes (NAEP, 1998, p. 9).

It is interesting to note that all six characteristics of good readers that NAEP identified are directly related to comprehension. Four years later the RAND Reading Study Group (2001) verified and amplified this message. Throughout the chapters of this book, the research base related to these characteristics is applied to classroom settings to provide insights and recommendations for improving comprehension instruction for all students.

Looking to the future, the RAND Reading Study Group (2001) recently formulated a proposal concerning the research that most urgently needs to be conducted over the next ten to fifteen years. The primary agenda of the RAND report is the promotion of skillful reading or reading with good comprehension. The primary message is that we need to increase our knowledge base concerning reading comprehension instruction.

What Is Reading Comprehension?

In this volume we define *reading comprehension* as acquiring meaning from written text—with *text* being defined as a range of material from traditional books to the computer screen. In this meaning-making process, the reader interacts with the print and is involved in making sense of the message. Readers comprehend text by acquiring meaning, confirming meaning, and creating meaning. In sum, reading comprehension is the process of meaning making.

For many students, good reading comprehension comes easily. For many others, it is a difficult and often confusing process. Teaching students to become better comprehenders is also a difficult and challenging task because reading is such a complex process. We know that students who are good comprehenders use specific strategies, become deeply engaged in what they are reading, monitor and evaluate what they are reading, and are able to apply what they read to their own lives.

Reading comprehension is an interactive process involving the reader, the text, and the context. This relationship is an ever-changing one. During the reading process, the reader may attend to the text-based information. At other times the reader may relate to the text in terms of his or her own experiences; as Pearson has so aptly put it, "we reach out to the text, grabbing whatever meaning we can before the text has a chance to fully assert its own" (Pearson, 2001, p. 79). In the first case the text dominates, while in the second the reader dominates. In both instances the social context influences what one reads, how one reads, and why one reads. That is, on different occasions, the comprehending reader may come away from a text with a very different understanding, sometimes reflecting more literally the text, sometimes filled with reader interpretations, and sometimes strongly biased by the surrounding social environment (for example, an unfavorable reading of a review of the movie version of *Lord of the Rings* while sitting in a class on Tolkien's writing).

Tracing the Development of Reading Instruction

When we trace the development of contemporary understandings of reading instruction from the nineteenth century, we witness a shift at the end of the century away from a predominant emphasis on decoding and recitation. During the first fifty years of the twentieth century, researchers and practitioners agreed that comprehension was the ultimate goal of reading and that instruction needed to engage students more deeply in the meaning-making process. Educators invented a number of different approaches to foster reader comprehension development. The most prevalent, the directed-reading activity, was developed by E. A. Betts in 1946 and soon became the almost universal means of comprehension instruction in U.S. schools. In addition, from the 1950s to the 1980s, the use of literal-level questions to develop students' understanding of text prevailed in basal manuals and elementary classroom reading instruction. During this era *reading* was implicitly defined as the ability to recall structural elements of a story and the ability to answer questions following reading. Approximately 70 percent of the questions that teachers asked students during reading instruction called for literal-level responses (Durkin, 1978–1979; Guszak, 1967).

Since the early 1980s, researchers and teachers have worked to extend this definition and expand the student's repertoire of comprehension skills. For example, in the late 1980s the National Assessment of Educational Progress (Applebee, Langer, & Mullis, 1987) suggested that reading instruction needed to emphasize thinking skills and strategies that provide the foundation for higher-level interpretative and reasoning abilities. Interest in comprehension instruction, or the lack thereof, increased during the 1980s. This interest was sparked to a large extent by the classic Durkin study (1978–1979), "What Classroom Observations Reveal About Reading Comprehension Instruction." Durkin observed that very little comprehension instruction was taking place in elementary classrooms and that teachers primarily "mentioned" or "assessed" comprehension, as opposed to teaching students to independently use strategies for enhancing comprehension. Following Durkin's study, reading researchers began to focus on comprehension-strategy instruction that resulted in increasing students' understanding of text. They made many studies of imagery, self-questioning, and summarization, in part stimulated by the awareness that little comprehension instruction was occurring in schools but that there were cognitive processes associated with greater understanding of text. Cognitive psychologists, in particular, felt that if child readers could only be taught to carry out the processes that good readers use on their own, reading comprehension would improve. That comprehension did improve when children learned to execute strategies like imagery, self-questioning, and summarization provided some validation for this perspective (Pressley, 2000).

The Priorities of Meaning-Enhanced Comprehension Instruction

Skilled comprehenders come to the reading process with rich exposure to literacy, well-developed oral language ability, well-developed world knowledge, competence in social interactions with others about text, efficient word identification skills, and effective comprehension strategies. Lack of attention to any of these factors will increase the likelihood that reading comprehension development will be impeded (Pressley, 2000). Thus, research on comprehension instruction broadened, including studies of vocabulary instruction, teaching or comprehension strategies in small groups, and enrichment of world knowledge to improve comprehension. Currently, research is emphasizing that in order to increase comprehension, educators must develop a motivational context for reading, provide interesting and appropriate texts, and teach research-based comprehension strategies. That is why these broad themes emerge throughout the chapters in this book.

Creating a Motivational Context for Comprehension Instruction

Motivation to read plays a crucial role in the development of comprehension skills (Gambrell, 2001). An important goal of reading instruction is to foster an intrinsic desire to read. Effective comprehenders must possess both the skill and the will to read, yet evidence suggests that as grade level increases, children tend to have less positive attitudes toward reading (McKenna, Ellsworth, & Kear, 1995; Mazzoni, Gambrell, & Korkeamaki, 2000). A robust finding in the motivation research is that students in kindergarten are the most motivated and those in high school the least motivated (Eccles & Midgley, 1989; Harter, 1990).

Not surprisingly, motivation and achievement are linked (Dweck, 1986; Elley, 1992; Flippo, 1998; Morrow & Gambrell, 1998; Guthrie et al., 1996). Why? As individuals read more, they read better and learn more about the world. The result is better comprehension—better achievement (Anderson, Wilson, & Fielding, 1988; Morrow, 1992; Taylor, Frye, & Maruyama, 1990).

Effective comprehension instruction increases students' motivation to read in several ways (Block & Pressley, 2001). Comprehension instruction can support the development of motivated readers by rewarding improvement and emphasizing effort.

Rewarding Improvement

Researchers have found that classroom competition reduces student motivation rather than increasing it (Ames, 1984; Nicholls, 1989). Particularly for struggling learners, competition undermines motivation: these students, who are not winners in competitions, typically give up. On the other hand, even proficient learners can suffer reduced motivation in competitive endeavors because it may take relatively little effort for these students to win.

Educators can structure comprehension instruction around recognizing and rewarding improvement in performance. When instruction centers on the goal of getting better versus the goal of doing better than others, students are more likely to attempt to understand at a deep level what they are reading (Nolen, 1988; Pressley, 2000).

Emphasizing Effort

Research supports the notion that academic motivation is undermined when students attribute success and failure to ability (Weiner, 1979). Less proficient learners often attribute failure to "being stupid" or if they are successful, to "luck." These attributions play a significant role in undermining motivation to learn. If students believe that ability explains achievement, then they are less likely to exert effort to learn. If, however, the student sees that success is related to effort, then there is an increased probability that the student will exert greater effort to learn (Carr & Borkowski, 1989; Deshler & Schumaker, 1988).

Educators can design comprehension instruction to reward student effort. Teaching students to recognize that effort pays off can positively influence their motivation to learn. Furthermore, instruction that supports students in recognizing the role of effort in learning is especially effective if combined with comprehension strategy instruction (Borkowski, Carr, Rellinger, & Pressley, 1990; Carr & Borkowski, 1989; Deshler & Schumaker, 1988).

Providing Interesting and Appropriate
Texts for Comprehension Instruction

Students are more motivated to sustain their engagement in reading when they find interesting and appropriate texts readily available (Gambrell, Wilson, & Gantt, 1981). The availability of interesting and appropriate texts increases the time spent reading and related literacy behaviors (Morrow, 1992; Morrow & Sharkey, 1993). During in-depth interviews with elementary-age students, Palmer, Codling, and Gambrell (1994) were able to identify a number of factors related to reading engagement. During these interviews students reported the positive influence of prior experiences with books and the role of choice. Students talked about how experiences such as hearing a peer talk about a book and hearing the teacher read a book aloud motivated them to read. In addition, these students reported that they were more motivated to read books they chose to read for themselves rather than books that teachers assigned to them.

The availability of interesting and appropriate narrative and informational text is a critical factor in comprehension. Beyond having a chance to read such texts, students need to develop strategies for comprehending both narrative and informational text. In fact, students of all ages, from elementary to high school, have difficulty comprehending the structure of informational text (McGee, 1982; Meyer, Brandt, & Bluth, 1980; Taylor, 1980). In the past young children have lacked sufficient exposure to informational text, which may account for the difficulties that child readers have when they do have to deal with expository materials. Given the dominance of narrative text in the early elementary grades (Duke, 2000), we cannot assume that students can or will transfer their ability to read narrative to the reading of informational text. Duke cautions that we should not, however, pit narrative against informational text, as such an approach would be self-defeating. Rather, we should balance instructional texts so that our students develop comprehension strategies that are effective and appropriate for high-level understanding of both genres.

Comprehension of informational text is becoming increasingly important in this century. Another important reason for increasing elementary students' exposure to informational text is that these texts can serve as a catalyst for literacy motivation. Some students are very interested in the topics that informational texts present. These nonfiction texts can capitalize on students' interests in these topics and can nurture motivation to read. Some kids like facts more than stories!

Teaching Research-Based Comprehension Strategies

Although the development of competent comprehenders requires much more than strategy instruction, researchers have identified many strategies that educators can teach readers in order to increase understanding and memory of texts. One of the goals of this book is to demonstrate how we can teach students a repertoire of comprehension strategies that they can apply at critical points during text reading (Anderson, 1992; Brown, Pressley, Van Meter, & Schuder, 1996; Collins, 1991). Providing comprehension-strategy instruction empowers readers to independently increase their understanding of text.

Among the first researchers to focus on teaching students a repertoire of comprehension strategies were Palincsar and Brown (1984). Their work on reciprocal teaching involved teaching groups of students to predict, question, clarify, and summarize. Instruction in reciprocal teaching included teacher modeling and explanation with eventual transfer to students who then would assume the role of leading the reading group in the use of the strategies. Reciprocal teaching resulted in positive effects on students' reading comprehension and independent application of strategies. Building on this work, Duffy and his associates (1987) proposed that strategy instruction should begin with direct explanation and modeling of strategies for students.

Pressley and his colleagues (1992) explored strategy instruction in three school settings that built on the work of Palincsar and Brown (1984) and Duffy and associates (1987). The features of instruction that Pressley and his colleagues (1992) identified in classrooms where effective strategy instruction was occurring included the following:

- Teachers taught students a small repertoire of comprehension strategies.
- They instructed students in how to use the strategies.
- Students practiced the strategies.

- Students modeled and explained strategy use for one another.
- Teachers conveyed to students information about when and where to use strategies.
- Teachers often used strategy vocabulary (clarification, summaries, and so on).
- Flexibility in students' use of strategies was apparent.
- Teachers continually sent the message that student thinking mattered.

Because the teachers in these classrooms responded to student needs for instruction, Pressley and his colleagues (1992) referred to this type of teaching as transactional strategies instruction. Qualitative and quantitative studies have documented the positive effects that teaching students transactional strategies can have on their comprehension competence (Anderson, 1992; Anderson & Roit, 1993; Brown, Pressley, Van Meter, & Schuder, 1996).

Block (1993) conducted a study with elementary-age children that focused on instruction designed to increase students' strategic knowledge and comprehension. Comprehension strategies that students learned included clarifying ideas, summarizing, making inferences, interpreting, evaluating, solving problems, and thinking creatively. Researchers randomly assigned classrooms of students to experimental or control treatment groups. In the comprehension-strategy instruction group, students participated in lessons twice weekly for thirty-two weeks. The lessons were conducted in two parts: (1) the teacher explained and modeled a thinking and reading comprehension strategy (for example, predicting, summarizing), and (2) the students selected literature and applied the strategy to it. In the control group, students received traditional instruction that did not emphasize these comprehension strategies. The comprehension-strategy instruction group outperformed the control group on the reading comprehension, vocabulary, and total battery sections of the Iowa Test of Basic Skills. Students in the comprehension-strategy instruction group also outperformed control students in the ability to transfer cognitive strategies to applications outside school and to measures of self-esteem and critical and creative thinking.

Next, Dole, Brown, and Trathen (1996) investigated the effects of strategy instruction on the comprehension performance of at-risk fifth- and sixth-graders. Researchers randomly assigned the students to one of three treatment conditions: strategy instruction, story content instruction, and basal control instruction. Immediate posttest and seven-week delayed posttest data revealed that the comprehension strategy group performed as well as the story content and basal control groups when students read texts after receiving instruction. However, the strategy group outperformed the other two groups when students were asked to read selections independently.

Subsequently, Baumann and Ivey (1997) conducted a qualitative study that explored what students learned about reading, writing, and literature in a program of strategy instruction integrated within a literature-based classroom environment. During the year-long study, Baumann was the full-time classroom teacher, and Ivey was a participant-observer in the classroom. Data sources included both researchers' personal journals; interviews with individual students, parents, and caregivers; videotapes of regular classroom literacy activities; and the teacher's daily plan book. A content analysis of the data sources revealed that students grew in overall reading performance and came to view reading as a natural component of the school experience. Most notably, students demonstrated high levels of engagement with books and developed skill in word identification, fluency, and comprehension, as well as written-comprehension abilities. Immersion in literature with ongoing strategy instruction enhanced students' reading and writing abilities.

In summary, both qualitative and quantitative studies provide evidence that teaching comprehension strategies based on reading research benefits and increases students' comprehension. Across these studies, strategy instruction increased students' willingness to read difficult material, discover meaning in text, and react to and elaborate on text meaning.

Summary

Learning to read with good comprehension is an enormously complex task. Since the 1970s, researchers have made much progress in understanding the components of reading comprehension and the role that instruction plays in helping students acquire strong comprehension skills. Good comprehension is more than understanding at the word, phrase, or sentence level, as thirty-nine researchers report in the recently published text *Comprehension*

Instruction: Research-Based Best Practices (Block & Pressley, 2001). According to all prior work, as Pressley (2000) succinctly stated, effective comprehension instruction enables students to also understand the gist—the big ideas in the text.

In this book the chapter authors propose specific methods by which to develop students' motivation, their repertoire of comprehension strategies, and their independent meaning-making abilities. They also provide substantial evidence that comprehension instruction makes a difference. Students can learn to comprehend at higher levels—to efficiently and independently use comprehension strategies such as predicting, questioning, mental imagining, and summarizing. During the 1980s and 1990s, researchers' quest to identify comprehension instruction that made a difference was a great adventure. We also believe that great adventures still lie ahead. Each chapter of this book concludes with a section on recommendations for comprehension instruction in the future.

There is still much to do, and much that we need to know, in order to assure that all students become competent comprehenders. We welcome you to our book. We want our book to assist you to become a catalyst so that every student becomes a good comprehender who is able to read with joy, ease, and rich understanding. We want this book to assist you in developing new research programs and instructional methods that empower all readers to gain meaning from the newly evolving technologically driven and text based resources of the future. The great adventure continues!

References

Ames, C. (1984). Competitive, cooperative, and individualistic goal structures: A motivational analysis. In R. Ames & C. Ames (Eds.), *Research on motivation in education* (Vol. 1, pp. 117–207). Orlando, FL: Academic Press.

Anderson, V. (1992). A teacher development project in transactional strategy instruction for teachers of severely reading-disabled adolescents. *Teaching and Teacher Education, 8,* 391–403.

Anderson, V., & Roit, M. (1993). Planning and implementing collaborative strategy instruction for delayed readers in grades 6–10. *Elementary School Journal, 94,* 121–137.

Anderson, R. C., Wilson, P. T., & Fielding, L. G. (1988). Growth in reading and how children spend their time outside of school. *Reading Research Quarterly, 23,* 285–303.

Applebee, A., Langer, J., & Mullis, I. V. (1987). *Learning to be literate in America: Reading, writing, and reasoning.* National Assessment of Educational Progress. Princeton, NJ: Educational Testing Service.

Baumann, J. F., & Ivey, G. (1997). Delicate balances: Striving for curricular and instructional equilibrium in a second-grade, literature/strategy-based classroom. *Reading Research Quarterly, 32,* 244–275.

Betts, E. A. (1946). Foundations of reading instruction. New York: American Book.

Block, C. C. (1993). Strategy instruction in a literature-based reading program. *Elementary School Journal, 94,* 139–151.

Block, C. C., & Pressley, M. (2001). *Comprehension instruction: Research-based best practices.* New York: Guilford Press.

Borkowski, J. G., Carr, M., Rellinger, E. A., & Pressley, M. (1990). Self-regulated strategy use: Interdependence of metacognition, attributions, and self-esteem. In B. F. Jones (Ed.), *Dimensions of thinking: Review of research* (pp. 53–92). Hillsdale, NJ: Erlbaum.

Brown, R., Pressley, M., Van Meter, P., & Schuder, T. (1996). A quasi-experimental validation of transactional strategies instruction with low-achieving second-grade readers. *Journal of Educational Psychology, 88,* 18–37.

Carr, M., & Borkowski, J. G. (1989). Attributional training and the generalization of reading strategies with underachieving children. *Learning and Individual Differences, 1,* 327–341.

Collins, C. (1991). Reading instruction that increases thinking abilities. *Journal of Reading, 34,* 510–516.

Deshler, D. D., & Schumaker, J. B. (1988). An instructional model for teaching students how to learn. In J. L. Graden, J. E. Zins, & M. J. Curtise (Eds.), *Alternative educational delivery systems: Enhancing instructional options for all students* (pp. 391–411). Washington, DC: National Association of School Psychologists.

Dole, J. A., Brown, K. J., & Trathen, W. (1996). The effects of strategy instruction on the comprehension performance of at-risk students. *Reading Research Quarterly, 31,* 62–88.

Duke, N. (2000). 3.6 minutes per day: The scarcity of informational texts in first grade. *Reading Research Quarterly, 35,* 202–224.

Duffy, G. G., Roehler, L. R., Sivan, E., Rackliffe, G., Book, C., Meloth, M., Vavrus, L. G., Wesselman, R., Putnam, J., & Bassiri, D. (1987). Effects of explaining the reasoning associated with using reading strategies. *Reading Research Quarterly, 22,* 347–368.

Durkin, D. (1978–1979). What classroom observations reveal about reading comprehension instruction. *Reading Research Quarterly, 14,* 481–533.

Dweck, C. S. (1986). Motivational processes affecting learning. *American Psychologist, 41,* 1040–1048.

Eccles, J. S., & Midgley, C. (1989). Stage/environment fit: Developmentally appropriate classrooms for early adolescents. In R. E. Ames (Ed.), *Research on motivation in education* (Vol. 3, pp. 139–186). Orlando, FL: Academic Press.

Elley, W. B. (1992). *How in the world do students read?* Hamburg, Germany: International Association for the Evaluation of Educational Achievement.

Flippo, R. F. (1998). Points of agreement: A display of professional unity in our field. *Reading Teacher, 52,* 30–40.

Gambrell, L. B. (2001). What we know about motivation to read. In R. F. Flippo (Ed.), *Reading researchers in search of common ground* (pp. 129–143). Newark, DE: International Reading Association.

Gambrell, L. B., Wilson, R. M., & Gantt, W. N. (1981). Classroom observations of task-attending behaviors of good and poor readers. *Journal of Educational Research, 74,* 400–404.

Guszak, F. J. (1967). *Reading comprehension development as viewed from the standpoint of teacher questioning strategies.* (ERIC Document Reproduction Service No. ED 010 984)

Guthrie, J. T., Van Meter, P., McCann, A. D., Wigfield, A., Bennett, L., Poundstone, C. C., Rice, M. F., Faibisch, F. M., Hunt, B., & Mitchell, A. M. (1996). Growth of literacy engagement: Changes in motivations and strategies during concept-oriented reading instruction. *Reading Research Quarterly, 31,* 306–332.

Harter, S. (1990). Cause, correlates, and the functional role of self worth: A life-span perspective. In R. J. Sternberg & J. Kolligian (Eds.), *Competence considered* (pp. 67–97). New Haven, CT: Yale University Press.

Mazzoni, S. A., Gambrell, L. B., & Korkeamaki, R. (2000). A cross-cultural perspective on early literacy motivation. *Reading Psychology, 20,* 237–253.

McGee, L. (1982). Awareness of text structure: Effects on children's recall of expository text. *Reading Research Quarterly, 17,* 581–589.

McKenna, M. C., Ellsworth, R. A., & Kear, D. J. (1995). Children's attitudes toward reading: A national survey. *Reading Research Quarterly, 30,* 934–956.

Meyer, B.J.F., Brandt, D. M., & Bluth, G. J. (1980). Use of top-level structure in text: Key for reading comprehension of ninth-grade student. *Reading Research Quarterly, 16,* 72–103.

Morrow, L. M. (1992). The impact of a literature-based program on literacy achievement, use of literature, and attitudes of children from minority backgrounds. *Reading Research Quarterly, 27,* 251–275.

Morrow, L. M., & Gambrell, L. B. (1998). How do we motivate children toward independent reading and writing? In S. Neuman & K. Roskos (Eds.), *Children achieving: Best practices in early literacy* (pp. 144–161). Newark, DE: International Reading Association.

Morrow, L. M., & Sharkey, E. A. (1993). Motivating independent reading and writing in the primary grades through social cooperative literacy experiences. *Reading Teacher, 47,* 162–164.

National Assessment of Educational Progress (NAEP). (1998). *Reading framework for the National Assessment of Educational Progress: 1992–1998.* Washington, DC: U.S. Department of Education, Office of Educational Research and Improvement.

Nicholls, J. G. (1989). *The competitive ethos and democratic education.* Cambridge, MA: Harvard University Press.

Nolen, S. E. (1988). Reasons for studying: Motivational orientations and study strategies. *Cognition and Instruction, 5,* 269–287.

Palincsar, A. S., & Brown, A. L. (1984). Reciprocal teaching of comprehension-fostering and comprehension-monitoring activities. *Cognition and Instruction, 1,* 117–175.

Palmer, B. M., Codling, R. M., & Gambrell, L. B. (1994). In their own words: What elementary children have to say about motivation to read. *Reading Teacher, 48,* 176–179.

Pearson, P. D. (2001). Life in the radical middle: A personal apology for a balanced view of reading. In R. Flippo (Ed.), *Reading researchers in search of common ground* (pp. 78–83). Newark, DE: International Reading Association.

Pressley, M. (2000). What should comprehension instruction be the instruction of? In M. Kamil, P. Mosenthal, P. D. Pearson, & R. Barr (Eds.), *Handbook of reading research* (Vol. 3, pp. 545–562). Hillsdale, NJ: Erlbaum.

Pressley, M., El-Dinary, P. B., Gaskins, I., Schuder, T., Gergman, J., Almasi, J., & Brown, R. (1992). Beyond direct explanation: Transactional instruction of reading comprehension strategies. *Elementary School Journal, 92,* 511–554.

RAND Reading Study Group. (2001). *Reading for understanding: Toward an R & D program in reading comprehension.* Technical report for the Office of Educational Research and Improvement.

Taylor, B. M. (1980). Children's memory for expository text after reading. *Reading Research Quarterly, 15,* 399–411.

Taylor, B. M., Frye, B. J., & Maruyama, G. M. (1990). Time spent reading and reading growth. *American Educational Research Journal, 27,* 351–362.

Weiner, B. (1979). A theory of motivation for some classroom experiences. *Journal of Educational Psychology, 71,* 3–25.

Chapter One

Reconceptualizing Reading Comprehension

Anne P. Sweet and Catherine Snow

In this chapter we discuss reading comprehension from a perspective that reflects the work of the RAND Reading Study Group (RRSG). This study group was formed in the year 2000, after the U.S. Department of Education's Office of Educational Research and Improvement (OERI) asked RAND to examine ways in which OERI might improve the quality and relevance of the education research funded by the agency. In response to this call, RAND convened study groups in the areas of reading and mathematics education to develop long-term programs of research in the two fields. The RRSG sets forth a framework for a program of research in reading comprehension that serves as a starting point for a major discussion among researchers, practitioners, and policymakers of needed research and development related to reading comprehension. We view the report as a "living document" that should be regularly revised over the course of the program.

In its revised report (RAND Reading Study Group, 2002), the study group formulates a proposal concerning the research issues that the community of reading researchers most urgently needs to address over the next ten to fifteen years. The proposal is an invitation to join a conversation about an area of great practical importance: reading development and reading instruction. It attempts to map the fields of knowledge relevant to a major educational goal—improving reading outcomes—and to identify some key areas in which research would help us reach that goal.

The proposed research agenda builds upon a number of recent efforts to summarize the knowledge base in the field of reading. These efforts include the National Research Council report titled *Preventing Reading Difficulties in Young Children* (Snow, Burns, & Griffin, 1998), the National Reading Panel (NRP) report *Teaching Children to Read* (2000), and the recently published edition of the *Handbook of Reading Research* (Kamil, Mosenthal, Pearson, & Barr, 2000). Given the availability of these and older sources, the RRSG did not attempt an exhaustive synthesis of the knowledge base concerning reading and its implications for instruction and assessment of the general population; in many cases the study group exemplifies its claims rather than documenting them comprehensively. The study group argues that major challenges in the area of reading include understanding how children become good comprehenders, how to design and deliver instruction that promotes comprehension, how to assess comprehension, and how to prevent comprehension failure.

The RRSG is composed of fourteen experts representing a range of disciplinary and methodological perspectives on the field of reading. This group functioned as an expert panel over two years (2000–2001) to establish a convergent perspective on what is known about reading, what the most urgent tasks in developing an integrated research base are, and what needs to be done to improve reading outcomes. The study group decided early in its deliberations to concentrate on the issue of promoting proficient reading, with a focus on the development of comprehension and the capacity to acquire knowledge through reading. This is a field in which the accumulated knowledge base is limited to particular areas and to particular populations of students. The RRSG recognizes the need to develop a more coherent model of reading comprehension. It began this task by attempting to lay out where the most urgent gaps in our knowledge are. The study group also recognizes two needs: (1) to develop networks of communication among researchers currently working in several different research traditions relevant to comprehension and (2) to work with teachers and teacher educators to build rigorous knowledge bases about both research and practice that are mutually accessible and usable. It laid the groundwork for this process by initiating a conversation with researcher and practitioner communities about its preliminary draft report published on the RAND Web site (http://www.rand.org/multi/achievementforall.org) and by presenting at numerous professional association conferences during 2000 and 2001.

What is the core problem within the field of research on proficient reading? At one level the core problem is the construction of a unifying theory of reading comprehension that acknowledges its complexity and is informed by the multiple perspectives (including educational, cognitive, linguistic, sociolinguistic, discourse analytic, and cultural) that have been brought to bear in the design and conduct of literacy research. Considerable research has been directed at issues of reading comprehension, but these research efforts have been neither systematic nor interrelated. At another level the core problem presents itself in a practical form when a sixth-grade teacher turns to research with the question "What should I do with my students who don't understand their history texts or can't learn from reading science texts?" Teachers with such questions encounter only a partial knowledge base. That knowledge base typically does not sufficiently acknowledge the exigencies of the classroom, does not attend simultaneously to the demands of reading to learn during content area instruction while the student is still learning to read, and may not be relevant to the reading profiles of many students in a diverse class. Given the enormous educational importance of promoting reading comprehension and learning among elementary and secondary students, we need to organize what we know about these topics, define what we need to know, and pursue the research that will help the most in improving teacher preparation, classroom instruction, and student achievement.

The purpose of the RRSG, then, has been to summarize the state of research and research-based practice in the field of reading comprehension, in order to generate a well-motivated agenda for future research that will inform practice in this area. Because the study group did not undertake the kind of extensive, expensive, exhaustive review that informed both *Preventing Reading Difficulties in Young Children* (Snow, Burns, & Griffin, 1998) and *Teaching Children to Read* (NRP, 2000), relying instead on consensus and on the distributed knowledge base of its members, the reader should see the study group report as a stimulus to discussion rather than a summative statement.

Issues Motivating the Report

The proposed research agenda is motivated by a number of overarching issues of concern to the research and practice communities.

The demand for literacy skills is high and increasing. Higher levels of literacy are associated with a wide range of outcomes, including higher levels of health, leisure reading, political participation, and reading to children (Smith, 1998). Moreover, ensuring advanced literacy achievement for all students is no longer a luxury but an economic necessity.

The level of reading skills is remaining stagnant. Reading scores of high school students, as reported by the National Assessment of Educational Progress, have not improved between 1970 and 2000.

There are multiple sources of difference in the reading comprehension process and outcomes. Comprehension is affected by differences in the construction and context of the reading task, often socially and culturally influenced, by differences in reader capacities, in texts, and in the reading activity.

Reading comprehension instruction is often minimal or ineffective. Materials in middle school and secondary classrooms are often too difficult or uninteresting for many students to read. Moreover, comprehension instruction tends to be emphasized less in subject-matter classrooms, where teachers focus on content.

The achievement gap between children of different demographic groups persists. The large and persistent gap in reading achievement in the later elementary and secondary grades relates to differences in achievement in other content areas and to differences in high school dropout and college entrance rates.

High stakes tests are affecting reading comprehension instruction in unknown ways. There are very few data on the impact of high stakes tests on student achievement overall; in particular, we do not know how poorer comprehenders deal with the test demands.

The preparation of teachers does not adequately address children's needs for reading comprehension instruction. Teacher preparation and professional development programs are inadequate in the crucial domain of reading comprehension, in part because the solid, systematic research base that should undergird teacher preparation does not exist.

Making good on the federal investment in education requires more knowledge about reading comprehension. The fourth-grade slump in reading achievement is a well-documented phenomenon (Chall, Jacobs, & Baldwin 1990). The recent federal investment through the Reading Excellence Act and its successor programs, Reading First and Early Reading First (totaling more than $5 billion over the next five years), in improving early reading achievement will not ensure long-term gains without further development of our knowledge base concerning reading comprehension.

What We Know

Although these various overarching issues may make the task of developing a research agenda that would contribute to the improvement of practice seem formidable, we are encouraged by the recognition that we already know a good deal about addressing the practical challenges of improving reading comprehension outcomes.

First, we know some of the prerequisites to successful reading comprehension. We know, for example, that reading comprehension capacity builds on successful initial reading instruction and that children who can read words accurately and rapidly have a good foundation for progressing well in comprehension. We know that children with good oral language skills (large oral vocabularies, good listening comprehension) and with well-developed stores of world knowledge are likely to become good comprehenders. We know that social interaction in homes and classrooms as well as communities and the larger sociocultural context influence motivation and participation in literate communities and help construct students' identities as readers, thus influencing their access to text. We know that children who have had rich exposure to literacy experiences are more likely to succeed. We know about several instructional practices that are related to good reading outcomes, although such knowledge is much more extensive for initial than for later reading. Finally, we know that instruction based on an appropriate and well-articulated alignment between curriculum and assessment can improve performance in reading as well as other areas.

We also know several approaches to education and to reading instruction that do not work. We know, for example, that many approaches to compensatory education for socially, economically, and educationally disadvantaged groups do not promote success in reading comprehension. We know as well that identifying children as learning disabled, without tailoring specific instructional treatments to their individual needs, fails to generate reading comprehension gains. We know that current approaches to teaching second-language learners, whether in English as a second language (ESL), bilingual, or all-English settings, often do not address the particular challenges of reading comprehension. We know that the enormous complexities of teaching and the brevity of teacher education programs have the unfortunate consequence that the majority of novice teachers are ill prepared to engage in practice that reflects the existing knowledge base about reading. We know this situation is particularly critical for special education, ESL, and bilingual teachers who, although they need an even deeper understanding of reading, language, curricula, and instructional practices than the mainstream teacher, in fact have even fewer opportunities in their preparation programs to acquire this expertise. We know that preservice preparation and professional development in the domain of early reading instruction are improving, increasingly incorporating information from research about the characteristics of good instruction, but that such is not the case for reading comprehension instruction in the later elementary grades. We know that a frequent consequence of failure on high stakes assessment—namely, retention in grade—does not improve long-term reading achievement without specialized instruction. Finally, although we have a fairly long list of instructional strategies that are effective in targeted interventions or experimental settings, we need to know how to implement these teaching approaches on a large scale, into a coherent reading program that spans the elementary, middle, and high school grades.

The Need for a Definition of Reading Comprehension

The larger agenda that concerns us and the RRSG is the promotion of proficient reading. We see achieving reading proficiency as a long-term developmental process; "reading well" is different at different points along the individual's developmental trajectory. The endpoint, proficient adult reading, encompasses the capacity to read with ease and interest a wide variety of different kinds of materials for varying purposes and to read with comprehension even when the material is neither easy nor intrinsically interesting. Adult reading involves reading for purposes of pleasure, learning, and analysis, and it is a prerequisite to many forms of employment, to informed participation in the democratic process, and to gaining access to cultural capital.

Our focus is on reading comprehension as it is traditionally conceived within educational settings. Teachers think of reading comprehension as what students are taught to do in reading instruction during the early school years and the capacities they are expected to display throughout the middle and high school years. Reading comprehension is usually a focus of instruction in the postprimary grades, after students have largely mastered word recognition skills, though comprehension of text should be an integral part of reading instruction with beginning readers as well; and instruction in oral language, vocabulary, and listening comprehension should be a focus starting in preschool and throughout the elementary grades.

The first task in formulating this research agenda was to define reading comprehension. A useful definition would generate a map of what we know and what we need to know about the process and development of skilled reading comprehension. We define *reading comprehension* as the process of extracting and constructing meaning through interaction and involvement with written language. The reading comprehension process includes three dimensions: the reader, the text, and the activity. These three dimensions define a phenomenon that occurs within a larger sociocultural context (see Figure 1.1), which shapes and is shaped by the reader, and which infuses each of the three elements, influencing the texts that are available and valued, the activities that are engaged in with those texts, and the identities and the profile of capacities of the readers. The sociocultural context mediates students' experiences, just as students' experiences influence the context.

We turn now to a more formal presentation of a definition for reading comprehension. Then we consider dimensions of variability in each of the elements; we include a discussion on variability in part to elaborate and exemplify how we and the study group think about these elements and in part to focus attention on the enormous and unwarranted degree of variability in comprehension outcomes associated with variation in reader preparation and instructional activities. Though the RRSG identifies three pressing components of a long-term research agenda—improving reading comprehension through attention to (1) classroom instruction, (2) teacher preparation and professional development, and (3) appropriate assessment of reading comprehension—in this chapter we limit our discussion to classroom instruction. We

Figure 1.1. Heuristic for Thinking About Reading Comprehension.

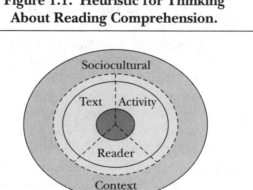

refer the reader to the RAND Reading Study Group report (2001) for a discussion of the other two components.

Defining Comprehension

Comprehension is extracting and constructing meaning from text. *Text* is broadly construed to include any printed text or electronic text. Comprehension entails three elements:

- The reader
- The text
- The activity

These three elements of comprehension interact within a broad sociocultural context that affects the elements and the nature of their interactions. We will elaborate each of these elements in more detail.

These three elements are interrelated in dynamic ways that vary across prereading, reading, and postreading. We consider each of these three "microperiods" in reading because it is important to distinguish between what the reader brings to reading and what a reader takes from reading. Each act of reading is potentially a microdevelopmental process.

The process of comprehension also has a macrodevelopmental aspect. It changes over time with experience and instruction. We focus on the potential impacts of instruction, particularly classroom instruction, in attempting to outline the research agenda needed to improve comprehension outcomes.

The interrelationship among these elements and the various phases of the reading process can be seen in Figure 1.1.

Reader

To comprehend, a reader must have a wide range of capacities and abilities. These include cognitive capacities; motivation; and types of knowledge like vocabulary, as well as other types of knowledge, including domain and topic knowledge, and linguistic and discourse knowledge; purpose; interest; and abilities like attention, memory, critical analytic ability, inferencing, and visualization ability. Of course, the specific cognitive and motivational capacities that any act of reading comprehension calls upon depend on the texts in use and the specific activity in which the reader is engaging.

Fluency is also important to reading comprehension. Good comprehenders are fluent—they have good word identification skills and can read orally with speed, accuracy, and appropriate expression. Fluency is distinct from comprehension. However, fluency does appear to be a prerequisite for good comprehension.

As the reader begins to read and completes whatever activity is at hand, some of the knowledge and capabilities of the reader change. For example, a reader might increase domain knowledge during reading. Similarly, vocabulary, linguistic, or discourse knowledge might also increase. Fluency could also increase as a function of the additional practice in reading. Furthermore, motivational factors such as student interest in reading or self-concept might change as well, either positively or negatively, during a successful or unsuccessful reading experience (Sweet, Guthrie, & Ng, 1998).

Another important source of changes in knowledge and capacities is the instruction a reader might receive. Appropriate instruction will foster reading comprehension; inappropriate instruction might interfere with learning to comprehend.

Text

The features of text have a large impact on comprehension. The proliferation of computers and electronic text has led us to broaden the definition of *text* to include electronic text and multimedia documents in addition to conventional print publications. Comprehension does not occur by simply extracting meaning from text. During reading the reader constructs different representations of the text that are important for comprehension. These representations include at least the *surface code,* consisting of the exact wording of the text and the *text base,* idea units representing the meaning.

Texts can be difficult or easy, depending on factors inherent in them, on the relation between the text and the knowledge and abilities of the reader, and on the activities in which the reader is engaged. For example, the content presented in the text has a critical bearing on reading comprehension, and a reader's domain knowledge interacts with that content to affect ease of comprehension. In addition, the vocabulary load of the text, its linguistic structure, discourse style, and genre also interact with the reader's knowledge. Text characteristics must match reader knowledge and abilities for optimal comprehension to occur. Furthermore, various activities are better suited to some texts than others. Electronic texts introduce some complications in defining comprehension because they require skills and abilities beyond those required for comprehension of conventional print.

The challenge of teaching reading comprehension is heightened because in the current educational era all students are expected to read more text and more complex texts. Schools can no longer track students so that only those with highly developed reading skills take the more reading-intensive courses. All students now need to read well to pass the high stakes exams and to make themselves employable.

Activity

Reading does not occur in a vacuum. It is done for a purpose, to accomplish some task. Activity refers to this dimension of reading. A reading activity involves one or more purposes, some operations to process the text at hand, and the consequences of performing the activity. Prior to reading, a reader has a purpose, which can be either externally imposed (for example, a class assignment) or internally generated (playing a video game). The purpose is influenced by a cluster of motivational variables, including interest, preference, and prior knowledge. These initial purposes can change as the reader reads. That is, the information a reader encounters might raise new questions that make the original purpose either incomplete or irrelevant.

When the purpose is externally mandated, as in instruction, the reader might accept the purpose and complete the activity; for example, if the assignment is to read a paragraph in order to write a summary, the compliant student will accept that purpose and engage in reading operations to address it. If the reader does not fully accept the mandated purpose, internally generated purposes may conflict. Such conflicts may lead to incomplete comprehension.

For example, this may occur in instructional activities when students fail to see the relevance of an assignment and do not read purposively to comprehend.

One important set of reading activities occurs in the context of instruction. In this context, instruction shapes the reader's purposes, operations, and consequences. The activities should be designed to promote learning how to comprehend across a wide variety of situations, texts, and contexts.

Context

From a sociocultural perspective, both the *process,* how instruction is delivered and the social interactions that contextualize the learning experience, and the *content,* focus of instruction, are of major importance. Learning and literacy are viewed as cultural and historical activities not just because they are acquired through social interactions but also because they represent how a specific cultural group or discourse community interprets the world and transmits this information. As adults, we belong to multiple discourse communities. However, the first discourse community into which children are socialized is their home and surrounding neighborhood. That community helps to shape the young reader's capacities, skills, and motivations, as well as to define appropriate texts and appropriate reading activities.

When discourse communities differ in their view of the world and in social practices that guide their children's instruction, conflicts are bound to occur. A sociocultural perspective is often invoked to help explain poorer literacy performance of students from groups traditionally not well served in U.S. schools, but in fact every act of comprehension is the expression of a particular cultural meaning. Reading research informed by a sociocultural perspective helps us to identify and deal with the various tensions that impact the reading comprehension development, engagement, and performance of both younger and older students.

The effects of contextual factors can be seen in oral language practices, in students' self-concepts, in the types of activities in which individuals engage, and in instructional history. The classroom learning environment (for example, organizational grouping, inclusion of technology, or availability of materials) is an important aspect of the context that can affect comprehension.

Variability

Variability in Reading Comprehension

There are multiple dimensions of difference in comprehension. These include differences in the construction of the reading activity that may be culturally or instructionally influenced, differences in the kinds of texts that people value and read, and differences in the capacities children bring to reading. We will now elaborate our definition of reading comprehension by giving examples of variation for the elements of reader, text, and activity. Of course, none of these elements operates independently of the other two in any authentic act of comprehension. However, we consider each in turn because each has an internal structure that deserves further consideration and that may clarify how the RRSG conceptualizes these elements of reading comprehension and the interface among them.

Variability in Readers

Proficient reading assumes a set of variables defining capabilities and dispositions that readers bring to the task of reading. Reader differences in capabilities such as fluency in word recognition, oral language ability, and domain knowledge, along with differences in dispositions such as the reader's motivation, goals, and purposes, are all important sources of variability in reading comprehension. Such variables interact with each other and with the text to which the reader is exposed (for example, narrative, expository, and so on) as determinants of performance on a given reading task (for example, acquiring knowledge in a domain, comparative analysis, problem solving). However, the capabilities and dispositions the reader brings to the task of reading, his or her engagement with and responses to given texts, and the quality of the outcomes produced by the act of reading for some purpose all take place within a broad sociocultural context and are themselves shaped by related factors such as cultural and subcultural influences, socioeconomic status, home and family background, peer influences, classroom culture, and instructional history. These multiple and interacting influences contribute to inter- and intra-individual differences in reading proficiency (for example, see Tabors &

Snow, 2001, for a review of language and literacy development in second-language learners). Any research agenda focused on reading comprehension will have to attend to the dimension of reader differences or perhaps more precisely to sources of variation in how outcomes relate to a purposive act of reading.

Variability in Text

Scholars have long recognized that texts should become more complex as reader capacities grow and also that the characteristics of various genres and subject matters create varying challenges for readers. Here, we consider the sources of varying challenge within text.

The texts that people read today are substantially more diverse than those in use thirty years ago. In the mid-twentieth century, children were assigned specific readings that were crafted for instructional purposes, or they were exposed to a select group of books in the narrative, descriptive, expository, or persuasive genres. The reading materials that made it into the canon did not even come close to representing a broad array of cultures and socioeconomic classes. U.S. society is experiencing an explosion of alternative texts that vary in content, readability levels, and genre; that incorporate multimedia and electronic options; and that pertain to a wider variety of cultures and groups. This will make it much more difficult for teachers to coordinate the selection and availability of texts for individual readers.

The study group's starting point in understanding variability in text is to map the large space in which texts that are potentially available to the readers are located. This space includes the following dimensions and categories:

Discourse genre, such as narration, description, exposition, and persuasion

Discourse structure, including rhetorical composition and coherence

Media forms, such as textbooks, multimedia, advertisements, hypertext, and the Web

Sentence difficulty, including vocabulary, syntax, and the propositional text base

Content, including different types of mental models, cultures, and socioeconomic strata, as well as age-appropriate selection of subject matter and the practices that are prominent in the culture

Texts with varying degrees of engagement for particular classes of readers

The assignment of texts to specific readers becomes more difficult as alternative texts grow in volume and diversity. Teachers will need computer technologies to meet the level of complexity that will be expected in schools of the future. The assignment of texts should provide a strategic balance among student interest in the subject matter, the student's level of development, particular challenges that the student faces, pedagogical goals in the curriculum, and availability of texts.

One salient challenge is the assignment of texts to children at different grade levels when curricula are developed on a broader institutional scale. We know that the assignments need to be diverse, but beyond that widespread consensus an incisive plan must reflect scientific and pedagogical agendas rather than a purely political agenda. The large gap between the available electronic and multimedia materials and teachers' understanding of how they should integrate these with the reading curriculum needs to be filled. Few textbooks are well written or promote understanding at a deep conceptual level, going beyond the shallow knowledge that has pervaded our school systems. The selected texts for a child need to be sufficiently challenging and engaging in addition to expanding comprehension proficiency. Otherwise, the children will not be intrinsically motivated to continue literacy development throughout their lifetimes.

Variability in Activity

A major issue of concern in U.S. schooling is how infrequent and ineffective instructional activities focused on teaching comprehension are (Durkin, 1978–1979). We know, though, that many instructional activities can improve comprehension. In the following section, we consider the nature of excellent comprehension instruction in order to develop a research agenda for improving comprehension outcomes.

We discuss instruction under the heading of activity even though activity is a larger category than instruction. *Activity* refers to the acts that a reader engages in with a text, and it is defined as encompassing purpose, operations, and consequences. Nonetheless, given the RRSG's focus on research to improve reading outcomes, we concentrate on instructional contexts for reading activity in this chapter.

The study group considered variation in activity generated by various purposes for reading (for example, reading for pleasure versus reading in order learn specific subject matter) as well as by focus on various operations while reading (for example, attention, fluency, monitoring comprehension). It considered, in particular, (1) the issue of how teacher-generated purposes conform or conflict with likely learner purposes and (2) the factors that influence teacher-imposed purposes. It also reviewed what scholars know about variability in attention, word reading, fluency, syntactic parsing, constructing a propositional text base, constructing mental models, generating inferences, monitoring comprehension, and using deep comprehension strategies. Each of these operations reflects specific reader capacities, and each at the same time is facilitated or impeded by features of the text being read.

Of course, it is variation in consequences that is of the greatest ultimate importance. Some classroom-structured reading activities generate important changes in the reader's capacity to comprehend an array of texts, whereas others may be limited to improving comprehension only of the text under consideration, and still others may have no long-term consequences at all (see Tierney & Cunningham, 1984, for a related distinction between learning to comprehend across texts versus comprehending a given text).

In sum, numerous dimensions of variability can be associated primarily with the reader, including sociocultural influences, group differences, interindividual differences, and intra-individual differences. Research evidence available on variability deriving from text or from activity, in comparison, is less apparent. Although previously articulated models of reading (Jenkins, 1976) have certainly pointed to reader, task, and text as three elements of interest (see Alexander & Jetton, 2000; Graves & Graves, 1994; Graves, Graves, & Braaten, 1996, for discussions of the tetrahedral model), research has nonetheless focused primarily on the reader, locating explanations for failure and targeting procedures for improvement there. The study group would argue that thinking creatively about the activity, in particular those activities in which readers are engaged with the purpose of improving their capacities to read with comprehension, and about the texts is equally important. The role and challenge of the text expands, furthermore, as novel electronic and multimedia texts become an increasingly important domain for reading.

Variability in Context

According to our model, contextual factors ranging from economic circumstances to social group membership to classroom organization can influence reading comprehension. We underscore that contextual factors operate at many levels to influence the reader, the text, and the activity in profound ways. For example, availability and variability of resources matter greatly; consider how the larger community, the school district, the school building, and the classroom vary singularly and in combination as a function of context. One of the more glaring aspects of the variability in context is the degree to which the quality of instruction in reading varies from schools serving economically secure, English-speaking, European American families and those serving economically marginalized families and those from other ethnic and linguistic groups. Not surprisingly, outcomes vary as radically. Reading comprehension, like instruction and learning, are inextricably linked to and infused by the larger context that defines them. Understanding the full complexity of reading comprehension requires understanding that it is a cognitive, linguistic, and cultural activity that is confounded with a range of contextual factors such as poverty.

What a Reader Looks Like
and How We Know She's Reading

According to our model, each reader is a bundle of complexity. Moreover, no two readers are necessarily the same bundle of complexity, although they are likely similar in essential ways. Put another way, a reader is like a fingerprint—each is unique but similar to others. Each is influenced by individual characteristics of the reader herself, the text, the activity, and the context. Teachers are challenged in many ways when teaching students to read with understanding and to learn from content text. The first part of the challenge is assessing each reader and the particular circumstances that influence the reader's disposition toward reading success. The second part of the challenge for teachers is providing sound reading instruction for all students—carefully structuring reading activities, selecting instructional texts, employing research-based instructional practices, and gauging students' reading progress along the way.

Teachers' making formative as well as summative assessments of how well students are reading is important. Some of these assessments can be informal, especially formative ones; others can be formal, most likely summative ones. At this point the tools available to teachers for use in assessing how well students read and understand what they read are wanting. Because knowledge, application, and engagement are crucial consequences of reading with comprehension, assessments that reflect all three of these are needed. Current thinking about the nature of reading comprehension, as illustrated in Figure 1.1, creates a demand for new kinds of assessment strategies and instruments that more robustly reflect the dynamic developmental nature of comprehension and represent adequately the interactions among the dimensions of reader, activity, text, and context.

Next, we turn to a more explicit consideration of the proposed research agenda. The overarching goal of this agenda is improving reading comprehension outcomes. We limit our discussion to the subtopic of instruction and classroom practices, leaving the reader to examine the RRSG report (2001) for the study group's discussion on teacher preparation and professional development and the assessment of reading comprehension.

A Research Agenda for Improving Reading Comprehension Instruction

Good instruction is the most powerful means of promoting the development of proficient comprehenders and preventing reading comprehension problems. Narrowly, the purpose of comprehension instruction is to promote the ability of a reader to learn from text. More broadly, comprehension instruction provides students access to culturally important domains of knowledge and a means of pursuing affective and intellectual goals.

Effective comprehension instruction is the process of enacting practices that reflect the orchestration of knowledge about readers, texts, purposeful activity, and contexts for the purpose of advancing students' thoughtful, competent, and motivated reading. This definition suggests that instructional decision making is a dynamic and highly interactive process. Drawing upon the literature that the study group uses to describe the many reader variables that are integral to proficient reading comprehension (see RRSG, 2001), we suggest that students can be characterized along a continuum from low need to high need of the instructional support they will require to become proficient comprehenders. However, this characterization of the reader must also take into account the nature of the text the student is reading, as well as the nature of the criterial task. We argue that any reader can be a high-need reader as a function of the degree of challenge of the text (that is, the text is poorly written, dense, contains a number of unfamiliar ideas) and as a function of how the reader is to demonstrate understanding of the text (for example, recall, reasoning, application, evaluation). Finally, the teacher must consider the broad range of contextual factors that will influence instructional opportunities for particular learners.

These contextual factors include but are not limited to community- and schoolwide factors, the culture of the classroom, the specific curriculum and instructional activities in which students are engaged, and the nature of the interaction between teacher and student as well as among students. Similarly, a student who may appear to be a high-need reader when we examine the reader variables in isolation may in fact be very successful in an instructional setting in which the teacher attends to this student's needs by selecting texts, designing criterial tasks, and making decisions about how to structure the context in a fashion that maximally supports the student's participation and learning.

One implication of this definition is that instructional researchers, regardless of the method they employ, need to attend to each of these features, if the research is going to yield usable knowledge. Careful descriptions of the participants need to be accompanied by careful descriptions of the texts used in the research and the specific nature of the task(s) for which students are using reading in the specific context of instruction. The context, in the case of classroom-based research, includes but is not limited to general classroom conditions (see Allington, 2000) that set the stage for effective instruction; the specific nature of the instructional activity (or activities) in which the learner is engaged; and the specific nature of the support provided by teachers, peers, and instructional tools (for example, computers).

What We Know

Although we prioritize research on comprehension instruction in this agenda, suggestions for future research are built on a knowledge base that is in some cases fairly well articulated.

PRINCIPLE 1: Instruction that is designed to enhance students' reading fluency leads to fairly significant gains in word recognition and fluency and only moderate gains in comprehension.

Most fluency instruction has consisted of repeated reading of the same text, using a variety of techniques. The NRP (2000) examined the wide-ranging literature on repeated reading and found that repeated reading was effective for normal readers through the fourth grade (there were no studies of normal readers beyond that grade) and for students with reading problems throughout high school. Most studies have found that reading connected text is necessary for effective fluency instruction, but one study (Tan & Nicholson, 1997) has indicated that reading isolated word lists also leads to increased fluency.

In addition to repeated reading techniques, another approach to promoting fluency involves ensuring that proficiency and fluency are acquired during instruction in all components of reading, starting with letter knowledge and phonemic awareness and moving to decoding and word recognition (Berninger, Abbott, Billingsley, & Nagy, 2001; Wolf & Katzir-Cohen, 2001). Both sets of investigators have developed intervention programs that address specific component skills, foster linkages among all relevant systems—orthographic, phonological, semantic, and morphological—and emphasize fluency at each step. These programs are very new, and no data on their success in promoting fluency exists yet.

PRINCIPLE 2: Instruction has been shown to be effective in providing students a repertoire of strategies that promote comprehension monitoring and foster comprehension.

Due to the experimental studies that the NRP (2000) reviewed, we know that the activity of engaging students in identifying the big ideas in a text and graphically depicting the relationships among these ideas improves readers' recall and comprehension of text. We also know that in grades three to five, question answering in the context of engagement in elaborative conversations improves students' comprehension of the text used in instruction and improves comprehension of a novel text as well. Teaching students in grades three to nine to self-question while reading text enhances their understanding of the text used in the instruction and of novel texts as well. Summarization studies conducted in the upper elementary grades indicate that learning to paraphrase text, identify the gist of text, and identify and integrate the "big ideas" enhanced students' recall of the text being taught and their capacity to understand novel text. Teaching students in grades three through six to identify and represent story structure improves their comprehension of stories. With this strategy, researchers found no evidence of transfer to new stories, and improvement was more marked for low-achieving readers.

PRINCIPLE 3: The explicitness with which teachers teach these strategies makes a difference in learner outcomes, especially for students who are low achieving and who profit from greater explicitness.

Results on the immediate impact of instructional programs have been quite positive, but we have less positive evidence that students continue to use the strategies in the classroom and outside of school after the conclusion of the instruction (Keeny, Cannizzo, & Flavell, 1967; Ringel & Springer, 1980) or that they transfer the strategies to new situations. Recent studies have underscored the importance of teacher preparation when the goal is to deliver effective instruction in reading comprehension strategies (Duffy et al., 1987; Brown, Pressley, Van Meter, & Schuder, 1996). This is especially important when the students are low performing. Implementation of a direct approach to cognitive strategy instruction in the context of the actual classroom has proved problematic. Proficient reading involves much more than using individual strategies. It involves a constant ongoing adaptation of many cognitive processes. Successful teachers of reading comprehension must respond flexibly and opportunistically to students' needs for instructive feedback as they read. Intensive teacher preparation has been shown to be effective in teaching teachers to deliver successful strategy instruction, and this has resulted in improved student outcomes on reading comprehension tests.

PRINCIPLE 4: Researchers have a number of working hypotheses about the role of instruction in explaining and addressing the problems of poor comprehenders.

Research has indicated that specific instruction, for example, prereading, can improve poor comprehenders' understanding of a difficult text. Researchers have used instructional scripts that provide students with essential background knowledge, key concepts, and vocabulary (Graves, Cooke, & LaBerge, 1983), or they have activated students' background knowledge through extended discussions (Langer, 1984). Researchers have also used such activities as story structures or graphic organizers to provide scaffolding for improved comprehension of a selected text (NRP, 2000). They have also used pre- and postwriting activities as effective instructional activities to promote comprehension for low-achieving readers. These instructional activities effectively address the problem of low-achieving readers' poor comprehension by providing instructional scaffolds to help them comprehend text.

The nature of the strategy taught seems less significant than the role that strategy instruction plays in engaging the reader in active interaction with the text (Chan & Cole, 1986). A synthesis of the research literature regarding the teaching of comprehension strategies to students with learning problems (Gersten, Fuchs, Williams, & Baker, 2001) indicates that successful comprehension instruction for the poor comprehender is characterized by explicit modeling by the teacher, the inclusion of additional opportunities for practice with feedback, skillful adjustments to the learner's level, and the reader's mindful engagement with the purposes for reading.

PRINCIPLE 5: The role of vocabulary instruction in enhancing comprehension is complex.

Vocabulary knowledge is strongly linked to reading comprehension (Freebody & Anderson, 1983), and vocabulary knowledge is an especially important factor in explaining the reading problems of second-language learners (García, 1991; Laufer & Sim, 1985). However, this relationship is extremely complex, confounded by the complexity of relationships among vocabulary knowledge, conceptual and cultural knowledge, and instructional opportunities.

The research in this area is vast, so we touch only upon a few key points. The NRP (2000) found that direct instruction of vocabulary improved students' reading comprehension. The effects of wide reading on vocabulary growth are, however, debatable. The NRP did not find compelling evidence that programs that are designed to increase independent reading, such as sustained silent reading, promoted vocabulary growth. Nevertheless, a powerful correlation exists between volume of reading and vocabulary growth among first-language learners (Stanovich & Cunningham, 1992), and book-flood studies with second-language learners have had powerful effects (Elley, 1991). Furthermore, a wealth of evidence relates children's oral language experiences to subsequent vocabulary growth (Dickinson & Tabors, 2001). Much of this evidence has been derived from studies of the effects of home and preschool on language development. Researchers know less about the effects of school-based oral language activities and vocabulary learning and growth, although researchers including Meichen-baum and Biemiller (1998) have argued that the fourth-grade slump we mentioned earlier in this chapter is caused at least in part by the failure of schools to promote oral language development while children are still working on the mechanics of reading.

Although scholars can make some generalizations about the characteristics of effective vocabulary instruction (Stahl & Fairbanks, 1986), the number of studies that have directly examined the effects of vocabulary instruction on reading comprehension is still relatively small. Some of the strongest demonstrations of the effects of vocabulary instruction on reading comprehension—the work of Isabel Beck and her colleagues (for example, Beck, Perfetti, & McKeown, 1982; McKeown, Beck, Omanson, & Pople, 1985)—used rather artificial texts heavily loaded with unfamiliar words. Little research addresses the question of the conditions—which types of texts, words, readers, and outcomes—constrain whether vocabulary instruction can actually improve comprehension.

PRINCIPLE 6: Teachers who provide comprehension strategy instruction deeply connected within the context of subject matter learning, such as history and science, foster comprehension development.

Teaching reading strategies, such as questioning, summarizing, monitoring comprehension, and using graphic organizers facilitate reading comprehension (NRP, 2000). Several quasi-experimental investigations show that when the strategy instruction is fully embedded in in-depth learning of content, students learn the strategies to a high level of competence (Guthrie, Van Meter, Hancock, Alao, Anderson, & McCann, 1998). If students learn that strategies are tools for understanding conceptual content of text, then the strategies become purposeful and integral to reading activities. Students' connection of cognitive strategies to their growing knowledge of an area of content enables them to increase their awareness and make deliberate use of the strategies as means for learning (Brown, 1997) in microgenetic analyses of instruction. Without the close linkage of strategies with knowledge and understanding in a content area, students do not learn strategies fully, do not perceive them as valuable tools, and are less likely to use them in new learning situations with new text.

Teachers can help students learn that gaining new ideas, increased understanding, and literary experience is an aim of reading and that strategies are a powerful way to accomplish that aim. This helps students to use strategies when they are appropriate. If educators teach comprehension strategies with an array of content and a range of texts that are too wide, then students do not fully learn the strategies. If educators teach strategies with too narrow a base of content or text, then students do not have a chance to learn how to transfer them to new reading situations (Rosenshine & Meister, 1994). The optimal balance enables students to learn that strategies are an important means for understanding but are not the main point of reading activities. The main purposes for reading are gaining meaning and knowledge.

An important aim of strategy development is to enable students to initiate the strategies independently (Alexander & Murphy, 1998). Students who spontaneously apply a strategy, such as questioning, when it is sensible will improve their comprehension. Thus, students must have motivation, self-efficacy, and ownership regarding their purposes for reading and strategies to be effective comprehenders.

PRINCIPLE 7: The use of various genres of text (that is, narrative and informational text) leads to important differences in instructional opportunities, as assessed by teacher and student discourse.

Knowledge of text structure is an important factor in fostering comprehension. Readers who are unaware of structure do not approach a text with any particular plan of action (Meyer, Brandt, & Bluth, 1980). Consequently, they tend to retrieve information in a seemingly random way. Students aware of text structure organize the text as they read, and they recognize and retain the important information it contains.

Simple exposure to stories is helpful, but explicit instruction is valuable. Children are taught to ask themselves generic questions that focus on the principal components of a story, which aid in the identification of the relevant and important information in stories (Mandler & Johnson, 1977; Stein & Glenn, 1979; Williams, 1993). In addition to the value of the questions as an organizational guide to the text structure, the questions also enhance active processing of the text, thus qualifying as comprehension-monitoring instruction. Such instruction improves the student's ability to see relationships in stories, answer comprehension questions, and retell in a focused fashion. Although stories form the bulk of reading material for instruction in early grades, scholars have made a case for greater inclusion of other text genres in instruction (Duke, 2000; Pappas & Barry, 1997). Such inclusion would allow for instruction that more closely matched the demands of reading in later grades.

The demands placed on readers change as they progress through school. At about the fourth grade, they are expected to read expository material in content instruction. Because expository text is often so dense with information and unfamiliar technical vocabulary, students must perform complex cognitive tasks to extract and synthesize its content (Lapp, Flood, & Ranck-Buhr, 1995). Expository text involves relatively long passages, less familiar content, and more complex and varied structures (Armbruster & Anderson, 1984) than narrative text. Explicit teaching about structure enables students to differentiate between common structures and to identify the important information in a text in a coherent, organized way (Armbruster & Armstrong, 1993). Researchers have used a variety of instructional techniques to aid in students' comprehension of expository text, including teaching children to self-question using generic questions (Wong & Jones, 1982), to analyze the text using mapping (Swanson, Kozleski, & Stegink, 1987; Boyle & Weishaar, 1997), to summarize (Nelson, Smith, & Dodd, 1992), and other simple strategies. These interventions have proved effective.

PRINCIPLE 8: Teachers who provide opportunities for student choices, challenging tasks, and collaborative learning increase motivation for reading and comprehension of text.

For students from grade one to grade twelve, classroom activities that enable and encourage students to take responsibility for their reading increase their reading achievement. For example, extensive observations of classroom instruction for primary students show that when teachers provide challenging passages for reading, students exert effort and persistence. Simultaneously, when students have a limited but meaningful choice about the learning activity, such as which part of a text to read, they invest higher energy in learning than if the teacher always prescribes the tasks (Turner, 1995). With elementary and middle school students, scholars have widely documented that teachers who provide meaningful choices and autonomy support increased motivation for reading and effortful attention to gaining knowledge from text (Reeve, Bolt, & Cai, 1999). The explanation for the benefit of autonomy support for reading comprehension is that students become more active learners when they have a minimal but meaningful choice in the topics, texts, activities, and strategies for learning.

Many investigators have documented the roles of motivation and engagement as a link between instruction and achievement (Skinner, Wellborn, & Connell, 1990; see Guthrie & Wigfield, 2000, for a review of empirical research). In brief, they have shown that engagement is a mediator of the effects of instruction on reading achievement. If instruction increases students' engagement, then students' achievement increases. In this literature *engagement* refers to a combination of the following: (1) students' use of cognitive strategies, (2) the presence of intrinsic motivation to read, (3) the use of background knowledge to understand text, and (4) the social interchanges in reading, such as discussing the meaning of a paragraph or the theme of a narrative. Therefore, instruction affects reading comprehension outcomes through the avenue of active engagement in frequent, thoughtful reading for understanding.

PRINCIPLE 9: Teachers nominated as effective teachers enact a wide range of instructional practices that they use in a thoughtful and dynamic fashion.

Effective teachers of reading engage in a diverse array of instructional practices (NRP, 2000; Pressley et al., 2001; Taylor, Pearson, Clark, & Walpole, 1999). This panoply of practices results in a complex environment that fosters comprehension. Effective

teachers used a variety of instructional practices related specifically to reading comprehension. For example, effective teachers
asked high-level comprehension questions, requiring students to
make inferences and to think beyond the text. Effective teachers
helped readers make connections between texts they read and
their personal lives and experiences. Effective teachers used small
group instruction to meet the individual needs of their readers. Effective teachers provided their readers with reading materials at their appropriate reading level. Effective teachers of young
readers monitored progress in reading through the use of informal assessments.

One critically important but thorny aspect of teaching reading
in general and comprehension in particular is the appropriate
balance between the teaching of skills and the use of literature.
Since the late 1970s, the reading field has vacillated between the
two—with fierce opposition between the camps. However, the
choice does not seem to be a concern to most teachers. In a survey of teacher practices, Baumann, Hoffman, Moon, and Duffy-
Hester (1998) reported that teachers believed both to be essential
for good teaching. In fact, teachers reported that they taught skills
and that they made extensive use of literature as well.

Principle 10: Despite the well-developed knowledge base re-
    garding the value of instruction designed to enhance compre-
    hension, typical classroom teaching spends inadequate time
    and attention on comprehension instruction in the primary
    and upper elementary grades.

In the late 1970s, research revealed that teachers devoted
only 2 percent of the classroom time designated for reading
instruction to actually teaching students how to comprehend
what they read (Durkin, 1978–1979). Over twenty years later, not
much has changed in the upper elementary (Pressley, 2000) or
primary grades (Taylor, Pearson, Clark, & Walpole, 1999). For example, Taylor and colleagues documented the limited opportunities that children in grades K–3 had to develop knowledge and
thinking even in the context of schools that were effectively beat-
ing the odds—that is, schools that were realizing higher early
reading achievement gains than would be predicted, given the

demographics of their student populations. Using survey and classroom observation data, they reported that only 16 percent of the teachers in the entire sample were reported to emphasize comprehension.

Despite the reputed role that inexperience with informational text plays in the fourth-grade slump (Chall, Jacobs, & Baldwin, 1990) and despite evidence that some young children prefer to read informational text (Pappas & Barry, 1997), primary-grade classrooms have a significant dearth of informational text (Duke, 2000). Beginning in grade four and throughout their formal education, students will spend the majority of their time reading expository text, yet their instruction in grades one to three has been primarily in narrative text. Recently a plethora of engaging informational texts, written for primary-grade students, has become available through publishers of school texts. However, these books are not yet in sufficient supply in primary classrooms, thus primary-grade teachers have not placed an emphasis on teaching students how to read informational text as compared to narrative text.

Other Topics

Although we do not broach the topic of teacher education and professional development in this chapter, as does the RRSG in its report (2001), we recognize that the teacher is central to discussions of how to improve comprehension instruction in schools today. Recent studies have underscored the importance of teacher preparation when the goal is to deliver effective instruction in reading comprehension strategies (for example, see Pressley, 1998). This is especially important when students are low performing. The question becomes, how can we bring about increased teacher quality and expertise in teaching reading comprehension? The report defines *increased teacher quality and expertise* as teachers who have a deep knowledge about the reading process and reading comprehension and who have the knowledge and skills to implement research-based instructional strategies in their teaching. For a discussion of this topic, we refer you to the report.

We also acknowledge the importance of assessments in the field of reading comprehension. A satisfactory assessment system is a prerequisite to making progress with all aspects of the proposed research agenda, and thus the RRSG (2001) argues that investment in improved assessments has very high priority. Of particular relevance in this chapter is the recognition that assessing the impact of changes in instruction depends on having valid, reliable, and sensitive assessments. The impact of assessment on instruction is a question that constitutes a research agenda of its own, particularly in this era of education reform, which is so highly oriented to accountability. For a discussion on assessment as it relates to a program of research on reading comprehension, see the RRSG report.

Finally, we submit that particular strategies for developing a research program on reading comprehension are also important. These strategies include establishing priorities in terms of mapping the territory for what new research directions constitute the best bets for improving comprehension instruction and reading outcomes. Additional and equally important considerations include ensuring programmatic efforts, developing a community of researchers, and making both research- and practice-based knowledge optimally usable for all. Our view, which is representative of the RRSG's view, is that researchers and practitioners must develop and nurture mechanisms for distinguishing excellence from mediocre practice, for reviewing and accumulating the knowledge of effective practitioners, and for incorporating effective practitioner expertise into the research process.

Three Recommendations for the Future

Our chapter portrays the design for a federally funded research effort on reading comprehension. A major premise behind this design is to promote a targeted research agenda that is sustainable, sizable, and cumulative. By *sustainable*, we mean that any research agenda on reading comprehension should continue uninterrupted over a long period of time. By *sizable*, we mean that research projects should be large in size and scope and should be supported by ample dollars. By *cumulative*, we mean that research studies should focus on particular problems, with each building on the findings of previous studies; that the program of research should unfold systematically over the long term; and creating a much-needed mechanism for regularly reviewing and synthesizing newly acquired knowledge.

The major goal of such a program, then, is to build new knowledge that will be helpful to all concerned with reading education—practitioners, teacher educators, policymakers, and parents. Given this charge, we conceive of three recommendations for the future in the form of three research questions that merit study.

What specific issues of educational urgency exist, and what are the most promising research directions for addressing them? Although the critical questions for a long-term research agenda in reading comprehension are many, we provide three examples of the most salient.

QUESTION 1: What instructional conditions should accompany strategy instruction to promote generative use of a strategic approach to learning across texts and tasks in diverse contexts and at different age levels? What specific instructional activities, materials, and practices are related to effective comprehension and engagement of students from various cultural and linguistic backgrounds at varying grade levels?

Much research shows that from the upper elementary grades onward students can learn to use strategies to advance their ability and inclination to independently learn from text (NRP, 2000). Despite this robust knowledge base, scholars have never described the appropriate embedding of strategy instruction into a larger program of reading comprehension instruction nor evaluated the effectiveness of strategy instruction across a variety of types of learners.

QUESTION 2: How should teachers of poor comprehenders in the general education setting allocate time and instructional emphasis among (1) promoting fluency, (2) teaching vocabulary, (3) instructing strategies, (4) providing extensive reading of informational and literary text, (5) encouraging writing based on reading, (6) using multimedia to support content learning, and (7) using computer programs to improve reading skills?

Teachers working in high-poverty schools need guidance about how to combine and prioritize various instructional approaches in the classroom and in particular about how to teach comprehension while attending to the often poor word-reading skills their students bring to the middle and later elementary grades. Guidance of this kind is absent in the available research literature.

QUESTION 3: For students who are learning ESL, what variations maximize their opportunities to acquire the knowledge, skills, and dispositions of successful comprehenders?

Teachers of English-language learners, like teachers of poor reading comprehenders, are challenged by selecting among various instructional practices for particular students and groups of students and by devoting appropriate amounts of time to them. Current published research offers little guidance.

Conclusion

In this chapter we have summarized a view of reading comprehension from the RRSG report (2001). This report is designed explicitly to serve as a foundation for conversation and consultation in the field of reading researchers, in order to generate a broad base of input to any federally funded research effort. Interested parties extensively commented on the first draft during 2000–2001, through solicited reviews, reactions posted to the Web site, and questions and comments during various conference presentations. The current draft, which has undergone extensive revision and is available on-line and in hard copy from RAND, reflects a deep rethinking of the issues that those many comments stimulated. Nonetheless, the draft is far from a final statement on these issues. Knowledge continues to accumulate; conclusions continue to be subject to revision; and hypotheses are designed to be disproven. Thus, neither we nor the study group wish to portray our proposals as a final product, but rather as a somewhat more advanced progress report.

References

Alexander, P. A., & Jetton, T. (2000). Learning from text: A multidimensional and developmental perspective. In M. L. Kamil, P. B. Mosenthal, P. D. Pearson, & R. Barr (Eds.), *Handbook of reading research* (Vol. 3, pp. 285–310). Mahwah, NJ: Lawrence Erlbaum.

Alexander, P. A., & Murphy, P. K. (1998). Profiling the differences in students' knowledge, interest, and strategic processing. *Journal of Educational Psychology, 90,* 435–447.

Allington, R. L. (2000). *What really matters for struggling readers: Designing research-based programs.* White Plains, NY: Longman.

Armbruster, B. B., & Anderson, T. H. (1984). Structures of explanations in history textbooks, or so what if Governor Stanford missed the spike and hit the rail? *Journal of Curriculum Studies, 16*(2), 181–194.

Armbruster, B. B., & Armstrong, J. O. (1993). Locating information in text: A focus on children in the elementary grades. *Contemporary Educational Psychology, 18*(2), 139–161.

Baumann, J., Hoffman, J., Moon, J., & Duffy-Hester, A. M. (1998). Where are teachers' voices in the phonics/whole language debate? Results from a survey of U.S. elementary teachers. *Reading Teacher, 51,* 636–652.

Beck, I. L., Perfetti, C. A., & McKeown, M. G. (1982). Effects of long-term vocabulary instruction on lexical access and reading comprehension. *Journal of Educational Psychology, 74,* 506–521.

Berninger, V. W., Abbott, R. D., Billingsley, F., & Nagy, W. (2001). Processes underlying timing and fluency of reading: Efficiency, automaticity, coordination, and morphological awareness. In M. Wolf (Ed.), *Dyslexia, fluency, and the brain.* Timonium, MD: York Press.

Boyle, J. R., & Weishaar, M. (1997). The effects of expert-generated versus student-generated cognitive organizers on the reading comprehension of students with learning disabilities. *Learning Disabilities Research and Practice, 12*(4), 228–235.

Brown, A. L. (1997). Transforming schools into communities of thinking and learning about serious matters. *American Psychologist, 52,* 399–414.

Brown, R., Pressley, M., Van Meter, P., & Schuder, T. (1996). A quasi-experimental validation of transactional strategies instruction with low-achieving second-grade readers. *Journal of Educational Psychology, 88,* 18–37.

Campbell, J. R., Hombo, C. M., and Mazzeo, J. (2000). *NAEP 1999 trends in academic progress: Three decades of student performance.* Washington, DC: National Center for Education Statistics.

Chall, J. S, Jacobs, V. A., & Baldwin, L. E. (1990). *The reading crisis: Why poor children fall behind.* Cambridge, MA: Harvard University Press.

Chan, L. K., & Cole, P. G. (1986). The effects of comprehension monitoring training on the reading competence of learning disabled and regular class students. *RASE: Remedial and Special Education, 7*(4), 33–40.

Dickinson, D. K., & Tabors, P. O. (Eds.). (2001). *Beginning literacy with language: Young children learning at home and school.* Baltimore: Brookes.

Duffy, G. G., Roehler, L. R., Sivan, E., Rackliffe, G., Book, C., Meloth, M. S., Vavrus, L. G., Wesselman, R., Putnam, J., & Bassiri, D. (1987). Effects of explaining the reasoning associated with using reading strategies. *Reading Research Quarterly, 22,* 347–368.

Duke, N. K. (2000). For the rich it's richer: Print environments and experiences offered to first-grade students in very low- and very high-SES school districts. *American Educational Research Journal, 37,* 456–457.

Durkin, D. (1978–79). What classroom observations reveal about reading comprehension instruction. *Reading Research Quarterly, 14,* 481–533.

Elley, W. B. (1991). Acquiring literacy in a second language: The effect of book-based programs. *Language Learning, 41*(3), 375–411.

Freebody, P., & Anderson, R. C. (1983). Effects of vocabulary difficulty, text cohesion, and schema availability on reading comprehension. *Reading Research Quarterly, 18,* 277–294.

García, G. E. (1991). Factors influencing the English reading test performance of Spanish-speaking Hispanic children. *Reading Research Quarterly, 26,* 371–392.

Gersten, R., Fuchs, L. S., Williams, J. P., & Baker, S. (2001). Teaching reading comprehension strategies to students with learning disabilities: A review of research. *Review of Educational Research, 71*(2), 279–320.

Graves, M. F., Cooke, C. L., & LaBerge, M. J. (1983). Effects of previewing short stories. *Reading Research Quarterly, 18,* 262–276.

Graves, M. F., & Graves, B. B. (1994). *Scaffolding reading experiences: Designs for student success.* Norwood, MA: Christopher-Gordon.

Graves, M. F., Graves, B. B., & Braaten, S. (1996). Scaffolded reading experiences for inclusive classrooms. *Educational Leadership, 53*(5), 14–16.

Guthrie, J. T., Van Meter, P., Hancock, G. R., Alao, S., Anderson, E., & McCann, A. (1998). Does concept-oriented reading instruction increase strategy use and conceptual learning from text? *Journal of Educational Psychology, 90,* 261–278.

Guthrie, J. T., & Wigfield, A. (2000). Engagement and motivation in reading. In M. L. Kamil, P. B. Mosenthal, P. D. Pearson, & R. Barr (Eds.), *Handbook of reading research* (Vol. 3, pp. 403–422). Mahwah, NJ: Lawrence Erlbaum.

Jenkins, J. J. (1976). Four points to remember: A tetrahedral model of memory experiments. In L. S. Cermak & F.I.M. Craik (Eds.), *Levels of processing in human memory.* Hillsdale, NJ: Erlbaum.

Kamil, M., Mosenthal, P. B., Pearson, P. D., & Barr, R. (Eds.). (2000). *Handbook of reading research* (Vol. 3). Mahwah, NJ: Lawrence Erlbaum.

Keeny, T. J., Cannizzo, S. R., & Flavell, J. H. (1967). Spontaneous and induced verbal rehearsal in a recall task. *Child Development, 38*(4), 953–966.

Langer, J. A. (1984). Examining background knowledge and text comprehension. *Reading Research Quarterly, 19,* 468–481.

Lapp, D., Flood, J., & Ranck-Buhr, W. (1995). Using multiple text formats to explore scientific phenomena in middle school classrooms. *Reading and Writing Quarterly: Overcoming Learning Difficulties, 11*(2), 173–186.

Laufer, B., & Sim, D. D. (1985). Measuring and explaining the reading threshold needed for English for academic purposes texts. *Foreign Language Annals, 18*(5), 405–411.

Mandler, J. M., & Johnson, N. S. (1977). Remembrance of things parsed: Story structure and recall. *Cognitive Psychology, 9,* 111–151.

McKeown, M. G., Beck, I. L., Omanson, R. C., & Pople, M. T. (1985). Some effects of the nature and frequency of vocabulary instruction on the knowledge and use of words. *Reading Research Quarterly, 20,* 522–535.

Meichenbaum, D., & Biemiller, A. (1998). *Nurturing independent learners: Helping students take charge of their learning.* Cambridge, MA: Brookline.

Meyer, B.J.F., Brandt, D. M., & Bluth, G. J. (1980). Use of top-level structure in text: Key for reading comprehension of ninth-grade student. *Reading Research Quarterly, 16,* 72–103.

National Reading Panel (NRP). (2000). *Teaching children to read: An evidence-based assessment of the scientific research literature on reading and its implications for reading instruction.* Washington, DC: National Institute of Child Health and Human Development and U.S. Department of Education.

Nelson, J. R., Smith, D. J., & Dodd, J. M. (1992). The effects of teaching a summary skills strategy to students identified as learning disabled on their comprehension of science text. *Education and Treatment of Children, 15*(3), 228–243.

Pappas, C. C., & Barry, A. (1997). Scaffolding urban students' initiations: Transactions in reading information books in the read-aloud curriculum genre. In N. J. Karolides (Ed.), *Reader response in elementary classrooms: Quest and discovery* (pp. 215–236). Hillsdale, NJ: Erlbaum.

Pressley, M. (1998). *Reading instruction that works: The case for balanced teaching.* New York: Guilford Press.

Pressley, M. (2000). What should comprehension instruction be the instruction of? In M. Kamil, P. Mosenthal, P. D. Pearson, & R. Barr

(Eds.), *Handbook of reading research* (Vol. 3, pp. 545–562). Mahwah, NJ: Lawrence Erlbaum.

Pressley, M., Wharton-McDonald, R., Allington, R., Block, C. C., Morrow, L., Tracey, D., Baker, K., Brooks, G., Cronin, J., Nelson, E., & Woo, D. (2001). A study of effective first-grade literacy instruction. *Scientific Studies of Reading, 5*(1), 35–58.

RAND Reading Study Group. (2002). *Reading for understanding: Toward an R&D program in reading comprehension.* Santa Monica, CA; Washington, DC: RAND Education.

Reeve, J., Bolt, E., & Cai, Y. (1999). Autonomy-supportive teachers: How they teach and motivate students. *Journal of Educational Psychology, 91,* 537–548.

Ringel, B. A., & Springer, C. J. (1980). On knowing how well one is remembering: The persistence of strategy use during transfer. *Journal of Experimental Child Psychology, 29*(2), 322–333.

Rosenshine, B., & Meister, C. (1994). Reciprocal teaching: A review of the research. *Review of Educational Research, 64,* 479–530.

Skinner, E. A., Wellborn, J. G., & Connell, J. P. (1990). What it takes to do well in school and whether I've got it: A process model of perceived control and children's engagement and achievement in school. *Journal of Educational Psychology, 82,* 22–32.

Smith, M. C. (Ed.). (1998). *Literacy for the twenty-first century: Research, policy, practices, and the National Adult Literacy Survey.* New York: Praeger.

Snow, C. E., Burns, M. S., & Griffin, P. (Eds.). (1998). *Preventing reading difficulties in young children.* Washington, DC: National Research Council, National Academy Press.

Stahl, S. A., & Fairbanks, M. M. (1986). The effects of vocabulary instruction: A model-based meta-analysis. *Review of Educational Research, 56*(1), 72–110.

Stanovich, K. E., & Cunningham, A. E. (1992). Studying the consequences of literacy within a literate society: The cognitive correlates of print exposure. *Memory and Cognition, 20,* 51–68.

Stein, N. L., & Glenn, C. (1979). An analysis of story comprehension in elementary school children. In R. Freedle (Ed.), *New Directions in Discourse Processing: Vol. 2. Advances in Discourse Processing* (pp. 53–120). Norwood, NJ: Ablex.

Swanson, H. L., Kozleski, E., & Steginck, P. (1987). Disabled readers' processing of prose: Do any processes change because of intervention? *Psychology in the Schools, 24*(4), 378–384.

Sweet, A. P., Guthrie, J. T., & Ng, M. (1998). Teacher perceptions and student reading motivation. *Journal of Educational Psychology, 90,* 210–223.

Tabors, P. O., & Snow, C. E. (2001). Young bilingual children and early literacy development. In S. B. Neuman & D. K. Dickinson (Eds.), *Handbook of early literacy research* (pp. 159–178). New York: Guilford Press.

Tan, A., & Nicholson, T. (1997). Flash cards revisited: Training poor readers to read words faster improves their comprehension of text. *Journal of Educational Psychology, 89,* 276–288.

Taylor, B. M., Pearson, P. D., Clark, K. F., & Walpole, S. (1999). Effective schools/accomplished teachers. *Reading Teacher, 53,* 156–159.

Tierney, R. J., & Cunningham, J. C. (1984). Research on teaching reading comprehension. In M. Kamil, P. Mosenthal, P. D. Pearson, & R. Barr (Eds.), *Handbook of reading research* (Vol. 3, pp. 545–562). Mahwah, NJ: Lawrence Erlbaum.

Turner, J. C. (1995). The influence of classroom contexts on young children's motivation for literacy. *Reading Research Quarterly, 30,* 410–441.

Williams, J. P. (1993). Comprehension of students with and without learning disabilities: Identification of narrative themes and idiosyncratic text representations. *Journal of Educational Psychology, 85,* 631–641.

Wolf, M., & Katzir-Cohen, T. (2001). Reading fluency and its intervention. *Scientific Studies of Reading, 5*(3), 211–239.

Wong, B.Y.L., & Jones, W. (1982). Increasing metacomprehension in learning disabled and normally achieving students through self-questioning training. *Learning Disability Quarterly, 5*(3), 228–240.

Chapter Two

The Thinking Process Approach to Comprehension Development

Preparing Students for Their Future Comprehension Challenges

Cathy Collins Block
and Rebecca B. Johnson

> *Dr. Block and Ms. Johnson, whenever you talk to teachers,*
> *would you tell them something for me? Would you tell them*
> *that when students read hard books they need someone*
> *who knows all the words always there beside them.*
> RUSTY, SECOND-GRADER, ST. LOUIS, MISSOURI

By second grade many children have not learned to decode and comprehend simultaneously. They cannot wield comprehension processes enjoyably and profitably even if their decoding skills are on grade level. If they cannot comprehend well after three years of instruction, continuing the same instruction will not likely raise their reading abilities to grade level, even if their decoding skills are on grade level (Block, 2000a; Hesselbrink, 1998; King, 1994). If ineffective instruction continues, many more students may fall behind in their comprehension abilities, as well as limit their world knowledge, power in our information society, aural and printed vocabularies, and motivation to read (Block, 2000b).

From prior research, we have learned that highly effective comprehension lessons are cognitively, socially, and pedagogically richer than ever before (Block & Pressley, 2002). We must no longer teach comprehension as a set of separate, segmented strategies. We must demonstrate it as a set of ever-changing interactions of thinking processes at specific points in a text. We must demonstrate the ebb and flow that occurs when the reader adds new thought processes to create complete, rich meanings. Many students can memorize strategies that they are shown, but they cannot transfer the strategic thinking independently. Teachers must show students how to make meaning for themselves.

Data suggest that many teachers find comprehension difficult to teach (Block, 2001a). This difficulty is in part due to new research that demonstrates the need to present comprehension as an ever-changing interaction of thought processes. Such instruction must be neither too prescriptive nor too free-flowing. When the teacher is too dominant, students may not learn how to apply skills without prompting (Block, 2000b; Taylor, Pearson, Clark, & Walpole, 1999; Wood, Willoughby, McDermott, Motz, & Kaspar, 1999). Alternatively, when instruction is sparse or unmonitored, pupils do not develop tools to think strategically as they read. Many struggle to attain a semblance of meaning, do not contemplate a detail's relevance, and create vague meanings of unfamiliar words in order to "keep on" reading. As a result, comprehension becomes such a challenge that these students disengage and refrain from making meaning.

We must base new methods of teaching on the strengths of prior, research-based practices (for example, Block & Pressley, 2002). The work in this chapter stems from the effectiveness of strategy-based comprehension instruction. The gains of this instruction have been well documented (for example, Brown, Pressley, Van Meter, & Schuder, 1996; Collins, 1991; Block, 1993; Block, 1999; Anderson, 1992; Anderson & Roit, 1993).

The thinking process approach to comprehension instruction is designed to overcome these difficulties. This approach is defined as the development of students' abilities to engage an effective set of thought processes at strategic points in a text to make rich, valid meanings. Robinson (2002) cites the thinking process approach as one of thirteen commonalities of effective reading programs of the past century. Moving beyond strategy-based comprehension instruction, this approach does more than remind students before they read to think about a comprehension strategy that they have learned. It does more than teach strategies with captivating, printed or teacher-made graphic organizers and modeled, minilessons. This approach empowers students to initiate their own comprehension processes continuously as they read. The following features characterize lessons in this approach:

- Students learn how to make meaning for themselves.
- Students verbalize when and where they elected to use one or more comprehension processes to make meaning.
- Students learn which processes are needed at specific points in a reading to enrich their understanding and combine two or more thinking processes to infer, summarize, predict, and so forth.
- These lessons differentiate comprehension instruction so that students can develop a broad and deep set of tools to assist them in making meaning.

The purpose of this chapter is to describe the research that led to the development of the thinking process approach to teaching comprehension. In addition, we present illustrative lessons and pose needs for future research and instruction.

Our study is based on two bodies of research (Beck & Dole, 1994; Block, 2000a). The first suggests that comprehension lessons should be differentiated so that students develop three distinct meaning-making abilities (Block, Schaller, Joy, & Gaine, 2002). These abilities are as follows: (1) students have time and opportunities to read alone in order to experience the satisfaction and accomplishment of making their own meanings without interruptions or promptings, (2) students learn how to verbalize the reasons why they are using specific comprehension processes at particular points in a text, and (3) students are taught new comprehension processes.

The rationale for the thinking process approach to comprehension development parallels the success of offering differentiated and distinct types of decoding lessons to students. For example, when we teach students to decipher print, we provide a wide variety of differentiated lessons to develop a broad repertoire of decoding processes for students (that is, we teach phonics, English letter pattern recognition, context and picture clue use, structural analysis abilities, content-specific and basic sight word knowledge, and so on). It seems reasonable to assume that when we teach comprehension, we should provide differentiated lessons so that students master an equally multifaceted set of tools that can assist them to make meaning.

A second body of research concerns expert readers' comprehension processes (see Pressley & Afflerbach, 1995; Block, 2001a, for reviews of this research). Among these processes are the ability to think metacognitively, reflect, and overcome comprehension difficulties independently. When we engage students in identifying, designing, and implementing instruction that builds comprehension processes that expert readers use, our lessons can include strategies used by individuals who have different reading needs, varied personalities, and diverse literacy abilities. From 2000 to 2001, we have developed and tested numerous expert readers' process-based comprehension lessons. When students mastered the processes contained in these lessons, their comprehension abilities increased significantly as measured by standardized and criterion-referenced test scores (Block, 2000a).

How to Teach the Thinking Process Approach

The thinking process approach provides more instruction than richly enhanced teacher-directed strategy lessons. Lesson One teaches students how to use two comprehension processes simultaneously. Lesson Two enables students to identify and interrelate text-specific thinking processes. Lesson Three leads students to teach others the comprehension processes they used and to describe what they want to learn next.

Lesson One: Set Two Process Goals (STPG) for Every Lesson to Keep Students' Minds Fully Engaged

Lesson One teaches students to develop the ability to apply and coordinate multiple comprehension processes sequentially. A comprehension process is the continued presence of ongoing mental effort to comprehend. The mental effort initiates and sustains several metacognitive thoughts that are necessary at specific points in a text by an individual to clarify and make meaning. The comprehension process approach uses the distinct steps in Lesson One to teach students to select and integrate more than one comprehension process at a time. Each step scaffolds students. Think alouds appear throughout the lesson as teachers describe the thoughts that occur in expert readers' minds when they read. Thinking process motions and graphics are also used to simulate the types of mental energy that is exerted and continued until distinct comprehension processes unveil a complete understanding. Lesson One consists of five steps:

1. Teacher describes the two thinking process goals for this lesson. Then she performs a think aloud of a first comprehension process to be taught and writes the directions for initiating that thought process on the board.
2. Teacher and students draw a diagram of the thinking process and practice using a motion to depict the process. For example, students draw an arrow on a Post-it® note pointing from left to right to depict inferencing forward onto the next page.
3. Teacher performs a think aloud of a second comprehension process and writes directions for initiating that thought process on the board.
4. Students and teacher diagram the second thinking process and perform a motion to depict the ongoing flow of mental energy that will occur each time this particular metacognition is required in a text. For example, drawing conclusions requires the mind to take a lot of information and pull it toward a single goal. The motion to depict this process is to make a funnel with one's hands or to graph it on paper. Next, teachers perform three think alouds using both comprehension processes at once.
5. Teachers continue to demonstrate the use of two processes three times before asking students to do so in small groups, and then the teacher asks students to read silently alone at their instructional reading levels.

To illustrate, Ms. Turner, a fourth-grade teacher, used Lesson One to teach students to think about the two comprehension processes of (1) to infer how the characters felt by connecting the historical and political context to characters' lives and (2) to combine literal meanings to build better inferences. We will look more closely at her methods in just a moment. Other implementations of Lesson One might teach students to (1) arrange facts into a sequence until the main ideas mold into a coherent body of knowledge, (2) relate main ideas vertically until themes emerge, (3) verify and make connections within and outside of a text during and after reading, or (4) draw conclusions and apply data to their lives as they read. Most important, Lesson One emphasizes that two of these processes (and eventually many processes) will be ongoing simultaneously and interrelate synergistically with one another as students become more able comprehenders.

To teach these lessons, a teacher will select two thinking processes. The educator then opens the lesson with a think-aloud demonstration of how to use these processes as students read. Students have the text before them (in a book or on an overhead screen, blackboard, felt board, or computer monitor) as the think alouds occur. After the teacher demonstrates the first process, the second process, and the combination of two processes to enhance comprehension of one paragraph, the students read four more paragraphs, as the teacher repeats this demonstration of two processes in action with each paragraph. All the while, the teacher describes how students are to combine the two processes when they read without the teacher's prompting to do so. These demonstrations continue for several minutes, using at least five subsequent paragraphs.

The next step is to ask students to volunteer to read a paragraph aloud to classmates and pause to describe the processes they are using to comprehend. When students are assessed, a teacher listens to them individually as they read a text. The teacher stops periodically and asks them to describe their comprehension processes. Paragraphs that can be used for these assessments are in Leslie and Caldwell (2001). These passages are marked at points where students should be able to describe how two or more thinking processes are being engaged simultaneously and successfully. The following example illustrates Ms. Turner's STPG lesson.

Ms. Turner elected to teach her fourth-graders (1) to infer how the characters felt by connecting the historical and political context to characters' lives and (2) to combine literal meanings to build better inferences. She selected a paragraph from the class history text that students were about to read. Before Ms. Turner displayed the paragraph on the overhead, she told the students that their minds would use many thinking processes as they worked to comprehend that text (Kintsch, 1988, describes each of these processes in more depth). She described the following processes. First, the mind puts individual word meanings together to determine the literal meaning in each sentence. She wrote "literal meaning" is "what I read" on the board. Second, the mind uses relational processes to generate a gist, which is the addition of several literal meanings to deduce the depth and direction toward which an author's thoughts are moving by the end of the paragraph. She wrote "gist" is "what I know about what the author is doing to communicate" on the board. Third, the mind uses inference processes to infuse human emotions into events as they unfold. She wrote "inference" is "what I know about this topic, authorial writing style, and life in general" on the board.

Next, Ms. Turner drew the graphic described in Figure 2.1 in order to demonstrate how these processes work together simultaneously to help the reader make meaning (see Figure 2.1). She wrote, "Build relationships between historical contexts and characters' lives while you read so as to unite literal meanings to authorial writing styles and life events to inference" as a title above the phrases and arrows. Then Ms. Turner began her first think

Figure 2.1. Lesson One: Depicting the Steps in an STPG Thinking Process Lesson.

What I Read and What I Know = Inference

Step 1   Do a think aloud of first comprehension process and write directions on board.
Step 2   Diagram thinking process with a motion, such as an arrow for inferencing forward.
Step 3   Do a think aloud of second comprehension process and write directions on board.
Step 4   Diagram second thinking process with a motion and do three think alouds using both comprehension processes at once.
Step 5   Demonstrate three times before you ask students to do so in group, then let them read silently alone with a checklist to monitor themselves.

aloud by referring to the history text. The text opened in 1929 with a description of two senior citizens. These historical context details were written around the title of the graphic described above, which the teacher had given each reader.

Her think aloud contained these parts:

1. She explained to the students how she used these two details to make inferences while she read the next sentence.
2. She read two sentences and did a think aloud that told how she identified the depth and direction of the author's writing style and how the choice of words created a gist of the purpose of this paragraph.
3. She adhered an adhesive note to the right corner on the bottom of the page of the text. On this adhesive note was ⟶ that she had written on the board. She demonstrated how to make an inference, explaining that she was able to infer because she combined literal meaning and historical context clues with the way the author wrote the first three sentences and how she would have felt if she had lived in 1929. She told the students what these clues had led her to infer in the next paragraph on the next page. She turned the page and then placed the adhesive note on the bottom of that page.
4. She repeated the think aloud three more times to show how to integrate historical context clues, literal meaning, gist, and authorial writing style to create inferences. Then she moved the adhesive note once more to the bottom of the next page.
5. After reading three full page with students, she asked the students to make inferences and tell how they made them. She passed out Post-it® notes to each student to remind them how to combine these comprehension processes as they read. She divided students into groups and asked them to stop at the end of each page and tell each other their inferences and how they united several comprehension processes to make each inference.

On the next day, Ms. Turner taught the students to identify when they needed each of the thinking processes. She also taught them how to initiate the processes of (1) uniting historical context clues with literal word meanings and (2) initiating inferences by recognizing the gist that arose from an author's writing style and the life events and emotions that the gist stimulated in their minds.

Then, Ms. Turner and her students read the following paragraph and described how they inferred what the characters felt by relating the historical context to literal meanings. Students read: "Their stomachs churned with fear and emotion. The old man and woman clasped each other's hands and looked up and down the enormous gray bank. There was no way to enter. They were paralyzed by fear, and all their lives' dreams flashed before them in an instant." Students discussed the processes they used to (1) infer something about the bank that must have frightened the people, (2) extract the gist, and (3) integrate the historical context clues that had appeared in previous paragraphs relative to 1929.

Next, she described the historical context that would have affected the meaning of the four sentences that they had just read. In 1929, when the story was set, most rivers swelled often, and few bridges existed to cross them. The U.S. economy fell in the same year, to create the most disastrous depression that the country had ever experienced. She asked the students to infer the characters' feelings depicted in the paragraph by relating them to one of the 1929 historical contexts. They were to read the paragraph as if these two following sentences had appeared right before it: "The old man and woman raised their heads and saw the bear at exactly the same instant. He was running toward their riverbank camp at top speed. Their stomachs churned with fear and emotion. The old man and woman clasped each other's hands and looked up and down the enormous gray bank. There was no way to enter. They were paralyzed by fear, and all their lives' dreams flashed before them in an instant."

Next, she asked students to read, infer, and relate the two comprehension processes of gaining information and understanding characters' emotional responses with the addition of the second set of historical context clues and to pay attention to the different inferences their minds were making.

She also asked them to pay attention to how the inference changed due to the interrelationship of the several comprehension processes. Next, she gave the following political context as if it had preceded the same paragraph: "It was October 29, 1929, now known as 'Black Tuesday,' the day that the biggest financial crisis occurred in America. As the old man and woman heard about the stock market crash, they drove all night from their New Hampshire farm to reach New York City's World Bank at dawn. Their stomachs churned with fear and emotion. The old man and woman clasped each other's hands and looked up and down the enormous gray bank. There was no way to enter. They were paralyzed by fear, and all their lives' dreams flashed before them in an instant."

Students wrote about how their minds used the differing historical contexts, literal meanings, author writing style, and gist to infer the differences in the fear felt by the people. For example, Tyler, one of the fourth-grade students, wrote:

> Ms. Turner taught me how to put two thoughts together when I don't understand something. I do that now. When I read something I do not know, I combine the meaning in each sentence to get a gist or main idea for the paragraph. I put those thoughts with what I've learned about life and the way the author writes to infer and overcome the thing I don't understand. You know, like the other day I came to the word "Indians." I did not know that word. Just sounding it out did not fill my mind enough. So I thought about the historical context and gist of the paragraph. The author was telling me about the first Thanksgiving and the people who were invited. Then, the word just came to me in an inference about what I already knew about Thanksgivings. Because the word began with the letter "I" and the people invited to the first Thanksgiving were "Indians," I inferred the word's meaning all by myself. I put the historical context, gist, and my own knowledge together, to learn new words. These were *three* comprehension processes that I've learned to use all at the same time. They helped me learn the word "Indian" all by myself and I'll never forget it either!

Graphics like the inference graphic in Figure 2.1, which depict the motion that the mind makes to inference, have been shown to assist students in integrating thinking processes and increasing their strategic decision making during reading (Block & Mangieri, 1996; Schuder, 1987). Moreover, when STPG (setting two comprehension goals for a single session) and graphics (depicting the integration of these processes) are included in comprehension instruction, teachers do not have to depend merely upon students' ability to practice or memorize comprehension strategies for them to reach deep levels of understanding.

STPG lessons teach how to use two or more comprehension processes in unison through think alouds, modeling, expanded explanations of two thinking processes, graphics that depict mental motions, and guided-practice exercises. They also enable teachers to avoid former difficulties that occurred during the strategy lessons of the 1990s. Many teachers did not learn how to implement specific thinking-processes-in-action. Many teachers had been led to believe that by merely asking questions, such as "What do you think the author meant?" students would learn to perform the thinking processes necessary to comprehend. Others began lessons by only citing definitions, such as "Inference is the ability to read between the lines," and they expected students to somehow be able to learn how to engage and sustain this inference type of thinking while they read.

Fortunately today, teachers who have repeatedly used STPG lessons report that their students are able to explain why they engaged a particular set of comprehension processes at specific points in a text and use several metacognitive thought processes to unlock meaning (Block, 2001b, 2001d).

Lesson Two: The First Two Pages Are Critical: Teaching Students Text-Specific Comprehension Strategies

Lesson Two is the second type of thinking process lesson. It develops the students' confidence that they can control the meaning-making process. The lesson also teaches the tools of selecting what is necessary to overcome a text's challenging sections. It teaches students that comprehending the authors' intent is more enjoyable than merely guessing at a meaning just to keep on decoding. Lesson Two teaches what Gee (1999a, 1999b, 2000, 2001) refers to as design grammar. *Design grammar* is the unique principles and patterns that writers use to communicate complex meanings within specific domains of knowledge. For example, scientists most often use an objective rather than a first-person, informal tone when reporting statistically analyzed data. Lesson Two enables teachers to develop students' use of design grammar as a new tool to comprehend individual domains of knowledge.

Lesson Two contains five steps, taught over several weeks. Because students are asked to practice each step of the lesson until it becomes an automatic comprehension tool, the amount of time spent in instruction for each step will vary. The five steps for teaching design grammar are the following:

1. Learn to follow the author's train of thought in the first two pages of a text by consciously attending to the way that the writer makes connections between the sentences in the first few paragraphs.
2. Consciously attend to the way that a writer makes connections between paragraphs as one reads from the third page and forward.
3. Mentally or literally diagram the method and frequency by which an author summarizes key tenets.
4. Identify the depth of an author's writing style.
5. Visualize literal intratext and intertext connections in a text.

Lesson Two's steps enable students to more fully engage in design grammar because they show students how to follow an author's sentence-to-sentence and paragraph-to-paragraph trains of thought. To teach these steps, teachers and students can engage in the following activities:

1. Diagram sentence-to-sentence connections within the first seven paragraphs. These visuals can illustrate how an author places single, simple ideas in relationship to broader, main concept sentences. For example, Patricia Lauber won awards for her scientific writing in *Volcano: The Eruption and Healing of Mount St. Helens* (1993). The design grammar that she used in most paragraphs throughout this book was as follows:

MAIN IDEA STATEMENT (SENTENCE ONE)
↓
DETAIL RELATED TO MAIN IDEA (SENTENCE TWO)
↓

EXAMPLE OF DETAIL (SENTENCE THREE)
↓
MORE DESCRIPTION OF THE EXAMPLE (SENTENCES
FOUR THROUGH END OF PARAGRAPH)

2. Diagram paragraph-to-paragraph connections from page 3 to page 7 of a text to determine the types of paragraphs used and number of paragraphs used to introduce, describe, illustrate, and conclude discussions of a main concept.
3. Diagram the author's summary method; that is, draw a box on a horizontal line for each paragraph before a summary paragraph occurs. Then, place a number inside each box to designate how many paragraphs will usually be written by this author before he draws a conclusion. Place the concluding summary box below the horizontal row of numbered paragraphs to complete the graphic of this author's summary design grammar.
4. Describe the depth of the author's style:
   Level 3 (very dense): Dense vocabulary, complex sentence structure, long paragraphs, many deep ideas
   Level 2 (average density): Average vocabulary, compound sentence structure, average paragraphs, some deep ideas per paragraph
   Level 1 (low density): Low vocabulary, simple sentence structure, short paragraphs, few deep ideas per paragraph
5. Diagram intratext and intertext connections.

To illustrate, if an author connects sentences by stating a main idea and then listing details related to that main point that are equal in value, students can diagram the train of thought by drawing a large arc across the top of the page with the main idea sentence written across it and arrows for each sentence as the handles to the umbrella. If every paragraph were of equal value, arrows could appear vertically beneath each other. If some paragraphs were of greater value, they could be drawn larger. By diagramming these connective trains of thought for several paragraphs, students can learn to predict the pattern that the author is likely to follow throughout the remainder of a text (see steps 1 to 3 above).

Step 4 is the process of teaching text-specific thinking to students. It describes the depth of an author's style of writing. This depth results from the density of vocabulary, complexity of sentence structure, length of paragraphs, and depth of ideas, as stated previously. Students learn to identify three levels of difficulty. In so doing, they not only develop the ability to describe the depth of every author's writing style, but they also recognize the depth at which they prefer to read, which in turn increases the likelihood that they will more frequently enjoy self-selected reading. As an example, one of the authors of this chapter most values authors whose depth corresponds to a Level 2 vocabulary density, Level 3 complexity of sentences, Level 2 paragraph length, and Level 3 idea density (a $V_2S_3P_2I_3$ pattern). Students enjoy saying these coded inscriptions of the books that they read. Lesson Two also assists poorer readers in refraining from diving into *every* text using the same undifferentiated, inflexible, and ineffective thinking processes. When taught design grammar, the comprehension of the less able readers improved (Block & Pressley, 2002).

Step 5 captures the most reluctant readers. Many benefit from creating their own diagrams showing the types of intratextual connections of their favorite authors. Once they depict these train-of-thought patterns, students also generate many intertextual connections to other books by the same author and to other authors, other topics, themselves, and the world.

This second lesson type is also important in assisting students in learning to read nonfiction. Nonfiction books cannot build momentum through the tool of story grammar that is used in fiction. Story grammar refers to the predictable sequence of events that occur in narrative text: (1) the setting, characters, and problem are introduced; (2) attempts to solve the problem occur; (3) the climax occurs; and (4) the sequence ends in a resolution. For this reason, we need to develop new methods so that students build the momentum and motivation to continue reading nonfiction books. Lesson Two provides these stimulants.

The tools that are taught in Lesson Two's five steps can be followed by two additional processes that we are including in our research. We call these processes "Tilling the Text" and "Scamper and Scan Until You Choose to Stop to Savor." Skimming and scampering over a nonfiction text can build motivation because students learn that they *can stop to savor pieces of information that are of most interest to them.* Scampering and scanning also develop the momentum to enjoy reading nonfiction. "Scamper and scan until they stop to savor" lessons begin by granting students the freedom to scan rapidly over information that they already know so that they have more time to process and learn information that is new to them. In so doing, momentum to keep on reading nonfiction occurs because students enjoy varying the rate at which they read. By teaching these two processes, nonfiction reading becomes more pleasant and distinct from fictional reading. As a result, students have demonstrated that they spend more time reading expository text (Block, 2001d). As their experiences with pleasurable nonfiction reading increase, students select texts that contain more new information. With all that is demanded of today's students, it is imperative that we teach students to "scamper and savor" to ensure that they master new knowledge efficiently and independently.

Tilling the text is reading with the goal of obtaining the gist of the content and structure of a nonfiction selection. Students can be taught to "till a text," just as farmers till the soil before they plant. Students who learn to till a text increase their understanding of informational text significantly above students who do not do so (Block, 2001c). *Tilling the text* enables students to better predict the facts that will appear on future pages of a text, build more accurate pictures in their minds when photographs are absent, and provide a quest to keep on reading.

To teach students to "till a text," you teach them to skim full nonfiction selections and note three things: (1) all subheads and points of emphasis, (2) level of density of ideas, and (3) content flow. With this information, students can establish the rate of reading speed and depth of thinking that they want to use with each text. Students can also identify which sections they will "scamper over" so that they can have the gist of the content when they reach the specific section of the text that they want to slowly digest and savor.

Lessons about tilling a text begin by teaching students to pause at difficult points in a text. Such a lesson could begin by saying: "Here's a difficult point in this story and one that will occur in other similar texts in the future. Whenever you come to this paragraph (and others like it in the future), I suggest that you call upon several processes such as . . . and do something like this to craft the deepest, most fulfilling meaning: _____."

In a fifth-grade class, for example, Ms. Mackey taught students to "till the text" with the following demonstration before students read. She told them to use the sea of thoughts surrounding a story as a context clue. Then she demonstrated how to let individual words that an author selects suggest the meanings in the next paragraph. For instance, Ms. Mackey said:

> The subtitles in this chapter have strange names—Arsenic, Venom, and Hemlock. I know that venom is poison in a snake. I think all of these names mean poison because they are all subtitles. Is he trying to tell me something about the commonalities between the natural phenomenons that will be described throughout this chapter? Maybe I should pay attention to what these types of poisons have in common because the author had to have a reason to group them all together in one chapter. I think he is depending on me to infer a lot from the details that describe each poison to gain a deeper meaning and to apply more global information to my life.

The freedom and skill that the tilling process develops enable students to vary the pace, breadth, and depth of their interrelated thought processes, which in turn increases the joy they receive from reading. Research has demonstrated that teaching two nonfiction texts about the same subject one after another also increases students' comprehension by 33 percent above what they experience after reading a fiction and nonfiction book about the same topic (Block, 2001b).

Comprehension instruction should provide varied tools that create a meaning-making process that is self-initiated, ever-changing, and free-flowing. Without effective differentiated lessons, poor readers state that reading becomes boring because of their inability to adapt comprehension processes for different contents and purposes (Block, 2001c). The readers' ineffective processing dulls their abilities to discover and savor subtle meanings, which limits their drive and desire to read.

Lesson Three: Student-Led Comprehension Process Groups (SLCPGs)

Lesson Three assists poor readers in overcoming their limitations. The lesson creates time for students to suggest what they want to learn. The teachers then teach these processes. The next day, students join a group in which a peer using a different book reteaches that comprehension process. Then students share a favorite book with a similar density of author's writing style.

During each SLCPG meeting, a different student describes in his or her own words the comprehension processes taught in Lessons One or Two. Next, all students share and ask questions about what they did to accomplish the comprehension processes. They demonstrate their thinking by performing think alouds after reading sections from their books. Last, participants in the SLCPGs offer suggestions for overcoming specific reading problems related to those comprehension processes. Students enjoy naming their groups according to the processes they are practicing.

For example, one of the students in a fifth-grade SLCPG reported: "Yesterday, during our 'meaning makers' group, our leader asked me what I wished I could do to comprehend better. For the first time, I realized that I wanted to cling to meanings more. My friends told me what they did to get a deeper understanding. What everyone suggested worked! Today, I'm reading the words more rapidly and the thoughts more slowly by stopping at the end of sentences to reflect. I don't read every word that the author says so slowly that I can't know each idea. Today, ideas just jump off the page. I must rush down the lines to capture them all as they leap into the pictures in my mind."

SLCPG meetings are normally held once a week. Between meetings, students practice the suggestions they learned and at the following meeting confer about what they did to apply the processes they previously discussed. At the second group meeting, students can make motion-filled icons or write down the steps they followed to unite two or more comprehension processes as they read a specific book. These graphics and lists (similar to the icons on computer bars) remind students of the comprehension tools they can use to become better comprehenders. Here are some of the names of the SLCPGs created by fourth-graders in a study by Block (1999):

Meaning makers	We want to learn how to understand better, make more in-depth responses to material, and learn how to inter-relate new thinking processes to craft understanding.
Transformer titans	We want to learn how to more rapidly apply what we read to our lives.
Word wanters	We want to learn more decoding strate-gies. We will bring a book we are reading to group meetings to model how we de-coded a difficult word. We will ask class-mates to find similar words and try out these strategies in their books.
Speed mongrels	We want to increase our speed of oral and silent reading.
Memory menders	We want to find ways to retain more of what we read.
Critical analyzers	We want to learn how to analyze what we read. We also want to learn how to reflect more on what we read.

Two examples of the products that arise when students meet together to learn how to comprehend better follow. The first was completed by fifth-graders on Sept. 2, 2001. Students discussed the need to recognize multiple causes and effects as they read. Students decided to select a topic of their choice and research it in teams. Then they recorded the different actions that could occur based on single decisions. (An example of such a diagram appears in Figure 2.2.)

The second example of an SLCPG lesson enabled students to initiate the thinking process of verifying information as they read. It began with pupils wanting to find multiple sources to verify single pieces of information (something that will become more important as students increasingly turn to the Internet). In this lesson students broke into SLCPGs and selected a topic to

Figure 2.2. Lesson Three Example: Multiple Outcomes.

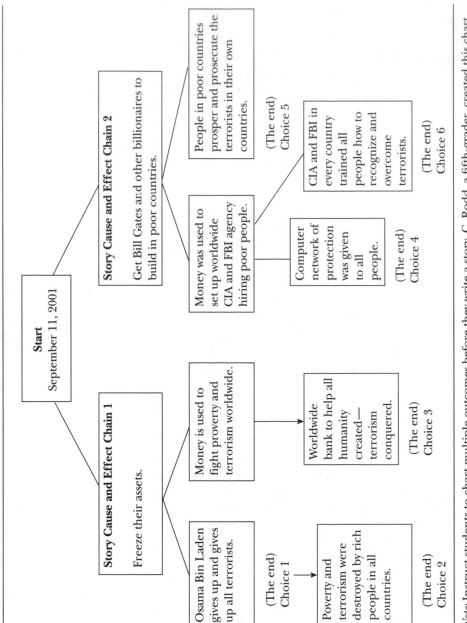

Note: Instruct students to chart multiple outcomes before they write a story. C. Rodd, a fifth-grader, created this chart, which he titled, "How President Bush Could Overcome Worldwide Terrorism."

research, formulated questions, and turned to two sources to answer their questions. For example, a group of fourth-graders who wanted to research information about volcanoes generated five questions and sought two different sources of information to answer each question (see Exhibit 2.1). After they had done their research, students met in SLCPG groups to describe how and why they called upon the verification process as they read silently and independently. As a result, the group reported that in the future they want and will enjoy reading more than one source before deciding upon answers to their questions.

Exhibit 2.1. Lesson Three Example: Record-Keeping Form for Verifying Information.

Research team members: Suzanna, John, Clarissa, Carl
Research book that began the study: *The Volcano* (Lauber, 1993)

Questions team wants to answer
1. How long had it been since Mount St. Helens had erupted?
2. What caused the volcano to erupt so suddenly without warning after having remained dormant for as long as team members had been alive?
3. How hot does lava become?
4. What is the largest volcano?
5. How many volcanoes are in the world?

Sources for answer to question 1
120 years as computed by Carl from data in *Encyclopedia Britannica* verified by seeking a second source in the *Volcano* (Lauber, 1993) and recalculating the numbers of years by John

Sources for answer to question 2
Earthquakes and seismic vibrations of the Earth's core south of Mount St. Helens had reduced the distance between the two plates beneath Mount St. Helens. This decreased space which increased the pressure upon magma forced it into the air. Source was http://volcano.und.novak.edu. Verification and names of the two plates were found in a diagram and text on pages 52 and 53 of *Volcano* (Lauber, 1993). Suzanna and Clarissa worked side by side, and both read all the information in both sources to provide increased verification.

(continued)

Exhibit 2.1. (*continued*)

Sources for answer to question 3

 2000 degrees at vent decreasing in intensity *very* slowly as it mingles with the 10 to 80 degrees in the atmosphere on the mountain slopes. It takes more than 1000 degrees to melt most rocks. Source 1 was *Reading Rainbow Video "Hill of Fire."* Source 2 was phone call to Museum of Science and History in which Carl spoke to the curator, Mr. Juan Paoblo. He verified the information in the video. All team members watched the video. Suzanna made the phone call. She asked John to confirm with her and record the information taken auditorally.

Sources for answer to question 4

 Mauna Loa, source was Mr. Juan Paoblo, in Suzanna and John's phone interview. Source 2 was http://volcano.und.novak.edu.

Sources for answer to question 5

 850 active volcanoes. Source was Mr. Juan Paoblo, but he said "about 600 or more." Because the information was vague, Carl and Clarissa sought two additional sources for verification. Two subsequent sources reported 850, and both sources converged to verify that number. Sources 2 and 3 were CD ROM: *Explorapedia* and http://volcano.urd.novak.edu.

Skills gained by the research team as a result of this project
 - Internet and CD ROM: Explorapedia and interviews with experts are rapid sources of factual information.
 - Vague information should be re-verified with at least two sources, and we saw how gossip in people's personal lives spreads when we don't follow this principle.
 - Videotapes are the best sources for experiencing large events, better than reading because our minds are freer to explore ramifications of, and pose questions about an event viewed because we don't have to be decoding and interpreting words.
 - It is important to have two people to verify.

On a separate page, write the grade you think you deserve and why.

Acknowledgment: The authors gratefully acknowledge the help of Rachel Escamilla in preparing this exhibit.

Three Recommendations for the Future

RECOMMENDATION 1: We must help students overcome the comprehension challenges they will face.

Students must be taught how to comprehend greater amounts of information exponentially faster than we did when we were their age. Many educators predict that by 2010, 100 percent of students will have access to the World Wide Web in unsupervised and unguided situations. They will be able to navigate the information superhighway before they can cross the street in front of their homes alone (AT&T, 1998). Because of this access, students must be taught how to discern fact, opinion, and bias when reading silently. They must learn not to be satisfied with creating and comprehending mere sound bites as the soul and scope of knowledge. How can we help students verify knowledge sources and place two nonfiction texts about the same subject matter in perspective? How can we convince children that unless they learn to synthesize a large body of nonfiction knowledge they will limit their world, their power in our Internet society, their vocabularies, and their intrinsic motivation to read (Block, 1999).

RECOMMENDATION 2: We must include more opportunities for students to learn how to overcome misunderstandings while they read silently alone. Students must be taught more lessons like those described in this chapter so that they can initiate comprehension processes unaided or prompted by their teachers.

World knowledge is increasing exponentially. By the year 2020, it will be doubling every seventy-three days ("Navigating the Internet Superhighway," 2001). When we combine this research with the dense information in nonfiction texts, we can appreciate the depth and complexity of information students must learn to comprehend *independently* when they become adults.

This explosion of knowledge is coupled with less time to comprehend it. This compression is expected to increase in the future. For example, the average length of a presidential candidate's statement on an evening news broadcast in 1968 was 42.3 seconds.

Twenty years later, the amount of time devoted to a single candidate's position and policies was compacted to only 9.8 seconds. In 1999, as the presidential election began, a new piece of news was broadcast every 3.5 seconds. As a result, the average length of time allocated to comprehend single candidate statements in the last thirty years decreased by 121 percent ("Navigating the Internet Superhighway," 2001).

Moreover, textbooks in all content areas are densely packed with facts. This density does not allow for authors to highlight, support, or elaborate upon intellectual ideas (Anderson, Armbruster, & Kantor, 1980; Block, 2001d). Unfortunately, most students have not learned how to study from or comprehend such dense expository texts (Pressley & Afflerbach, 1995). Similarly, students can read instant worldwide communications more often than students two decades ago. They no longer are protected or buttressed by, or have to wait for adults to interpret, expository data and media for them. We must teach *them* how to independently analyze data critically.

RECOMMENDATION 3: We must involve students in making decisions about what reading difficulties they want to overcome.

In the future, involving students in making decisions will become increasingly important. We can do so one-to-one or by involving whole classes. In a recent research study, we asked 450 students what they needed to comprehend nonfiction. Most could describe specifically what they wanted to learn next to become better comprehenders (Block, 2001b).

Summary

This is an exciting time to be teaching and researching in the field of reading comprehension. We are discovering how to teach comprehension more effectively than at any other time in history. In this chapter we proposed that comprehension should be taught through a thinking process approach. We recommend beginning by teaching students three differentiated lessons to improve their comprehension: (1) STPG, (2) initiating text-specific thinking on the first two pages, and (3) student-led comprehension group lessons.

References

Anderson, R. C., Armbruster, B., & Kantor, C. (1980). Recall of previously unrecalled information following shift in perspective. *Journal of Verbal Learning and Verbal Behavior, 17,* 1–12.

Anderson, V. (1992). A teacher development project in transactional strategy instruction for teachers of severely reading-disabled adolescents. *Teaching and Teacher Education, 8,* 391–403.

Anderson, V., & Roit, M. (1993). Planning and implementing collaborative strategy instruction for delayed readers in grades 6–10. *Elementary School Journal, 94,* 121–137.

AT&T. (1998). *Classroom of the future.* Research Report 119. Washington, DC: AT&T Research and Development Center.

Beck, I., & Dole, J. (1994). Engaging readers in nonfictional text. In C. Collins & J. Mangieri (Eds.), *Teaching thinking: An agenda for the twenty-first century* (pp. 233–254). Hillsdale, NJ: Erlbaum.

Block, C. C. (1993). Strategy instruction in a literature-based program. *Elementary School Journal, 94,* 103–120.

Block, C. C. (1999). Comprehension: Crafting understanding. In L. Gambrell, L. Morrow, S. Neuman, & M. Pressley (Eds.), *Best Practices in Literacy Instruction* (pp. 98–118). New York: Guilford Press.

Block, C. C. (2000a). The case for exemplary instruction especially for students who come to school without the precursors for literacy success. *National Reading Conference Yearbook, 49,* 155–167.

Block, C. C. (2000b). Reading instruction in the new millennium. In A. Costa (Ed.), *Developing Minds* (3rd ed., pp. 472–490). Alexandria, VA: Association for Supervision and Curriculum Development.

Block, C. C. (2001a). *Teaching the language arts* (3rd ed.). Needham Heights, MA: Allyn & Bacon.

Block, C. C. (2001b, May). *Comprehending non-fiction: Reading to learn.* Paper presented at the annual meeting of the International Reading Association, New Orleans, LA.

Block, C. C. (2001c). Teaching students to comprehend non-fiction. *California Reader, 21*(2), 1–12.

Block, C. C. (2001d). What effective teachers did to sustain reading growth. *The Colorado Communicator, 25*(1), 9–21.

Block, C. C., & Mangieri, J. (1996). *Reason to read: Thinking strategies of life through literature* (Vols. 1–3). Menlo Park, CA: Addison-Wesley.

Block, C. C., & Pressley, M. (Eds.). (2002). *Comprehension instruction: Research-based best practices.* New York: Guilford Press.

Block, C. C., Schaller, J. L., Joy, J. A., & Gaine, P. (2002). Process-based comprehension instruction: Perspectives of four reading educators.

In Block, C. C., & Pressley, M. (Eds.), *Comprehension instruction: Research-based best practices* (pp. 42–61). New York: Guilford Press.

Brown, R., Pressley, M., Van Meter, P., & Schuder, T. (1996). A quasi-experimental validation of transactional strategies instruction with low-achieving second-grade readers. *Journal of Educational Psychology, 88,* 18–37.

Collins, C. (1991). Reading instruction that increases thinking abilities. *Journal of Reading, 34,* 510–516.

Hasselbrink, T. (1998, May). *Overcoming the cycle of reading failure.* Paper presented at the annual meeting of the International Reading Association, Orlando, CA.

Gee, J. P. (1999a). Review of the "learning paradox" manuscript. *American Educational Research Journal, 36*(1), 87–97.

Gee, J. P. (1999b). The future of the social turn: Social minds and the new capitalism. *Research on Language and Social Interaction, 32*(1–2), 61–68.

Gee, J. P. (2000). The limits of reframing: A response to Professor Snow. *Journal of Literacy Research, 32*(1), 121–129.

Gee, J. P. (2001). Reading as situated language: A sociocognitive perspective—Comprehension of written and verbal language is as much about experience with the worlds of home, school, and work as it is about words. *Journal of Adolescent and Adult Literacy, 44*(8), 714–726.

Hesselbrink, T. (1998). Comprehending in a technologically-driven environment. Paper presented at the annual meeting of the International Reading Association, New Orleans, LA.

King, A. (1994). Guiding knowledge construction in the classroom: Effects of teaching children how to question and how to explain. *American Educational Research Journal, 31*(2), 338–368.

Kintsch, W. (1998). The role of knowledge in discourse comprehension: A construction-integration model. *Psychology Review, 95*(2), 163–182.

Lauber, P. (1993). *Volcano: The Eruption and Healing of Mount St. Helens.* New York: Macmillan.

Leslie, L., & Caldwell, J. (2001). *Qualitative Reading Inventory—3.* Needham Heights, MA: Allyn & Bacon.

"Navigating the Internet superhighway." *Wall Street Journal,* June 23, 2001, p. A3.

Palincsar, A., & Magnusson, R. (2000). Effects of comprehension strategy instruction on non-fictional text understanding. Paper presented at the annual meeting of the National Reading Conference, Scottsdale, AZ.

Pressley, M., & Afflerbach, P. (1995). *Verbal protocols of reading: The nature of constructively responsive reading.* Hillsdale, NJ: Erlbaum.

Robinson, R. (2002). *Classics in literacy education.* Newark, DE: International Reading Association.

Schuder, T. (1987). The SAIL Program: Effects on students; reading achievement. *Educational Leadership, 44*(6), 345–349.

Taylor, B. M., Pearson, P. D., Clark, K. F., & Walpole, S. (1999). Effective schools/accomplished teachers. *Reading Teacher, 53,* 156–159.

Wood, E., Willoughby, T., McDermott, C., Motz, M., & Kaspar, V. (1999). Developmental differences in study behavior. *Journal of Educational Psychology, 91,* 527–536.

Chapter Three

From Good to Memorable

Characteristics of Highly Effective Comprehension Teaching

Ellin Oliver Keene

Early June heat and light streamed through the narrow library windows at Bunker Elementary in Newark, California, a bedroom community on the east side of the San Francisco Bay. Thousands of immigrants and low-wage workers who serve in the hotels and restaurants, ubiquitous office parks, and construction sites of Silicon Valley have brought their families to live in Newark. Their children speak one of twenty-six languages and have flooded into a maze of temporary classrooms set up on school campuses to accommodate children in small primary classrooms (California statute stipulates a ratio of twenty students to one teacher) and terribly overcrowded intermediate classrooms.

On this morning Newark's twenty-three literacy coordinators listened as one of their own conducted a demonstration lesson with a class of twenty first-graders, many of whom were just learning English. Lynne Gurnee used Eve Bunting's picture book (1996), *Going Home,* to teach questioning, one of the metacognitive strategies researchers have suggested should be standard fare in the K–12 comprehension curriculum (Pearson, Roehler, Dole, & Duffy, 1992).

Gurnee read the first few pages in a lively animated way, pausing to think aloud when she became conscious of a question in her mind relevant to the plot. The group of twenty children was spellbound, watching Gurnee as she read, paused, glanced to the ceiling, and wondered aloud. Hands shot up, and voices in several languages offered answers to her question.

"How do they know what she asked?" one of the literacy coordinators murmured to a colleague. "I know those three," she pointed discreetly, "speak only Mandarin." Her colleague shrugged without looking away from the group on the floor. It was getting uncomfortably warm in the room, but no one seemed to notice.

Gurnee declined to call on anyone. "No," she said, "I don't want to answer that question. I just want to listen to it in my mind for a while. I know if I answer now, I don't get to keep thinking about it. I really want to keep thinking about my question because it makes me think about lots of answers and even some new questions." The adults in the room heard the children sigh. One of the children said, "We should wait then."

As the literacy coordinators debriefed, they asked Gurnee dozens of questions, and she fielded them with the agility of a presidential press secretary. She had given careful thought to planning the lesson; she had paid close attention to her questions as they floated into her consciousness during the lesson; she had used a think-aloud teaching strategy to show children how a proficient reader uses questions to understand more thoroughly, but there was something she just couldn't quite explain. What was it about Gurnee's lesson that seemed to transcend languages and speak directly to the children gathered before her? When Gurnee invited the children to return to their independent reading to try for themselves what they observed in her lesson, why did they scramble to their tables almost desperate for their shot at questioning? What catapulted the lesson from merely effective to memorable?

Gurnee is not alone. Throughout this country, I've been privileged to meet teachers who have read *Mosaic of Thought* (Keene & Zimmermann, 1997) and other publications on teaching comprehension strategies in K–12 classrooms and, instead of just shuffling through the pages in search of a few good ideas, have taken the charge to teach comprehension very seriously. They have studied comprehension research and discussed with colleagues ways in which they can translate it into their classrooms. They have lent their creative energy to ingenious adaptations of concepts proposed in *Mosaic* and elsewhere and have delighted in their students' successes.

Through all those interactions, a set of questions continues to haunt me. I recorded them in order to reflect on them later.

Why are some teachers breathtakingly effective in teaching comprehension strategies?

Why is it riveting to observe?

What do they do to ensure unprecedented levels of student engagement?

What have they done to ensure their students' lasting and independent application of each comprehension strategy in increasingly difficult text and in a wide variety of genres?

What teaching tactics do they use when discussing thinking that permits their students to articulate abstract thought processes with real insight?

How is it that their students can represent their thinking in a wide variety of ways and can describe how using the strategy helped them understand more than if they hadn't used the strategy?

Why do their students ache to read and talk about their insights?

How can these small miracles happen both in first grade and in a last-chance reading course in high school?

Is it possible to identify those qualities, and are these qualities that other teachers can learn and adapt?

Recently, I sat down in silence and tried to record what I have observed in hundreds of classrooms around the country in an attempt to answer those questions. I made some progress before deciding that my questions warranted a fuller exploration. I began to go to the source, not for a formal study, but to converse and review student data with teachers whose comprehension teaching transcends good and reaches well into exceptional. My overriding question was: What characterizes highly effective comprehension teaching?

I chose seventeen teachers whom I have observed with great admiration but who also had collected a significant body of student evidence to substantiate their effectiveness with children. Those who work with older children had norm- and criterion-referenced assessments in addition to a massive amount of student work samples they had collected and analyzed, but all had compiled evidence to satisfy themselves that their approach to comprehension instruction was not only professionally interesting and challenging but resulted in observable growth for their students.

For example, students in these classrooms had made greater than anticipated progress on a wide variety of instruments including state standards assessments and individualized reading inventories such as the Qualitative Reading Inventory III (Leslie, 2001) and on a comprehension-strategy assessment, the Major Point Interview for Readers (Keene, Goudvis, & Schwartz, 1996). Teachers also reported significant improvements in students' classroom work, level of engagement, and retention of concepts from books.

The teachers with whom I spoke teach first through twelfth grade and come primarily, but not exclusively, from low-income urban schools in six states.

From those observations and conversations, I define and describe a set of qualities all possess, despite their vastly different settings and circumstances. But I must admit that there is an elusive quality to memorable teaching. Shall we call it magic? I won't even try to pin that one down. Despite the level of student maturity in these seventeen classrooms and the wide range of schools in which they teach, these exemplary comprehension instructors shared seven common traits.

TRAIT 1: Superb teachers take the time to understand each strategy in their own reading.

When I queried teachers about how they get kids to think deeply using the comprehension strategies researchers have suggested are important for comprehension learning, they gave one response more frequently than others: the teachers take the time to use and understand the strategy to be taught. Research does not always define the nuances and subtleties of each strategy, so these teachers have filled this void by committing to study their own thinking during reading. They have decided that to teach effectively they must determine all the ways in which they use every strategy to better understand the text they read.

Researchers have confirmed what teachers of reading may have observed in themselves and in their students, namely, that thoughtful, active, proficient readers are *metacognitive:* they think about their own thinking during reading.

Proficient readers know what and when they comprehend and when they do not comprehend; they can identify their purposes for reading and identify the demands that a particular text places on them. They can identify when and why the meaning of the text is unclear to them and can use a variety of strategies to solve comprehension problems or deepen their understanding of a text (Bunting et al., 1987; Paris, Cross, & Lipson, 1984).

Metacognitive Reader's Comprehension Strategies

Activates relevant prior knowledge (schema) before, during, and after reading text. Proficient readers "use prior knowledge to evaluate the adequacy of the model of meaning they have developed," to enhance and make personal their interpretation of text, and to store newly learned information with other related memories (Pearson et al., 1992, p. 154; see also Gordon & Pearson, 1983; Hansen, 1981).

Determines the most important ideas and themes in a text. (Afflerbach & Johnston, 1986; Baumann, 1986; Tierney & Cunningham, 1984; Winograd & Bridge, 1986). Proficient readers use their conclusions about important ideas to focus their reading and to exclude peripheral or unimportant details from memory.

Asks questions of him- or herself, the authors, and the texts (Andre & Anderson, 1979; Brown & Palincsar, 1985). Proficient readers use their questions to clarify and to focus their reading and subsequent responses to reading.

Creates visual and other sensory images from text during and after reading. These images may include visual, auditory, and other sensory connections to the text. Proficient readers use these images to deepen their understanding.

Draws inferences from text. Proficient readers use their prior knowledge (schema) and textual information to form critical judgments and create unique interpretations from text. Drawing inferences involves literally creating a meaning as the reader reads. Inferences may occur in the form of conclusions, predictions, or new ideas (Anderson & Pearson, 1984).

Synthesizes what he or she has read. Proficient readers often combine information from different sources to create succinct restatements of central messages or information from text. To do so, they attend to the most important information, their background knowledge, and to the clarity of the synthesis itself. Readers synthesize in order to better understand what they have read (Brown & Day, 1983).

Uses a variety of fix-up strategies to repair comprehension when it breaks down. Proficient readers select appropriate fix-up strategies from one of the six language systems (pragmatic, schematic, semantic, syntactic, lexical, or graphophonic) to best solve a given problem in a given reading situation (Garner, 1987).

To determine for themselves the ways in which they use every strategy to better understand the text they read, many teachers gather in study groups or hold informal conversations with colleagues prior to teaching a comprehension strategy. They read short challenging adult text, paying careful attention to and recording the myriad ways they use the strategy. For example, at Foster Elementary in Jefferson County, Colorado, teachers found that they had become so unaware of their own comprehension processes, they needed to read the text, highlight and code it, and discuss ways in which they comprehended before beginning to teach a particular strategy.

The Foster staff decided to focus on the same comprehension strategy schoolwide, differentiating for students' needs with a huge variety of texts and genres to which they would ask children to apply the strategy. Before beginning a long-term strategy study focused on using sensory images to better understand what they read, they spent two after-school study group sessions scrutinizing their own use of sensory images in text that was challenging to them. As they read and discussed their reactions with their colleagues, they recorded not just specific images that came to mind as they read but the ways in which those images enhanced their comprehension. Their teacher-generated list of ways that readers form and use images to help them comprehend became a list of minilessons for the classroom. The Foster teachers focused several days' instruction on each element of the strategy, as they had described it, over the term of the strategy study—usually between six and nine weeks. Similarly, these teachers asked their students to create their own working definition of the strategy as they study it. The students added to charts around the classrooms that became compilations of ways in which using sensory images helped them comprehend more completely.

TRAIT 2: The most effective comprehension instruction is incorporated into a predictable daily, weekly, and monthly readers' workshop.

Teachers for whom comprehension instruction transcends the commonplace are teachers who have given careful thought to the structure of the workshops in which they engage their children. These teachers understand that there is no one perfect way to configure the time they spend with children in reading, writing, and discourse—so much, of course, depends on the needs of a particular group of learners. They have learned the hard way, though, that without a set of goals for comprehension learning and a predictable schedule to ensure that those goals are met, their classrooms feel unfocused and chaotic.

Many of the teachers with whom I have spoken about this issue tell me they find it useful to think about each component they want to include in the workshop according to how frequently it needs to be accomplished. For example, what is essential enough that it must be built into the daily schedule? Few would argue that a minilesson for the class during which the teacher demonstrates use of a comprehension strategy by thinking aloud is essential fare nearly every day. Each of the teachers with whom I spoke ensures that children have abundant time to read independently every day. (In nearly every case, the period of time set aside for independent reading far exceeded the amount of time typically set aside for students at that grade level—perhaps this has something to do with the students' growth on classroom work and more formal assessments!) Each of these teachers made time to confer with individual students a daily priority, something I don't encounter nearly as much in other classrooms. Finally, each felt that it is critical to have some kind of opportunity for students to share their thinking every day, even if that sharing takes place only between pairs of students.

In highly effective classrooms, teachers set aside time each week to work more intensively with children in small needs-based groups. Most children meet at least twice a week in "invitational" groups, a term introduced in *Mosaic of Thought* (Keene & Zimmermann, 1997) to describe small temporary groups assembled by the teacher to address some area of shared need. For example, if six or seven children were having difficulty describing how asking questions helps them comprehend, their teacher might pull them together in an invitational group to support the development of this skill. In addition, many of the teachers to whom I spoke ensure that students read in at least two genres each week, depending on the age of the children; without exception, these teachers had set aside some time for book clubs or literature circles to meet at least once a week.

The distinction between these highly effective classrooms and many others I've visited seems to revolve around how many priorities teachers try to squeeze into each day and week. These highly effective teachers chose to address priorities that many teachers view as essential weekly or even daily tasks in great depth but on a biweekly or monthly basis. Most set aside time at least once a month for students to spend class time reflecting on their progress toward goals they had set. These teachers made it a practice to ask students to review the list of texts they had read, the responses to books they shared, the insights recorded on charts around the room, and their own written reflections on their progress as readers and to comment on their progress that month. Some teachers asked their students to collect their reflections in a portfolio; others asked students to write a letter home; still others asked the children to share their reflections with small peer groups who gave them feedback. In some way, however, each of these highly effective teachers asked children to step back and find a way to summarize in order to understand more deeply their progress in using comprehension strategies.

Each teacher's sense of daily, weekly, and monthly essentials was slightly different, but all were clear that it is impossible to address everything one considers essential every day or even every week. These teachers preferred to engage students in more in-depth exploration of ideas less frequently. For example, they often explored students' understanding in books with weighty themes such as the Holocaust, immigration, or slavery for weeks rather than a day or two. They created time, not only to discuss the content in the books, but also to discuss the ways in which children used comprehension strategies in order to more deeply understand that content. They felt equally committed to retaining a predictable schedule. They understood that children thrive in an environment that is simultaneously predictable and rigorous. For them, setting daily, weekly, and monthly instructional priorities and sticking to them created the luxury of time for their children to think deeply and consider ideas for more than a fleeting moment.

TRAIT 3: Teachers ask children to apply each comprehension strategy in a wide variety of texts and text levels.

I have had hundreds of conversations with teachers about the perfect books to use when teaching a particular comprehension strategy. I emphasize that there is no perfect set of books to use for instruction on a given comprehension strategy but that they should (1) consider using texts with challenging and profound themes, even for the youngest children, (2) select texts that are beautifully written, and (3) generally choose pieces that can be read in their entirety during a minilesson. When I spoke to other teachers about this question, they emphasized two additional elements to consider.

Text Variety. Highly effective teachers with whom I spoke were unanimous in their belief that comprehending well means that a student can use the previously outlined strategies in a wide variety of texts, not just in the genres most familiar to him or her. The student can determine importance in expository text as well as fiction, use sensory images not just to understand the nuances in poetry but to better understand the characters in a novel, synthesize not only in a magazine article but also in a persuasive essay, use background knowledge to better understand biography as well as a textbook.

The lesson from highly effective teachers is clear. Many of us teach students to use comprehension strategies but fail to ask them to apply the strategies in a wide variety of texts and contexts. One of the ways we can ensure that students have truly internalized the strategies we've taught is to ask them to think aloud or otherwise demonstrate how they use a strategy in several genres. We might ask them how they use a strategy such as determining importance, for example, differently in fiction than in expository text. To the degree that they are able to show and defend their use of a strategy in a wide range of texts, we can generally expect that they will continue to apply that strategy independently after our instructional focus has changed to another strategy (see Table 3.1).

Table 3.1. How Proficient Readers Use Comprehension Strategies.

Comprehension Strategy	Proficient Reader's Action
Sensory images	Creates images during and after reading. These images, rooted in prior knowledge, may include visual, auditory, and other sensory as well as emotional connections to text. Draws conclusions and creates unique interpretations of text. Images from reading frequently become part of reader's writing; images from reader's personal experience frequently become part of reader's comprehension. Clarifies and enhances comprehension. Immerses self in rich detail while reading, which gives depth and dimension to the reading, engaging reader more deeply, making text more memorable. Adapts images in response to shared images of other readers.

(continued)

Table 3.1. (*continued*)

Comprehension Strategy	*Proficient Reader's Action*
	Adapts images while continuing to read and revises them to incorporate new information revealed through the text and new interpretations as reader develops them.
Determination of what is important in text	Identifies key ideas or themes while reading.
	Distinguishes important from unimportant information in relation to key ideas or themes in text. Proficient reader can distinguish important information at word, sentence, and text level.
	Uses text structure and text features (such as bold or italicized print, figures, and photographs) to help distinguish important from unimportant information.
	Uses knowledge of important and relevant parts of text to prioritize in long-term memory and synthesize text for others.
Inferences	Uses background schema (prior knowledge) and textual information to draw conclusions and form unique interpretations from text.
	Makes predictions about text, confirms predictions, and tests developing meaning while reading.
	Knows when and how to use text in combination with background knowledge to seek answers to questions.
	Creates interpretations to enrich and deepen experience in a text.
	Develops opinions and beliefs about content of reading and may try to persuade others to share those opinions.
Schema	Spontaneously activates relevant prior knowledge before, during, and after reading text.
	Assimilates information from text into schema and makes changes in that schema to accommodate new information.
	Uses schema to relate text to world knowledge, text knowledge, and personal experience.
	Uses schema to enhance understanding of text and to store text information in long-term memory.
	Uses schema for authors and their style to better understand text.

Comprehension Strategy	Proficient Reader's Action
	Recognizes when he or she has inadequate background information and knows how to create it—to build schema—to get information needed.
Questions	Spontaneously generates questions before, during, and after reading.
	Asks questions for different purposes including clarifying meaning; making predictions; determining author's style, content, or format; locating specific answer in text; or considering rhetorical questions inspired by text.
	Uses questions to focus attention on important components of the text.
	Is aware that other readers' questions may inspire new questions for him or her.
Monitoring for meaning	Knows when text makes sense, when it does not, what does not make sense, and whether the unclear portions are critical to overall understanding of the piece.
	Identifies when text is comprehensible and degree to which he or she understands it. The proficient reader can identify ways in which a text becomes gradually more understandable by reading past an unclear portion or by rereading parts or the whole text.
	Is aware of the processes reader can use to make meaning clear. Reader checks, evaluates, and revises the evolving interpretation of the text while reading.
	Identifies confusing ideas, themes, or surface elements (words, sentence or text structures, graphs, tables, and so on) and can suggest a variety of different means to solve the problems reader encounters.
	Is aware of what he or she needs to comprehend in relation to the purpose for reading.
	Learns how to pause, considers the meanings in text, reflects on understandings, and uses different strategies to enhance understanding. Readers best

(*continued*)

Table 3.1. (*continued*)

Comprehension Strategy	Proficient Reader's Action
	learn this process by watching proficient models think aloud and gradually taking responsibility for monitoring their own comprehension as they read independently.
Synthesizing	Maintains cognitive track of the major ideas, themes, and topics while reading. Reader monitors overall meaning, important concepts, and themes in text while reading and is aware of ways text elements fit together to create that overall meaning and theme. Reader uses knowledge of these elements to make decisions about the overall meaning of a passage, chapter, or book.
	Retells what he or she has read. Reader attends to the most important information and to the clarity of the synthesis itself. Reader synthesizes in order to better understand the material.
	Capitalizes on opportunities to share, recommend, and criticize books read.
	Responds to text in a variety of ways, independently or in groups of other readers. These include written, oral, dramatic, and artistic responses and interpretations of text.
	Extends synthesis of the literal meaning of a text to the inferential level.
Fix-up strategies	Uses the six major systems of language (graphophonic, lexical, syntactic, semantic, schematic, and pragmatic) to solve reading problems. When not comprehending, reader asks self questions: Does this make sense? Does the word I'm pronouncing sound like language? Do the letters in the word match the sounds I'm pronouncing? Have I seen this word before? Is there another reader who can help me make sense of this? What do I already know from my experience and the context of this text that can help me solve this problem?
	Has and selects a wide range of problem-solving strategies and can make appropriate choices in a given reading situation (that is, skip ahead or reread, use the context and syntax, sound it out, speak to another reader, consider relevant prior knowledge, read the passage aloud, and so on).

Text Level. Since the mid 1990s, much professional conversation has focused on ensuring that children are reading text that is at an appropriate instructional level, and I have been eager to ascertain whether highly effective teachers relied heavily on text-leveling practices. I have observed too many children reading texts far too easy or far too difficult for them, and there is consensus in the field that children make optimal progress when they read text that is challenging but not overwhelming for them, when it is at their instructional level.

The teachers with whom I spoke told me this: for children to comprehend as proficient readers do, actively and assertively, they must read text in which not just the words but also the ideas and concepts are appropriately challenging. If a child struggles with, let's say, one-seventh of the words but is completely familiar with the text structure, concepts, and ideas, is that text challenging enough for him? Probably not. If a child reads every word accurately but has no schematic (or prior knowledge) background to help her understand the concepts in the text, is that text too easy? Definitely not. This presents a challenge for young children and those who struggle at any age. What if the child finds identifying words in a particular book far too challenging but its themes appropriately complex? These teachers emphasized that we must rely more on reading aloud to such children and that it is important to select books with extremely challenging ideas. They extract small sections of those books and encourage children, following the read aloud, to "practice read" that section of text with a partner until they can more easily identify the words.

Many elements make a text readable. Highly effective teachers suggest that we must be aware of all of these components and teach children to independently identify text that is appropriately challenging in relation to most if not all those elements. When our goal is comprehension, the complexity of ideas and themes in the text is critically important if children are to deepen their understanding and interpretation of text.

What makes a text readable? Effective teachers consider the following brief list of elements when they teach children to select books wisely:

- Background knowledge or schema for the text content, structure, and author

- Text size, features, graphics (including photographs)
- Familiarity with the text's genre
- Interest in the concepts and ideas presented in the text
- Prereading discussions (or lack thereof)
- Ability to use a range of fix-up strategies to solve word problems such as pronunciation or unusual word usage

How do superb teachers ensure that every child's text is appropriately challenging? In a third-grade classroom in the Denver area, the teacher asks children to keep track of the books they read at home and at school. Each month they have a reading checkup just like an annual physical. They share their lists with a partner who asks some key questions:

Which of the books was hardest?

What made it hardest?

What "new kind of hard" can you try next month?

How many different genres are represented in your checkup this month?

What new genre will you try next month?

Do you usually get stuck on words or ideas?

Can you try books in which you get stuck in a whole new way next month?

After both partners have shared, each student writes a short plan detailing the ways in which she will diversify her reading repertoire in the coming month—in genre and text level. Then each child adds book titles and details about her recommendations to a large classroom chart. The chart has space not only for titles but for types of challenge, making it possible for any child in the classroom to consider challenges others have faced and consider new challenges for him- or herself.

TRAIT 4: Outstanding teachers skillfully vary the size of groupings for strategy instruction.

The most successful teachers of comprehension know when to use particular kinds of grouping strategies. They've found that different group sizes and configurations help them focus on different purposes in comprehension instruction. These successful teachers use large group and small group instruction as well as individual conferences. They use these grouping configurations flexibly depending on their instructional goals and knowledge of the children.

Highly effective teachers know that large group instruction is particularly useful when using think alouds to model how proficient readers use comprehension strategies in order to understand text more deeply. They know they need not separate children who struggle from the others when thinking aloud. All children need comprehension strategies and instruction pertaining to those strategies—what differs from child to child and grade to grade is the text in which the child applies those strategies. They also know that the most insightful responses often come from children not considered the most able readers. They understand that all children can think effectively, and the teachers use large groups to encourage all children to take the floor to share their thinking.

Large groups are most often the appropriate venue in which to

- Introduce a new strategy
- Think aloud to show children how a proficient reader uses that strategy
- Think aloud using the same strategy in a new genre
- Allow children to share their independent use of the strategy

Small (invitational) groups are particularly effective when the goal is to

- Provide more intensive instruction for children who, after several weeks of instruction on a new strategy, are not using it independently
- Introduce children who are unusually quick in applying the strategy independently to more challenging texts and new genres
- Introduce new means that children can use to share their thinking, such as new types of maps, charts, thinking notebooks, sketches, logs, or dramatic representations of thinking

- Meet and discuss books and the comprehension strategy they are studying without teacher involvement

  Conferences are particularly effective when the goal is to

- Check a child's understanding of how to apply the strategy they are studying to their own books
- Provide intensive strategy instruction in a particular text that may be unusually challenging for a child
- Coach a child in the means he or she might use to reveal thinking to others (for example, should a child use written, oral, artistic, or dramatic means to share her use of synthesis?)
- Push a child to use a strategy to think more deeply than he might have imagined he could

When I consider this range of exceptional classrooms, I note that all the teachers manipulate groupings rather than letting a rigid schedule of groupings manipulate them. They capitalize on different group sizes to capture the intellectual imagination of all students when they are learning to use a comprehension strategy.

Trait 5: Consistently effective teachers gradually release responsibility for application of a comprehension strategy to students.

I clearly recall observing a superb first-grade teacher in Denver at work early in the school year during her students' independent reading time. I watched her carefully, initially believing that she was adroitly moving around the room solving problems before they happened. The more carefully I observed, however, the more I realized that she wasn't solving or even preventing problems for children. She was reminding them that they already knew and had assumed responsibility for solving knotty intellectual problems.

When a child approached her to complain that he or she couldn't read the assigned book or, conversely, had read every book in the classroom (or the world) and just didn't know what to do next, this brilliant teacher refused to solve the problem for the child. She simply said, "I wonder how you'll solve that problem."

The bewildered six-year-old often took a few moments before replying, "Oh, I can go look on the book recommendation list or in my mailbox to see if someone has recommended a book for me, or I can . . ." How powerful those children felt—how responsible.

Reading comprehension expert David Pearson (1985) proposed a model for conceptualizing in-depth instruction that, decades later, still provides an important framework for helping children assume responsibility for using a complex new skill or strategy. The gradual release of responsibility model is a way of planning for long-term instruction that suggests that instruction on any new concept, but particularly a complex new idea such as a comprehension strategy, begins with a great deal of teacher modeling and explicit instruction that gradually gives way to student independence in using the strategy. Over several weeks (up to twelve or more in many of the best classrooms I've observed) teachers using this model create opportunities for students to practice a comprehension strategy such as using sensory images, first with a great deal of teacher guidance, then in small groups with other children, and finally independently in increasingly more challenging contexts, for example, in tougher books or in new genres.

The outstanding teachers I've observed all use some variation on the gradual release of responsibility model. They report that the model helps them plan for long-term strategy instruction. But perhaps more interesting, they also report that keeping such a model in mind helps them avoid solving kids' problems and providing too much support when the most important lesson that students can learn is that they are quite capable of solving their own learning problems. Use of the model reminds these teachers that their instruction begins intensively and ends with a light touch as children take responsibility for using a new skill such as a comprehension strategy and proving that they can do so.

TRAIT 6: Highly skilled teachers ask students to demonstrate their use of each comprehension strategy in a variety of ways.

Many of the finest teachers I've been privileged to observe have an enviable knack for using a wide variety of learning tools to encourage students to record their thinking so that others might benefit from it. Not incidentally, this provides the teacher with a rich source of assessment data on the child's emerging use of the strategy being taught!

These teachers use learning tools such as two-column journals, Venn diagrams, sketches, charting, skits, book clubs, and letters to the author not as an activity that children use to fill time but as a way to record their thinking and to make that thinking permanent. They reason that if a student can capture his or her thinking long enough to analyze how using a strategy such as inferring helped him or her deepen comprehension, the chances are good that the student will continue to use that strategy independently and in a wide variety of texts.

Instead of using a double-entry diary to record a quote and a response to the quote, for example, they may first ask children to record in one column a word or phrase from text that they were reading at the moment when they became aware of using a comprehension strategy and in the second column, to record how they used the strategy to better understand the passage. Or rather than asking children to meet with a book club to discuss general impressions of a book they've all read, these teachers ask children to come to their book club prepared to discuss their use of a comprehension strategy and to defend how they used that strategy to better understand the material they read.

Several of the teachers refer to these learning tools as records of thought and divide them into three categories:

Written	*Artistic*	*Oral*
Post-it® notes	Sketching	Four-way share—an
Two-column journals	Group depictions of	oral sharing strategy
Fluency responses—	text concepts	in which four stu-
writing down as	Artistic metaphors	dents quickly share
quickly as possible	Artistic timelines	their thinking by
everything that a	Photographs of the	moving clockwise
student thought of	mind—a technique	around the group
while he read a short	in which the student	Think-pair-share—a
section of text	completes a very	sharing strategy in
Venn diagrams	quick sketch that	which two students
Column charts	"freezes" the action	share their thinking,

Written	Artistic	Oral
Letters to other readers and authors	in the book or in her mind like a photograph	they then join two others to extend their thinking, and the group of four joins another group of four to further the process
Highlighting to show important ideas or themes		
Story maps or webs		Book clubs and literature circles
Transparency text— copying short sections of text, making transparencies so that students can use markers to show obstacles to understanding or places in which they used a comprehension strategy		Large and small group sharing
		Notice and share—a sharing method in which students work alone first, noticing a telling or salient detail in their reading, and then meet with a partner to determine its significance in the text as a whole
Coding text—using letters or symbols in text or on sticky notes to indicate connections, questions, inferences, images, or an area that was difficult to understand		Strategy study groups
		Dramatic: Student-created dramatic representations of text content or particular use of a strategy
Timelines		
Bar and line graphs		

The teachers model the use of a record of thought once or twice and then invite the students to choose when they use that particular means to capture their thinking. Students can select which record of thought best represents their use of a strategy and submit it as part of a portfolio for analysis by other students and their teacher.

TRAIT 7: Superb teachers understand why they teach comprehension strategies and how comprehension strategy instruction fits into their overall literacy goals.

Recently, I've been relearning to play the piano after years of hiatus. I enjoy immensely the times of practicing in the living room in the quiet of the late evening. When I hear doors closing elsewhere in the house, shutting out the noise from the living room, I try not to take it personally. But when my piano teacher comes for our weekly lesson, I falter. I play what I have practiced so carefully and believe that I'm doing well until she says gently, "Remember, pianissimo. OK, now crescendo here, or the left hand really leads here." I am tempted to say, "Just let me play it!" But she has a larger purpose. She wants me to learn to understand and use the tools that proficient pianists use. Slowly I am learning to integrate them into habitual use. The names of the tools she is teaching me are important, but what matters most is what those tools permit me to do when I play.

I think the same is true with teaching. We learn a new set of skills, such as teaching comprehension strategies and become so intent on making our initial trials successful that we may lose sight of the reason for teaching the strategy in the first place. These successful teachers were unanimous in their ability to articulate to children and to me why they teach comprehension strategies. They teach the strategies not so that the children can recite them but in order that children can manipulate them to understand more deeply and consider ideas more completely than they otherwise would. Simple. Clear. No variation from that commitment.

Comprehension strategy instruction is intoxicating because we find children thinking and saying things we didn't imagine possible. The insight and depth revealed in a simple conversation between two readers astonishes us. It reminds us why we teach. Comprehension instruction has been for so many teachers a way into the complexity and sophistication of thinking, even among the youngest children.

But comprehension instruction is only part of the overall reading program, and great teachers understand that. Word learning and learning to understand must be taught simultaneously. Comprehension strategy instruction for children who aren't yet able to pronounce words independently is just as critical but is primarily listening comprehension instruction. As children become more proficient in recognizing and pronouncing words, comprehension takes a more prominent role and is taught in the form of listening and independent reading comprehension.

Great teachers have always known that there are no silver bullets or simple answers, no packaged programs that take the place of thoughtful reflective teaching. While grounding themselves in a rich and intriguing new type of teaching, these teachers wisely remember the big picture. They take stock regularly. What activities take precious instruction time that could be eliminated? Which are absolutely essential to children's literacy learning? These teachers reserve a great deal of time for comprehension instruction, but they and their children live in a classroom community where reading, in its entirety, is well understood and where there is ample time to develop all the strategies that characterize proficient readers.

Three Recommendations for the Future

The qualities that characterize the fine teachers whose work I observed and reflected on in this chapter bring to mind several priorities in improving comprehension instruction. First, we should consider an entirely new way of conceptualizing comprehension itself. Unlike the teachers I've described in this chapter, too many U.S. teachers still define comprehension as the ability to answer questions about text or to retell what has been read. The teachers I've described in this chapter have a very different working definition of comprehension. They want children not only to be able to retell and respond to questions but to manipulate their own thinking in order to comprehend text more deeply. They expect children to comprehend in a wide variety of texts including nonfiction, and they expect children to struggle for insight rather than being satisfied with superficial understandings. They understand that comprehension is not the use of a compendium of discrete skills but the purposeful and deliberate use of a few comprehension strategies to extend and expand meaning.

Because they define comprehension differently, these educators teach it differently. They model frequently, emphasizing that comprehension is more than completing a given assignment or understanding the book that students are currently reading. They demonstrate so that children can witness ways in which they can use comprehension strategies later in a wide variety of texts and contexts, including other content areas. Teachers who have a more traditional definition of comprehension will inevitably teach to that definition. In order to make large-scale improvements in comprehension instruction, we must carefully reexamine our perceptions about what it is.

Second, we must weave effective comprehension instruction into the instructional program from the beginning to the end of a child's schooling. Comprehension learning is an ongoing process that deserves ample instructional attention for very young children as well as those perceived to be very competent readers in the latter stages of their high school experience. In too many U.S. classrooms, teachers postpone comprehension instruction until after children understand sound and symbol correspondence and can read fluently aloud. Children have little opportunity in these classrooms to delve into the fascinating and engaging ideas so prevalent in fine children's literature, and by the time they reach second and third grade, they are detached and unmotivated readers. Effective comprehension instruction must be carefully balanced with other instructional priorities such as word learning for young children and understanding nonfiction text elements and genre study for older students.

Primary teachers should seek a balance, as do the teachers described in this chapter, between (1) helping children learn strategies to identify and pronounce words and read fluently and (2) helping children comprehend what they read. We may wonder if children as young as five or six are developmentally ready to comprehend texts with subtle themes and powerful messages. We should be cognizant that although very young children may not yet have the language to define and describe their ideas, they are nonetheless quite capable of understanding very complex text. Our responsibility is to teach the language that proficient readers use to define and describe the thought processes associated with comprehension—comprehension strategies. Once we do, children will use that language to call the strategies into action each time they read.

Upper elementary and secondary teachers also need to balance the instructional attention they give to comprehension learning as they begin to help children read in an increasingly wide variety of genres and as they help their students manage the staggering amount of content presented in textbooks. Ironically, comprehension instruction often takes a backseat to studying particular titles from literature and reading in a particular content area precisely at the time when it is most desperately needed. Older students faced with the need to read much more text and text that is schematically unfamiliar to them need ongoing demonstrations from proficient readers who can show them how to use comprehension strategies to help them understand more effectively. Comprehension instruction is a shared responsibility for all of us.

Finally, as I travel to schools around the country I find teachers hungry for guidance in effective comprehension instruction. Many have not enjoyed the exposure to highly effective practice that drove the teachers described in this chapter to refine their practice. Teachers need ongoing opportunities for classroom-based professional development if they are to more closely align their teaching practices with research in effective comprehension instruction. The teachers about whom I wrote in this chapter did not become effective only by taking a graduate class, reading professional books, or even participating in a study group with colleagues. Their professional learning took all these forms, and in addition they had ample opportunity to observe highly effective teachers in the classroom.

Many of the teachers described in this chapter participated in lab classroom training in which they observed in the same classroom as many as eight times during the course of a year. They were able to see how a more experienced colleague set up the classroom at the beginning of the school year and to observe the class throughout the year as the children's sophistication in using comprehension strategies increased. In lab classrooms, observing teachers spent the morning watching the host teacher at work and had the afternoon of each visit to debrief with other observers and the host teacher.

In addition, each of the seventeen teachers had at least occasional on-site support from a staff developer who modeled lessons and coached them as they attempted new practices and considered ways to refine their existing practice. They were able to coteach with a colleague whose experience in comprehension instruction exceeded their own and to learn through experimentation with their own students while the staff developer provided feedback. These teachers describe these processes as immeasurably important to their professional growth in comprehension instruction.

Understanding is elusive. Did you fully understand *Beowulf* or the *Brothers Karamazov*? Did your high school English teacher return your response to *Death of a Salesman* with red marks all over it? For that matter, do you understand your adolescent child? Do you understand why you went into teaching or married your spouse or why your aunt has the power to annoy you as she does?

The teachers I respect so much remind us all that comprehension strategy instruction is a way to equip children with tools they can use independently, purposefully, actively, aggressively even, to understand more deeply and remember more permanently. And they would like us to know that it is hard. It takes a long time. But since when is teaching easy? And if we have the opportunity to help our children tussle with complex concepts and be tenacious in their quest to understand the world, shouldn't we take it? If we don't, who will?

References

Afflerbach, P. P., & Johnston, P. H. (1986). What do expert readers do when the main idea is not explicit? In J. F. Baumann (Ed.), *Teaching main idea comprehension* (pp. 49–72). Newark, DE: International Reading Association.

Anderson, R. C., & Pearson, P. D. (1984). A schema-theoretic view of basic processes in reading. In P. D. Pearson (Ed.), *Handbook of reading research* (pp. 255–292). White Plains, NY: Longman.

Andre, M.E.D.A., & Anderson, T. H. (1979). The development and evaluation of a self-questioning study technique. *Reading Research Quarterly, 14,* 605–623.

Baumann, J. F. (1986). The direct instruction of main idea comprehension ability. In J. F. Baumann (Ed.), *Teaching main idea comprehension* (pp. 133–178). Newark, DE: International Reading Association.

Brown, A. L., & Day, J. D. (1983). Macrorules for summarizing texts: The development of expertise. *Journal of Verbal Learning and Verbal Behavior, 22,* 1–14.

Brown, A. L., & Palincsar, A. S. (1985). *Reciprocal teaching of comprehension strategies: A natural history of one program to enhance learning* (Tech. Rep. No. 334). Urbana: University of Illinois, Center for the Study of Reading.

Bunting, E. (1996). *Going Home.* New York: HarperCollins.

Bunting, E., Duffy, G. G., Roehler, L. R., Sivan, E., Rackliffe, G., Book, C., Meloth, M. S., Vavrus, L. G., Wesselman, R., Putnam, J., & Bassiri, D. (1987). Effects of explaining the reasoning associated with using reading strategies. *Reading Research Quarterly, 22,* 347–368.

Garner, R. (1987). *Metacognition and reading comprehension.* Norwood, NJ: Ablex.

Gordon, C. J., & Pearson, P. D. (1983). *The effects of instruction in metacomprehension and inferencing on children's comprehension abilities* (Tech. Rep. No. 277). Urbana: University of Illinois, Center for the Study of Reading.

Hansen, J. (1981). The effects of inference training and practice on young children's reading comprehension. *Reading Research Quarterly, 16,* 391–417.

Keene, E. O., Goudvis, A., & Schwartz, W. (1996). Major Point Interview for Readers.

Keene, E. O., & Zimmermann, S. (1997). *Mosaic of thought: Teaching comprehension in a reader's workshop.* Portsmouth, NH: Heinemann.

Leslie, L. (2001). Qualitative Reading Inventory III. White Plains, NY: Longman.

Paris, S. G., Cross, D. R., & Lipson, M. Y. (1984). Informed strategies for learning: A program to improve children's reading awareness and comprehension. *Journal of Educational Psychology, 76,* 1239–1252.

Pearson, P. D. (1985). Changing the face of reading comprehension instruction. *Reading Teacher, 38,* 724–738.

Pearson, P. D., Roehler, L. R., Dole, J. A., & Duffy, G. G. (1992). Developing expertise in reading comprehension. In J. Samuels & A. Farstrup (Eds.), *What research has to say about reading instruction* (pp. 145–199). Newark, DE: International Reading Association.

Tierney, R. J., & Cunningham, J. W. (1984). Research on teaching reading comprehension. In P. D. Pearson (Ed.), *Handbook of reading research* (pp. 609–654). White Plains, NY: Longman.

Winograd, P. N., & Bridge, C. A. (1986). The comprehension of important information in written prose. In J. F. Baumann (Ed.), *Teaching main idea comprehension* (pp. 18–48). Newark, DE: International Reading Association.

Chapter Four

The Guided Reading Lesson

Explaining, Supporting, and Prompting for Comprehension

Gay Su Pinnell

All reading instruction is directed toward helping students expand their ability to read texts with ease and understanding. Let's look at an example of a guided reading lesson in a second-grade classroom.

> Erik, who is teaching a small group of students, asks: "Some of you have read a Cam Jansen book before. Who can explain to Samantha what kinds of things might happen in this book?"
>
> Joseph responds by saying, "It's a mystery. Cam Jansen is like a detective, and she has a mental camera."
>
> Erik questions, "That's interesting. What do you mean by a 'mental camera'?"
>
> Joseph continues, "She just looks at something and goes 'click' like a camera, and she can remember everything for, like, ten hours!"
>
> Erik elaborates, "Her mind *is* like a camera. When she goes 'click,' it's like she is taking a photograph, and she can remember all the details. That's why they call her Cam. So what will you expect to happen in this book?" Students reply that there is going to be a mystery for Cam to solve. [They have discussed the structure of mysteries with their teacher before.]
>
> "Well," says Erik, "You'll need to find out what the mystery is and think about how to solve it. Have any of you ever been to a circus?"

In this example, the teacher reminded students of their previous experience and asked them to make their thoughts explicit in order to focus on the particular structure of the text they were to read, thus becoming more conscious of the way the text organized the information. *Cam Jansen and the Mystery of the Circus Clown* (Adler, 1983), a simple chapter book of realistic fiction (a mystery), is one of a series of books involving the same characters and similar text structure. Helping the students "see the bones" of the text sets their expectations as to the kind of strategies that would be required to understand the text: noticing and remembering details, defining the mystery and trying to solve it, making predictions, bringing background knowledge to bear, understanding what the characters are like, and so on.

The quoted conversation from Erik's classroom seems casual, but the teaching is intentional, and the points are preplanned. The teacher is always thinking about how to explain, demonstrate, and support comprehension strategies. Introducing the text was an important component of Erik's guided reading lesson. It involved about five minutes of lively interaction, during which time Erik unlocked the text for the students without preempting their individual roles in processing, searching, and problem solving. He explained pertinent vocabulary, activated students' prior knowledge, invited discussion of text structure, asked students to recall important details from previous reading, and prompted them to analyze the text and make predictions.

Instruction within guided reading varies from the teacher's direct demonstration and explanation of effective reading strategies to his or her prompting, guiding, and reinforcing students' use of strategies as they read texts that offer opportunities to learn. In this chapter I will examine the ways teachers explain, prompt for, and support comprehension strategies within the instructional context of guided reading.

What Does It Mean to Comprehend a Text?

We may grow tired of hearing about just how complex the reading process really is, but as teachers, that is exactly the understanding we need as a foundation for effective instruction. In response to the demands of a text, readers draw on both cognitive and linguistic strategies as well as a range of information within and outside the text.

Early in the development of a reading process, children learn how to look at print, hear sounds in words, and make matches between sounds and letters (Adams, 1990; Snow, Burns, & Griffin, 1998). In very easy texts, they begin to match oral language with print and develop basic concepts about how print works, such as left-to-right directionality and word-by-word matching (Clay, 1991). They develop the "working systems" that allow them to notice and correct mismatches and to check on themselves by using visual information in combination with language and meaning (Clay, 2001).

Readers build strategies over time. As they process more complicated texts, those texts make greater demands on readers' processing systems. The whole process is driven by readers' search for meaning. Effective readers

- Recognize quickly and automatically a large body of words while reading for meaning
- Problem-solve words by applying a variety of decoding skills while reading for meaning
- Process the text with fluency and phrasing, noticing and using punctuation and reproducing the writer's intended syntax
- Vary reading rate and attention according to purpose and the particular demands of the text
- Have questions in mind before, during, and after reading and search for answers
- Recognize, attend to, and remember important ideas and details
- Form sensory images as an extension of understanding
- Make connections between the text and their own lives, their world experience and knowledge, and other texts they have read
- Integrate the information gained from reading into their own understandings
- Extend the meaning of the text, where appropriate, through inference
- Use multiple sources of information, including background knowledge, personal experience, literary experience, visual

and letter-sound information, and language in a smooth and orchestrated way

As competent adult readers, we are for the most part almost completely unaware of these strategies in our heads that make it possible for us to bring meaning to print and construct meaning from it. Any discussion of reading strategies probably oversimplifies the process, because we do not employ cognitive actions in an isolated or linear way, yet it seems important to examine this range of strategies (see Table 4.1) so that we can demonstrate and prompt students to use them (Fountas & Pinnell, 1996, 2001).

Table 4.1. Strategies for Comprehending Written Texts.

Strategies for Sustaining Reading

Solving words	Using a range of strategies to take words apart and understand what words mean while reading continuous text
Monitoring and correcting	Checking on whether reading sounds right, looks right, and makes sense
Gathering	Picking up important information
Predicting	Thinking about what will follow while reading continuous text
Maintaining fluency	Integrating sources of information in a smoothly operating process that results in expressive phrased reading
Adjusting	Reading in different ways as appropriate to purpose for reading and type of text

Strategies for Expanding Meaning

Making connections: personal, world, text	Searching for and using connections to knowledge that readers have gained through their personal experiences, learning about the world, and reading other texts

(continued)

Table 4.1. (*continued*)

Strategies for Expanding Meaning

Inferring	Going beyond the literal meaning of a text to think about what is not there but is implied by the writer
Summarizing	Putting together important information while reading and disregarding irrelevant information
Synthesizing	Putting together information from the text and from the reader's own background knowledge in order to create new understandings
Analyzing	Examining elements of a text to know more about how it is constructed
Critiquing	Evaluating a text based on the readers' personal, world, or text knowledge

Source: Adapted from Figure 18-5 in Fountas and Pinnell (2001). Copyright © 2001 by Irene Fountas and Gay Su Pinnell. Published by Heinemann, a division of Reed Elsevier Inc., Portsmouth, NH.

Strategies for Sustaining the Reading Process

All readers must read words, solving them by a variety of means. If an individual is reading a text fluently, then the reader is recognizing most words, or parts of words, quickly and automatically, freeing the reader's attention to think more deeply about the meaning of the text (Clay, 2001). Certainly, automatic decoding plays an important role in comprehending: if readers are struggling to solve words, the process will break down to the point that they are simply meeting and attempting to pronounce one word at a time, with little energy left to actively search for meaning. Word-level comprehension, to a great extent, depends on readers' ability to recognize words and solve their meanings rapidly (Gough, 1984). Good evidence shows, moreover, that decoding that uses common letter patterns or parts of words makes for a more efficient process (Ehri, 1991, 1992; Ehri & Robbins, 1992).

Sustaining the reading process requires recognizing words, knowing what they mean (Beck & McKeown, 1991), and picking up or gathering the basic and important information from print while reading continuous text. Readers must also constantly check on their word recognition and decoding by asking themselves whether the reading is making sense, sounding right, and looking right given their current understanding of the structure and patterns in words. Successful processing means that the reader is constantly monitoring and checking using all these sources of information and may have self-correcting strategies that work together for accuracy. They use the same sources of information to make predictions at the word-, sentence-, and longer text–level that propel them through the piece of written material. Readers maintain fluency, keeping the rate of reading going as well as accessing phrase patterns that are deeply related to the meaning of the text, and they adjust rate and style of reading as needed. For example, good readers slow down to give attention to detail, notice literary language or other features of text, answer a question, or solve a particular word, and then speed up again. Poor readers sometimes develop a constant habit of reading very slowly.

Readers also have strategies that allow them to constantly expand their understanding of the concepts and ideas presented in a text. Every reader who comprehends is going beyond the given text to understand it in a truly unique manner. Although a culture tends to share common meanings and any text usually has accepted or bottom-line interpretations, readers also have their own unique remembered images and interpretations of the world, and they bring these to their reading. Scholars have identified prior knowledge as a key factor in comprehension. Anderson and Pearson (1984) have proposed that knowledge is stored in schemata, which represent an interrelated set of concepts and details. Readers access these schemata, and they form a context for understanding what they read; for example, a reader who knew what a circus is like would have a foundation that would enhance the meaning of *Cam Jansen and the Mystery of the Circus Clown* (Adler, 1983).

Another way to look at the process is that readers rapidly and automatically relate the ideas in a text to one another and to their own understandings to create networks of meaning, gradually working toward an overall understanding of the text. They are constantly developing and expanding their store of information, called propositions. Good readers make the connections that are necessary to expand the meaning of any given text, discarding those connections that do not make sense, are not necessary for understanding, or that might even interfere with understanding (Pressley, 1998). Readers connect what they read in texts with their own experiences, often in very personal, even emotional ways (Rosenblatt, 1978). A reader may find, for example, that he is interested in reading a novel like *Beach Music* (Conroy, 1996) but have a very personal response if he recognizes family relationships like those the author treats or if he loves the outer banks of South Carolina.

Knowledge of the world also figures into readers' understandings. Having knowledge of Middle Eastern culture or of biblical texts, for example, will provide a rich backdrop for reading a novel like *The Red Tent* (Diamant, 1997) and provides for fascinating mental cross-referencing. Moreover, readers not only bring background information to the reading of a text but they summarize the information they gather and synthesize it with their own knowledge, expanding and changing their concepts, perceptions, and views of the world as a result of the process. As they gain experience in comparing and contrasting texts, readers can analyze texts for certain features, such as writing style, organization, and literary language; they also begin to critique texts for authenticity and quality. At every level, understanding the organization of the text, that is, how it works, is an important factor (Berkowitz, 1986).

Readers do not learn reading strategies one at a time in a linear way, nor can the teacher plan a series of lessons that "covers" them as a curriculum. Some have said that children first learn to decode words and then develop comprehension strategies, but that is not the case. Young readers do indeed find decoding challenging, and their beginning strategies may be slower, more laborious, and more easily observed than those of more sophisticated readers; however, from the beginning, children must engage in the use of multiple sources of information. Readers must never abandon the idea that reading carries meaning for the reader to comprehend. Reading without meaning undermines the development of an effective reading process.

Readers develop strategies as they engage in successful processing of continuous text, but that is not to say that simply reading is enough to help most students become good readers (Pressley, 1998). If that were true, then designating an hour per day for self-selected reading would do the trick. For most students, several components are essential:

- Readers must have high quality, designated, dedicated time for reading continuous texts.
- They must read texts that they can process easily, with a few problems to solve so that they have the opportunity to apply strategies.
- They must receive explicit and supportive instruction.

The first two elements are necessary but not sufficient to assure that students develop as readers; the third, instruction, is the key.

Guided Reading: A Supportive Context

Guided reading is an instructional approach in which a teacher brings together a small group of students who are similar in their development of a reading process. By sampling and assessing oral reading, engaging students in talking and writing about what they read, and applying a range of assessment tasks, teachers determine the strategies readers control and the level of text that is appropriate. The teacher can then bring together small groups of students who are similar enough that they can be taught together. These groups are not static entities; they change periodically based on students' needs.

Groups do not follow each other through a set sequence of texts. Instead, teachers use a gradient of text difficulty to assist them in selecting texts that are appropriate for each group on a daily and weekly basis. The text is "just right" in that students can read it successfully with supportive teaching. A text that is just right for a group of students, for example, would be one that

- Has content and ideas that are available to them based on their background experience and previous texts read
- Has potential for engaging them as readers
- Includes vocabulary that they either know or can derive from context
- Provides language patterns and text structures that are possible for students to articulate and understand

- Has potential for expanding students' problem-solving strategies

Using the gradient, teachers gradually increase text difficulty so that students encounter varied demands for comprehension. Text selection sets the scene for effective instruction because it assures that the text is accessible with teaching. The idea is to provide for a great deal of reading, accompanied by the instruction that will allow for successful processing; the more successful they are and the more they read, the better they will get at reading (Stanovich, 1986).

A guided reading lesson is highly structured and predictably organized so that the teacher can provide different kinds and levels of teaching to help students successfully process these increasingly demanding texts. Components of the lesson are as follows:

- Introducing the text
- Reading the text
- Discussing and revisiting the text
- Teaching for processing strategies
- Extending the meaning of the text (optional)
- Working with words (optional)

I will describe each of these components, along with their relevance to the development of comprehension strategies.

Introducing the Text

The introduction to text should support students' successful processing of a text that is just a little more difficult than they could process independently. The introduction is conversational and depends on the teacher's analysis of what students need to know as they engage with the text. This analysis has three components, including the teacher's

- Analysis of the demands of this text in terms of word solving and comprehension
- Analysis of what this group of readers knows and needs to know
- Knowledge of the reading process

The teacher may indicate difficult words, explain concepts, elicit what students already know (about a topic, type of text, setting, or theme), foreshadow a problem (given the setting, genre, and so on), point out something interesting, get students to start wondering about what might happen in the story, and do anything else that will support readers as they begin to process the text.

A closer observation of Erik's introduction of *Cam Jansen and the Mystery of the Circus Clown* (Adler, 1983) to his second-graders, for example, reveals that he elicited information from students so that they could share background experiences in reading a particular genre and series, and he also explained key concepts that would help students understand the text.

> Erik inquires about previous experience reading text: "I think most of you have read a Cam Jansen book, haven't you?"
>
> The students nod, except for Samantha
>
> Erik invites the students to share experiences. He activates background knowledge of genre and series. "Who can tell Samantha what might be happening in this story?"
>
> Joseph says, "She has a mind like a camera."
>
> Andrea adds, "She solves mysteries."
>
> "With her friend Eric," says Marjeta.
>
> Roberto explains, "She has a photographic memory."
>
> Erik then draws attention to key concepts related to the nature of the story and the main character. "Wait a minute—what do you mean by a mental camera?"
>
> Roberto answers, "She just goes 'click,' and she remembers everything for, like, ten hours."
>
> "So Cam Jansen is very good at remembering things," says Erik. "She just looks at something, and it's like she's taking a picture of it. So that's why she says 'click,' and that's why they call her . . . "
>
> "Cam," says Joseph.
>
> Erik explains this key concept and elicits background information about the setting. "Yes, [Cam is] short for *camera,* although that is not her real name. Have any of you been to the circus?

Marjeta answers, "Yes, there are clowns, and I don't like the clowns. They just run around."

Roberto adds, "There are lots of people, and there are clowns and people."

Erik provides background information. He draws attention to difficult words in print and uses them in conversation. He also provides information about how to interpret a character's actions. "I see most of you know what a circus is. Well, in this story, Cam and her friend Eric go to the circus with Cam's Aunt Molly. Aunt Molly travels a lot, and sometimes she gets things mixed up. Look at page 3. She says, 'I went to Milwaukee, or maybe it was Mexico, or Minnesota.' Put your finger on *Milwaukee*. Say that word."

The students say, "Milwaukee."

"Now put your finger on *Mexico*. I think you know that word. And now, *Minnesota*."

Erik goes on to present key vocabulary and elicits the readers' prior knowledge. "Aunt Molly talks about all those places, and they all begin with *M*. At a circus you sometimes see acrobats. Do you know what acrobats are?"

Joseph answers, "They walk across a rope," and he mimics a tightrope walker.

Erik clarifies the concept and draws attention to the difficult word in print. Then he explains the concept: "Sometimes there are tightrope walkers that walk across ropes, but these acrobats do somersaults and fly through the air on trapezes and turn flips. They are part of a troupe. The troupe is a group of acrobats, and this troupe is called the Elkans Troupe. Find those words on page 6. They are all members of a family called Elkans, and they are a troupe of acrobats who do tricks."

Erik reminds the readers of the text genre and structure. He directs them to make predictions based on their analysis of the structure. Erik goes on to explain that in the first three chapters, the readers will find out what the mystery is. He assigns them to read the first three chapters, determine what the mystery is, and then write a prediction about what they think will happen next.

In preparation for introducing this book to his students, Erik had analyzed the entire text, as well as the portion of text that he would ask the readers to process. He thought about the following:

The information, concepts, and vocabulary these students probably already had that he would not need to explain [When in
doubt, Erik asked them to share with each other what they already knew, an activity that would get students helping each
other, articulating their thoughts, and also provide him with
critical information.]

The information, concepts, and vocabulary that students would
probably need in order to read the text with ease and understanding [Erik explained or demonstrated these concepts, often with reference to places in the text.]

The information, concepts, and vocabulary that students could
work out on their own as they processed the text [Erik would
not overtly explain or demonstrate these concepts, but he
might revisit them with the class after reading to assure that
students understood.]

Erik's goal in the introduction was to provide supportive information and untangle any confusions that students might have. For
some concepts, he checked with students to be sure they had a beginning understanding (or schema) of the setting and the nature
of the genre—mystery. Uncovering confusions through the conversation, Erik had the opportunity to add or elaborate on essential information.

Because the introduction is always particular to the students in
the group—what they know and what they need to know—it is not
possible to script these introductory comments. Teachers tend,
however, to become skilled in analyzing texts, particularly those
they select and use over and over, so that they understand the potential challenges and demands of a text and find it easy to tailor
the introduction in accordance with their knowledge of students.

The introduction may focus on any kind of demand that the
text makes on readers' comprehension and word-solving strategies. Categorizing texts along a gradient of difficulty provides
a guide for teachers in matching books to readers. Fountas and
Pinnell (1996; 2001) have defined and described a gradient of
text difficulty from A to Z. Texts are analyzed using a combination
of factors related to text difficulty: genre, text structure, content, themes and ideas, language and literary features, vocabulary,

sentence complexity, and book and print features. Levels are matched to grade level but provide a more precise way of matching books to readers. The gradient allows teachers to categorize a particular text as to the level of difficulty. Adler's Cam Jansen book (1983) is level M, about second- or third-grade level. But even with an extremely simple book like *Lunch* (Pinnell, 2000), level A, the teacher will need to unlock the structure of the text and show students how it works. *Lunch* is a very simple book that has patterned text and clear, uncluttered illustrations; uses the same words frequently (high frequency words); and has one content word (for example, "apple") per page that is clearly illustrated by the picture. Students need only to understand that the book is about different kinds of food that they might have for lunch:

page 2	"I like apples."
page 3	"I like sandwiches."
page 4	"I like bananas."
page 5	"I like pizza."
page 6	"I like cookies."
page 7	"I like milk."
page 8	"I like lunch."

A picture on each page provides a clear clue that the reader can check with the print. The content is familiar for most young children. Challenge is introduced with the idea that *bananas* and *sandwiches* are both three-syllable words (requiring pointing only once, although you hear three breaks). The challenge lies in the fact that children will hear the syllable breaks in oral language and treat each syllable as a one-syllable word. They need to learn that a word may have one, two, or even more parts that you can hear. Because the new words being introduced are at the end of the sentence, readers may think that they have run out of words. They are matching the natural breaks they hear with the clusters of letters on the page, but encountering a multisyllable word at the end of the line signals a mismatch in that they begin to realize that they must be looking at one cluster of letters even though they are saying a word with several syllables. The book's last word, *lunch,* departs from the pattern by being a larger and more abstract concept and so introduces more challenge.

As I introduced *Lunch* (Pinnell, 2000) to a group of kinder-garten readers, I wanted to make sure that they understood to match one spoken word with one cluster of letters ("read the spaces") and that both picture and word must "match" for the reading to be accurate. I also helped them predict both the over-arching concept and the specific words within the text.

"This book is all about lunch. You eat lunch every day, don't you? What are some of the foods you eat?"

"Sandwiches," says Joachim.

"Potato chips," says Jimmy.

Other students offer a list of foods.

"Well, in this story a little girl is saying that she likes the foods she has for lunch. On every page she says that she likes something that she has for lunch. Look at page 1. She's having something there for lunch. What [letter or sound] would you expect to find at the beginning of the word *like?*"

The students call out, "L."

"Find the word *like* with your finger." The students do so. "She's saying, 'I like . . .'"

"Apples!"

"You are noticing the apples in the picture, aren't you? And what would you expect to see at the beginning of *apples?* Say that word and think about the first sound."

The students respond that *apples* has an *a.*

The teacher writes the word on the whiteboard. "Say that word *apples* again. What do you hear at the end?"

Students say the word and respond that there is an *s.*

"Check the word again. Do you see an *a* at the beginning and an *s* at the end? On every page of this book, the little girl says, 'I like *something,*' and it will be something that you might have for lunch. What does she like on page 2?"

"Sandwiches," say the students.

"What would you expect to see at the beginning?"

> Carola replies, *"s."*
>
> "Check the word to be sure you are right. So you will need to check the picture and the word to be sure it looks right and makes sense."
>
> The teacher has children name a few of the items in the pictures and check one or two of them with the word in print by thinking first about the sound. She leaves the last page for children to work out.

I knew that the concepts in this book would be easy for children to understand, but since they were just beginning to read, I wanted them to use the visual information in print and to notice mismatches by cross-checking the print with the concept word. In other words, for these readers to be confident in processing even this simple text, they had to

- Have in mind the setting—the words that actually would fit with the structure and overall meaning of the text
- Understand a larger concept and concepts that fit within it
- Look closely at the print and use word recognition skills, as well as letter-sound connections in word solving
- Use meaning as a check on word solving and vice versa

Without reference to a known schema or to connected propositions (such as having a set of words related to food), problem solving would be much harder for these new readers.

The introduction engages students and sets the scene for meaningful and purposeful reading, but it does much more. It foregrounds comprehension so that problem solving takes place against a backdrop of accurate, meaningful reading.

Reading the Text

Following the introduction each student reads the text (or a unified portion of it) softly or silently, processing it independently. During this time the teacher samples oral reading from each student, recording observations that provide evidence of the strategies they are using. Also, the teacher may interact briefly with individuals, prompting students to use strategies that the teacher has previously demonstrated and taught.

While students read, the teacher collects information that provides feedback on the effectiveness of the text selection and introduction. For example, when Jamie was reading *Lunch* (Pinnell, 2000), on page 7 she read, "I like m- . . . " and then stopped and appealed to me to supply the word. I said, "You know that it starts with *m*, don't you? Could it be *milk?* Immediately Jamie said, "Yes!" and finished the sentence. After she was done reading, I asked her to return to a page that was tricky, and she immediately went back to page 7, saying, "It's *milk* because it starts like that and also because that's something you would have for lunch." I pointed out that the picture would help also because it showed something to drink, although certainly illustrations provide only partial information to readers.

While Erik's students read *Cam Jansen and the Mystery of the Circus Clown* (Adler, 1983), he sampled oral reading from all six students; next he let the group read silently for about five more minutes while he attended to other students in the class. Erik listened to Samantha read. The text was, "I do seem to lose things. Once when I was reading in the library, I took my shoes off and I didn't notice it until I stepped in a puddle" (p. 16). Noticing that Samantha read the two sentences, ignoring the period, Erik intervened, saying, "Wait just a minute. You read the words, but what is that after the word *things?*" Samantha responded by saying that she saw a period, and she and Erik briefly discussed the need for the reader to stop at a period and let the voice fall, then begin a new sentence with *Once.* Erik demonstrated how to read the selection and explained that Aunt Molly was telling about a time that illustrated her tendency to lose things, an important concept within the story. Samantha reread the selection, and Erik said, "Now do you see how that helps you understand it better?" These brief interactions provide a time to demonstrate use of strategies but also to prompt students to use what they have previously learned.

Discussing and Revisiting the Text

After reading the text, the teacher engages the students in a conversation about the meaning of the text. With the reading fresh in their minds, students may offer opinions and ideas, revisiting the text to find supporting evidence. The teacher guides them to make explicit their connections to other texts and their own experiences and to bring forward their own opinions.

Students give close attention to the text to summarize and synthesize information, make hypotheses, express opinions, benefit from the interpretations of others, resolve dilemmas, relate the text to other reading, search for new information, and think critically about what they have read.

After reading a book like *Lunch* (Pinnell, 2000), students might not engage in a deep discussion, but certainly they would talk about the kinds of things that the little girl in the book likes to eat and might express their own preferences about foods. After reading *Cam Jansen and the Mystery of the Circus Clown* (Adler, 1983), Erik brought his group back to a discussion of the mystery, which students articulated. Engaging in discussion is especially important for Eric's students, all of whom are English-language learners.

After reading the first three chapters, Eric asked the group, "What do you think?"

Elisa answered, "The clowns are doing it."

Joseph added, "Or the woman that was standing there."

Elisa replied, "The clown that bumped them was doing it."

Erik prompted, "What's the mystery?"

"Everything's disappearing," answered Roberto.

"Everything is disappearing?" asked Erik.

Elvis said, "The wallets of everyone. I know what happened."

Erik prompted again, "So the mystery is that wallets are disappearing. You seem to have it figured out, Roberto."

Elvis went on, "The clown bumped the man and Aunt Molly, and when he bumped them, he just took the wallet out of the pocket."

"You know," said Erik, "you should be a detective! You've got it all figured out. What do some of the rest of you think?"

Given the expectations he set before the reading, Erik asked students to articulate the mystery or problem of the story and then to produce hypotheses based on evidence.

Teaching for Processing Strategies

The teacher's observations and interactions with students over time provide a profile of the strategies the students control, as well as the instruction that will be helpful in expanding their capabilities. Examples from the text the group has read serve as a basis for demonstrating and having students try effective strategies. Erik told the class about Samantha's paying attention to the sentences' punctuation and had her demonstrate this to the group. Reading the punctuation was one of Erik's goals for the group of students.

After reading *Lunch* (Pinnell, 2000) to the kindergarten students, I prompted them to say the word *like* and quickly locate this high frequency word on three of the pages of the text, pointing out that knowing words would help them read quickly. I had them check their reading for sounds they could hear—*l*, *i*, and *k*. I also drew attention to page 3, asking students to clap the rhythm of the word *sandwiches* and notice that it had three parts and began and ended with *s*. One student commented that the *s* at the beginning sounded like *s*, but the one at the end sounded like *z*, which was good noticing of letters and sounds within words.

Extending the Meaning of the Text (Optional)

At the end of the lesson, the teacher may decide to engage students in writing, charting, or other ways of organizing information to extend their understanding, for example, analyzing characters or exploring concepts from different perspectives, using graphic organizers (diagrams, charts, and other visually organized devices that help students make comparisons and connections among ideas), gathering further information, or engaging in extended discussion. Through extension, readers have the opportunity to look at a text from different perspectives so that they can think more about it. They examine the text in different ways and make new connections. Readers begin to understand that reflecting on a text and connecting it with their lives are key aspects of reading.

To extend the meaning of *Lunch* (Pinnell, 2000), I quickly made a fold book for each child by folding in half a piece of 8½-by-11-inch paper and then folding it once more. The result was a four-page book (front page, two inside pages, and the back). On the front of each book, I wrote *I like* and asked each child to write his or her name. On the left inside page, I wrote *I like* and had each child write (some with help) the name of some kind of food and draw a picture. Children could copy *I like* on the other pages. To help them write the names of foods, I asked children to say the word slowly and think what letters to write. I filled in letters that children didn't know and ended by saying, "Bring your books to reading tomorrow, and we will read them to each other." Children had the opportunity to hear sounds in words, to use again two useful high frequency words, and to think about letters and sounds within other words that fit within the concept of food.

Erik had asked students to write predictions of the mystery story, which they would later share with each other. This beginning chapter book took the group only three days to read. By the third day, Erik made a group chart (see Exhibit 4.1) to help students understand how mysteries work.

Summarizing the details they noticed and deciding whether they were good clues or not helped the students bring to conscious attention the kinds of mental processes they would need to use to fully comprehend and enjoy mysteries. By prompting students to employ these strategies on a simple accessible text and making them explicit, Erik was helping them to establish a mindset for reading other texts in this genre.

Working with Words (Optional)

For one or two minutes, the teacher asks the students to closely examine words and by working with them, learn how they work. Word work involves explicit demonstrations of how words are related to each other. Students have the opportunity to notice word parts; to make new words by substituting letters and letter clusters at the beginning, middle, and end of words; and to make connections between words. Students may work with magnetic letters, or the teacher may write examples on a chart, chalkboard, or whiteboard. The teacher does not relate word work to the text students have read but preplans it based on students' needs.

Although not all students will need this explicit work with words, many need to learn to pay close attention to words, word parts, word patterns, and letters within words. For example, for the

**Exhibit 4.1. Group Chart Extending the Meaning
of *Cam Jansen and the Mystery of the Circus Clown* (Adler, 1993).**

Genre: Mystery

Purpose: To help students learn more about the organizational structure of a mystery

Extension: As children read the story, their teacher asked them to write predictions based on clues that helped Cam Jansen solve the mystery. Before reading the last chapter, they shared the clues they had uncovered. The teacher wrote the clues on a group chart and asked children to talk about why they were important.

Cam Jansen and the Mystery of the Circus Clown

Clues	Why is it a clue?	Was it a good clue?
A clown bumped people.	When you bump people, you might be able to take things without their noticing.	yes
The clown has red hair.	They could look for someone with red hair.	no
Clowns can take off makeup.	If clowns take off makeup, they look just like anybody else.	yes
It's hard to take off makeup.	You can look for some paint left on somebody's face.	yes
The robber had a shopping bag.	You can look for a shopping bag.	?

Source: Erik's second-grade class.

group that read *Lunch* (Pinnell, 2000), I placed the magnetic letters *i* and *s* on the whiteboard and asked them to tell me the word I had made. All the children identified the word *is*. Then this sequence followed:

> "Watch what I do. I'm going to take away the *s* and put a *t* after the *i*. This word is *it*. I can make *is*, then take away the *s* and put in a *t*, and I have *it*. Now you do that."
>
> The children had magnetic letters *i, s,* and *t*. They formed *is* and *it* quickly.
>
> "Now watch again. This time I'm going to take away the *s* and put an *n* after the *i*. What word did I make?"
>
> The children said, "In." They then made *is, in,* and *it*, taking turns saying which word everyone should make.
>
> "Now watch really closely. I'm going to take away the *i* and put an *a* at the beginning. This word is *at*. You make it."

This lesson establishes a simple substitution routine and is varied over time as children grow in their ability to recognize patterns and make connections between words.

Erik also chose to work on words with his group of second-graders, all of whom are English learners; their first language was Spanish. These children had just transitioned to English during their second-grade year. In word study, Erik had been helping children understand that words could sound the same but look different and have different meanings.

Using magnetic letters, he started with *no* and *know* (which some of the children called *now*). Erik explained that words can sound the same but look different and have different meanings. After discussion of the principle, he made the word *red* on a small metal board and asked children to read the word and use it in a sentence. Then he made *read*, inserting the *a*, and asked the children to recognize the word. They responded by saying that it could be *read* (as in "I can read a book") or *read* (as in "I read a book yesterday"). The children discussed the fact that words could be spelled differently and sound the same; Erik emphasized the importance of realizing what a word means to be sure they are saying it correctly. Erik also showed the children the word *reed,* which referred to a kind of plant or grass.

Erik was not teaching word recognition; he was helping children understand an important principle. They will be on the lookout for examples that fit the principle and will gradually enlarge their knowledge of homophones. Erik spends one to two minutes on word work at the end of each guided reading lesson. He has worked with the children on phonogram patterns, recognizing onsets and rimes, breaking up multisyllable words for analysis, and other strategies related to solving words. An onset is the first part of a word and the rime is the last part. For example, in the word *start,* the onset is *st* and the rime is *art.* The word *rime* is similar to the word *rhyme,* and that is no accident because words with the same ending rimes also rhyme.

The goals of this preplanned word work are to help children make powerful connections between words, learn to recognize word parts and patterns, and realize that they can manipulate the letters and sounds. Rapid flexible recognition of word patterns facilitates comprehension because it frees the reader's attention to think more deeply about the meaning.

Guided Reading Within a Comprehensive Language and Literacy Framework

In this chapter I have described components of guided reading, which is a structured small group lesson for children who are similar in their development of a reading process. Teachers select texts that are within readers' control and that they can successfully process with teaching. Success in reading, of course, means reading with accuracy, ease, and comprehension. Table 4.2 summarizes the components of guided reading and their contributions to comprehension.

Within this supportive context, teachers can use instructional approaches to help readers expand comprehension strategies; however, guided reading is only one component of a comprehensive language and literacy framework. Developing the ability to construct meaning is not limited to small group instruction but crosses the elements of an excellent language and literacy program. A comprehensive language and literacy curriculum consists

Table 4.2. Guided Reading: Contributions to the Development of Comprehending Strategies.

Element	Steps	Teaching for Comprehending Strategies
Introducing the text	The teacher introduces the text, pointing out important concepts, organizational design, or key vocabulary words in a way that will help students to process with understanding a text that represents greater challenge and one that holds the opportunity for learning.	Teacher provides key information that assures that students process the text with understanding. Teacher guides students' thinking so that they may become aware (or partially aware) of effective reading strategies. Teacher demonstrates and prompts for deeper understanding and thinking while reading.
Reading the text	Students read the text softly or silently for themselves while the teacher observes and interacts briefly with individuals.	Students apply and expand comprehending strategies by processing an entire text or a unified portion of it. Students encounter new demands related to word solving, parsing the text into phrases and meaningful units, relating ideas to one another within the text, and understanding the larger ideas and basic concepts of a text. Teacher prompts for behaviors that he or she has previously taught and demonstrated.
Discussing and revisiting the text	After reading the text (or a unified part of a longer text) the teacher talks with students about the meaning, inviting them to make connections. They may revisit the text to search for more information or to find evidence for their inferences, predictions, and conclusions.	Students give close attention to the text as they summarize or synthesize information. Students make hypotheses, express opinions, relate the texts to others they have read, search for new information, analyze the text for literary quality, or think critically about the text. Students benefit from hearing the ideas of others.

Element	Steps	*Teaching for* *Comprehending Strategies*
		Teacher guidance and group discussion support and extend individuals' thinking.
Teaching for processing strategies	Using examples from the text and observations of students' reading, the teacher highlights one or two important processing strategies, providing explicit demonstrations.	Teacher provides explicit explanations and demonstrations of effective reading behaviors related to in-the-head strategies. Students expand their reading strategies, taking on new learning that they can apply in further reading, with the goal not simply of reading this book but learning principles that they can apply widely as part of a reading process.
Extending the meaning of the text (optional)	The teacher engages students in writing or organizing information to extend their understanding, for example, analyzing characters or exploring concepts from different perspectives, using graphic organizers, gathering further information, or engaging in extended discussion.	Readers act on text in different ways so that they can think more about it. Readers take on different perspectives. Readers process information in different ways by talking or writing about it. Readers begin to understand that reflecting on a text and connecting it with their own lives are key aspects of understanding what they read.
Working with words (optional)	For one or two minutes, the teacher asks the students to closely examine words by using magnetic letters or writing several examples on a chart, chalkboard, or whiteboard. The teacher preplans word work based on students' needs, related to the teachers' observation of the students' spelling and reading skills.	Teacher demonstrates principles of how words work in a very specific, explicit, and concrete way. Students have the opportunity to manipulate words themselves with close teacher attention. Students learn principles that they can apply in both reading and writing. Students have the opportunity to become flexible, rapid word solvers.

of three blocks of time, each with specialized study that directly affects students' comprehending abilities. Teachers can use these blocks in any order, but they must set aside time to fully explore the different aspects of literacy.

Block One: Language and Word Study

The language and word study block provides opportunities for students to experience and study language from the text level to the level of word parts and patterns. Teachers interact with students as they read aloud in order to help them process, discuss, and comprehend texts that are beyond what they can read independently or texts that offer excellent and clear examples of different genres and writing styles. Hearing written language read aloud, students can concentrate fully on the meaning, stretching their thinking as well as internalizing more complex patterns of language and new vocabulary.

Also, as part of the language and word study block, teachers visit the conventions of language through interactive editing and shared or modeled writing. They may involve students in shared reading or readers' theater, which focuses on group interpretation of the meaning and rhythm of text. They also provide a specific word study minilesson to help students understand how words work. In the upper elementary grades, students may be involved in public speaking or presentation.

Block Two: Reading Workshop

Students in kindergarten to about the middle of grade two are involved in small group instruction such as the lessons described in this chapter. While the teacher is working with a small group, other students are engaged in independent work, which may include writing assignments, a word study or phonics activity (related to the minilesson), or independent reading.

For upper elementary students, the reading workshop involves a minilesson on any aspect of reading, followed by silent reading of texts that students have chosen. The minilesson is brief, concise, and direct; it focuses on an important principle that students can apply in their reading. During this time students also may write in a reading response journal, exploring their thinking in a letter to the teacher, who then responds in a way that helps them to extend their thinking. During the reading workshop block, the teacher also brings together small groups of students reading at a similar level for guided reading lessons. While the teacher works with a small group, the other students either read silently or write in their response journals. Another small group activity in the reading workshop, one that is heterogeneous in nature, involves students in extended discussion of children's literature. Students in a literature discussion group will be reading on different levels (defined by the text gradient), but all of them need to engage with age-appropriate material. Students who cannot read at the level of the text to be discussed can have access to the text by listening to a tape or to an adult reading aloud.

Block Three: Writing Workshop

The writing workshop block deeply engages students in exploring the writer's craft by keeping a writer's notebook in which they write and revise their own pieces. Using examples from interactive read-aloud sessions, independent reading, guided reading, and literature study, students can learn to notice aspects of the writer's craft and apply it to their own writing.

Learning Across the Framework

Within this balanced language and literacy framework, students are actively thinking all the time—making connections across many different language and literacy contexts. They may meet a word, concept, or abstract theme in one area but connect with it again and again as they write, talk, and read together. Such connections will not occur without careful teacher planning, guidance, explanation, and demonstration. Instruction is the key to students' reading success: deeply comprehending texts.

Three Recommendations for the Future

I propose three recommendations, all related to our professional development as teachers. Creating schools in which all children learn competent (and ideally joyful) literacy and develop as effective users of language requires expert teaching. No materials, not even scripts, can replace the kinds of interactions that intensify and support learning from moment to moment. I propose teacher development of great skill and understanding in three areas.

RECOMMENDATION 1: Increase teachers' knowledge of language systems and of the reading and writing processes.

Extensive knowledge of the semantic, syntactic, and phonological systems of language (as well as the relationships between oral and written language) provide a strong foundation for designing lessons for students from kindergarten through the elementary grades. Phonological awareness is an important component of literacy learning, but we also want children to learn the complex ways that readers use oral language and visual information to read for meaning. For teachers, this knowledge is built over time as they both work with children and study language processes.

RECOMMENDATION 2: Increase teachers' ability to analyze the demands of texts.

When we look closely at the texts we are using, we are really thinking about what must happen in the brain of the reader. This ability to analyze texts is critical to supporting students as they increase and expand their reading strategies. Teachers may use guides (such as a book list graded for difficulty), but thinking about each particular text will provide more powerful interactions with students.

RECOMMENDATION 3: Increase teachers' ability to observe and analyze readers' strengths and needs.

Teachers are wise to collect program assessment data, but daily, systematic, close observation provides the best guide for teaching. Listening to students read orally, noting accuracy as well as fluency and phrasing, provides good information. Engaging them in conversation and having them write about their reading will provide more information about what students are thinking as they read. This information, matched against knowledge of texts and of interconnected reading strategies, creates a base for helping students develop their reading process.

Teaching is a career that requires lifelong development of expertise within an established culture of learning and inquiry. Professional development that provides support to teachers in schools while they are teaching is important. Teachers should participate in ongoing sessions to learn more about language, reading, writing, and learning; they should also receive in-class coaching to put the new practices into action (Lyons & Pinnell, 2001). According to Darling-Hammond and McLaughlin (1996, p. 203), "effective professional development is . . . sustained, ongoing, and intensive, supported by modeling, coaching, and collective problem solving around specific problems of practice." Comprehensive, ongoing professional development programs are the best investment for the future of education and of our children.

References

Adams, M. J. (1990). *Beginning to read.* Cambridge, MA: Harvard University Press.

Adler, D. A. (1983). *Cam Jansen and the Mystery of the Circus Clown.* New York: Puffin Books, Penguin.

Anderson, R. C., & Pearson, P. D. (1984). A schema-theoretic view of basic processes in reading. In P. D. Pearson, R. Barr, M. L. Kamil, & P. Mosenthal (Eds.), *Handbook of reading research* (pp. 255–291). White Plains, NY: Longman.

Beck, I. L, & McKeown, M. (1991). Conditions of vocabulary acquisition. In R. Barr, M. L. Kamil, P. Mosenthal, & P. D. Pearson (Eds.), *Handbook of reading research* (Vol. 2, pp. 789–814). White Plains, NY: Longman.

Berkowitz, S. J. (1986). Effects of instruction in text organization on sixth-grade students' memory for expository reading. *Reading Research Quarterly, 21,* 161–178.

Clay, M. M. (1991). *Becoming literate: The construction of inner control.* Portsmouth, NH: Heinemann.

Clay, M. M. (2001). *Changes over time in literacy learning.* Portsmouth, NH: Heinemann.

Conroy, P. (1996). *Beach music.* New York: Bantam Books.

Darling-Hamond, L., & McLaughlin, M. W. (1996). Policies that support professional development in an era of reform. In M. McLaughlin & I. Oberman (Eds.), *Teacher learning: New policies, new practices* (pp. 202–218). New York: Teachers College Press.

Diamant, A. (1997). *The red tent.* New York: Picador.

Ehri, L. C. (1991). Development of the ability to read words. In R. Barr, M. L. Kamil, P. B. Mosenthal, & P. D. Pearson (Eds.), *Handbook of reading research* (Vol. 2, pp. 383–417). White Plains, NY: Longman.

Ehri, L. C. (1992). Reconceptualizing the development of sight word reading and its relationship to recoding. In P. B. Gough, L. C. Ehri, & R. Treiman (Eds.), *Reading acquisition* (pp. 107–143). Hillsdale, NJ: Erlbaum.

Ehri, L. C., & Robbins, C. (1992). Beginners need some decoding skill to read words by analogy. *Reading Research Quarterly, 27,* 12–27.

Fountas, I. C., & Pinnell, G. S. (1996). *Guided reading: Good first teaching for all students.* Portsmouth, NH: Heinemann.

Fountas, I. C., & Pinnell, G. S. (2001). *Guiding readers and writers, grades 3–6: Teaching comprehension, genre, and content literacy.* Portsmouth, NH: Heinemann.

Gough, P. B. (1984). Word recognition. In P. D. Pearson, R. Barr, M. L. Kamil, & P. Mosenthal (Eds.), *Handbook of reading research* (pp. 225–254). White Plains, NY: Longman.

Lyons, C. A., & Pinnell, G. S. (2001). *Systems for change in literacy education: A guide to professional development.* Portsmouth, NH: Heinemann.

Pinnell, G. S. *Lunch.* (2000). New York: Scholastic.

Pressley, M. (1998). *Reading instruction that works: The case for balanced teaching.* New York: Guilford Press.

Rosenblatt, L. M. (1978). *The reader, the text, the poem: The transactional theory of the literary work.* Carbondale: Southern Illinois University Press.

Snow, C. E., Burns, M., & Griffin, S. (Eds.). (1998). *Preventing reading difficulties in young children.* Washington, DC: Committee on the Prevention of Reading Difficulties in Young Children, Commission on Behavioral and Social Sciences.

Stanovich, K. (1986). Matthew effects in reading: Some consequences of individual differences in the acquisition of literacy. *Reading Research Quarterly, 21,* 360–407.

Chapter Five

Instructional Components for Promoting Thoughtful Literacy Learning

Pamela J. Dunston

Teachers have the power to produce readers who are capable of thinking beyond the level of recognition, recall, and recitation. They have the power to develop readers who think and question, feel and react, reflect and imagine. The ability to think deeply about ideas presented in texts and summarize, synthesize, analyze, and evaluate those ideas is what Allington (2001, p. 90) calls "thoughtful literacy." However, recent research suggests that to produce readers who engage in thoughtful literacy, teachers must first rethink three things: (1) their curriculum—what they teach, (2) their reading instruction—how they teach, and (3) their classroom organization—how they use instructional time and classroom space (for example, Allington, 2001; Guthrie, Schafer, Wang, & Afflerbach, 1995; Morrow, Tracey, Woo, & Pressley, 1999; Taylor, Pearson, Clark, & Walpole, 1999). Although curriculum, instruction, and classroom organization are equally important in fostering thoughtful literacy, this chapter will focus on discussion of reading instruction.

Specifically, the author will examine three components of reading instruction: effective teaching practices, instructional text, and peer discussion. The purpose of this chapter is twofold: (1) to discuss findings from research from 1995 to 2001 concerning important components of instruction that have the potential to produce positive effects in students' comprehension and thoughtful literacy and (2) to provide an example of how educators can incorporate these components into a literacy lesson. Classroom instruction is complex, multifaceted, and well researched. This chapter does not provide a thorough and extensive review of the bodies of research pertaining to classroom instruction or reading comprehension. The author limited research for this discussion to instructional practices that affect comprehension and thoughtful literacy.

Effective Teaching Practices

What can teachers do to develop and encourage students' thoughtful literacy? The answer seems clear: they can provide meaningful instruction that includes activation of prior knowledge, modeling, and opportunities to apply knowledge through purposeful activities that interest and motivate children (Allington, 2001). What constitutes meaningful instruction? Researchers have investigated instructional practices that produce successful readers and writers (for example, Morrow et al., 1999; Taylor et al., 1999; Wharton-McDonald, Pressley, & Hampston, 1998; Wharton-McDonald, Pressley, Rankin, Mistretta, Yokoi, & Ettenberger, 1997). Findings from this line of research indicate that effective reading instruction involves

- Teachers repeatedly modeling and demonstrating strategies in the context of school-related and real-world-related reading
- Concentrating on one strategy over an extended period of time
- Assigning tasks that require students to apply their knowledge

Thoughtful literacy requires students to think at higher levels and use their knowledge. However, the majority of activities currently being used in classrooms tend to assess students' recall of facts and details rather than their ability to think (Allington, 2001). An activity that teachers commonly use involves students completing a worksheet on cause and effect after reading about the message in *Charlotte's Web* (White, 1952). A typical worksheet includes beginnings of statements (for example, "Wilbur was given lots of food because . . . ") followed by multiple-choice answers. On the other hand, application tasks require students to write about or discuss why Charlotte wrote the message, what it means, and what will happen to Wilbur once Lurvy sees it. For other examples of tasks that promote higher-order thinking, see Headley and Keeler (Chapter Ten) in this volume.

Where do teachers find meaningful, interesting, and motivational activities that require application of knowledge? Each year publishers issue numerous books and professional journals containing innovative and worthwhile activities aimed at improving students' reading comprehension. Research conducted in classrooms has found many of the activities these publications offer to improve students' reading comprehension significantly. The key is to look for activities that require students to apply their knowledge and think at higher levels.

Teachers already know much of the information presented in the preceding paragraphs, yet principles of effective instruction, exemplary teaching, and balanced literacy have received much attention in recent years. Why? Because what we know about teaching reading and improving comprehension does not necessarily match what teachers are doing in practice. Why? In part, the mismatch is the result of public concern over teacher effectiveness and the quality of public education in the United States (Allington, 2001) and the influence this concern exerts on what and how teachers teach. Research has closely tied teacher effectiveness to student achievement as measured by standardized tests (Hoffman, Assaf, & Paris, 2001; Brophy & Good, 1986). The increased use of standardized tests and the use (or misuse) of test results has led teachers to believe that what counts as effective teaching is higher standardized test scores. Teachers know that standardized, multiple-choice tests target lower-level thinking skills rather than application of knowledge. As a result, they have adopted classroom practices aimed at improving students' test performance rather than improving their understanding and thoughtful literacy. Although many have voiced concern over testing and its influence on instruction for years (National Commission on Testing and Public Policy, 1990), Hoffman and colleagues (2001) reported that teachers continue to feel the pressure of testing and adjust instructional practices in an effort to improve test scores.

This would be the perfect time to tell teachers that standardized test scores will most assuredly improve if students receive instruction and engagement in thoughtful literacy tasks. Unfortunately, little scientifically based reading research will back up such a statement. Only a few researchers have investigated the effects of thoughtful literacy instruction using standardized tests. Dole, Brown, and Trathen (1996) compared at-risk fifth- and sixth-grade students' achievement using the Stanford Achievement Test (SAT) following students' participation in one of three instructional treatments for reading. Students in one group received story content instruction that focused on activating prior knowledge and building declarative knowledge. The second group received instruction for using strategies to improve comprehension during independent reading. Instruction for the third group followed the traditional basal lesson. Findings suggest that at-risk students who learned procedures for using strategies during independent reading performed significantly better on the SAT comprehension measures than did students from other treatment groups. Modeling and collaboration in the strategy instruction group played an important role in the five-week study. Students modeled to one another for two weeks, worked in small groups for one week, and worked in pairs and independently for two weeks. Students in the other treatment groups did not have these same opportunities. Findings from the study support the need for extended instruction with multiple modeling episodes.

A study by Fuchs, Fuchs, Kazdan, and Allen (1999) found the positive effect of peer collaboration, summarization, and prediction on second-, third-, and fourth-grade students' performance on a standardized comprehension tests. Fuchs and colleagues were interested in the effects of higher-performing students assisting lower-performing classmates as compared to students in other classrooms who did not participate in peer tutoring. Findings suggest that quick-paced, peer-directed lessons that include intense oral reading, summarization, and prediction improved comprehension scores on the Stanford Diagnostic Test.

In sum, the results of effective teaching practices can and do improve students' standardized test performance because they promote higher-order thinking and understanding. The instructional practices advocated here may concern some teachers, who may worry about fitting in all the material that they must cover in a school year if they spend lengthy periods teaching each strategy. Teachers may argue that students will perform poorly on tasks that require application of knowledge because they are not accustomed to such tasks. They may argue that tasks of this type do not match the tasks and knowledge that standardized tests evaluate. Allington (2001) contends that students will engage in higher-order thinking if expected to do so. Teachers who expect students to engage regularly in higher-order thinking can anticipate improved performance in students' lower-level thinking as students use and move beyond lower-level thinking to reach higher levels of understanding. Many teachers would engage in effective teaching practices that promote thoughtful literacy if they had the freedom to do so. That freedom comes from administrators and policymakers who understand that effective teaching is what counts.

Books and Reading Instruction

To become better readers, kids need to read. For years researchers have investigated the correlation between time spent reading and reading achievement. The findings are clear: time spent reading leads to improved reading ability. In-school reading time is particularly important and should involve connected text rather than reading single sentences or isolated words. How much time should teachers devote to in-class reading? Allington (2001) recommends ninety minutes per day for kindergarten through sixth-grade students. According to Taylor, Frye, and Maruyama (1990), even fifteen minutes a day makes a significant difference. Although they conducted their study over ten years ago, their findings are important even today. The researchers found that fifth- and sixth-grade students' comprehension scores on the Gates-MacGinitie Reading Test improved when students engaged in extended periods of in-class reading. Students read assigned and self-selected material for an average of only fifteen minutes per day, yet their comprehension improved significantly. Interestingly, the study found that students' independent, at-home reading time did not result in a statistically significant increase in reading comprehension.

Providing in-class reading time is an important factor in improving students' comprehension and thoughtful literacy. Providing high quality reading materials is another. Texts for independent reading and reading instruction abound. Large textbook companies publish a variety of texts for every grade level and subject area imaginable. Hundreds of children's and adolescents' trade books are published each year (Galda & MacGregor, 1992). However, quality trade books that motivate children to read and provide teachers with a medium for classroom instruction are sometimes difficult to find. Several professional organizations and groups provide annual awards or lists of selected books that have been identified as important contributions to children's literature. Published annually by the American Library Association, "Notable Children's Books" is one example of a list that identifies quality books for children. The International Reading Association publishes annual lists titled "Children's Choices" (October 2001 issue of *The Reading Teacher*), "Young Adult's Choices" (November 2001 issue of the *Journal of Adolescent and Adult Literacy*), and "Teacher's Choices" (November 2001 issue of *The Reading Teacher*) that are additional resources for teachers.

When one is selecting books, an important question is: Will kids want to read them? "Children's Choices" and "Young Adult's Choices" are lists of newly published, grade-level appropriate books that kids have read and voted as their favorites. However, teachers may view some books on these lists as inappropriate for classroom use due to content or language. The fact is that kids enjoy reading materials that adults sometimes view as inappropriate or noneducational. Worthy, Moorman, and Turner (1999) found that sixth-grade students' top reading preferences included scary stories, cartoons and comic books, and magazines (for example, teen, music, video, and car magazines). The researchers concluded that a wide gap exists between reading materials available in schools and students' reading preferences. Classroom use of "texts" that students prefer has been virtually nonexistent to this point and merits discussion.

In recent years the idea of text has expanded beyond printed words and now includes signs, symbols, and images (Stevens, 2001). Hagood (2000, p. 312) argues that technological changes and cultural diversity have led to a definition of literacy that "encompass[es] interrelations of print, visual, and audio texts of cultural and linguistic diversity." Alvermann and Hagood (2000) define *text* as written messages, visual images, and sound bites. In their exploration of adolescents' after-school literacy, Alvermann, Hagood, and Williams (2001) identified e-mail, compact disc (CD) inserts, lyrics, Internet Web sites, and other popular culture texts that students use in their daily lives outside of school. Parents and teachers (even students) may not view interaction and engagement with these texts as true reading. Academics tend to define meaningful, purposeful, and worthwhile reading narrowly, and they generally perceive it as the act of acquiring information or knowledge from print. When we view reading in a broader sense and expand it to include e-mails, CDs, lyrics, Web pages, instant messages, and the like, we find that students are engaged in reading more than parents and teachers (and they) think. A powerful example of an individual's perceptions of what counts as reading and the influence these perceptions can have on an individual's self-concept and school performance can be found in Alvermann's (2001) discussion of and insights from her work with an African American adolescent male. The student in the study professed his dislike of reading, reportedly had trouble reading textbooks, and scored in the lowest quartile on school-administered reading tests. He did not participate fully in group literacy activities in the after-school media club and had rejected Alvermann's attempt to entice him to read a magazine. However, he actively engaged in e-mail communications and eagerly read a Pokémon trainer's manual. This student's in-school reading identified him as a struggling reader, a classification that may have affected his self-esteem and view of himself as a reader and student. When considering the student's successful interactions with popular culture texts, Alvermann concedes that her own impressions of the student were primarily based on inaccurate assumptions.

The literate activities in which adolescents regularly and spontaneously engage may not be considered valuable or real to some, but when we examine them closely, these activities provide students with opportunities to learn and use sophisticated strategies for constructing and communicating meaning. Fabos and Lewis (1999) found that teenage girls altered tone, voice, word choice, and topics when writing electronic instant messages to boys. The girls in the study demonstrated clear understanding of the principles and power of communication through writing. They used voice and word choice to manipulate boys' thinking and perceptions. That is, when corresponding with young adult males, adolescent girls in the study were able to characterize themselves as mature young women who were experienced in matters relating to dating and personal relationships by using writing styles and word choices that conveyed the images the girls wanted to produce.

Selecting texts for literacy instruction, whether from traditional or popular culture, requires time and thought. When teachers decide to use popular culture texts, Stevens (2001) acknowledges the need for teachers to (1) make judgments and decisions about appropriate topics for public discourse and (2) create links between curriculum and popular culture. Traditional texts like trade books are considered for inclusion in the curriculum more often than popular culture texts. However, parents and administrators may even object to traditional texts because they sometimes address issues related to sexuality, violence, drugs, obscenity, and other adult themes or can misrepresent the cultures and experiences of specific groups (Mikulecky, 1998). Teachers must address and resolve parents' and administrators' concerns about any text included in the curriculum within the context of the school and community.

The Double-Edged Sword of Peer Discussion

Peer discussion takes different forms (for example, book clubs, electronic discussion groups, and collaborative learning experiences) and serves a variety of purposes (for example, constructing meaning from texts, promoting awareness of cultural diversity, and motivating students). Researchers have found that peer-led discussion groups have a positive effect on students' comprehension and attitudes about reading (Samway, Whang, Cade, Gamil, Lubandina, & Phommachanh, 1991) and can engage diverse learners in meaningful learning experiences (Goatley, Brock, & Raphael, 1995). Peer discussion offers students social, cognitive, and motivational benefits (Alvermann et al., 1996). Although many teachers express interest in using discussion and believe discussions within book clubs provide students with important ways to learn about literature, few of them actually use book club discussion groups in their own classrooms (Commeyras & Degroff, 1998).

If peer discussion improves comprehension and attitudes about reading, how is it a double-edged sword? The double edge of the peer discussion sword lies in the challenges teachers face in successfully implementing it in their classrooms. Challenges with grouping kids for discussion, getting kids to talk about instructional topics, and managing behavior to stay on-task and on-topic are issues that teachers must address. Deciding which students will productively work together is the first challenge. Grouping students with similar personalities or communication styles may not be in the students' best interest. Alvermann (1995–1996) questions the hierarchical nature of "like" groupings but feels that peer approval, acceptance, and self-esteem are issues to consider when grouping less vocal or less popular students with highly vocal or popular students. Getting kids to talk once they are in groups is the next challenge. Teachers use a variety of strategies to engage students in constructive classroom discussions. Guiding discussions through activities that involve controversy, assigning students specific tasks or roles, and allowing students to work things out are some strategies that teachers use to get kids talking. Alvermann and her colleagues (1996) found that assignments and topics influence students' participation in discussion and that students prefer topics that are interesting, debatable, and enjoyable. Students in the study reported that working in small groups, knowing and liking group members, contributing to the discussion, and staying on topic are important in promoting discussion. Students' ability to stay focused on discussion topics is a third challenge for teachers who use peer discussion. Teachers' ability to manage on-task and on-topic conversations and peer interactions is an important aspect of peer discussion. Students must be taught to construct links between old and new topics and examine new topics in depth through discussion (Almasi, 1995; Almasi, O'Flahavan, & Arya, 2001). In addition, they must be taught to "recognize and resolve their own interaction dilemmas" (Almasi et al., p. 117).

Peer discussion is a powerful tool that can help students understand what they read, but subtle and potentially harmful aspects of discussion have recently come to light. A growing body of research (for example, Alvermann, 1995–1996; Alvermann, Young, Green, & Wisenbaker, 1999; Evans, Alvermann, & Anders, 1998) suggests that issues of power, privilege, gender, and voice are important considerations in students' negotiations during discussion. Social interactions within peer-led discussion groups tend to determine (1) who does or does not speak; (2) whether males or females get

more or less time to talk; (3) whether males or females speak more
or less often; and (4) how other group members accept, reject,
value, or devalue one another's thoughts and opinions. The interactions these researchers observed in classroom discussions tend
to reflect social issues apparent in larger social contexts. For
example, Alvermann, Young, Green, and Wisenbaker (1999) concluded from their study of adolescents' participation in an after-
school book club that adolescents in the group ascribed to and
perpetuated gender-related stereotypes (girl talk versus boy talk)
and social class boundaries found in society (for example, a
mother felt that some reading material was beneath her daugh-
ter's social and economic status). Evans, Alvermann, and Anders
(1998) found that fifth-grade boys challenged female group members' right to talk within a discussion group but did not challenge
other boys. Girls in the group attempted to retain power and express their views to varying degrees of success. Alvermann (1995–
1996) contemplates the effect that classroom discussions have
on peer acceptance, approval, and self-esteem when conversations
weave in threads of gender, power, and voice. For example, students
who seek peer acceptance and approval must weigh their desire to
be accepted and classmates' opinions of them against their desire
to express their opinions and their ability to phrase their thoughts
within the constraints of socially accepted views of their gender
and social position.

Peer-led discussion requires teachers to take risks, share classroom power, and provide effective instruction. Almasi, O'Flahavan, and Arya (2001) provide helpful guidelines for using peer-led
discussion:

- Allow time for groups to gel
- Teach students how to recognize and resolve problems with
  their own interactions
- Provide explicit instruction and modeling on how to make
  topics cohere

For peer discussions to be successful and aid students in constructing meaning from text, students need interesting and enjoyable
tasks that can lead to debate. Perhaps most important, teachers

need to monitor discussions and be aware of students' comments and behaviors that threaten others' power, gender, and voice.

Three Recommendations for the Future

Administrators, policymakers, and stakeholders control much of the power needed to make changes that will improve literacy teaching and learning in the United States. The role and importance of standardized tests in education, for example, rests primarily with administrators, policymakers, stakeholders, and politicians. However, the power to make the most important changes that will positively and immediately affect children's literacy is in the hands of classroom teachers. Teachers have the power to change what they do in their classrooms. They have the power to change what and how they teach, and those changes can have immediate and lasting effects on their students' literacy. For teachers to evoke change in students' thoughtful literacy, they must critically examine and adjust three aspects of their classroom instruction.

First, to develop students' thoughtful literacy, teachers must reevaluate their instructional practices. They must move away from teaching practices that target lower-level thinking and rote memorization and actively employ classroom practices that engage students in meaningful literacy tasks. They must move away from the practice of teaching only tested objectives and move toward the goal of literacy instruction—a goal that is to produce independent, lifelong adult readers and writers. Current testing practices in the United States are driving curriculum and classroom instruction. Teachers must realize the reading tests they administer do not represent authentic reading tasks and, therefore, do not measure students' skilled reading. Future classroom literacy instruction must include meaningful, interesting, and motivational activities that require students to apply their knowledge.

Second, to improve students' thoughtful literacy, educators must broaden their definitions of *text* to include a variety of forms of visual and audio signs, symbols, and images (e-mails, Internet Web sites, popular culture texts, and so on). These texts merit consideration for use in the classroom due to the role they play in the lives of children and adults. In addition, the frequency with which children and adults interact with these texts is rapidly increasing. Teachers must provide students with opportunities to read and interact with a variety of texts that are not only interesting and motivating but will aid in preparing them for the adult world.

Third, future literacy instruction needs to include peer-led classroom discussions that provide students with opportunities to exchange opinions and consider alternative explanations and interpretations of reading material. Through classroom discussions, students have the opportunity to learn respect for others and the views, values, and beliefs they hold. They learn to share power, take risks, and express their own views, values, and beliefs. And they begin to take an active role in the learning process.

These three instructional components have the potential to positively influence students' thoughtful literacy. Adapting current teaching practices to accommodate the suggestions offered in this chapter does not require teachers to purchase trade books or popular culture texts, revamp curriculum, or redesign their instructional day. The suggestions do, however, require teachers to take risks and adjust instructional goals to include the development of thoughtful literacy in addition to mastering standardized test objectives. They do require teachers to invoke their power to produce change and improve students' literacy.

An Example of Thoughtful Literacy in the Classroom

Thoughtful literacy instruction includes three things: (1) effective teaching practices, (2) instructional texts that represent high quality literature and popular culture texts, and (3) thoughtful consideration to the use and role of peer discussion. To illustrate how these components of reading instruction can interact and play out in a classroom, an example of a literacy lesson is provided in Table 5.1. For the sake of brevity, the directives are short and concise. The example is designed for students in grades four through six and is based on the popular culture text *Harry Potter and the Sorcerer's Stone* by J. K. Rowling (1997). Many of the teaching activities mentioned in the table (opinionnaire-questionnaire, character perspective charts, literary report cards, and contrast charts) originate in *Literature-Based Activities* by Yopp and Yopp (2001).

Table 5.1. Literacy Lesson: *Harry Potter and the Sorcerer's Stone* (Rowling, 1997).

	Instruction	Reading Materials	Student-Directed Activities Discussion
Prereading	1. Students interview one another using an opinionnaire-questionnaire. Ask such questions as: How do parents demonstrate love, disappointment, and pride in children? How do classmates feel about people who are different? How do classmates describe bullies? How can classmates cure bullies? 2. Students independently read several modern fantasies. Assist them in identifying characteristics of fantasy. Pairs write a fantasy and illustrate.	Comic books World Wide Web Modern fantasy books (wide variety) Magic and magician books	1. Discuss responses to opinionnaire-questionnaire. Discuss and list different ways people express emotion (for example, verbally or nonverbally), celebrate holidays (family traditions, foods, hobbies), and deal with problems.
During reading	1. Discuss summarizing and model with short passages. Discuss what is included and excluded in summaries. Students form groups, summarize a chapter from the book and an overall summary to this point. 2. Discuss imagery, explaining its role in comprehension, how key words and phrases enhance imagery. Model imagery with short descriptive passages, noting words or phrases that produce images. Students select passages, read aloud, discuss words and phrases used to visualize characters, setting, or events. Assign students character roles (main characters only);	Encyclopedias Reference books Popular teen magazines Music magazines CDs CD covers Comic books	1. Discuss differences in characters' responses to character perspective chart. Discuss characters' traits. Design a literary report card grading main characters on a variety of behaviors or attributes (such as honesty sportsmanship, obedience, trustworthiness). 2. Discuss ideas for coats of arms. Persuade, negotiate, and justify use of individual ideas. House members must be able to explain meaning of coat of arms. Other

(continued)

Table 5.1. (*continued*)

	Instruction	Reading Materials	Student-Directed Activities Discussion
	several students can be the same character. Students complete character perspective charts based on character assignment. Include questions like: Who are the character's friends? What is the character's goal? What does the character do to solve the problem or achieve the goal? 3. Divide class into the four houses of Hogwart's. House members read about and work to design a coat of arms (search for tattoos, graffiti, and other symbols to incorporate) and select a musical theme representing their house.		houses guess significance of coat of arms' elements and overall meaning. Follow same procedures for musical themes.
Postreading	1. Review and model summarizing. Students summarize independent reading of modern fantasies to partners. Students discuss descriptive words for summarizing the plot (boring, exciting, humorous, scary) and motivating others to read the book. Share descriptive words using trade books as examples. House members list most exciting, memorable, and important events in book (in order of occurrence). Pairs construct plot profile using descriptive words to rate each event. Write new summary for book from perspective of publisher who wants to sell the book. Students e-mail summaries to parent, friend, family member.	Dust jackets from a variety of books Book reviews and best-seller lists from newspapers E-mail Reference books	1. After students have completed a contrast chart of Albus Dumbledore and Voldemort, discuss similarities and differences. 2. List main characters' names. Investigate meaning of each. Discuss possible meaning of names and other important words: Diagon Alley, the mirror of Erised, Nimbus Two Thousand, and so on.

References

Allington, R. L. (2001). *What really matters for struggling readers: Designing research-based programs.* White Plains, NY: Longman.

Almasi, J. F. (1995). The nature of fourth graders' sociocognitive conflicts in peer-led and teacher-led discussion of literature. *Reading Research Quarterly, 30,* 314–351.

Almasi, J. F., O'Flahavan, J. F., & Arya, P. (2001). A comparative analysis of student and teacher development in more and less proficient discussions of literature. *Reading Research Quarterly, 36,* 96–120.

Alvermann, D. E. (1995–1996). Peer-led discussion: Whose interests are served? *Journal of Adolescent and Adult Literacy, 39,* 282–289.

Alvermann, D. E. (2001). Reading adolescents' reading identities: Looking back to see ahead. *Journal of Adolescent and Adult Literacy, 44,* 676–690.

Alvermann, D. E., & Hagood, M. C. (2000). Critical media literacy: Research, theory, and practice in "new times." *Journal of Educational Research, 93,* 193–205.

Alvermann, D. E., Hagood, M. C., & Williams, K. B. (2001, June). Image, language, and sound: Making meaning with popular culture texts. *Reading Online* [On-line], *4*(11). Available: http://www.reading online.org/newliteracies/lit_index.asp?HREF=/newliteracies/action/alvermann/index.html

Alvermann, D. E., Young, J. P., Green, C., & Wisenbaker, J. M. (1999). Adolescents' perceptions and negotiations of literacy practices in after-school read and talk clubs. *American Educational Research Journal, 36,* 221–264.

Alvermann, D. E., Young, J. P., Weaver, D., Hinchman, K. A., Moore, D. W., Phelps, S. F., Thrash, E. C., & Zalewski, P. (1996). Middle and high school students' perceptions of how they experience text-based discussions: A multicase study. *Reading Research Quarterly, 31,* 244–267.

Brophy, J. E., & Good, T. L. (1986). Teacher behaviors and student achievement. In M. C. Wittrock (Ed.), *Handbook of research on teaching* (3rd ed., pp. 328–375). Old Tappan, NJ: Macmillan.

Commeyras, M., & Degroff, L. (1998). Literacy professionals' perspectives on professional development and pedagogy: A national survey. *Reading Research Quarterly, 33,* 434–472.

Dole, J. A., Brown, K. J., & Trathen, W. (1996). The effects of strategy instruction on the comprehension performance of at-risk students. *Reading Research Quarterly, 31,* 62–80.

Evans, K. S., Alvermann, D. E., Anders, P. L. (1998). Literature discussion groups: An examination of gender roles. *Reading Research and Instruction, 37,* 107–122.

Fabos, B., & Lewis, C. (1999, December). *Chatting on-line: Uses of instant message communication among adolescent girls.* Paper presented at the meeting of the National Reading Conference, Orlando, FL.

Fuchs, L. S., Fuchs, D., Kazdan, S., & Allen, S. (1999). Effects of peer-assisted learning strategies in reading with and without training in elaborated help giving. *Elementary School Journal, 99,* 201–219.

Galda, L., & MacGregor, P. (1992). Nature's wonders: Books for a science curriculum. *Reading Teacher, 46,* 236–245.

Goatley, V. J., Brock, C. H., Raphael, T. E. (1995). Diverse learners participating in regular education "book clubs." *Reading Research Quarterly, 30,* 352–280.

Guthrie, J. T., Schafer, W., Wang, Y. Y., & Afflerbach, P. (1995). Relationships of instruction to amount of reading: An exploration of social, cognitive, and instructional connections. *Reading Research Quarterly, 30,* 8–25.

Hagood, M. C. (2000). New times, new millennium, new literacies. *Reading Research and Instruction, 39,* 311–328.

Hoffman, J. V., Assaf, L. C., & Paris, S. G. (2001). High-stakes testing in reading: Today in Texas, tomorrow? *Reading Teacher, 54,* 482–492.

Mikulecky, L. (1998). Diversity, discussion, and participation: Comparing Web-based and campus-based adolescent literature classes. *Journal of Adolescent and Adult Literacy, 42,* 84–97.

Morrow, L. M., Tracey, D. H., Woo, D. G., & Pressley, M. (1999). Characteristics of exemplary first-grade literacy instruction. *Reading Teacher, 52,* 462–476.

National Commission on Testing and Public Policy (1990). *From gatekeeper to gateway: Transforming testing in America.* Chestnut Hill, MA: National Commission on Testing and Public Policy, Boston College.

Rowling, J. K. (1997). *Harry Potter and the sorcerer's stone.* New York: Scholastic.

Samway, K. D., Whang, G., Cade, C., Gamil, M., Lubandina, M. A., & Phommachanh, K. (1991). Reading the skeleton, the heart, and the brain of a book: Students' perspectives on literature study circles. *Reading Teacher, 45,* 196–205.

Stevens, L. P. (2001). *South Park* and society: Instructional and curricular implications of popular culture in the classroom. *Journal of Adolescent and Adult Literacy, 44,* 548–555.

Taylor, B. M., Frye, B. J., & Maruyama, G. M. (1990). Time spent reading and reading growth. *American Educational Research Journal, 27,* 351–362.

Taylor, B. M., Pearson, P. D., Clark, K. F., & Walpole, S. (1999). Effective schools/accomplished teachers. *Reading Teacher, 53,* 156–159.

Wharton-McDonald, R., Pressley, M., & Hampston, J. M. (1998). Literacy instruction in nine first-grade classrooms: Teacher characteristics and student achievement. *Elementary School Journal, 99,* 101–128.

Wharton-McDonald, R., Pressley, M., Rankin, J., Mistretta, J., Yokoi, L., & Ettenberger, S. (1997). Effective primary-grades literacy instruction = Balanced literacy instruction. *Reading Teacher, 50,* 518–521.

White, E. B. (1952). *Charlotte's web.* New York: Harper.

Worthy, J., Moorman, M., & Turner, M. (1999). What Johnny likes to read is hard to find in school. *Reading Research Quarterly, 34,* 12–21.

Yopp, R. H., & Yopp, H. K. (2001). *Literature-based activities* (3rd ed.). Needham Heights, MA: Allyn & Bacon.

Part Two

New Comprehension Lessons Across the Curriculum

Chapter Six

Differentiating Reading and Writing Lessons to Promote Content Learning

Karen D. Wood

Without question, one of the primary concerns of classroom teachers throughout the nation is how to meet the ever increasing diverse learning needs of students in our classrooms today. Research on the status of diverse learners reveals that these concerns are valid:

Between the years 1986 and 1996, the percentage of children with disabilities who were educated in regular classrooms increased by nearly 20 percent (U.S. Department of Education, National Center for Education Statistics [USDE], 2000).

The number of students who participated in federal programs for students with disabilities has risen 51 percent between 1977 and 1996 (USDE, 1998).

The foreign-born population, for whom English is a second language, accounts for virtually all of the national increases in public school enrollment over the last two decades (Center for Immigration Studies, 2001).

Students at risk for educational failure and students for whom English is a second language represent the fastest growing student population in the country (USDE, 1995, 2000).

Fortunately, with decades of research behind us and more under way, we have learned a lot through the years about helping diverse learners, particularly those students who are struggling with print. This chapter will discuss five areas we need to emphasize if we are going to include diverse learners within the classroom community. More specifically, the focus will be on comprehension strategies that teachers can adapt to encourage participation and improve the literacy of students of all ability levels. This chapter will present the five areas of emphasis by briefly reviewing the research and then translating the research into classroom practice.

Read Every Day in Every Class Period

Research has clearly shown that students must have access to good literature and opportunities to engage in authentic reading experiences as often as possible (Donahue, Voelkl, Campbell, & Mazzeo, 1999; Hiebert, 1996; Neuman, 1999; Routman, 1996). Yet extensive classroom observational research suggests that struggling readers do not get to read very much (Allington, 1983; Allington & Walmsley, 1995; Collins, 1986). Many times, students who need the most experiences with print are receiving a daily dosage of drill and practice in skills, with little or no opportunities to read whole sentences, paragraphs, and texts—this, despite the fact that a combined approach of daily reading supplemented with skill and strategy instruction has proven to lead to increased reading performance (Dahl, Scharer, Lawson, & Arogan, 1999; Hiebert, 1996; Roller, 1996; National Reading Panel, 2000; Routman, 1996).

Students must have the opportunity to read connected discourse as often as possible, preferably every day and in every class period. This section describes three ways to engage students in more frequent reading:

- Employ alternative approaches to round-robin reading
- Include strategies for increasing reading fluency
- Provide opportunities to read for pleasure and information

Employ Alternative Approaches to Round-Robin Reading

One way to increase the amount of time students spend engaged in reading is to eliminate, or at least reduce, the practice of round-robin reading, which is alive and well and has been "flying" around our classrooms since the turn of the twentieth century. Table 6.1 compares round-robin reading with alternative approaches to oral reading. The middle column represents the text itself, which could be a page, a paragraph, or a sentence depending upon the grade and ability level of the student. The right-hand column shows how the round-robin reading lesson proceeds with Kevin reading paragraph one, Lamar reading paragraph two, and so on. Typically, while Lauren is reading, the next student is reading ahead rehearsing his lines but certainly not paying attention to the text. When a reader misses a word, the group immediately supplies it, leaving her little or no opportunity to use the meta-cognitive fix-up strategies necessary to help her become a strategic, independent reader. Next, as a slow laborious reader struggles through the text, the students become restless. Fearful of losing the attention of the class, the teacher cuts his reading time, thereby, as research indicates (Allington, 1983; Weaver, 1994), giving the student who needs the most help fewer opportunities to read connected text.

Table 6.1. Comparison of Approaches for Oral Reading.

Varied Approaches	Text	Round-Robin Reading
Choral	Paragraph 1	Kevin
Whisper	Paragraph 2	Lamar
Paired	Paragraph 3	Lauren
Mumble	Paragraph 4	Juan
Imitative	Paragraph 5	Stacey
Cloze	Paragraph 6	Mario
Assisted	Paragraph 7	Kevin

The left-hand column of Table 6.1 shows the same lesson with alternative approaches (excerpted from Wood & Algozzine, 1994) incorporated throughout.

PAIRED OR ASSISTED READING: A group of two or more students read aloud in unison. In fact, McCauley and McCauley (1992) indicate that methods in which students are paired together to assist one another in reading have been proven effective for ESL students who often benefit from not having to go it alone.

MUMBLE READING: Cunningham's mumble reading (1978) is a variation of oral reading that appeals to students at all grade levels. Merely telling students to mumble read (read aloud under the breath) to the top of a page can enliven a reading lesson and motivate reluctant readers.

WHISPER READING: *Whisper reading* means carefully pronouncing the words but doing so in a lowered voice. This can be done alone or with a partner.

IMITATIVE READING: Imitating the vocal patterns of the teacher can help beginning or struggling readers with pacing and fluency. The teacher reads a segment of a story (usually dialogue) in an exaggerated tone and then calls on one or more students to read the same segment in a similar manner.

CHORAL READING: When used in moderation, and preferably in combination with some of the other reading methods, choral reading is an excellent way to maintain the interest and enthusiasm of the class. Having the group or class read in unison at just the right moment in a story can heighten the suspense or emphasize an important event.

CLOZE PROCEDURE ORAL READING: The teacher reads a story aloud as the students follow with their copies of the text. When the teacher pauses, the students collectively respond with the missing word. This method helps students stay focused on the task of reading, while encouraging them to see and hear the match of speech to print.

Note, however, that teachers should combine one or more alternatives with silent reading because students will read silently most often both in and out of school. Throughout the lesson, the teacher can also encourage students to retell what they read to partners or group members, elaborating on the content and sharing related information.

Include Strategies for Increasing Fluency

Often overlooked in the debate between phonics and whole language (Bear, 1991), fluency has been a neglected aspect of literacy instruction (Allington, 1983). Being able to read connected text with smoothness, rhythm, and ease indisputably allows students to concentrate on what they have read and may be an essential element for comprehension and appreciation (Nathan & Stanovich, 1991). Reducing the demands on readers' use of the graphophonic cueing system leads the way for paying more attention to the semantics, understanding and recalling the content (Richards, 2000). One method for providing students with fluency practice is the adaptation of Koskinen and Blum's strategy (1986) of paired reading for fluency. In this strategy, the teacher pairs students who are having difficulty with print. Ideally, the pairing would include two students in need, with one slightly more proficient than the other, to provide mutual help during the lesson. The students read a short passage related to the topic that the rest of the class is studying. One student begins by reading the passage three times to the partner. As Exhibit 6.1 indicates, the students first evaluate themselves and then each other by circling the appropriate figure on the page. Then each indicates how the partner's reading improved. Together they can write a few sentences summarizing the information in the passage. This strategy has the potential to help diverse learners read material on current class topics, contribute to class discussions and activities, and simultaneously receive practice in fluency and smoothness of reading.

Provide Opportunities to Read for Pleasure and Information

Researchers in literacy have for decades recommended that teachers give students time daily to read for both pleasure and information. To promote this practice, the professional literature has described numerous strategies including sustained silent reading

Exhibit 6.1. Partner Reading and Retelling Exercise.

Name: __Antonio_____ Partner: __Marcus_____

Date: __November 11__ We read: __p. 14 Lions Pair-it Book_____

Reading #1 #2 #3

How well did you read?　　　Score!　　Good!　　OK　　Try Again

How did your partner's reading improve?

　　Read more smoothly　　_____

　　Knew more words　　_____

　　Read with more expression　　_____

Tell your partner one thing that was better about his or her reading. __His reading is smooth. He sounds like a pro._____

With the aid of your partner, retell what you have learned: __Baby cubs are born blind. They drink milk and learn to eat meat later. We learned in class that they live in groups called prides._____

Source: Adapted from Koskinen and Blum (1986).

(Berglund & Johns, 1983), reading workshop (Atwell, 1987), book clubs (McMahon & Raphael, 1997), literature circles, and more recently the Talking About Books (TAB) in the content area approach (Harmon & Wood, 2001). Traditionally, teachers of reading, language arts, and English have implemented book clubs in their classrooms. The TAB approach allows teachers to use book clubs in the content areas as well by connecting literature to topics under study. TAB integrates reading, talking, and writing in several ways to help students comprehend informational texts as they work in small groups. Although preliminary experiences with the TAB approach have been with middle school students reading below grade level, the approach is appropriate for students of all ability levels. For example, a social studies teacher might use the TAB book club approach to integrate five works of literature in that content area: *So Sings Blue Deer* (McGee, 1994), *The People Shall Continue* (Ortiz, 1994), *Cherokee Summer* (Hoyt-Goldsmith, 1994), *Sarah Winnemucca* (Zanjani, 2002), and *The Rattle and the Drum: Native American Rituals and Celebrations* (Sita, 1994).

Capitalize on Students' Interests and Abilities

Promote Understanding Through a Nonprint Medium

We often see learners struggle with print but excel in other forms of self-expression such as painting, drawing, charting, or describing content (Gambrell, Dromsky, & Mazzoni, 2000; Sadowski & Paivio, 2001; Sidelnick & Svoboda, 2000; Wood & Algozzine, 1994). One way to elicit students' thinking and prior knowledge on a topic is through the use of visual imagery. Research has shown that getting students to create images of what they read before, during, and after reading is a beneficial means for improving understanding (Gambrell & Bales, 1986; Peters & Levin, 1986; Pressley, 1976; Sadoski & Paivio, 2001). Two strategies for achieving this purpose are talking drawings (McConnell, 1993) and imagine, elaborate, predict, and confirm (IEPC) (Wood, 2001; Wood & Endres, 2001).

In talking drawings, students begin by closing their eyes, allowing their minds to form a mental picture of a particular, teacher-assigned topic (see Exhibit 6.2). Then they are asked to draw what they see, using labels to depict parts, location, characters, and so on as they apply. Next, they share their drawings with at least one other person, talking about what they depicted and why. They then share this information with the entire class and display the results on the board or on a transparency in the form of a semantic map, for example. The students read the assigned selection with their pictures in mind. After reading the targeted selection, students make another drawing showing what they learned, discuss their drawings with partners and then with the entire class. To further extend the activity from McConnell's original idea (1993), creative teachers have incorporated writing with the lesson. In one classroom, students were asked to tell what was different about their before and after pictures. Talking drawings becomes an engaging way to frame the pre- and postreading portions of a lesson and give all students, particularly diverse learners, another modality through which to excel. In Exhibit 6.2, a limited-English-proficient student and an English-speaking partner drew a picture of an ant in preparation for a discussion on insects in science class.

IEPC (Wood, 2001; Wood & Endres, 2001) is a whole class strategy designed to take the predictive process back to its origins in the imagination and extend it throughout the prereading, reading, and postreading stages of an instructional lesson.

The IEPC begins with the *imagine phase,* in which the teacher tells the students they are going to explore the pictures in their heads by closing their eyes and imagining everything they can about the selection they are about to read. The teacher may base the imagining on the cover of a book, a title, or a topic and encourages the students to use sensory experiences by imagining feelings, taste, smell, sight, and surroundings. The teacher writes the students' responses from this phase and all of the phases on the blank IEPC form displayed on the board or an overhead projector.

In the *elaboration phase,* the teacher models for the students how to use their visual images and to add details, anecdotes, prior experiences, sensory information, and so on. In the *prediction phase,* the teacher talks about at least one sample prediction, based upon prior visual images, and encourages the students to do the same. The students are to think about these predictions as they read or listen to the selection. After the reading they return to the predictions to gauge whether their predictions were correct.

Exhibit 6.2. Talking Drawings Lesson.

Partners: <u>Carlos and Ryan</u>

1. Close your eyes and think about an ant. Now open your eyes and
   draw what you saw. Talk about your drawing with at least one other
   person.

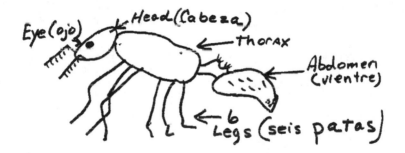

2. Read the selection on "Ants" from Chapter 6; then draw a second
   picture to show what you learned.

3. In the space below, tell what you have changed about your before
   and after pictures.

   *At first, we only drew the ant having two parts, the head (cabeza) and his
   body (cuerpo). We drew his antenna (antenna), so we got that part right.
   We also only drew him having four legs (quatro patas) in the first
   drawing. We learned that the ant has a head (cuerpo), and abdomen
   (vientre) that make up his body. We also learned that the ant has six legs
   (seis patas) instead of four (quatro). We also learned that even though he
   has eyes (ojos), he uses his antenna (antenna) to feel around with and
   move things.*

Table 6.2. Imagine, Elaborate, Predict, and Confirm (IEPC) Lesson for *Lon Po Po* (Young, 1989).

	Imagine	Elaborate	Predict	Confirm
Teacher's instruction to students	**Close your eyes. Imagine the scene, character, and events. What do you see, feel, hear, and smell?**	**Elaborate: tell, describe, or give details of what you see in your mind.**	**Use these ideas to make some predictions or guesses about the passages you will read.**	**Read to confirm or change your predictions about the passage.**
Students' responses	Wolf coming to eat Sandstorm Boat, water, tornado Family saying goodbye House far away, in the country King has a son looking for a wife. In Roxaboxen Boy is almost falling off a cliff. People are living in a house	Walking Cloudy, foggy Footsteps coming Sound of crickets at night Quiet, fear, scared Hear the wind blowing through the trees. Snowstorm is coming; smell food cooking. Rocks tumbling down the cliff into the water, splash, splash Smell animals	Son, daughter living in a house with no parents. Parents left them because the mother doesn't like them. A boy is playing with his friend; a toy went over a cliff; boy tries to get the toy. Three people sacrifice themselves to the wolf.	Mother goes to grandmother's house. She likes her kids. Wolf falls out of a tree three times. Wolf did try to eat three girls but was unsuccessful. No storms Wolf does come in the house at night, not in the daytime.

Wolf is going to a house.
Family lives in the desert and landed in a strange place.

People are in the house, and a storm is dangerous and picks up the house and moves it to Neptune.
Sunshine shines through the house in the morning.
Parents die; children want to capture the wolf somehow.
Storm comes leaving no power; they have to use candles.
Sandstorm comes; house is covered with sand, and people are trapped inside.
Hunter saves children; he doesn't think straight.
Pirate ship comes by the cliff.

Wolf does not kill parents; children do capture the wolf.
They use candles; wolf blows out the candles and lantern.
Mother leaves children alone in house with orders not to open the door.
No hunter, kids save themselves.
A wolf comes by the house.

Source: Joni Turner contributed this example.

Depending upon the ability levels of the students and the degree of teacher support they need, the teacher may ask students to read in pairs and retell segments to partners or group members or to read silently and engage in whole class discussions. After reading, students enter the *confirmation phase*. The teacher and students modify the original predictions to coordinate with the newly learned information. Thinking aloud and giving some sample responses is always helpful here. To further enhance understanding, the teacher should model for the students how to go back to the key parts of the text to confirm or refute the predictions.

The IEPC strategy, to date, has been field-tested in over thirty classrooms from kindergarten through the community college level. Teachers have commented that after using IEPC, they have noticed not only an increased interest from the students but also an improvement in their ability to write more elaborate passages in preparation for state assessment (Wood & Endres, 2001). Table 6.2 shows a sample IEPC lesson for *Lon Po Po* (Young, 1989).

Write Every Day in Every Class Period

Because reading and writing are reciprocal processes, practice in either communication process has a positive effect on the other (Tierney & Shanahan, 1991). Research has also indicated that the more quality time students spend in reading and writing activities, the higher their achievement test scores (Gambrell, Morrow, Neuman, & Pressley, 1999; Greenwald, Persky, Campbell, & Mazzeo, 1999; Rhodes & Dudley-Marling, 1996; Routman, 1996; Wood & Algozzine, 1994).

Provide Opportunities for Formal and Informal Writing Practice

As with any skill, proficient writing takes many practice sessions, including sessions that are not under the watchful eye of a teacher or evaluator. Although teachers need not grade all their students' writing efforts, the students themselves should check them all. This process may be as simple as asking students to reread journal entries to assess what could be termed their sound. How does the passage sound when read aloud or silently? Does it make sense? Does it need a word inserted or deleted? Do the ideas flow? Or proofreading may be engaging in peer editing, in which students oversee the grammar, punctuation, and cohesiveness of a selection.

In still other cases, more formal writing practice should take place involving close teacher scrutiny and, above all, feedback for improving the piece of writing. This increasing variation in the degree of evaluation of a writing assignment is depicted in the continuum shown in Figure 6.1.

One approach that fits in the third degree of the continuum is communal writing (Wood, 1994; Wood & Harmon, in press), getting four or five students to compose a single product together. The teacher groups students heterogeneously and asks them to collaborate on a single written assignment. Afterward group members may either reread and informally check the piece, or they may engage in the peer editing process. Communal writing is beneficial because (1) it is expedient; (2) students participate actively in the process; (3) students assist one another and serve as models for the writing process; (4) it enables teachers to monitor and assist where needed; (5) it serves as a practice writing exercise;

Figure 6.1. Continuum of Informal and Formal Writing Evaluation.

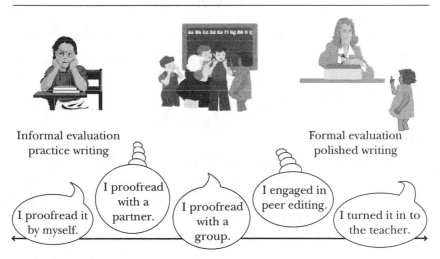

Informal evaluation
practice writing

Formal evaluation
polished writing

I proofread it
by myself.

I proofread
with a
partner.

I proofread
with a
group.

I engaged in
peer editing.

I turned it in to
the teacher.

and (6) students can engage in peer editing to polish their work (Wood, 1999). Communal writing, because it is a collaborative effort, involves all students in the learning experience. Giving ESL students ample opportunities to interact with other readers, both novice and proficient, helps them acquire a broader understanding of the conventions and purposes of print (Fitzgerald, 1993; Grabe, 1991).

Educators can adapt communal writing to many different writing strategies. One strategy that has been particularly successful in classrooms at varied grade levels is exchange-compare writing (Wood, 1994). In exchange-compare writing, the teacher pulls out from six to fifteen key terms, characters, or phrases (depending on the grade and ability level of the students) about a selection that they will study and writes them on a transparency, board, or handout. Working in their preassigned heterogeneous groups, students predict how the words will be used to convey information in the selection to be read. They put their heads together to construct a passage, reflecting what they think will be in the selection to follow. The teacher circulates and monitors to provide assistance. Afterward the groups can share their predicted passages with the class. Next the students read the passage silently, orally, or in a combination of both methods, being certain to focus on the way the author uses the significant terms. The teacher can then engage the students in a discussion of how the passage used the terms. To further reinforce the new concepts, the teacher asks the groups to use them in a composition that reflects or summarizes the targeted passage. Exhibit 6.3 is a sample exchange-compare writing exercise for science on the topic of sharks.

Incorporate Flexible Grouping

Use a Combination of Whole Class, Small Group, and Individual Learning

Scholars have established that collaboration, not segregation, improves learning (Rhodes & Dudley-Marling, 1996; National Reading Panel, 2000; Paratore & McCormack, 1997; Risko & Bromley, 2001; Wood, McCormack, Lapp, & Flood, 1997). Research conducted over one hundred years and spanning numerous continents

Exhibit 6.3. Exchange-Compare
Writing Exercise for Science: Sharks.

1. Key concepts or phrases

food chain

natural predators

cartilage

sixth sense

no bones

detect prey

whale shark

plankton

tiger sharks

eat most anything

twenty years

reproductive age

2. Predicted passage [with key terms italicized]

Whale sharks are at the top of the *food chain* and have no *natural predators.* The *tiger shark* eats sea *plankton* but the *whale shark* will *eat most anything.* Sharks do not have *bones* and are made mostly of *cartilage.* They also have a *sixth sense* that they use to *detect prey.* Some sharks live to be *twenty years* old before they reach *reproductive age.*

3. Passage based on actual selection

Sharks are at the top of the ocean's *food chain,* which means most of the more than 350 species have few *natural predators* except humans. Sharks don't have *bones.* Instead their internal frames are made of *cartilage.* Sharks have what some call a *sixth sense.* They can sense electrical and magnetic fields, which help them *detect prey.* Sharks' diets vary widely. The largest of the bunch, the whale shark, feeds mostly on *plankton. Tiger sharks* will *eat most anything.* Most species grow slowly and mature late. It can take up to *twenty years* for some species to *reach reproductive age.*

Source: Susannah Dwight contributed this example.

has shown that collaborative learning is a beneficial means of improving students' academic performance. Specifically, researchers (Fuchs, Fuchs, Mathes, & Simmons, 1997; Johnson & Johnson, 1991; Kagan, 1994; Paratore & McCormack, 1997; Slavin, 1995) have demonstrated that collaborative learning in the form of flexible grouping

- Increases students' self-esteem and motivation
- Improves peer relationships
- Aids students in accepting diversity
- Improves achievement scores
- Improves performance in all subject areas
- Improves performance of all ability levels

This is not to suggest that all learning and instruction should be collaborative. On the contrary, the most effective instruction takes place when teachers use a combination of whole class, small group, and individualized instruction (Zemelman, Daniels, & Hyde, 1993). One strategy that employs all of these approaches in a single lesson is the collaborative listening viewing guide (CLVG) (Wood, 1994; 2001; Wood, McCormick, Lapp, & Flood, 1997). Unlike instructional frameworks for a reading lesson such as the Directed Reading Thinking Activity (DRTA) (Stauffer, 1969), guided reading (Fountas & Pinnell, 1996), or the stages of an instructional lesson outlined by Readence, Bean, and Baldwin (1995), no widely disseminated framework exists in the professional literature to help students learn from what they see or hear. The CLVG is an instructional framework for taking notes designed for that purpose. At varied grade levels, the CLVG is useful within subject areas: for observing experiments in science class; demonstrating procedures to be followed, for example, in math class; listening to a lecture or outside speaker in health; taking a field trip in social studies; or watching a videotape.

The CLVG has five phases:

1. Preview or review information (whole class)
2. Record or take notes (individual)
3. Elaborate (small groups)

4. Synthesize (whole class)
5. Extend (in pairs)

The first, preview or review information, is a preview of coming attractions that may involve brainstorming or eliciting the whole class's input about a topic, or it may call for the teacher to preteach key concepts and vocabulary. The second phase, record or take notes, requires students independently to keep track of any significant ideas, concepts, or phrases by writing, charting, or drawing them as they view or hear the content. In the third phase, elaborate, students work in preassigned heterogeneous groups to share, condense, and elaborate on their individual notes. The teacher encourages them to extend ideas, add personal anecdotes, draw analogies, and discuss observations. In the fourth phase, synthesize, the groups contribute their elaborated knowledge as a class, providing a broader view of the topic and content. The teacher may find it helpful to organize the newly learned information in the form of a chart or graphic organizer. The fifth phase, extend, is an optional follow-up phase that allows students to work in pairs (or in interest groups) to design a project, research an issue, or compose a paragraph about the topic under study. Exhibit 6.4 gives an example of a CLVG for a social studies video lesson on the Mississippi River.

Present Content in Meaningful Segments

Students who are struggling with print often benefit from information presented in meaningful segments, that is, a page, a paragraph, or a sentence or two, for example (Readence, Bean, & Baldwin, 1995; Rhodes & Dudley-Marling, 1996; Wood, 1986; Wood, Lapp, & Flood, 1992), rather than as a whole page, chapter, lesson, or topic. Presenting content in unit format can take various forms. For example, the teacher may want to employ a phased transfer or gradual release model of instruction that involves the gradual lessening of students' reliance on the teacher. Another approach is to chunk (or group) the amount of print students must deal with at a given time through reading or study guides.

Exhibit 6.4. Collaborative Listening Viewing Guide (CLVG) Lesson for Social Studies: Mississippi River.

Class_Mr. Evans   Date_May 15, 2001

Topic_Mississippi river

Student's Name_Nathaniel   Group Members_Antonio, Jenny

Partner_Tonya

We know that: —The Mississippi is the largest river in the United States.
—It empties into the Gulf of Mexico.

My Notes	Our Group's Notes
People use the water from the river for many things.	The water from the Mississippi is used for drinking, cooking, and cleaning. Farmers also need it to water their crops.
There are several dams.	Dams are used to make electricity.
	Near the end of the river, it is almost a mile wide.
It is 2,348 miles long. The Mississippi is like a highway for boats.	Boats travel all the way down the river from Minneapolis to New Orleans carrying passengers and cargo to different parts along the way.
St. Louis is the busiest port.	St. Louis is the busiest port and also known as the gateway to the West because many pioneers traveled through it on their way west.
New Orleans is also a large port.	New Orleans is downstream from St. Louis. In New Orleans cargo is transferred from barges to sea freighters and then carried to ports in other countries.

We learned that: The Mississippi River is very important to the United States. It is a major gateway to the rest of the world for trade to and from other countries.

We will find out: More about important trade routes in and outside of the United States.

Source: Suzannah Dwight contributed this example.

Employ a Phased Transfer or Gradual Release Model of Instruction

A phased transfer model (Wood, 2001; Wood & Endres, 2001) or gradual release model (Pearson, 1983) is a way to present content in meaningful units by phasing the teacher out and allowing the students to apply the new learning to other contexts on their own, independently. Both models advocate that the teacher scaffold the instruction, providing the necessary modeling, demonstrating, and practice needed to allow the student to use the strategy independently. The phased transfer model, however, incorporates flexible grouping throughout to further provide support and scaffolded instruction through peers and with teacher monitoring and assistance, teaching the process over several weeks.

1. The teacher displays a finished product, the end result of the class or learner's efforts. For example, if the goal of the instruction is to help students learn to write descriptive paragraphs in preparation for the state writing test, the teacher might display a sample paragraph on an overhead projector.
2. The teacher and the class analyze the finished product to determine its organization and key elements.
3. The teacher thinks aloud a sample description, writing these lines on the board or transparency for analysis and modification.
4. The teacher enlists the aid of the class and begins releasing responsibility to the students, asking them to come up with some responses to another prompt. The teacher writes their responses on the board or transparency while providing guidance, direction, and prompting where necessary.
5. The teacher preassigns students to heterogeneous groups of four or five. Given a different prompt on a similar or varied topic, the students engage in communal writing (Wood, 1994), working together to compose a single paragraph by using the targeted elements the class has previously discussed.
6. The teacher assigns the students to pairs, ensuring that the dyads are similar in ability to both help each other and benefit from the collaboration on a single composition. They can pass

the practice passages to another dyad for editing and share them with the whole class. During the small group, pair, and individual phases, the teacher circulates and monitors to provide assistance.

7. Students practice individually. The teacher decides when to ask the students to respond to a writing prompt or engage in the targeted form of writing on their own. The teacher may choose to have students engage in peer editing or have them turn the papers in for grading and editing.

8. At this point or sooner, the teacher can integrate the descriptive writing pattern (or other variations) by asking the class to apply what they have learned to the writing of a passage in science, social studies, health, or some other subject area.

Chunk the Amount of Print Presented at a Given Time

Reading or study guides are one way to make textbook or other material more comprehensible by chunking (or grouping) the amount of print students must read at a given time. This practice differs from asking students of all ability levels, especially those struggling with print, to read an entire chapter and answer questions at the end. In this way, students do not really know where they are going until they get to the end. Reading guides use questions and other activities to lead students through segments of the text, helping them to focus on the significant information and key concepts. Consequently, Wood & Mateja (1983, p. 494) has called reading guides "tutors in print form."

The professional literature (Wood, Lapp, & Flood, 1992) describes numerous reading guides, but the interactive reading guide (Wood, 1988) has particular merit because it uses a variety of whole class, small group, and individualized activities to guide students through the reading of printed material. As with any strategy, the uses and purposes of the interactive reading guide should be explained and modeled thoroughly before beginning. Exhibit 6.5 is an excerpt from an interactive reading guide used in a sixth-grade social studies class.

Exhibit 6.5. Interactive Reading Guide for Social Studies: Eastern Europe.

Codes: ● Individually ◐ Pairs ◕ Group ● Whole Class

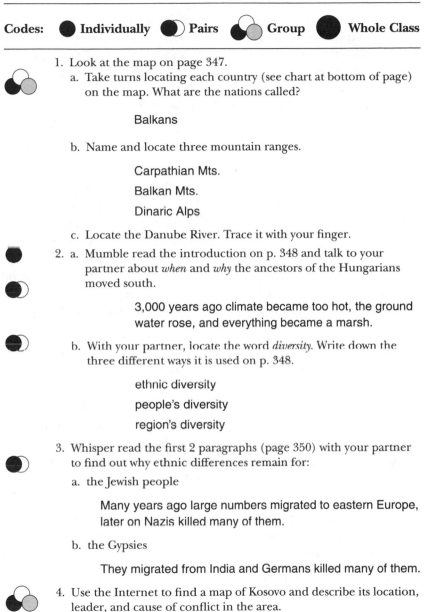

1. Look at the map on page 347.
   a. Take turns locating each country (see chart at bottom of page) on the map. What are the nations called?

      Balkans

   b. Name and locate three mountain ranges.

      Carpathian Mts.

      Balkan Mts.

      Dinaric Alps

   c. Locate the Danube River. Trace it with your finger.

2. a. Mumble read the introduction on p. 348 and talk to your partner about *when* and *why* the ancestors of the Hungarians moved south.

      3,000 years ago climate became too hot, the ground water rose, and everything became a marsh.

   b. With your partner, locate the word *diversity*. Write down the three different ways it is used on p. 348.

      ethnic diversity

      people's diversity

      region's diversity

3. Whisper read the first 2 paragraphs (page 350) with your partner to find out why ethnic differences remain for:
   a. the Jewish people

      Many years ago large numbers migrated to eastern Europe, later on Nazis killed many of them.

   b. the Gypsies

      They migrated from India and Germans killed many of them.

4. Use the Internet to find a map of Kosovo and describe its location, leader, and cause of conflict in the area.

Source: Sally Cameron contributed this example.

Three Recommendations for the Future

The message in the professional literature is clear: students functioning below grade level comprise the fastest-growing student population in the country. The best way to help struggling learners improve their reading and writing abilities is to give them ample opportunities throughout the school day for practice. This chapter recommends that educators take three steps to improve students' comprehension in the future.

RECOMMENDATION 1: Have students read and write every day in every class period.

Students' reading performance can improve if we increase the amount of time they spend reading text, provide instruction in fluency and comprehension where needed, and allow opportunities for reading for pleasure and information every day. Similarly, students' writing performance can improve if we integrate writing activities across the curriculum with a combination of formal and informal guided practice sessions throughout the day.

RECOMMENDATION 2: Incorporate flexible grouping to enable students to benefit from one another.

Ample evidence exists in the professional literature for the benefits of collaborative learning. Teachers must strategically use a repertoire of grouping strategies to meet instructional goals. Peer cooperation and assistance enable the teacher to monitor, circulate, and provide help where needed.

RECOMMENDATION 3: Capitalize on students' interests and abilities by presenting content in a meaningful manner.

This requires using multiple content sources and presenting information in a developmentally appropriate manner that includes modeling, demonstration, scaffolding, practice, and transfer with support from both teacher and peers.

References

Allington, R. (1983). The reading instruction provided readers of differing reading abilities. *Elementary School Journal, 83,* 548–559.

Allington, R. L., & Walmsley, S. A. (Eds.). (1995). *No quick fix: Rethinking literacy programs in America's elementary schools.* New York: Teachers College Press.

Atwell, N. (1987). *In the middle.* Portsmouth, NH: Heinemann.

Bear, D. R. (1991). Learning to fasten the seat of my union suit without looking around: The synchrony of literacy development. *Theory into Practice, 30,* 149–157.

Berglund, R. L., & Johns, J. L. (1983). Primer on uninterrupted sustained silent reading. *Reading Teacher, 36,* 534–539.

Center for Immigration Studies. (2001). Immigrants in the U.S.—2000: A snapshot of America's foreign-born population. Washington, DC: Center for Immigration Studies.

Collins, C. (1986). Is the cart before the horse? Effects of preschool reading instruction on four-year-olds. *Reading Teacher, 40,* 332–339.

Cunningham, P. M. (1978). Mumble reading for beginning readers. *Reading Teacher, 31,* 409–411.

Dahl, K. L., Scharer, P. L., Lawson, L. L., & Arogan, P. R. (1999). Phonics instruction and student achievement in whole language first-grade classrooms. *Reading Research Quarterly, 34,* 312–341.

Donahue, P. L., Voelkl, K. E., Campbell, J. R., & Mazzeo, J. (1999). *National assessment of educational progress, 1998 reading report card for the nation and the states.* Washington, DC: NAEP.

Fitzgerald, J. (1993). Literacy and students who are learning English as a second language. *Reading Teacher, 46,* 638–647.

Fountas, I. C., & Pinnell, G. S. (1996). *Guided reading: Good first teaching for all children.* Portsmouth, NH: Heinemann.

Fuchs, D., Fuchs, L. S., Mathes, P. G., & Simmons, D. C. (1997). Peer-assisted learning strategies: Making classrooms more responsive to diversity. *American Education Research Journal, 32*(1), 174–206.

Gambrell, L. B., & Bales, R. (1986). Mental imagery and the comprehension-monitoring performance of fourth- and fifth-grade poor readers. *Reading Research Quarterly, 21,* 654–664.

Gambrell, L. B., Dromsky, A., & Mazzoni, S. A. (2000). Motivation matters: Fostering full access to literacy. In K. Wood & T. Dickinson (Eds.), *Promoting literacy in grades 4–9: A handbook for teachers and administrators* (pp. 128–138). Needham Heights, MA: Allyn & Bacon.

Gambrell, L. B., Morrow, L. M., Neuman, S. B., & Pressley, M. (1999). *Best practices in literacy instruction.* New York: Guilford Press.

Grabe, W. (1991). Current developments in second language reading research. *TESOL Quarterly, 25,* 375–406.

Greenwald, E. A., Persky, H. R., Campbell, J. R., & Mazzeo, J. (1999). *National assessment of educational progress 1998 writing report card for the nation and the states.* Washington, DC: U.S. Dept. of Education, Office of Educational Research and Improvement.

Harmon, J., & Wood, K. D. (2001). The TAB book club approach: Talking (T) about (A) books (B) in content area classrooms. *Middle School Journal, 32*(3), 51–57.

Hiebert, E. H. (1996). Revisiting the question: What difference does reading recovery make to an age cohort? *Educational Researcher, 25*(7), 26–28.

Hoyt-Goldsmith, D. (1994.) *Cherokee Summer.* New York, NY: Holiday House.

Johnson, D. W., & Johnson, R. T. (1991). *Learning together and alone* (3rd ed.). Needham Heights, MA: Allyn & Bacon.

Kagan, S. (1994). *Cooperative learning.* San Juan, CA: Kagan Cooperative Learning.

Koskinen, P. S., & Blum, I. H. (1986). Paired repeated reading: A classroom strategy for developing fluent reading. *Reading Teacher, 40,* 70–75.

McCauley, J. K., & McCauley, D. S. (1992). Using choral reading to promote language learning for ESL students. *Reading Teacher, 15,* 526–533.

McConnell, S. (1993). Talking drawings: A strategy for assisting learners. *Journal of Reading, 36,* 260–269.

McCracken, M. (1973). *A circle of children.* Philadelphia: Lippincott.

McGee, C. (1994). *So Sings Blue Deer.* New York, NY: Simon & Schuster.

McMahon, S. I., & Raphael, T. E. (1997). *The book club connection: Literacy learning and classroom talk.* Newark, DE: International Reading Association.

Nathan, R. G., & Stanovich, K. E. (1991). The causes and consequences of differences in reading fluency. *Theory into Practice, 30,* 176–184.

National Reading Panel (2000). *Teaching children to read: An evidence-based assessment of the scientific research literature on reading and its implications for reading instruction.* Washington, DC: National Institute of Child Health and Human Development.

Neuman, S. B. (1999). Books make a difference: A study of access to literacy. *Reading Research Quarterly, 34,* 286–310.

Ortiz, S. J. (1994). *The People Shall Continue.* San Francisco, CA: Children's Book Press.

Paratore, J. R., & McCormack, R. L. (1997). *Peer talk in the classroom: Learning from research.* Newark, DE: International Reading Association.

Pearson, P. D. (1983). Changing the face of reading comprehension instruction. *Reading Teacher, 38,* 724–738.

Peters, E. E., & Levin, J. R. (1986). Effects of mnemonic imagery strategy on good and poor readers' prose recall. *Reading Research Quarterly, 21,* 161–178.

Pressley, M. (1976). Mental imagery helps eight-year-olds remember what they read. *Journal of Educational Psychology, 68,* 355–359.

Readence, J. E., Bean, T. W., & Baldwin, R. S. (1995). *Content area reading: An integrated approach.* Dubuque, IA: Kendall/Hunt.

Rhodes, L. K., & Dudley-Marling, C. (1996). *Readers and writers with a difference: A holistic approach to teaching struggling readers and writers* (2nd ed.). Portsmouth, NH: Heinemann.

Richards, M. (2000). Be a good detective: Solve the case of oral reading fluency. *Reading Teacher, 53,* 534–539.

Risko, V. J., & Bromley, K. (2001). *Collaboration for diverse learners: Viewpoints and practices.* Newark, DE: International Reading Association.

Roller, C. M. (1996). *Variability not disability: Struggling readers in a workshop classroom.* Newark, DE: International Reading Association.

Routman, R. (1996). *Literacy at the crossroads: Critical talk about reading, writing, and other teaching dilemmas.* Portsmouth, NH: Heinemann.

Sadowski, M., & Paivio, A. (2001). Imagery and text: A dual coding theory of reading and writing. Hillsdale, NJ: Erlbaum.

Sidelnick, M. A., & Svodboda, M. L. (2000). The bridge between drawing and writing: Hannah's story. *Reading Teacher, 54,* 174–184.

Sita, L. (1994). *The Rattle and the Drum: Native American Rituals and Celebrations.* Brookfield, CT: Millbrook Press.

Slavin, R. (1995). *Cooperative learning* (2nd ed.). Needham Heights, MA: Allyn & Bacon.

Stauffer, R. G. (1969). *Directing reading maturity as a cognitive process.* New York: HarperCollins.

Tierney, R. J., & Shanahan, T. (1991). Research on the reading-writing relationship: Interactions, transactions, and outcomes. In R. Barr, M. L. Kamil, P. Mosenthal, & P. D. Pearson (Eds.), *Handbook of reading research* (Vol. 2, pp. 246–280). White Plains, NY: Longman.

U.S. Department of Education (USDE), National Center for Education Statistics. (1995). *The condition of education.* Washington, DC: Author.

U.S. Department of Education (USDE), National Center for Education Statistics. (1998). *The condition of education.* Washington, DC: Author.

U.S. Department of Education (USDE), National Center for Education Statistics. (2000). *The condition of education.* Washington, DC: Author.

Weaver, C. (1994). *Reading process and practice: From socio-psycholinguistics to whole language* (2nd ed.). Portsmouth, NH: Heinemann.

Wood, K. D. (1986). The effects of interspersing questions in text: Evidence for slicing the task. *Reading Research and Instruction, 25*(4), 295–307.

Wood, K. D. (1988). Guiding students through the reading of informational text. *Reading Teacher, 41,* 912–920.

Wood, K. D. (1999, October). *Including diverse learners in the classroom community.* Paper presented at the eastern regional conference of the International Reading Association, Dover, DE.

Wood, K. D. (1994). *Practical strategies for improving instruction.* Columbus, OH: National Middle School Association.

Wood, K. D. (2001). *Strategies for integrating reading and writing in middle and high school classrooms.* Needham Heights, MA: Allyn & Bacon.

Wood, K. D., & Algozzine, B. (1994). Using collaborative learning to meet the needs of high risk learners. In K. D. Wood & B. Algozzine (Eds.), *Teaching reading to high-risk learners: A unified perspective.* Needham Heights, MA: Allyn & Bacon.

Wood, K. D., & Endres, C. (2001). *Imagine, elaborate, predict, and confirm (IEPC): A strategy for improving comprehension.* Manuscript submitted for publication.

Wood, K. D., & Harmon, J. (2002). *Strategies for integrating reading and writing in middle and secondary classrooms.* Columbus, OH: National Middle School Association.

Wood, K. D., & Mateja, J. A. (1983). Adapting secondary level strategies for use in elementary classrooms. Reading Teacher, *36*(6), 492–496.

Wood, K. D., McCormack, R. L., Lapp, D., & Flood, J. (1997). Improving young adolescent learning through collaborative learning. *Middle School Journal, 28*(3), 26–34.

Wood, K. D., Lapp, D., & Flood, J. (1992). *Guiding readers through text: A review of study guides.* Newark, DE: International Reading Association.

Young, E. (1989). *Lon Po Po.* New York: Philomel.

Zanjani, S. S. (2002). *Sarah Winnemucca.* Lincoln: University of Nebraska Press.

Zemelman, S., Daniels, H., & Hyde, A. (1993). *Best practice: New standards for teaching and learning in America's schools.* Portsmouth, NH: Heinemann.

Chapter Seven

Parsing, Questioning, and Rephrasing (PQR)

Building Syntactic Knowledge to Improve Reading Comprehension

James Flood,
Diane Lapp,
and Douglas Fisher

Good readers need sophisticated knowledge about the workings of language in order to make sense of texts. In addition to decoding knowledge (graphophonemic knowledge) and rich vocabularies (semantic knowledge), students also need a vast storehouse of syntactic knowledge that will enable them to comprehend difficult texts. In short, children need to understand the way language works, its underpinnings, and its structural framework (Lapp, Flood, Brock, & Fisher, in press). Just as readers need to know when and how to access their topical knowledge and their cognitive strategies, so too do they need to know when and how to access their syntactic knowledge. This is done best through practice with parsing sentences, paragraphs, and complete texts. Students need to develop their syntactic skills so that they can use them when they are struggling with texts, especially with texts in which they easily decode and understand all of the words.

Word Callers

We've all heard about *word callers,* students who decode the words of a text flawlessly but fail to comprehend what they are reading. Throughout our careers as educators, we have lived through periods when researchers flatly stated that "There's no such thing as a word caller" and periods when researchers confirmed the word-calling phenomenon, particularly in the case of second-language students. We authors have long believed that the phenomenon does, in fact, exist for first-language as well as second-language students. But it exists on a continuum from almost no understanding of a text to limited understanding. We have found that almost all students who can decode the words of a text have some sense of the meaning of the text.

For example, take the case of the ten-year-old boy who reads this simple word problem: "John runs three miles in eighteen minutes while Mary runs four miles in twenty-two minutes. How long will it take each of them to complete a ten-minute run if they continue at the pace they are currently running?" He doesn't miss a word in terms of decoding and vocabulary, but he can't answer the question. He sits blankly, unable and perhaps unwilling to attempt an answer.

Is he a word caller, one who can say the words but can't understand the text? Yes, to a degree, he is. Through questioning, his teacher becomes convinced that the student understands the meaning of every word and even understands that both John and Mary are running in a race. But he is unable to answer the question; he is unable to perform the tasks that are required of a competent comprehender—parsing the text, asking questions of the text, paraphrasing the ideas included in the text, and manipulating the ideas in ways that make them comprehensible.

Although some might argue that his problem is not faulty comprehension but an inability to do mathematics, we argue that, yes, the student probably has issues of mathematical understanding, but these mathematical deficits are inseparable from his comprehension problems. As he sits and stares at the problem, it becomes increasingly obvious that he has not parsed the text; he does not know what it is saying—what it is asking of him. Without parsing the problem, he cannot possibly answer the question.

A second example of the word-calling phenomenon came to our attention recently when a young teacher told us about her experiences with the *Babysitter's Club* series when she was a third-grader. She remembers her experiences and laughs as she tells a sobering story of her development as a reader. Although she can hardly believe it now, she vividly remembers her embarrassment when she realized that reading the *Babysitter's Club* books was more than a decoding or vocabulary exercise:

> As my friends gathered on the playground to retell (and respond to) the latest book, I suddenly realized that I wasn't doing what the other girls were doing—comprehending the stories. I felt confused at first because I dutifully "read" each book; sometimes I even read the words aloud to my mother, but it never dawned on me that I was supposed to be getting the story. Probably this was also happening in my classroom reading—I was probably hearing the other children's answers to questions and piecing the story together that way. The whole notion of working toward comprehension passed me by. I had no idea that I was supposed to understand each phrase and each sentence. I never tried to make sense of the story by putting the pieces together. I barely remembered the names of the girls in the stories. I didn't understand that each sentence was supposed to make sense, and I never dreamed that the sentences were related to one another. Now I can look back at that experience and say: "Thank God I heard the other girls retelling and analyzing the stories." I'm sure my social antennae told me to get with it, to start reading for meaning if I wanted to be part of the group.

In this chapter we will focus on the needs of children who have adequate and even superior decoding and vocabulary skills but still need help accessing their syntactic knowledge as they try to comprehend the texts that they are reading. However, before we discuss instructional ideas for these children, we need to explain that the trichotomy between (1) decoding skills, (2) vocabulary skills, and (3) comprehension is rarely as clean as we have suggested to this point. Most children need help with all three cueing systems—decoding, vocabulary, and syntax—as they try to make sense of the books they read.

Decoding and Comprehension

Overwhelming evidence shows that children who learn automatic decoding in the early years of schools become good comprehenders (Juel, Griffith, & Gough, 1986), and strong evidence shows that well-developed word recognition skills predict later reading comprehension success (Juel, 1988). The converse is also true, however: children who do not learn to decode automatically continue to have comprehension problems throughout their school years.

Gough and Tunmer (1986) go so far as to argue that learning to comprehend is almost exclusively a problem of learning to decode. They assert that children who can decode words in texts will be able to comprehend them. Other researchers make similar connections between decoding and comprehending but do not go so far as to say that the ability to decode automatically results in the ability to comprehend. Rather, they argue the connection from the opposite direction: word-level decoding is critical for comprehending a text; if readers cannot decode words, they will not be able to comprehend them (Adams, 1990; Metsala & Ehri, 1998; and Pressley, 1998).

Although several researchers have demonstrated that extensive training in decoding did not necessarily result in improved comprehension (Fleisher, Jenkins, & Pany, 1979; Yuill & Oakhill, 1991), others have found that extensive training, which produces highly skilled decoders, does result in better comprehension because children who are truly automatic decoders have more mental "space" for focusing on comprehension (Tan & Nicholson, 1997).

Although the debate will undoubtedly continue for years to come, evidence shows that skilled comprehenders use multiple cueing systems in their efforts to make meaning. The primacy of the graphophonemic system remains intact, according to the currently available research data (Nicholson, 1991), but evidence also shows that competent comprehenders use syntactic and semantic cues to make meaning (Weaver, 1994).

Vocabulary and Comprehension

Nagy (1988) documented the relationship between word knowledge and reading comprehension, cogently arguing that understanding oral and written language without knowing what most of the words in a text mean is very difficult. Researchers have demonstrated that a student's vocabulary (receptive and expressive) is a measure of his or her world knowledge and active ability to comprehend (Nagy, 1988; Nagy & Herman, 1987). Many studies have demonstrated the interrelation between vocabulary knowledge and reading comprehension (Nagy, Anderson, & Herman, 1987; McKeown, Beck, Omanson, & Pople, 1985), and researchers have drawn a straightforward conclusion: the greater the reader's knowledge of vocabulary, the deeper the comprehension of texts will be (Baumann & Kameenui, 2002).

Although scholars give consistent evidence that vocabulary can be directly taught (McKeown, Beck, Omanson, & Pople, 1985), others have also reported that readers learn most vocabulary words incidentally as a function of encounters with words in oral and written contexts (Sternberg, 1987). This finding helps to explain a phenomenon that several researchers have found—readers who read most frequently and most widely possess the greatest vocabularies (Cunningham & Stanovich, 2002). Reading and knowledge of information are interdependent—the more one reads, the greater is his or her knowledge; the greater the knowledge, the better the comprehension.

Text Comprehension

Storehouses of Knowledge

In addition to good decoding skills and rich vocabularies, students need storehouses of knowledge about many topics that they can access when they are reading. This knowledge is organized in their minds in such a way that readers can get at knowledge to help them make sense of print. This knowledge, sometimes called schema knowledge, serves as a structure for organizing relations between and among ideas (Anderson & Pearson, 1984).

For example, competent readers may have schema knowledge for a restaurant: they know its purpose (eating), where it's done (a building), by whom (customers), and when it's done (certain hours of the day). Specific customs are embedded within the schemata, for example, waiting to be seated, ordering from the menu, paying the bill, and leaving a tip.

Schema knowledge helps people understand the relationships among events easily as soon as they identify one small piece of the schema (readers know to access their restaurant schema as soon as the word *waitress* is used in the text). Bauer and Fivush (1992) have shown that even very young children have schemata for events in their own lives (bedtime rituals, dinner routines, game rules) that help them make inferences as they hear and read stories with events that match their knowledge. Thus, the wider the child's experiences, the greater his or her ability to comprehend texts.

Although schema theory is a decidedly top-down model of meaning making, comprehension sometimes occurs from bottom-up processing (Graesser, 1981). For example, a reader may be lost in the text until a specific word or familiar image (such as a barking dog, a twirling dancer, a speeding car) clarifies what went before. These familiar words and images evoke a connection between the text and the reader's prior knowledge.

Strategies

A great deal of research has documented the importance of using well-developed cognitive strategies during reading (Lapp, Flood, Brock, & Fisher, 2002). Although there are many lists of strategies, the most effective strategies seem to boil down to these seven (Keene & Zimmermann, 1997):

- Activation of prior knowledge
- Prioritizing information (deciding the big ideas)
- Questioning the author and the text
- Evoking sensory images
- Drawing inferences
- Retelling or synthesizing
- Using fix-up strategies to repair comprehension

In our master's thesis seminar the other evening, we began discussing this issue of word callers, and one teacher explained that she wanted to do her master's project on comprehension strategies because she believed that many of her children were becoming word callers. She explained that many of her third-graders were having great difficulty with understanding their books—their leveled readers, their independent reading books, and their content area texts—because they lacked comprehension strategies rather than decoding or vocabulary skills. She told us that she wanted to teach what she called "tried and true" comprehension strategies to her students and then look at the ways that they transferred the strategies from one text to another. We asked her whether she thought the learning of her list of tried and true strategies would enable every child to comprehend. "Yes, I do," she replied. We asked her to talk more about her proposed topic. As she began to talk, some of the other students in the seminar joined in; some weren't so sure that strategies instruction was the only silver bullet that she and her students would need:

TEACHER A: I think teachers often teach children the "right" strategies like the one's discussed in *Teaching Reading to Every Child* (2003)—visualizing, inferring, etc.— and even ask them to demonstrate that they can do the strategy, but then they don't check to see if the children actually use the strategies when they come to their own textbooks. That's what I want to look at in my study.

TEACHER B: Well, I think teachers get so frustrated with content area texts because they're so hard to read that they teach the children the content they need by telling them the concepts and then never even ask them to read their books. So I'm not sure that they really learned the strategies.

TEACHER C: I'm not sure that we really know the right strategies that all children need. I think some of the strategies that we all talk about are good for nonfiction texts but not so useful for narratives. And I think the strategies that we all talk about aren't always the answer.

> Sometimes the textbook or article or even the story is hard because of the author's style; I mean voice. Sometimes the author is presenting a very sophisticated, complex, downright confusing argument that students can't follow, no matter how hard they try. I think they need strategies for making each sentence make sense.

TEACHER D: Yes, I agree, and I also think the problem is that students never really get a chance to "own" the strategies. They don't get enough chance to practice them to transfer them from the teaching lesson to the textbook.

TEACHER E: Sometimes the whole thing breaks down because we ask students to do assignments that are impossible because the text doesn't even include information that they need to answer our questions. And sometimes they actually understand the information in the text, but we ask them to write a paper that is so unfamiliar to them—like if the text lists the facts about Hammurabi's Code and Confucius's philosophy, then we ask them to compare their styles of leadership. Well, where did the textbook talk about that?

TEACHER F: I think students sometimes get so lost in a sentence or a paragraph that they stop trying. They can't figure out whether the author is for or against the point that is being discussed. They don't get the notion of point of view or perspective very well. I'm always amazed when I ask students if the author likes a character that he is writing about, and they have no idea. That makes the text pretty difficult to comprehend.

In this brief exchange the teachers succinctly and effectively outlined many of the problems of comprehending and the challenges of teaching comprehension to students who have adequate decoding and vocabulary skills. The issues they raised include

Student behaviors while comprehending within and across texts from student knowledge of language content and strategies to motivation

Text features from author's purposes, perspectives, points of view, and writing styles to content, vocabulary, and presentation of ideas

Tasks from deciphering meaning at the phrase, sentence, and paragraph level to writing assignments

Although strategies are important for reading, our students and many researchers argue that strategies are good only when they are used judiciously and correctly. Students need practice deciding when to use a specific strategy, and they need to learn which strategy to use with each text. Our students and many researchers have also pointed out that cognitive strategies alone are not a magic potion that will make all things right. They remind us that the text also plays a critical role in comprehension. Just as no two children are alike, no two texts are alike. Each must be worked on to be understood. Children need to use their language skills as well as their cognitive strategies to make meaning.

Parsing for Understanding

When teachers ask students to read materials that are difficult for them, they sometimes need help at the most basic level of figuring out what's going on as the text begins—they often need to parse the text in order to grasp the syntactic relations between and among the words and the sentences. If they lose their footing in the first few sentences, they are often unable and unwilling to try to comprehend the rest of the text. The following first paragraph of W. W. Jacobs's short story "The Monkey's Paw," frequently anthologized for intermediate and middle schoolers, introduces the characters and the setting of the story and sets the tone for what is to come. Understanding this paragraph is critical for comprehension of the entire story; when students don't understand the message of these first two sentences, they rarely make sense of the story. The story begins: "Without, the night was cold and wet, but in the small parlor of Lakesnam Villa the blinds were drawn and the fire burned brightly. Father and son were at chess, the former, who possessed ideas about the game involving radical changes, putting his king into such sharp and unnecessary perils that it even provoked comment from the white-haired old lady knitting placidly by the fire."

Many children can read all of the words in these two sentences; many children have a rudimentary grasp of the concepts of chess and understanding of words like *parlor* and *placidly.* Yet they can't understand the paragraph. Some simply drift away because the language is unfamiliar (and complex); others try to understand but are baffled by the syntax and writing style, unable to hold so many different ideas in their heads at once.

What can we do to help these children? One approach might be to chuck this text for an easier one. Yes, that's a possibility, but there will come a time when we, as teachers, are sure that a particular text is so important for our students that we want them to learn to read it (for example, texts like the U.S. Constitution). Let us suppose for a moment that is a text that you believe your students need to read. What can you do?

Parsing, Questioning, Rephrasing (PQR)

PQR is a process of parsing, questioning, and rephrasing a text. This strategy enables children to slowly and gradually develop their understanding of sentences, paragraphs, and complete texts. PQR is based on the belief that children need to be engaged as they read texts by being challenged continually to derive meaning from the text. Flood, Lapp, and Fisher designed this technique to enable children to construct meaning in stages; the reader constantly evaluates and revises meaning as the process unfolds. We have found that this technique helps readers to

- See the underlying relations between words, sentences, and paragraphs in a text
- Pose their own questions of the text
- Predict events to come in the text
- Evaluate their own progress in meaning making
- Redirect their attention when it wanders
- Stay tuned into the author's nuances and perspective changes

Although PQR is a text-driven process in which readers work at comprehending an author's message, it is also a constructive process in which readers work to build meaning that is based on their own experiences and knowledge. At its core it requires a close analysis of the text. Former President Jimmy Carter frequently talked about a similar method that he used when he found a text difficult—he "diagrammed" each sentence that he didn't understand and claimed that the painstaking process increased his comprehension. We are not proposing his time-consuming, overly complex method, but we are proposing a process that makes students look carefully and critically at ideas that are included within and across sentences.

PQR consists of three steps (parsing, questioning, and rephrasing) with a bonus step (explaining or extending [E]), in which the teacher can introduce external information into the discussion that helps to explain or extend understanding of a concept. The teacher can incorporate this step into the process at any time. After the teacher has prepared the students for the text by having them access appropriate prior knowledge and focus on potentially difficult vocabulary items, she and the children read the text. Once it becomes clear from questioning that the students are stumped in their efforts to comprehend, the teacher uses the PQR strategy. The steps begin with these two:

1. PARSING: The teacher and the children parse the text together, proceeding through the text chunk by chunk.
2. QUESTIONING: The teacher questions the students as they parse the text sentence by sentence. She reminds them that sentences have subjects and predicates, which include the verb and the complement. Together they look for the subject, the verb, and the object or descriptor. The teacher asks the students to fill in the guide sheet (Exhibit 7.1) by moving children through the portion of the text that is troubling them. The guide has room for five big ideas per sentence, but the number of ideas will vary for each sentence. For example, the first sentence of "The Monkey's Paw" contains two big ideas.

Exhibit 7.2 gives an example of the way that one teacher and her students filled in the guide for the first sentence of "Monkey's Paw" (Jacobs, 1906).

Exhibit 7.1. Guide for Parsing Through Questioning and Rephrasing (PQR).

Sentence: [Write sentence to be analyzed here.]

Idea 1

Subject (Who, What)	Verb (Is, Do)	Object or Descriptor (Who, What, When, Where, How)

Idea 2

Subject (Who, What)	Verb (Is, Do)	Object or Descriptor (Who, What, When, Where, IIow)

Idea 3

Subject (Who, What)	Verb (Is, Do)	Object or Descriptor (Who, What, When, Where, How)

Idea 4

Subject (Who, What)	Verb (Is, Do)	Object or Descriptor (Who, What, When, Where, How)

Idea 5

Subject (Who, What)	Verb (Is, Do)	Object or Descriptor (Who, What, When, Where, How)

Exhibit 7.2. Guide for PQR: "Monkey's Paw," Sentence 1.

Sentence: "Without, the night was cold and wet, but in the small parlor of Lakesnam Villa the blinds were drawn and the fire burned brightly."

Idea 1

Subject (Who, What)	Verb (Is, Do)	Object or Descriptor (Who, What, When, Where, How)
Outside house	is	cold and wet

Idea 2

Subject (Who, What)	Verb (Is, Do)	Object or Descriptor (Who, What, When, Where, How)
Inside house	is	warm

Idea 3

Subject (Who, What)	Verb (Is, Do)	Object or Descriptor (Who, What, When, Where, How)

Idea 4

Subject (Who, What)	Verb (Is, Do)	Object or Descriptor (Who, What, When, Where, How)

Idea 5

Subject (Who, What)	Verb (Is, Do)	Object or Descriptor (Who, What, When, Where, How)

Exhibit 7.3. Guide for PQR: "Monkey's Paw," Sentence 2.

Sentence: "Father and son were at chess, the former, who possessed ideas about the game involving radical changes, putting his king into such sharp and unnecessary perils that it even provoked comment from the white-haired old lady knitting placidly by the fire."

Idea 1

Subject (Who, What)	Verb (Is, Do)	Object or Descriptor (Who, What, When, Where, How)
Father and son	play	chess

Idea 2

Subject (Who, What)	Verb (Is, Do)	Object or Descriptor (Who, What, When, Where, How)
Father	puts	king in peril

Idea 3

Subject (Who, What)	Verb (Is, Do)	Object or Descriptor (Who, What, When, Where, How)
Mother	sits	by fire

Idea 4

Subject (Who, What)	Verb (Is, Do)	Object or Descriptor (Who, What, When, Where, How)
Mother	criticizes	father

Idea 5

Subject (Who, What)	Verb (Is, Do)	Object or Descriptor (Who, What, When, Where, How)

In step 3, rephrasing (R), the teacher asks the students to create a text impression log by rephrasing (and summarizing) the information contained in the text. The teacher may also ask students to visualize the scene by drawing or enacting it. In the text impression log for sentence 1, students might write

Outside of house cold and wet

Inside of house warm

The teacher repeats the process with the second sentence of the Jacobs text (1906). Together the teacher and her students start to parse the text. Next they question the text (Exhibit 7.3 shows their completed guide sheet). Afterward the teacher asks the students to rephrase the text by continuing their text impression log:

Outside of house cold and wet

Inside of house warm

Father and son playing chess in parlor

Father puts king in peril

Mother silently criticizes father for risk taking

The teacher uses the bonus E (explanation or extension) step. At this point she wants to make sure that the students are realizing that the author is setting up the story in these first sentences, so she uses one of her E bonuses. In this case the author is foreshadowing what is to come in the story, but the foreshadowing is not explicitly stated, and the teacher doesn't want her children to miss it. She wants the children to know that the contrast between the outside of the house (cold and wet) and the inside of the house (warm and safe) is important to what will happen—perhaps evil from the outside will strike their cozy world. She also wants them to know that the old lady (perhaps the mother) does not approve of the daredevil risk-taking ways of the father. She wants her students to know that the story's conflict is being established in these first two sentences. The text doesn't specify any of these things, so she needs to enter into the comprehension processes of her students by explaining the meaning of foreshadowing and extending their existing knowledge of the concept.

Getting Started with PQR

Teachers can use the PQR strategy for small chunks of text as in this case (the first paragraph consisting of two sentences) or with larger chunks of text. We recommend that the teacher start with a target chunk, a piece of the text that is especially important: the first paragraph of a story or text, the section of the text that explicitly or implicitly states the main idea, or the sections of the story that include the climax and resolution.

Once children are familiar with the strategy, we suggest that the teacher use larger chunks of text. The teacher must be careful when making this jump to larger chunks of texts because he or she may be tempted to move directly to summarizing and skip the rephrasing stage. Even when the summaries seem to be complete, we suggest that the teacher still ask the students to rephrase important sentences within the large chunks in order to help assess whether they are continually parsing the text for understanding. Students might get lucky and say the few things that the teacher wants to hear, but they may not really be as comfortable with the relations of all of the ideas in the chunks as their summary might suggest.

Three Recommendations for the Future

Teachers and students need to continue their focus on developing children's use of the graphophonemic and semantic systems for comprehending, but they must also reemphasize the third pillar of the foundation for comprehension—the syntactic system. PQR is a first step in that direction. Other steps include

Developing writing exercises that parallel the discourse style and structure of the text that students are reading. By composing texts that are similar to the one being read, students are focusing on the underlying structures that help to organize and build a text.

Experimenting with using PQR on a detailed textbook that contains many chapters.

Inviting children to experiment with and manipulate sentences and paragraphs through structural as well as semantic paraphrasing. Students who receive instruction in sentence combining techniques are well on their way to understanding the importance of syntactic knowledge in reading.

References

Adams, M. J. (1990). *Beginning to read.* Cambridge, MA: Harvard University Press.

Anderson, R. C., & Pearson, P. D. (1984). A schema-theoretic view of basic processes in reading. In P. D. Pearson, R. Barr, M. L. Kamil, & P. Mosenthal (Eds.), *Handbook of reading research* (pp. 255–291). White Plains, NY. Longman.

Bauer, P. J., & Fivush, R. (1992). Constructing event representations: Building on a foundation of variation and enabling relations. *Cognitive Development, 7,* 381–401.

Baumann, J., & Kameenui, E. (2002). Vocabulary. In J. Flood, D. Lapp, J. Squire, & J. Jensen (Eds.), *Handbook of research on teaching the English language arts* (2nd ed.). Hillsdale, NJ: Erlbaum.

Cunningham, A., & Stanovich, K. (2002). Reading, comprehension and knowledge. In J. Flood, D. Lapp, J. Squire, & J. Jensen (Eds.), *Handbook of research on teaching the English language arts* (2nd ed., pp. 666–678). Hillsdale, NJ: Erlbaum.

Fleisher, L., Jenkins, J., & Pany, D. (1979). Effects on poor readers' comprehension of training in rapid decoding. *Reading Research Quarterly, 15,* 30–48.

Flood, J., & Lapp, D. (1994). Using conceptual mapping for improving comprehension. *Reading Teacher, 41,* 780–783.

Gough, P. B., & Tunmer, W. E. (1986). Decoding, reading, and reading stability. *Remedial and Special Education, 7,* 6–10.

Graesser, A. C. (1981). *Prose comprehension beyond the word.* New York: Springer-Verlag

Jacobs, W. W. (1906). *The lady of the barge.* New York: Harper & Brothers.

Juel, C., Griffith, P. L., & Gough, P. B. (1986). Acquisition of literacy: A longitudinal study of children in first and second grade. *Journal of Educational Psychology, 78,* 243–255.

Juel, C. (1988). Learning to read and write: A longitudinal study of fifty-four children from first through fourth grade. *Journal of Educational Psychology, 80,* 437–447.

Keene, E. O., & Zimmermann, S. (1997). *Mosaic of thought: Teaching comprehension in a reader's workshop.* Portsmouth, NH: Heinemann.

Lapp, D., Flood, J., Brock, C., & Fisher, D. (in press). *Teaching reading to every child* (4th ed.). Hillsdale, NJ: Erlbaum.

Martin, A. M. (1988–2000). *Babysitter's club mysteries.* (Series). St. Alban's, VT: Little Apple Press.

McKeown, M. G., Beck, I. L., Omanson, R. C., & Pople, M. T. (1985). Some effects of the nature and frequency of vocabulary instruction on the knowledge and use of words. *Reading Research Quarterly, 20,* 522–535.

Metsala, J., & Ehri, L. (Eds.). (1998). *Word recognition in beginning reading.* Hillsdale, NJ: Erlbaum.

Nagy, W. E. (1988). *Vocabulary instruction and reading comprehension* (Tech. Rep. No. 431). Champaign, IL: University of Illinois, Center for the Study of Reading.

Nagy, W., Anderson, R., & Herman, P. (1987). Learning word meanings from context during normal reading. *American Educational Research Journal, 24,* 237–270.

Nagy, W. E., & Herman, P. A. (1987). Breadth and depth of vocabulary knowledge: Implications for acquisition and instruction. In M. G. McKeown & M. E. Curtis (Eds.), *The nature of vocabulary acquisition* (pp. 17–25). Hillsdale, NJ: Erlbaum.

Nicholson, T. (1991). Do children read words better in context or in lists? A classic study revisited. *Journal of Educational Psychology, 83,* 444–450.

Pressley, M. (1998). *Reading instruction that works: The case for balanced teaching.* New York: Guilford Press.

Sternberg, R. J. (1987). Most vocabulary is learned from context. In M. G. McKeown & M. E. Curtis (Eds.), *The nature of vocabulary acquisition* (pp. 89–105). Hillsdale, NJ: Erlbaum.

Tan, A., & Nicholson, T. (1997). Flashcards revisited: Training poor readers to read words faster improves their comprehension of text. *Journal of Educational Psychology, 89,* 276–288.

Weaver, C. (1994). *Understanding whole language: From principles to practice* (2nd ed.). Portsmouth, NH: Heinemann.

Yuill, N., & Oakhill, J. (1991). *Children's problems in reading comprehension.* Cambridge: Cambridge University Press.

Chapter Eight

Using Writing to Improve Comprehension

A Review of the Writing-to-Reading Research

Bena R. Hefflin
and Douglas K. Hartman

For three decades scholars have made considerable study of the reading-writing relationship (Carroll, 1966; Dyson & Freedman, 1991; Langer & Allington, 1992; Scardamalia & Bereiter, 1986; Shanahan & Tierney, 1990; Squire, 1984; Tierney & Shanahan, 1991). For better or worse, both parts of this relationship have been wedded in a rather curious way: reading takes place before writing. A very common instructional practice is to have students read a selection (or have it read to them) and then respond to it by writing or drawing (Durkin, 1978–1979, 1984; Farr, 1993; Goodlad, 1984; Olson, 1996). Rarely does the opposite occur, with students writing before reading a selection. Similarly, the reading-to-writing pattern is reflected in the design structure of most instructional research (Beach & Hynds, 1991). To the extent that the reading-to-writing "order of things" reflects political, cultural, theoretical, historical, or practical assumptions about the relative importance of each process (Foucault, 1970), our work in this chapter is to reorder these things by looking at reading-writing research

Acknowledgment: For helpful feedback during critical points in the development of this chapter, we'd like to thank Richard Donato of the University of Pittsburgh.

askance—from writing to reading—and review the research on using writing to improve comprehension.

Approach

We began by asking the question: Does scholarly work examine the temporal flip side of the reading-writing relationship? Has anyone studied what we might call the "reading-writing-reading-writing-reading-writing-reading-writing" activity chain by segmenting it into writing-to-reading units? As we scoured the literature, we immediately confronted two issues: (1) defining what writing and reading are and (2) determining when writing and reading begin and end.

Although defining what writing and reading are might seem like a straightforward proposition, our task was complicated by the presence of different writing types used across studies. Is spelling *writing*? Is scribbling a word or phrase? Is penciling a sentence? Is composing a paragraph, short story, or report? Or sketching a semantic map? Rather than limit writing to any restrictive sense, we operationalized it so that writing referred to any symbolic representation—linguistic, graphic, pictorial, or otherwise—that was peripheral, contributory, or central to the reading that followed. Similarly, we adopted a broad definition of *reading* so that any form of response, comprehension, or apprehension to print could be construed as reading.

Even more difficult—at least conceptually—was the issue of determining where writing and reading begin and end. To be sure, there is a point when a writer's pen first presses against the page (or the writer's fingers press on the keyboard) and etches its way until the ideas or pages are no more. And to be sure, there is a point where the reader's eyes first fixate and progressively saccade and regress their way across the page (or monitor) until there is no more print or time (Hartman, 1992). But such notions of beginnings and endings are cultural constructions that have evolved for pragmatic, methodological, or other reasons. Doesn't a writer read while writing? And doesn't a reader think like a writer while reading (Pearson & Tierney, 1984; Tierney & Pearson, 1983)? Questions like these blurred the boundaries between the writing-to-reading sequence in practice. Given this blurriness, we adopted an inclusive conception of beginning and ending that extends along a continuum of sorts—from studies with a more linear writing-to-reading design at one end to those with a more recursive design or analysis at the other.

Rationale

While grappling with these issues, we attended to a second question: Why look at writing as the starting point in the reading-writing connection? What would be gained? The obvious reason—that it apparently has not been done—was not completely satisfactory. At the heart of our review was a more compelling reason: in everyday practice writing often initiates a chain of exchanges with reading. For example, filling out a job application starts a series of reading and verbal events that may lead to being hired. Jotting down a grocery list leads to locating and reading environmental print (for example, cereal boxes, store signage) on items to be purchased from a store. And scrawling a few thoughts about a topic for a research paper prior to exploring the library shelves provides some initial direction and purpose to the investigative reading that follows. Even the writing of this chapter began with our committing to paper words, phrases, and sketches of possible relations from writing to reading before we searched and read any of the studies cited.

As these and other everyday examples indicate, the rootedness of writing-to-reading practices is everywhere. As a construct and practice, it is imbued with an authenticity and ecological validity that has been so central to the formation of literacy curriculum, methods, and standards in the last decade. Thus, our reason for looking at the literature on the relationship of writing to reading is a desire to better understand how this particular segmenting of the writing-to-reading chain—so rooted in everyday life—has been articulated for school-related purposes.

A secondary reason for looking at the writing-to-reading sequence is to facilitate further research. Reviews such as this one make visible what is present and absent in the research literature, providing a freeze-frame for referencing what researchers have done and what they could do.

We begin our review by surveying what has been done, offering a brief description of writing-to-reading procedures with an even shorter account of the research on the effects of the procedure.

The representative studies we cite are nonsectarian in method, including whatever approaches are present in the literature itself. Following the review of literature is a discussion section, where we tease out patterns and assumptions across the spectrum of writing-to-reading literature.

Writing-to-Reading Practices

Our initial step was to sort the studies according to the nature of the writing-to-reading relationship: linear or recursive (see Table 8.1). As the labels suggest, linear writing-to-reading practices are unidirectional, whereas recursive practices loop and fold back into preceding others. Within each category, we located specific practices along a continuum that depicts the extent of the writing that feeds or folds into subsequent or prior reading. We reasoned that by foregrounding the practice (writing, in this case) that initiates the writing-to-reading segment of the chain, we could best highlight the differences that follow across the various approaches. The continuum ranges from abbreviated forms of writing on one end (words, phrases, sentences, diagrams, or sketches) to expanded forms in the middle (story synopsis or descriptive paragraph) to extended forms on the other end (story, report, or

Table 8.1. Writing-to-Reading Practices Scheme.

	Linear	*Recursive*
Abbreviated	List-group-label Prereading plan K-W-L Semantic maps Probable passages	Language experience approach Reading recovery

Expanded	Story impressions
	Guided writing
	   procedure
		Dialogue journals
		Reading-writing
		   workbench

Extended		Authoring cycle Writing workshop Label-less practices

book). Taken together, this two-tiered approach—highlighting both the nature and form of writing-to-reading approaches—provides a finer-grained depiction of the features that differentiate the literature we reviewed.

Linear Practices

Linear practices of writing to reading mark clear temporal and activity boundaries between the two: writing (in some form) occurs first, followed by reading. In the literature we reviewed, a linear practice uses writing as a contributory activity—not the focal activity; writing is instrumental to the reading that follows. As a contributory activity, writing practices ranged from abbreviated or truncated forms of writing (words, phrases, sentences, or diagrams) to more expanded, connected forms of prose. In both cases the premise for asking students to write (or sketch) prior to reading is that activating and building their knowledge about a concept before they read enhances their comprehension of the text to be read (see Anderson & Pearson, 1984, for a review of this research).

Abbreviated

Five procedures typify the ways in which educators use abbreviated or truncated writing as a prereading activity: list-group-label; prereading plan; K-W-L; semantic maps; and probable passages.

LIST-GROUP-LABEL. The earliest use of writing prior to reading we found in the literature is Taba's list-group-label procedure (1967). She originally conceived of this as a way to help students better learn and remember concepts in social studies and science prior to reading the text. The three-part strategy involves students'

Brainstorming in response to a stimulus concept while the teacher writes their contributions on a chalkboard, overhead projector, or butcher paper

Breaking the large brainstormed list (in small working groups or as individuals) into smaller lists of common conceptual groupings and assigning a label or title that represents the shared attribute of the group-word members

Sharing the groups of words and their labels with the rest of the
class (the teacher writes these on another section of the chalkboard, transparency, or piece of butcher paper) and explaining why they have categorized the words in this way

Given the long history and widespread recommended use of
the list-group-label procedure, we expected to find a number of
studies that examined the effects of the procedure on concept development, comprehension, and learning. We found none. Aside
from Taba's original work (1967) on elementary social studies,
with its anecdotal accounts, the effects of the list-group-label procedure remain unstudied.

PREREADING PLAN. Langer (1981, 1982) developed the prereading plan to engage students in a discussion about key concepts in
a text before they read it and to provide teachers with a framework
for analyzing the level of knowledge that students have about
those concepts central to the text they will read. The two-stage
procedure involves

1. Students generating, explaining, and reformulating what they
   know about a concept while the teacher writes what they discuss on the chalkboard
2. The teacher analyzing students' responses

Langer's guidelines for analysis categorize student responses as ill-
formed, partly formed, or well-formed knowledge structures about
the concept(s).

With one exception, the research basis for the prereading plan
has exclusively focused on the validity of using the procedure as a
means for assessing prior knowledge (Langer, 1980; Langer &
Nicolich, 1981). Only Molner (1989) studied the relation between
this plan and improvements in passage comprehension, concept
development, or strategy use and found that the prereading plan
had positive effects on delayed memory of text that students read
and that the procedure benefited students who had more prior
knowledge of specific subject matter. Kiewit (1997), who used a
modified version of the plan, found that the prereading writing
activities statistically improved the recall of college students.

K-W-L. Ogle (1986a, b) developed K-W-L as a framework to elicit students' prior knowledge and engage interest before, during, and after reading expository text. The three-step procedure involves students'

1. Brainstorming ideas in response to a concept as the teacher writes them on the board, a chart, or overhead projector and generating category labels for the ideas
2. Developing questions that the teacher writes down for students to answer while reading the text
3. Writing down what they learned in response to the questions they posed at the outset

Others have since extended the procedure to include students' use of summarization and mapping (K-W-L plus) (Carr & Ogle, 1987) and identification of where to find resources to answer their questions (K-W-W-L) (Bryan, 1998).

Claims in the published work on K-W-L (Carr & Ogle, 1987; Ogle, 1986a, b) indicate that the procedure effectively helps students to

- Better remember what they have read over time
- Become more active in their reading
- Better elicit their own background knowledge and organize it
- Become better readers of expository text

The same studies claim that K-W-L helps teachers develop a more interactive teaching style.

Although these early claims about K-W-L's effectiveness were supported by limited evidence, a number of studies in the last decade indicate that K-W-L affects the comprehension of students in a marked way (Burns, 1994; Drew, 1995; Hall, 1994; Jared, 1993).

SEMANTIC MAPS. Semantic mapping (also called webbing or clustering) is a way to organize brainstormed ideas graphically, indicating the relationships among ideas and a key concept by labeling lines, boxes, circles, and other geometric shapes with words that are strategically positioned to represent their semantic syntax. As a prereading writing activity, semantic mapping has taken on many forms (see, for example, Heimlich & Pittelman, 1986; Pearson & Johnson, 1978; Rico, 1983). Three steps usually compose any mapping practice:

1. Students brainstorm what they know about a key concept.
2. The teacher writes their ideas and experiences on the board or overhead.
3. Students shape their ideas and experiences into a graphic form, designed by either the teacher or the students themselves.

Little published research on the use of student-generated semantic maps has been done (although considerable research on direct teacher use of them to teach text-specific vocabulary during prereading does exist; see Moore & Readence, 1984). In one of the few studies we located, Dyer (1985) found that the writing and sketching done through semantic maps prior to reading greatly improved the comprehension of the text that followed. Stahl and Vancil (1986) further refined their use by examining the role of discussion in tandem with the mapping procedure.

PROBABLE PASSAGES. Wood (1984) developed probable passages to use writing as a vehicle to learn key concepts about a basal selection prior to reading. Probable passages involve a series of four stages that span two or three days of instruction: preparation, prereading, reading, and postreading.

In the first stage, the teacher selects key words or concepts from a story (for example, apartment, Pittsburgh, fight, and Roberto) and categorizes them according to the structure of the selection (for example, setting, characters, problem, events, and solution). Using the words and categories, the teacher develops an incomplete probable passage that provides stem statements for each of the story categories followed by a blank space (for example, "The story takes place in _____").

In the second stage students write key words under the story categories (setting, problem, and so on) to complete the outline of a good story (for example, setting: Pittsburgh, apartment; characters: Roberto). Once they are done, the teacher assigns them the task of writing a logical probable passage using the incomplete passage the teacher has written (for example, "The story takes place in an apartment in Pittsburgh, Pennsylvania").

Students read (or listen to) the story in the third stage, verifying the accuracy of their probable passage. During the fourth stage, students discuss how they need to recategorize the words and revise their probable passage.

Readence, Bean, and Baldwin (1989) adapted the procedure to use with expository text. However, we could find no research that examined the efficacy of the probable passage writing on reading comprehension, concept development, or response to narrative or expository text.

Expanded

Two procedures typify the ways in which extended, connected writing is used as a prereading activity: story impressions and the guided writing procedure.

STORY IMPRESSIONS. McGinley and Denner (1987) developed story impressions as a prereading writing activity. Students use key concepts from a story to develop their own impression of what the story will be like by building an anticipatory model that they can confirm or modify when they encounter the real text. The procedure's four steps are

1. The teacher develops a vertical list of ten to fifteen story-specific idea clues (in the form of clue words or phrases).
2. Students brainstorm how the ideas could connect into a possible story while the teacher jots them down on the chalkboard or an overhead.
3. Collaboratively they develop a class story (on the board or overhead) that ties the clues together.
4. Students read the actual story and discuss how their story compares.

Several studies indicate that the story impression prestory writing procedures make marked improvement in the comprehension of narrative text in elementary and middle school students (Denner & McGinley, 1989; Denner, 1992). Bligh (1995) has found it especially helpful in improving the comprehension of less able learners.

GUIDED WRITING PROCEDURE. Smith and Bean (1980) designed the guided writing procedure to activate and assess students' prior knowledge of a text's key concept(s) before they read and to evaluate and teach written expression in a content area. The multiday procedure involves two parts:

1. Students brainstorm thoughts about a key concept while the teacher writes on the board or overhead. Students then vote to distinguish major from minor ideas, design an outline or semantic map of the ideas, and individually write a one- or two-paragraph draft description of what they know using the outline or map. The teacher collects these drafts and quickly analyzes them for organization, style, mechanics, and content while the students read the assigned text.
2. The teacher displays an illustrative draft on the board or overhead and guides students through editing the draft. Students then edit their own first drafts and prepare a second draft for submission.

Research on the guided writing procedure indicates that it significantly improves students' writing and content learning (Konopak, Martin, & Martin, 1987; Martin, Konopak, & Martin, 1986). Searfoss, Smith, and Bean (1981) adapted the procedure to better suit the needs of second-language learners and found similarly strong results.

Recursive Practices

Recursive practices of writing to reading mark less clear temporal and activity boundaries between the two: writing (in some form) occurs first but can be followed by any number or pattern of reading-writing paths. In the literature we reviewed, a recursive practice uses writing as central, integral, and constitutive to the literacy activity that students engage in—it is not merely instrumental to the reading that follows. As part of recursive literate activity, writing practices ranged from abbreviated to expanded to extended forms of connected prose.

Abbreviated

Two approaches typify the ways in which abbreviated or truncated writing is integral to writing to reading: the language experience approach and reading recovery.

LANGUAGE EXPERIENCE APPROACH. A number of approaches fall under the label of language experience approach (Ashton-Warner, 1958; Stauffer, 1970; Allen, 1976). Collectively, they emphasize an eclectic set of procedures that take advantage of the intellectual, linguistic, social, cultural, political, and social capital that students bring to school with them so that the transfer from oral to written language can be easily made. Regardless of approach, three general features mark the procedure: (1) dictated experience stories, (2) word banks, and (3) creative writing.

Dictated experience stories, the first feature, begin when a teacher or student provides a stimulus (an object, event, or idea) within or just beyond the students' experiential reach to stir discussion and careful observation. Once the group is fully engaged, the teacher invites students to tell their ideas about the stimulus and writes them on the chalkboard, chart, overhead projector, or computer. The class reads the stories over several days: first the teacher reads to students, followed by the students reading in groups, pairs, or individually. Word banks, the second feature, are individual folders where students deposit words from the dictated stories to use in a game, skill, strategy, or other composing activity. The third feature, creative writing, offers students a space to compose a piece of writing (for example, a name, sentence, paragraph, or story) individually or with a classmate or teacher by drawing upon words, ideas, spellings, and punctuation from a word bank; this in turn can animate an idea for another stimulus for a dictated story experience.

A number of research reports indicate favorable findings of the language experience approach compared to traditional instructional programs (Kendrick & Bennett, 1966; Stauffer & Hammond, 1967, 1969) and basal word lists (Packer, 1970). Other studies find the approach to strongly benefit students of varying reading abilities (Duquette, 1972), students who are dual-language speakers (Spanish-English) (Riojas-Clark, 1995), and students who are language delayed (Alagna, 1993); another study finds it to strongly support student growth when teachers exhibit particular instructional behaviors while using the procedure (Eichenberger & King, 1995). Stauffer (1970) has abstracted a compendium of additional research.

READING RECOVERY. Reading recovery originated with Clay (1979, 1988) in New Zealand and is largely aimed at first-graders who are not progressing sufficiently in learning to read. A central tenet of this one-on-one early intervention program is that reading and writing work together to enhance the development of both processes. The five-part lesson framework includes

- Reading two or more familiar books
- Writing messages and stories, then rereading them
- Hearing sounds
- Cutting up stories
- Introducing and attempting new books

Writing to reading comes into play in the second part of this lesson framework. Every day the teacher encourages the student to tell a story about a topic that the student chooses (perhaps a book that he or she has read). The teacher encourages the student to write as much as he or she can alone (usually a sentence or two). When the student comes to a problem word, the teacher prompts him or her to predict and isolate sounds (that is, segment phonemes) so that this supports the writing process. After the student has finished writing, the teacher may return to a word and uncover parts of the word slowly to see if the student can decode it, or have the student practice writing selected words that the teacher thinks the student should know. The student then reads the story independently, with the teacher offering support as needed. Finally, the story is typed by the student or teacher and subsequently read or used for instructional purposes in future lessons.

Most of the research shows that reading recovery increases reading achievement, moves students back to regular classroom instruction, and moderately sustains academic benefits beyond the tutoring (Clay, 1982; Ross, Smith, Casey, & Slavin; 1995); very few studies show little or no improvement (Collins & Stevens, 1997). A few studies have focused on the writing-to-reading aspect of the lessons: Walters (1996) finds that message or story writing has a strong impact on student reading performance, and Mott (1994) examines the evolving effects that various teacher-student interactions during the message- or story-writing time have within and across the other parts of the lesson framework.

Expanded

Two approaches typify the ways in which expanded, connected writing is integral to writing to reading: dialogue journals and reading-writing workbench.

DIALOGUE JOURNALS. Dialogue journals take many forms (Atwell, 1984; Harste, Short, & Burke, 1989; Staton, 1980) but share the common thread of providing students an informal space to write to the teacher or another student about things that are on their minds and have them respond with no threat of reprisal or evaluation.

The procedure involves two general phases: getting started and reciprocal responding to journals. In the fist phase, the teacher outlines the types of things that students can write about and explains how the writing exchange will take place. The second phase involves the orchestrated dance of responding to and fro—writing and reading again and again—in mutually respectful and nonevaluative ways. Kluin (1996) has extended the use of dialogue journals to students with special needs. Luft (1997) and Wang (1996) have discussed taking the journals to the electronic medium, with dialogues occurring through e-mail.

A number of studies have examined the beneficial effects of dialogue journals on the writing-to-reading exchange of students of all sorts: students from young children to those of college age (Markman, 1985; Staton, 1984; Staton, Shuy, Peyton, & Reed, 1988); students outside the United States learning English as a foreign language (Song, 1997); and family literacy participants (Linder, 1996). Others have focused on the downside of the procedure (for example, Holmes, 1995). A newsletter titled *Dialogue* has been published to espouse the uses, benefits, theory, and research of dialogue journals (Staton, Kreeft, & Gutstein, n.d.).

READING-WRITING WORKBENCH. The reading-writing workbench (Tierney, Caplan, Ehri, Healy, & Hurdlow, 1989) uses writing as a prereading activity to initiate a cycle of writing and reading around a theme or topic. The procedure involves three phases: (1) exploring personal experiences, (2) experimenting with reading and writing, and (3) reflecting and assessing. During the first phase, students discuss an experience related to a key concept, write a description of the experience, and then share and discuss their writing with others in class. In the second phase, students read a selection that articulates the key concept in some manner and pursue activities that prompt them to consider the text they have written in light of the one they have read. Students then revise the text they have written, reading and gathering other texts in the revising process. In the final phase, students reflect on what they have learned and its potential use for further writing to read.

The systematic study of this procedure is limited: only Burris (1988) examined the effects of the reading-writing workbench on middle school students. Other work has examined this approach's effect on teacher decision making (Dorsey, 1988) and the development of those designing the procedure (Thistlewaite, 1988).

Extended

Three approaches typify the ways in which extended, connected writing is integral to writing to reading: authoring cycle, writing workshop, and a grouping of what we might call label-less studies.

AUTHORING CYCLE. The authoring cycle was developed by Short, Harste, and Burke (1996) as a curricular framework for helping students understand how writing and reading relate to reasoning and learning. Seven features of the cycle mark the ebb and flow of writing-to-reading transactions in the framework:

- Life experiences
- Uninterrupted writing and reading
- Author's circle
- Self-editing
- Outside editing
- Publishing and celebrating authorship
- Invitations and language strategy instruction

By drawing upon life experiences, students initiate themselves into a series of uninterrupted engagements to construct meaning through various expressive and interpretative sign systems (writing, reading, drawing, painting, viewing, dramatizing, dancing, singing, listening, and so on). With a circle of other authors, students explore, negotiate, and reflect on their constructions, making self- and peer-directed revisions to better articulate the substance and form of the vision they are authoring. Finally, they share and present the product of authoring (whether a dance, piece of writing, or some other work) with others to enjoy and examine the process used to construct it, leading students to invite themselves and others into other authoring ventures.

Research on the authoring cycle has shown the framework to be a powerful procedure for students to construct stories from their lives with others and to learn how authoring tools and various sign systems function in learning content for students of many age groups: preschoolers (Rowe, 1986), first-graders (Short, 1986), intermediate students (Short, 1992), and mixed-age learners (Heine, 1990). Kemp (1993) has examined the authoring experiences in hypertext computing medium.

WRITING WORKSHOP. A number of educators have articulated and developed the writing workshop (Atwell, 1987; Calkins, 1986; Graves, 1983). The workshop is a designated time during the school day when students write (individually or collaboratively) on topics of their own choosing and for their own purposes. A typical workshop has three phases: minilessons, writing time, and sharing time. During the minilesson the teacher offers instruction on a topic that is essential to students' being successful with writing they are or will be doing. The minilessons can focus on procedural matters (such as how to work in writing groups), literary concepts (developing setting, characters, plot, and so on), and writing skills and strategies (such as usage, spelling, or punctuation). In the second and longest phase, students work on pieces while the teacher also writes and holds brief conferences with them to give feedback and encouragement on a specific draft. Small groups of students can also meet during this time to read and respond to one another's works in progress. During the last phase, the whole class gathers to hear a handful of peers share their writing out loud.

Although careful and extensive work has gone into the developing and use of the writing workshop, little systematic documentation and analysis of this effort appears in the educational literature. We found three studies: Tuemmler (1993) carefully examined the writing workshop's impact on the comprehension of middle schoolers of mixed ability; Power (1996) analyzed how teachers often gloss over the central features of the writing workshop; and Calkins (1983) wrote a case study of one child's development as a writer and reader through the workshop approach.

Label-less Approaches. A number of studies describe the writing-to-reading practices as they supposedly naturally occur in a given setting or task environment (Pearson & Gallagher, 1983). They leave the writing-to-reading process without a label (label-less) in favor of providing a thick description of how people actually use writing along with reading to make sense and represent meaning. The scholars provide no catchy acronym or phrase to name the practice. These studies capture a wide range of literate practice, from those using traditional print to more esoteric symbolic activity.

In the more traditional vein is Many's research (1996a, b) in which eleven- and twelve-year-olds use writing as a way to explore a historical topic, reading more as they realize through writing the things they need to know more about in order to complete their compositions. By tracing the intertextual patterns, the researcher highlights the self-directed nature of these writing-reading practices. Many paints a complex portrayal of how students transformed information when moving from writing to reading and the various perspectives they considered while doing so.

In the more esoteric realm are studies by Dyson (1992, 1994, 1997) that examine children writing with a wide range of cultural symbols and sources. Through symbolic means children compose enactments of cartoon superhero scenarios or gender roles in dialogue with peers that they view weekly on TV shows. Dyson's existential descriptions of writing to reading show writing and reading to be based on more than print and inclusive of a broad range of materials and practices that children can compose, comprehend, and respond to.

What interests us about these label-less descriptions about writing-to-reading practices is that they are aimed at providing theoretical and conceptual accounts of what students do in particular contexts. The authors of these studies make few explicit pedagogical connections for everyday practice. Implied in their purpose, however, is the move to extend and complete our views of what researchers might consider next in the study of specific approaches to writing to reading.

Three Recommendations for the Future

Given the boundaries we have drawn between the linear and recursive nature of writing-to-reading practices, as well as the continuum of writing forms from abbreviated to expanded to extended, what patterns can we identify, and what do they imply for the future?

Macropatterns

At the global level, three patterns stand out. First, the amount of published research on any approach is minimal, with the exception of the language experience approach (most of this work was done prior to 1970). Although the existence of a large number of studies does not necessarily mean that an approach is efficacious, a paucity of studies raises questions about the certainty with which one might recommend an approach or practice. Are two or three well-conceived and well-executed studies showing strong positive effects sufficient to support the widespread recommendation of the method? Do scholars know enough about the approach to give practitioners ways to use it in context? Scholars have long been concerned about the fallacies of "misplaced concreteness" and "misplaced confidence" (Whitehead, 1925). A study or two can create an impression of certainty and conclusiveness about an approach, when in fact the conditions under which practitioners use the approach and the effects it creates can vary widely from one application to another. Application miscues result, and practitioners use (and perceive) the approach as a method to fit all classes, children, content, communities, and cultures. Given that all the linear and recursive approaches we reviewed receive considerable coverage in methods books and professional journals, we expected to find more systematic study of how each approach worked under certain conditions, in varying contexts, with students across many developmental levels, and so on. But we found none.

Second, the studies focused almost exclusively on a conception of writing that emphasized printed text. Granted, much of our history and school practice value proficiency in writing connected print discourse. However, given the widespread recommendations that teachers use graphic organizers, semantic maps, and other sign systems, we thought to find considerable research on other systems of writing that allow students to represent their understandings in other forms and modes. We found very little.

Finally, computer technology as a tool for linking writing to reading is absent in the literature. The obvious connections and possibilities for wedding writing (broadly conceived) to reading (also broadly conceived) left us wondering: Shouldn't there be work that examines how K-W-L, the writing workshop, or the language experience approach work with computer technology as the primary instrument for writing and reading? And given the ubiquitous World Wide Web, shouldn't there be work that examines the authoring cycle that student builders of Web pages use for reading? We found no such work in the literature.

Microquestions

At the local level, a number of questions cut across approaches and suggest directions for further research. Who does the writing? What role does talk play in the act of writing? What is selected to write? Who selects what students write? What are the critical features for directing instruction? What is being activated or constructed by writing? And what supports the bridge between what students write and read? The answers to these questions and the role those answers play in making the approaches we reviewed efficacious or not—given various goals, materials, student backgrounds, linguistic competencies, developmental levels, and so on—would provide a more comprehensive conception of when and how best to use these approaches.

A subset of the studies, the label-less ones, bring to mind one question: How can the findings and interpretations of these more theoretical or conceptual descriptive studies better inform the use of linear and recursive writing-to-reading practices in the classroom? Any sort of connection between strictly descriptive and solely pedagogic work was absent in the literature we reviewed. To our way of thinking, a feedback loop that uses the work of Many (1996a, b) and Dyson (1992, 1994, 1997) to reanimate existing approaches (such as list-group-label, story impressions, dialogue journals, and the authoring cycle) and animate new writing-to-reading approaches would move the reading-writing connection literature and practice to a new level.

Methodological Issues

In methodological terms, one issue stands out: the limited range of tools used to study writing-to-reading practice. The limitation is clear in the conception, collection, and analysis of data. For example, the conception of data has exclusively been framed in terms of *substance* (the material or content) or *process* (what is done to or with the substance), not the two together. As early as 1956, Russell provided a conceptual frame for examining the two as they co-occur. Others have rearticulated the frame in a number of forms, most recently in Hefflin's study (1996) of student responses to culturally specific African American children's literature. We can think of no theoretical or pragmatic reasons why scholars would not use this conception of data to frame the combinatorial uses of writing to reading.

Furthermore, none of the research we reviewed used the sophisticated process-tracing microanalytic methods for collecting data that the reading-to-writing research of McGinley (1992) and Kamberelis and Scott (1992) used. Given the insight that this and other data-collecting procedures have stimulated in the reading-to-writing research, we wondered why researchers would not use it to extend our vision with writing-to-reading approaches. We can think of no theoretical or pragmatic reasons why this and other data collection approaches should not be used as a window into the flip side of the reading-writing relationship.

Finally, we found that scholars used a limited lens on complexity when analyzing the data. None of the studies we reviewed examined writing to reading in the layered and multidimensional ways that Hartman (1996) and Bloome and Egan-Robertson (1993) did. Their analytic means captured the nested and *heterarchical* relations (that is, flatter and less rigid in the chain of command as opposed to *hierarchical*) of the cognitive, social, cultural, and historical dimensions that play against and with each other in reading and writing. Again, we can think of no theoretical or pragmatic reasons why scholars could not use this and other data analysis procedures in studying writing-to-reading approaches. In all three cases—conception, collection, and analysis of data—the expanded range of methodological tools would begin to address the macropatterns and microquestions we discussed in the two preceding sections.

Final Thoughts

To move to a new level, especially in thinking about writing to reading, we think scholars should explore two conceptual directions. The first is toward a framework (or frameworks) that outlines the critical features for instructional decision making and curricular design. Knowing when (and when not) to use K-W-L, story impressions, and writing workshop—and when and how to adapt each—given particular curricular goals, time constraints, student backgrounds, developmental levels, and so on requires a framework of sorts to ferret out the features that matter for making informed decisions. Paris, Lipson, and Wixson (1983) refer to such knowledge as *conditional knowledge:* knowing when, where, and why to use or adapt an approach. To date, we know of no knowledge framework for writing-to-reading practices. The content of this chapter points toward an initial outline for discussing such a framework. But unless a more refined framework marks the critical features of writing-to-reading approaches, hegemonically generic writing-to-reading procedures will mask the particulars and contingencies of classroom literacy practice. To begin with, we think that such a framework should include features like the quantity of writing and reading, the nature of the writing, the purpose for reading, the requirements of writing tasks, the link between writing and reading, the amount of time to complete a task, the structure of a task, the nature of instructional support necessary to complete a task, the level of collaboration, the concept density of the subject matter, and the topic's interest for students.

What would such a framework look like? And how would it be useful for teaching? Figure 8.1 is one way to frame the ideas of this chapter into a working set of guidelines for deciding which

Figure 8.1. Instructional Decision-Making Process for Using Writing-to-Reading Approaches.

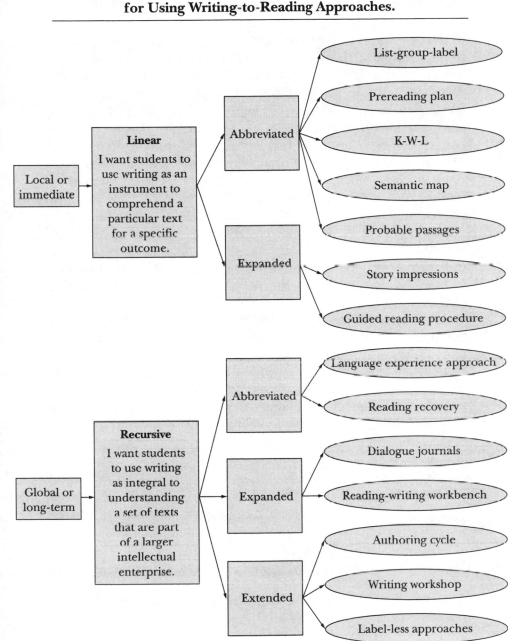

writing-to-reading approaches to use with particular curricular goals, time constraints, student backgrounds, and developmental levels. Starting at the left side of the figure, a teacher can decide which goal and nature of writing will best fit the direction she plans to take. Following the flow of arrows, she can then decide on which form of writing fits the time and task demands she has in mind. Finally, she can select the writing-to-reading approach that makes use of that form. As a decision-making tool, the figure highlights the critical features of goal, nature, and form so that the teacher can use these to make a principled decision about a specific approach. Our experience is that conceptualizing the writing-to-reading approaches in a framework like this one will make for better practice—because teachers can select a method based on the features that matter most to their curriculum and students.

The other conceptual direction is toward pedagogical approaches that link the writing-to-reading practice to real-world, everyday literacy. As we indicated in the rationale portion of this chapter, the writing-to-reading segment of the reading-writing chain is rooted everywhere in everyday literacy practices. The language experience approach and the writing workshop, for example, make the link in sometimes profound ways. But other approaches do so incidentally or not at all. Only by linking such procedures as the prereading plan, list-group-label, guided writing procedure, and others to everyday writing-to-reading practices can any of us make the claims of relevance, authenticity, and power in these approaches in good faith. And only then can we understand the order of things more fully and not askance.

References

Alagna, M. M. (1993). *Language-based reading perspective: A connection between linguistic and reading processing.* Unpublished doctoral dissertation, D'Youville College.

Allen, R. V. (1976). *Language experiences in communication.* Boston: Houghton Mifflin.

Anderson, R. C., & Pearson, P. D. (1984). A schema-theoretic view of basic processes in reading. In P. D. Pearson, R. Barr, M. L. Kamil, & P. Mosenthal (Eds.), *Handbook of reading research* (Vol. 1, pp. 255–292). White Plains, NY: Longman.

Ashton-Warner, S. (1958). *Spinster.* New York: Simon & Schuster.

Atwell, N. (1984). Writing and reading literature from the inside out. *Language Arts, 61,* 240–252.

Atwell, N. (1987). *In the middle: Writing, reading, and learning with adolescents.* Portsmouth, NH: Heinemann.

Beach, R., & Hynds, S. (1991). Research on response to literature. In R. Barr, M. L. Kamil, P. Mosenthal, & P. D. Pearson (Eds.), *Handbook of reading research* (Vol. 2, pp. 453–489). White Plains, NY: Longman.

Bligh, T. (1995). Using story impressions to improve comprehension. *Reading Horizons, 35*(4), 287–298.

Bloome, D., & Egan-Robertson, A. (1993). The social construction of intertextuality in classroom reading and writing lessons. *Reading Research Quarterly, 28,* 304–333.

Bryan, J. (1998). K-W-W-L: Questioning the known. *Reading Teacher, 51,* 618–620.

Burns, P. M. (1994). *The effects of the K-W-L reading strategy on fifth graders' reading comprehension and attitude.* Unpublished doctoral dissertation, Temple University.

Burris, G. (1988, December). *Student as decision maker: Power of the reading writing model.* Paper presented at the annual meeting of the National Reading Conference, Tucson, AZ.

Calkins, L. M. (1983). *Lessons from a child: On the teaching and learning of writing.* Portsmouth, NH: Heinemann.

Calkins, L. M. (1986). *The art of teaching writing.* Portsmouth, NH: Heinemann.

Carr, E., & Ogle, D. M. (1987). K-W-L plus: A strategy for comprehension and summarization. *Journal of Reading, 30,* 626–631.

Carroll, J. B. (1966). Some neglected relationships in reading and language. *Elementary English, 43,* 577–582.

Clay, M. M. (1979). *Reading: The patterning of complex behavior.* Portsmouth, NH: Heinemann.

Clay, M. M. (1982). Reading recovery: A follow-up study. In M. M. Clay (Ed.), *Observing young readers: Selected papers* (pp. 1–15). Portsmouth, NH: Heinemann.

Clay, M. M. (1988). *The early detection of reading difficulties.* Portsmouth, NH: Heinemann.

Collins, J. D., & Stevens, L. M. (1997). Does "reading recovery" work? *American School Board Journal, 84*(6), 38–39.

Denner, P. R. (1992). Effects of prereading activities on junior high students' recall. *Journal of Educational Research, 86*(1), 11–19.

Denner, P. R., & McGinley, W. J. (1989). Effects of story impressions as a prereading/writing activity on story comprehension. *Journal of Educational Psychology, 82*, 320–326.

Dorsey, S. (1988). *Teacher as decision maker: The power of the reading-writing model.* Paper presented at the annual meeting of the National Reading Conference, Tucson, AZ.

Drew, M. E. (1995). *Effects of the K-W-L Plus strategy on college developmental readers' recall of expository text.* Unpublished doctoral dissertation, Southern Illinois University, Carbondale.

Duquette, R. J. (1972). Research summary of Barnette-Duquette study. *Childhood Education, 48*, 438–440.

Durkin, D. (1978–1979). What classroom observations reveal about reading comprehension instruction. *Reading Research Quarterly, 14*, 481–533.

Durkin, D. (1984). Is there a match between what elementary teachers do and what basal reader manuals recommend? *Reading Teacher, 37*, 734–744.

Dyer, P. (1985). *A study of the effect of prereading mapping on comprehension and transfer of learning.* Unpublished doctoral dissertation, University of California, Berkeley.

Dyson, A. H. (1992). The case of the singing scientist. *Written Communication, 9*(1), 3–47.

Dyson, A. H. (1994). The Ninjas, the X-Men, and the ladies: Playing with power and identity in an urban primary school. *Teachers College Record, 96*(2), 219–239.

Dyson, A. H. (1997). *Writing superheroes.* Teachers College Press.

Dyson, A. H., & Freedman, S. W. (1991). Writing. In J. Flood, J. M. Jensen, D. Lapp, & J. R. Squire (Eds.), *Handbook of research on teaching the English language arts* (pp. 754–774). Old Tappan, NJ: Macmillan.

Eichenberger, C., & King, J. R. (1995). Two teacher roles in language experience: Scaffold-builder and gatekeeper. *Reading Research and Instruction, 35*(1), 64–84.

Farr, R. (1993). Writing in response to reading: A process approach to literary assessment. In B. E. Cullinan (Ed.), *Pen in hand: Children become writers* (pp. 64–79). Newark, DE: International Reading Association.

Foucault, M. (1970). *The order of things: An archaeology of the human sciences.* New York: Pantheon.

Goodlad, J. (1984). *A place called school: Prospects for the future.* New York: McGraw-Hill.

Graves, D. H. (1983). *Writing: Teachers and children at work.* Portsmouth, NH: Heinemann.

Hall, K.A.J. (1994). *The effects of reading strategies and cooperative learning on eighth-grade students' recall of expository text.* Unpublished doctoral dissertation, University of Missouri, Kansas City.

Harste, J. C., Short, K. G., Burke, C. (1989). *Creating classrooms for authors.* Portsmouth, NH: Heinemann.

Hartman, D. K. (1992). Intertextuality and reading: Reconceptualizing the reader, the text, the author, and the context. *Linguistics and Education, 1*(3–4), 295–311.

Hartman, D. K. (1996). Eight readers reading: The intertextual links of proficient readers reading multiple passages. *Reading Research Quarterly, 30,* 520–561.

Hefflin, B. R. (1996). *African American children's literature and its connections to enriching learning.* Unpublished doctoral dissertation, University of Pittsburgh.

Heimlich, J. E., & Pittelman, S. D. (1986). *Semantic mapping: Classroom applications.* Newark, DE: International Reading Association.

Heine, P. J. (1990). *Writers supporting writers.* Unpublished doctoral dissertation, Indiana University, Bloomington.

Holmes, V. L. (1995). A contrarian view of dialogue journals: The case of a reluctant participant. *Journal of Second Language Writing, 4*(3), 223–251.

Jared, E. J. (1993). *The effects of the K-W-L Plus comprehension strategy on the achievement of preservice teachers.* Unpublished doctoral dissertation, University of Missouri, Columbia.

Kamberelis, G. S., & Scott, K. D. (1992). Other people's voices. The co-articulation of texts and subjectivities. *Linguistics and Education, 4*(3–4), 359–403.

Kemp, S. J. (1993). *The medium: An inquiry into the nature of the authoring process in a computing medium.* Unpublished doctoral dissertation, University of Alberta.

Kendrick, W. M., & Bennett, C. L. (1966). A comparative study of two first-grade language arts programs. *Reading Research Quarterly, 2,* 83–118.

Kiewit, S. F. (1997). *The relationship of prior background knowledge to the summarization skills of developmental college students.* Unpublished doctoral dissertation, University of Akron.

Kluin, T. N. (1996). Getting hearing and deaf students to write to each other through dialogue journals. *Teaching Exceptional Children, 28*(2), 50–53.

Konopak, B. C., Martin, S. H., & Martin, M. A. (1987). An integrated communication arts approach for enhancing students' learning in the content areas. *Reading Research and Instruction, 26,* 275–289.

Langer, J. A. (1980). Relation between levels of prior knowledge and the organization of recall. In M. L. Kamil & A. J. Moe (Eds.), *Perspectives in Reading Research and Instruction* (pp. 23–33). Washington, DC: National Reading Conference.

Langer, J. A. (1981). From theory to practice: A prereading plan. *Journal of Reading, 25,* 14–19.

Langer, J. A. (1982). Facilitating text processing: The elaboration of prior knowledge. In J. Langer & M. Smith-Burke (Eds.), *Reader meets author: Bridging the gap.* Newark, DE: International Reading Association.

Langer, J. A., & Allington, R. L. (1992). Curriculum research in writing and reading. In P. Jackson (Ed.), *Handbook of research on curriculum* (pp. 687–725). Old Tappan, NJ: Macmillan.

Langer, J. A., & Nicolich, M. (1981). Prior knowledge and its effect on comprehension. *Journal of Reading Behavior, 13,* 375–388.

Linder, P. E. (1996). *A qualitative analysis of dialogue journal responses of parents in a family literacy program.* Unpublished doctoral dissertation, University of Akron.

Luft, P. (1997). Using electronic dialogue journals to model whole language procedures. Monograph of collected papers from the annual conference of the Association of College Educators—Deaf and Hard of Hearing, Santa FE, NM. (ERIC Document Reproduction Service No. ED 406 780). Reprinted from Egelston-Dodd, J. (Ed.) (1997). Windows-97 on the New Standards. Monograph of collected papers from the annual conference of the Association of College Educators—Deaf and Hard of Hearing. Rochester, NY: Rochester Institute of Technology, National Technical Institute for the Deaf (BBB20927 and ED 406 768).

Many, J. E. (1996a). Patterns of selectivity in drawing on sources: Examining students' use of intertextuality across literacy events. *Reading Research and Instruction, 36*(1), 51–63.

Many, J. E. (1996b). Traversing the topical landscape: Exploring students' self-directed reading-writing-research processes. *Reading Research Quarterly, 31,* 12–35.

Markman, M. (1985). *Teacher-student dialogue writing in a college composition course: Effects upon writing performance and attitude.* Unpublished doctoral dissertation, University of Missouri, Columbia.

Martin, M. A., Konopak, B. C., & Martin, S. H. (1986). Use of the guided writing procedure to facilitate reading comprehension of high school text materials. In J. A. Niles & R. V. Lalik (Eds.), *Solving problems in literacy: Learners, teachers, and researchers* (pp. 66–72). Rochester, NY: National Reading Conference.

McGinley, W. J. (1992). The role of reading and writing while composing from sources. *Reading Research Quarterly, 27,* 226–248.

McGinley, W. J., & Denner, P. R. (1987). Story impressions: A pre-reading/writing activity. *Journal of Reading, 31,* 248–253.

Molner, L. A. (1989, December). *Developing background for expository text: PReP revisited.* Paper presented at the annual meeting of the National Reading Conference, Austin, TX.

Moore, D. W., & Readence, J. E. (1984). A quantitative and qualitative review of graphic organizers research. *Journal of Educational Research, 78,* 11–17.

Mott, L. U. (1994). *Generating ideas during story negotiation: Inter-action and intra-action.* Unpublished doctoral dissertation, Texas Women's University.

Ogle, D. M. (1986a). K-W-L: A teaching model that develops active reading of expository text. *Reading Teacher, 38,* 564–570.

Ogle, D. M. (1986b). K-W-L group instruction strategy. In A. M. Palincsar, D. M. Ogle, B. F. Jones, & E. G. Carr (Eds.), *Teaching reading as thinking* (pp. 22–31). Alexandria, VA: Association for Supervision and Curriculum Development.

Olson, C. B. (1996). Strategies for interacting with text. In C. B. Olson (Ed.), *Practical ideas for teaching writing as a process at the elementary and middle school levels* (pp. 231–235). Sacramento: California Department of Education.

Packer, A. B. (1970). Ashton-Warner's key vocabulary for the disadvantaged. *Reading Teacher, 23,* 559–564.

Paris, S. G., Lipson, M., & Wixson, K. (1983). Becoming a strategic reader. *Contemporary Educational Psychology, 8,* 293–316.

Pearson, P. D., & Gallagher, M. C. (1983). *The instruction of reading comprehension* (Tech. Rep. No. 297). Urbana: University of Illinois, Center for the Study of Reading.

Pearson, P. D., & Johnson, D. D. (1978). *Teaching reading comprehension.* Austin, TX: Holt, Rinehart and Winston.

Pearson, P. D., & Tierney, R. J. (1984). On becoming a thoughtful reader: Learning to read like a writer. In A. Purves & O. Niles (Eds.), *Becoming readers in a complex society.* Chicago: National Society for the Study of Education.

Power, B. M. (1996). Nutshells, monkeys, and the writer's craft. *Voices from the Middle, 3*(2), 10–16.

Readence, J. E., Bean, T. W., & Baldwin, R. S. (1989). *Content area reading: An integrated approach.* Dubuque, IA: Kendall/Hunt.

Rico, G. L. (1983). *Writing the natural way.* Los Angeles: Tarcher.

Riojas-Clark, E. (1995). "How did you learn to write in English when you haven't been taught in English?": The language experience approach in a dual language program. *Bilingual Research Journal,* *19*(3–4), 611–627.

Ross, S. M., Smith, L. J., Casey, J., & Slavin, R. E. (1995). Increasing the academic success of disadvantaged children: An examination of alternative early intervention programs. *American Educational Research Journal, 32*(4), 773–800.

Rowe, D. W. (1986). *Literacy in the child's world: Preschoolers' explorations of alternate sign systems.* Unpublished doctoral dissertation, Indiana University, Bloomington.

Russell, D. H. (1956). *Children's thinking.* Waltham, MA: Blaisdell.

Scardamalia, M., & Bereiter, C. (1986). Research on written composition. In M. C. Wittrock (Ed.), *Handbook of research on teaching* (3rd ed., pp. 778–803). Old Tappan, NJ: Macmillan.

Searfoss, L. W., Smith, C., & Bean, T. W. (1981). An integrated language strategy for second language learners. *TESOL Quarterly, 15*(4), 283–289.

Shanahan, R., & Tierney, R. J. (1990). Reading-writing connections: The relations among three perspectives. In J. Zutell & S. McCormick (Eds.), *Literacy theory and research: Analyses from multiple paradigms* (pp. 13–34). Chicago: National Reading Conference.

Short, K. G. (1986). *Literacy as a collaborative experience.* Unpublished doctoral dissertation, Indiana University, Bloomington.

Short, K. G. (1992). Researching intertextuality within collaborative classroom learning environments. *Linguistics and Education, 4*(3–4), 313–333.

Short, K. G., Harste, J. C., & Burke, C. (1996). *Creating classrooms for authors and inquirers* (2nd ed.). Portsmouth, NH: Heinemann.

Smith, C., & Bean, T. W. (1980). The guided writing procedure: Integrating content reading and writing improvement. *Reading World, 19*, 290–298.

Song, M. (1997). *The effect of dialogue journal writing on overall writing quality, reading comprehension, and writing apprehension of EFL college freshmen in Korea.* Unpublished doctoral dissertation, Indiana University of Pennsylvania.

Squire, J. (1984). Composing and comprehending: Two sides of the same process. In J. M. Jensen (Ed.), *Composing and comprehending.* Urbana, IL: National Conference on Research in English.

Stahl, S. A., & Vancil, S. J. (1986). Discussion is what makes semantic maps work in vocabulary instruction. *Reading Teacher, 40*, 62–67.

Staton, J. (1980). Writing and counseling: Using a dialogue journal. *Language Arts, 57*, 514–518.

Staton, J. (1984). *The interactional acquisition of practical reasoning in early adolescence: A study of dialogue journals.* Unpublished doctoral dissertation, University of California, Los Angeles.

Staton, J., Kreeft, J., & Gutstein (Eds.). (n.d.). *Dialogue.* Washington, DC: Center for Applied Linguistics.

Staton, J., Shuy, R., Peyton, J. K., & Reed, L. (1988). *Dialogue journal communication: Classroom, linguistic, social, and cognitive views.* Norwood, NJ: Ablex.

Stauffer, R. G. (1970). *The language-experience approach to the teaching of reading.* New York: HarperCollins.

Stauffer, R. G., & Hammond, W. D. (1967). The effectiveness of language arts and basic reader approaches to first grade reading instruction—extended into second grade. *Reading Teacher, 20*, 740–746.

Stauffer, R. G., & Hammond, W. D. (1969). The effectiveness of language arts and basic reader approaches to first grade reading instruction—extended into third grade. *Reading Research Quarterly, 4*, 468–499.

Taba, H. (1967). *Teacher's handbook for elementary social studies.* Reading, MA: Addison-Wesley.

Thistlewaite, A. (1988, December). *The evolution of the Columbus reading-writing initiative.* Paper presented at the annual meeting of the National Reading Conference, Tucson, AZ.

Tierney, R. J., Caplan, R., Ehri, L., Healy, M., & Hurdlow, M. (1989). Writing and reading working together. In A. Dyson (Ed.), *Writing and reading: Collaboration in the classroom?* Urbana, IL: National Council of Teachers of English.

Tierney, R. J., & Pearson, P. D. (1983). Toward a composing model of reading. *Language Arts, 60*, 568–580.

Tierney, R. J., & Shanahan, T. (1991). Research on the reading-writing relationship: Interactions, transactions, and outcomes. In R. Barr, M. L. Kamil, P. Mosenthal, & P. D. Pearson (Eds.), *Handbook of reading research* (Vol. 2, pp. 246–280). White Plains, NY: Longman.

Tuemmler, L. S. (1993). *Comparative study of writers' workshop at Loma Junior High School.* Unpublished doctoral dissertation, University of Southern California.

Walters, M. L. (1996). *The relationship between reading recovery story-writing activity and student achievement and acceleration rate.* Unpublished doctoral dissertation, University of Southern Mississippi.

Wang, Y. (1996). *E-mail dialogue journaling in an ESL reading and writing classroom*. Proceedings of selected research and development presentations at the national convention of the Association for Educational Communications and Technology, Indianapolis, IN. (IR 017 960 and ERIC Document Reproduction Service No. ED 397 845)

Whitehead, A. N. (1925). Science and the modern world. Old Tappan, NJ: Macmillan.

Wood, K. D. (1984). Probable passages: A writing strategy. *Reading Teacher, 37,* 496–499.

Chapter Nine

Research-Based Comprehension Practices That Create Higher-Level Discussions

Janice F. Almasi

Traditionally, postreading discussion has been the primary means by which elementary teachers assist and assess children's comprehension of text (Barr & Dreeben, 1991). Typically, these discussions occur after students have read a text. Following their reading, the teacher engages students in a discussion of the text. These discussions may be with the whole class or with small groups of students. Generally, the purpose of these discussions is to help students understand the text better (assist comprehension) and to determine how well students have understood what they read (assess comprehension).

Cazden (1986) and Mehan (1979) examined the discourse associated with such postreading discussions and found that they typically follow a participation structure that they identified as initiate-respond-evaluate (IRE). During such discussions the teacher maintains a central role: initiating discussion topics by asking questions (initiate), soliciting student responses to those questions (respond), and evaluating student responses (evaluate).

Not surprisingly, research conducted in authentic classroom contexts (compare Almasi, 1995) and survey research at the national level (for example, Foertsch, 1992; Langer, Applebee, Mullis,

& Foertsch, 1990) have found that these discussions are dominated by teacher talk (up to 85 percent of all discourse) and re-
current sequences of teacher questions and student responses.
Teachers' questions during these interactions often require students to recall factual, known-answer, or literal information about
the text. When teachers repeatedly ask the same types of literal
questions, students adjust their expectations and values accord-
ingly. Thus, when teachers tend to ask literal questions, their students tend to focus on literal reading and recall of texts rather
than critical, higher-level, or interpretive readings.

Dillon's research (1985) found that teacher questioning di-
minished students' cognitive, affective, and expressive responses.
Likewise, teacher questioning stalled and interrupted student discourse to such an extent that it led to decreased motivation, cognitive disengagement, and passivity. In essence, students in such
environments are relatively passive, both cognitively and socially.
Research on question-asking behaviors in grades K–12 has suggested that certain teacher behaviors associated with the IRE
participation structure (for example, calling on some students less
often, providing less wait time for some students, providing evalu-
ative feedback) induce passivity among low-achieving students in
particular. For these students, nonparticipation and passivity become an alluring alternative to cognitive engagement because they
would rather remain passive to avoid making mistakes in public
(Good, Slavings, Harel, & Emerson, 1987). For other students, passivity occurs primarily by design. When students are engaged in
postreading discussion in which the teacher initiates the discussion by asking questions that are important to her, seeks responses
from students of her choice to those questions, and evaluates the
so-called correctness of students' responses, students have little opportunity for involvement and little need for cognitive engagement. If by chance a student should happen to get called on to
answer a question, the student quickly becomes engaged in the
discussion. Prior to and immediately after that point, however, the
student can elect to be cognitively disengaged. Thus the context
of teacher-centered discussions does not necessarily enable students to be optimally engaged.

Proficient comprehension, however, is contingent upon active
cognitive engagement, which requires that students use metacog-

nitive and self-regulatory strategies (Meece, Blumenfeld, & Hoyle, 1988). Metacognition involves the ability to monitor progress toward achieving one's goal (Flavell, 1979), and it involves the control one has over one's own learning and thinking (Baker & Brown, 1984). In reading, the ultimate goal is comprehension, thus metacognition requires one to be aware of incoming information to such an extent that one can monitor whether it is congruent or incongruent with prior information and interpretation. When an incongruity or comprehension difficulty occurs, proficient readers are metacognitively aware that something has happened to disrupt their comprehension and know to enact a repair strategy such as rereading or reading ahead (Garner, 1987). Unfortunately, the same younger and less proficient readers who prefer to remain passive during classroom discussions are also less able to monitor and regulate their performance (Baker & Brown, 1984; Garner, 1987; Markman, 1977) than older and more proficient readers (Baker & Anderson, 1982; Winograd & Johnston, 1982). Students' inability to monitor and regulate their reading often has a negative effect on their comprehension. Developing an internal monitoring system in which readers can recognize and resolve textual incongruities is essential to proficient comprehension (Baker & Brown, 1984; Paris, Wasik, & Turner, 1991; Pressley, Symons, Snyder, & Cariglia-Bull, 1989). Thus, educators are faced with the dilemma of designing an instructional context that enhances comprehension by fostering student involvement and active cognitive engagement.

Research has shown that peer discussion provides such an instructional context (Almasi, 1995; Almasi, McKeown, & Beck, 1996; Almasi, O'Flahavan, & Arya, 2001; Fall, Webb, & Chudowsky, 2000). Peer discussion is a classroom event in which students collaboratively construct meaning or consider alternate interpretations of texts to arrive at new understandings. During peer discussions students gather to talk about, critique, and understand texts with minimal teacher assistance. They determine their own topics of conversation and negotiate the procedural rules and social conventions that govern their discussion. Discourse is lively and focuses on personal reactions, responses, and interpretations of what they have read. Students in these environments enjoy gathering with their peers to discuss their interpretations, confusions, and misgivings about texts because the environment is safe. Rather than being afraid to let the teacher know that they do not understand the text or are confused by part of the text, students in peer discussions willingly share those aspects of the text that were confusing to them and are eager to chat with peers to resolve their dilemmas. Students also use a variety of strategic reading behaviors (for example, comprehension monitoring, imagery, prediction, and summarization) and higher levels of abstract and critical thinking (for example, making intertextual connections and critiquing the author's craft) to participate meaningfully in discussions and to overcome confusion (Almasi, in press).

The most recent National Assessment of Educational Progress (NAEP) results (Donahue, Voelkl, Campbell, & Mazzeo, 1999) report that students who explain their understanding or discuss interpretations of what they read with friends at least once or twice a week had higher reading achievement than students who reported doing so less frequently. Research has shown that peer discussion provides opportunities for children to grow cognitively, socially, and affectively. More specifically, when students engage in peer discussion, the quality of their discourse, their ability to recognize and resolve comprehension dilemmas, and the cognitive processes associated with higher-level thinking (for example, comprehension monitoring and metacognition) are enhanced (Almasi, 1995). Peer discussion fosters meaning construction and evokes more natural conversation; in addition, students' extensive talking in peer discussion helps them confirm, extend, and modify their interpretations of text (Alpert, 1987; Eeds & Wells, 1989; Leal, 1992). Students exhibit a larger repertoire of types of responses, and they exhibit positive dispositions when engaged in discussions of this nature (Martinez, Roser, Hoffman, & Battle, 1992; McGee, 1992). Likewise, students themselves find peer discussion valuable in helping them understand what they read, and they view it as a valuable social outlet for trying out new ideas on subjects within their peer community (Alvermann et al., 1996).

New Directions in Peer Discussion Research

My previous research (1995) examined and compared peer discussion contexts and more traditional teacher-led discussion contexts. This work described the nature of sociocognitive conflict

(Mugny & Doise, 1978) as it occurred in peer and teacher-led discussions. During an episode of sociocognitive conflict, an individual experiences an overt conflict in understanding or interpreting text. Thus, we can liken sociocognitive conflict to a comprehension dilemma that occurs in a social setting. Recognition and resolution of sociocognitive conflict require the same metacognitive and self-regulatory abilities that proficient comprehension and active cognitive engagement require. Fourth-grade students in peer discussion contexts were able to recognize and resolve sociocognitive conflicts significantly better than their counterparts in teacher-led discussions. My research (1995) showed that students' discourse in peer discussions was also more elaborate and more complex than students' discourse in teacher-led discussions. Thus, peer discussion settings provided a context that enabled students to learn and use strategies for monitoring and regulating their comprehension better than did traditional teacher-led discussions.

Given the success of the peer discussion context in facilitating students' metacognitive and self-regulatory abilities, it then became important to examine the influence of that context on active cognitive engagement. Working with colleagues McKeown and Beck (1996), I sought to describe those elements that were essential to engaged reading from students' and teachers' perspectives. This work found that the context of the literacy act and the culture of the classroom play a significant role in engaged reading. Contextual factors such as those present in peer discussion (that is, providing the opportunity to respond to and challenge each others' interpretations, the author's style, and the meaning of the text in a student-centered environment) were critical to student engagement. Likewise, the literary features of the text also contributed greatly to student engagement.

Although research has clearly indicated that peer discussion has a positive influence on higher-level comprehension and engagement with text, and teachers recognize its value, research by Commeyras and DeGroff (1998) found teachers rarely use peer discussion in classrooms. Thus, the next phase of my research sought to understand and describe what proficient peer discussions looked like, how teachers were able to create such contexts over time, and why some teachers might have difficulty implementing it in their classrooms. With colleagues O'Flahavan and

Arya (2001), I studied differences between a highly proficient peer discussion group and a less proficient peer discussion group across a semester. We found that more proficient peer discussion groups were better able to recognize and resolve social interaction dilemmas (for example, obtaining the floor without interrupting, listening to others, responding to others' comments) and that the teacher's ability to effectively teach students how to recognize and resolve such dilemmas without dominating was key. Teachers who handed the situation back to the students to resolve were more effective than teachers who resolved the dilemmas for them. In addition, students in more proficient peer discussions were better able to sustain topics of discussion by making linkages to old topics and by embedding topics within one another than were students in less proficient peer discussions.

My present research extends previous work by examining how children attain and develop higher levels of social, cognitive, and affective functioning within peer discussion contexts. The first line of research examines how social, cognitive, and affective processes develop on a moment-by-moment (or microgenetic) basis as students participate in peer discussion. That is, we are examining how students affect and are affected by one another socially, cognitively, and affectively moment by moment.

Inherent to any examination of the moment-by-moment development that occurs as students discuss text is the close scrutiny of how students interact with one another to construct meaning. The teacher plays an important role in that the classroom context determines how students will interact with one another. In a series of studies aimed at examining the patterns of interaction and discourse that emerge as students discuss informational texts, we found that peer discussion can have a strong teacher influence even without the teacher being present physically in the discussion (Almasi & Russell, 2000; Almasi, Russell, Guthrie, & Anderson, 1998). That is, although the teacher in this series of studies was not present physically during the peer discussions, she provided assistance to the group in other ways. In essence, a shared culture emerged among students in the group in which the teacher (and her authority) were present semiotically (that is, symbolically).

For the purposes of these studies, we viewed authority as the ability to manipulate discourse related to literacy in an acceptable speech genre. Teachers typically maintain such authority in class-rooms because they possess a speech genre of appropriate and adult literacy. They decide which language to use in a given task, and they design the environment in which the class will undertake the task. When the teacher is not physically present within a group, as in peer discussion, the students themselves negotiate the boundaries and speech genres that they will use. At times teachers attempt to assist this process by scaffolding students' language and the manner in which they interact with one another. In these studies (Almasi & Russell, 2000; Almasi et al., 1998) we attempted to examine how such teacher scaffolding affected third-grade students' discourse. The teacher in these studies used several scaffolds to assist students' peer discussions. These scaffolds ultimately became ways in which the students attempted to attain authority and status within the group: (1) using the language of the task (for example, students would read and reread the assigned task to convince others in the group about the nature of the work to be completed), (2) using the authority of their teacher-assigned roles, and (3) using formulaic teacher language.

The shared worlds that emerged from these discussions arose from participants enacting a multitude of voices (Almasi & Russell, 2000; Almasi et al., 1998). But these students' voices often lacked the procedural and declarative knowledge necessary to make them functionally dialogic (Bakhtin, 1986; Mannheim & Tedlock, 1995). The students employed a mimetic faculty to assume or get hold of a semiotic conception of "teacher." The students met with varying degrees of success. At times students' behaviors and language were ritualistic or performative (Harré & Van Langenhove, 1991; Mannheim & Tedlock, 1995). More often their behaviors and discourse indicated that their "teacher" positions lacked authenticity. Some students tried to get close to a power that was not inherently theirs. For example, they attempted to act and speak as if they were the teacher, when they clearly did not have teacher-like powers or authority in the group. This resulted in student discourse that challenged their attempts rather than student discourse that was aimed at constructing meaning. Students met these challenges with a variety of responses that illustrated their frustration and bewilderment at the daunting task of trying to understand the language and literate behaviors required to participate meaningfully in discussions that were influenced strongly by teacher scaffolding rather than by authentic student inquiry and interest in constructing meaning.

These findings highlight the fragile and delicate balances that exist within peer discussion. In our attempt to enhance children's social and cognitive development within peer discussions, we offer scaffolds by modeling language, encouraging (or even assigning) students to assume a variety of roles, and providing topics and tasks to foster discussion. However, these studies (Almasi & Russell, 2000; Almasi et al., 1998) reveal that these scaffolds may not permit an indigenous, authentic, and dynamic communication system to emerge. Instead the ensuing discourse is characterized by one-way exchanges rather than the type of dialogic exchanges that we desire (Mannheim & Tedlock, 1995).

The second line of research is a three-year study of children in grades K–3. This series of studies is just beginning and will examine how social, cognitive, and affective processes develop across childhood (that is, ontogenesis) as a result of participating in peer discussions. Thus we will gain insight into how students' participation in peer discussion affects their social interaction; comprehension, word recognition, and critical thinking; and motivation for reading over time. Such research will enable us to more fully understand the impact of student-centered learning environments on children's growth and development.

Three Recommendations for the Future

RECOMMENDATION 1: Students must be active sociocognitive participants in their comprehension.

Research has consistently shown that students must be active cognitive participants in order for proficient comprehension to occur. Students cannot sit by as passive, disengaged participants while the teacher does all the cognitive work involved in comprehension. Students must be thoughtful as they read. They must have opportunities to think and talk about what makes sense and what does not make sense. This means that students must have opportunities to ask questions about text that they, rather than the teacher, wonder about. They must have opportunities to learn how to wonder, to learn how to inquire, and to learn how to monitor and regulate their own comprehension. This means creating classroom contexts that permit such opportunities.

RECOMMENDATION 2: Teachers must create classroom contexts that enable students to be active sociocognitive participants.

Classroom contexts that enable active sociocognitive participation require that teachers make space for students to engage in student-centered activities such as peer discussion. Such spaces must enable students to think, examine, critique, and inquire about the texts they read. This means that teachers themselves need to relinquish some of the control that they typically maintain in such contexts. Rather than asking questions and pursuing topics they feel are important for comprehending text, teachers must trust and value students' questions. Teachers need to limit their desire to provide scaffolding that might hinder student dialogue. Instead they must teach students how to recognize when they do not understand text and how to resolve such comprehension dilemmas on their own. Teachers who have been successful in such endeavors often model and teach students how to monitor their understanding by using sticky notes to record things they wonder about or are confused by. As students read text, they jot down their wonderings and confusions on the notes and use those notes to formulate topics for consideration during peer discussions. In this manner the topics for discussion come from students; therefore, students are more active cognitively and are more engaged. The peer discussion group then becomes the site in which students share and resolve such comprehension dilemmas for themselves. Such contexts create independent, self-regulated readers and thinkers.

RECOMMENDATION 3: Teachers must teach students to monitor comprehension while reading and preparing for peer discussion.

The following is a sample lesson that demonstrates how teachers might teach students to monitor their comprehension in preparation for peer discussions of text.

Context

Whole class read aloud followed by small group peer discussions of the text

Grade Levels

1–5

Goals

Upon completion of the lesson, student will learn to (1) recognize when text does not make sense and (2) generate topics from text for use in peer discussion.

Materials

Sticky notes

Pencils

Chart paper

Hey Al by Arthur Yorinks (1986)

Introduction

Begin the lesson by asking students to think of a time when something didn't make sense to them. Have students share their experiences and what they do to help them understand. List the things that students do to help them understand on chart paper. Explain that sometimes when we read, the text might not make sense. Explain that today we are going to learn how to recognize when the text we are reading does not make sense, and we will learn what we can do about it.

Description of Instructional Experience

Begin by introducing the book *Hey Al* by Arthur Yorinks. Have students examine the cover closely. Begin to think aloud about the thoughts that cross your mind as you examine the cover. For example, you might state, "When I look at this cover, I wonder why there are so many birds. I also wonder why the book is called *Hey Al*. Could Al be that man?" Explain that these wonderings are good questions to think about as we read and that good readers are continually thinking and wondering about the text and the pictures as they read. Explain that you are going to jot down your wonderings on a sticky note so that you can remember them later. Write the questions down on a sticky note and place it on the cover of the book. Explain that students can also jot down their wonderings on sticky notes as you read the book to them. Have students share any wonderings they might have related to the cover and title of the book. Encourage students to use their sticky notes to jot down their wonderings. Be sure to praise and encourage those students who elect to jot wonderings down. You might say things such as, "I'm so glad to see that you are thinking so much!" or "Wow, you are really wondering! I'm so happy. You are doing just what good readers do while they read."

Begin reading the book aloud. Stop at various points to share your wonderings or confusions with the class. Be sure to model how to write down these ideas on sticky notes. Each time you stop, ask students whether they are wondering anything or whether they are confused by anything. Encourage students to jot these wonderings or confusions on sticky notes. If students are anxious to share their wonderings or confusions, encourage them to briefly share or talk about their ideas with a partner; then resume the read aloud. Continue reading in this interactive manner. You might consider stopping midway through the text to permit students to engage in a peer discussion of their wonderings and confusions, or you might wait until you have read the entire text aloud.

Once you reach a stopping point, explain that there are lots of ways to get help when you are wondering about what you have read or are confused about something you read. One thing you can do is talk about your wonderings and confusions with your friends so that they can help you understand. Explain and demonstrate how you might start a conversation using your sticky notes. Explain that when one person brings his or her wondering and confusion to the discussion, everyone in the group should work together to try to help that person. Explain that they might need to refer back to the book to help a person understand or they might need to share some ideas from their own background to help them understand, but the conversation should not shift to a different topic until the person who raised the wondering or the confusion is satisfied.

Divide the class into small groups of four or five students and have them discuss their wonderings and confusions.

Conclusion

After each group has concluded its peer discussion, sit in with each group and chat with group members about how the peer discussion went. On a piece of chart paper, jot down those things that the group feels worked well in its peer discussion and those things that group members feel they should improve.

This sheet of chart paper can become a road map for the group in terms of how to enhance their peer discussion the next time. At the next peer discussion, the teacher reviews the suggestions prior to beginning the discussion about the text.

Assessment

You will know whether students are able to recognize when they do not understand the text when you read the content of their sticky notes.

You will know whether students are able to generate topics for discussion and use them by listening to and taking anecdotal notes as each small group engages in peer discussion.

References

Almasi, J. F. (in press). Peer discussion. In B. Guzzetti (Ed.), *Literacy in America: An encyclopedia.* New York: ABC.

Almasi, J. F. (1995). The nature of fourth graders' sociocognitive conflicts in peer-led and teacher-led discussions of literature. *Reading Research Quarterly, 30,* 314–351.

Almasi, J. F., McKeown, M. G., & Beck, I. L. (1996). The nature of engaged reading in classroom discussions of literature. *Journal of Literacy Research, 28*(1), 107–146.

Almasi, J. F., O'Flahavan, J. F., & Arya, P. (2001). A comparative analysis of student and teacher development in more and less proficient discussions of literature. *Reading Research Quarterly, 36,* 96–120.

Almasi, J. F., & Russell, W. S. (2000, November). *Positioning for power: The female pariah in peer discussions of text.* Paper presented at the annual meeting of the National Reading Conference, Scottsdale, AZ.

Almasi, J. F., Russell, W. S., Guthrie, J. T., & Anderson, E. (December, 1998). *Scaffold to nowhere? Appropriated voice, metatalk, and personal narrative in third graders' peer discussions of informational text.* Paper presented at the annual meeting of the National Reading Conference, Austin, TX.

Alpert, B. R. (1987). Active, silent, and controlled discussions: Explaining variations in classroom conversation. *Teaching and Teacher Education, 3*(1), 29–40.

Alvermann, D. E., Young, J. P., Weaver, D., Hinchman, K. A., Moore, D. W., Phelps, S. F., Thrash, E. C., & Zalewski, P. (1996). Middle and high school students' perceptions of how they experience text-based discussions: A multicase study. *Reading Research Quarterly, 31,* 244–267.

Baker, L., & Anderson, R. I. (1982). Effects of inconsistent information on text processing: Evidence for comprehension monitoring. *Reading Research Quarterly, 17,* 281–294.

Baker, L., & Brown, A. L. (1984). Metacognitive skills and reading. In P. D. Pearson, R. Barr, M. L. Kamil, & P. B. Mosenthal (Eds.), *Handbook of reading research* (Vol. 1, pp. 353–394). White Plains, NY: Longman.

Bakhtin, M. M. (1986). In C. Emerson & M. Holquist (Eds.), *Speech genres and other late essays.* Austin: University of Texas Press.

Barr, R., & Dreeben, R. (1991). Grouping students for reading instruction. In R. Barr, M. L. Kamil, P. B. Mosenthal, & P. D. Pearson (Eds.), *Handbook of reading research* (Vol. 2, pp. 885–910). White Plains, NY: Longman.

Cazden, C. B. (1986). Classroom discourse. In M. C. Wittrock (Ed.), *Handbook of research on teaching* (3rd ed., pp. 432–463). Old Tappan, NJ: Macmillan.

Commeyras, M., & DeGroff, L. (1998). Literacy professionals' perspectives on professional development and pedagogy. A national survey. *Reading Research Quarterly, 33,* 434–472.

Dillon, J. T. (1985). Using questions to foil discussion. *Teaching and Teacher Education, 1,* 109–121.

Donahue, P. L., Voelkl, K. E., Campbell, J. R., & Mazzeo, J. (1999, March). *NAEP 1998 reading report card for the United States.* Washington, DC: U.S. Department of Education, Office of Educational Research and Improvement, National Center for Education Statistics.

Eeds, M., & Wells, D. (1989). Grand conversations: An exploration of meaning construction in literature study groups. *Research in the Teaching of English, 23,* 4–29.

Fall, R., Webb, N. M., & Chudowsky, N. (2000). Group discussion and large-scale language arts assessment: Effects on students' comprehension. *American Educational Research Journal, 37*(4), 911–941.

Flavell, J. H. (1979). Metacognition and cognitive monitoring: A new area of cognitive-developmental inquiry. *American Psychologist, 34,* 906–911.

Foertsch, M. A. (1992, May). *Reading in and out of school: Factors influencing the literacy achievement of American students in grades 4, 8, and 12, in 1988 and 1990* (Vol. 2). Washington, DC: National Center for Education Statistics.

Garner, R. (1987). *Metacognition and reading comprehension.* Norwood, NJ: Ablex.

Good, T. L., Slavings, R. L., Harel, K. H., & Emerson, H. (1987). Student passivity: A study of question asking in K-12 classrooms. *Sociology of Education, 60,* 181–199.

Harré, R., & Van Langenhove, L. (1991). Varieties of positioning. *Journal for the Theory of Social Behaviour, 21*(4), 393–407.

Langer, J. A., Applebee, A. N., Mullis, I.V.S., & Foertsch, M. A. (1990). *Learning to read in our nation's schools: Instruction and achievement in 1988 at grades 4, 8, and 12*. Princeton, NJ: Educational Testing Service.

Leal, D. (1992). The nature of talk about three types of text during peer group discussions. *Journal of Reading Behavior, 24*(3), 313–338.

Mannheim, B., & Tedlock, D. (1995). Introduction. In D. Tedlock & B. Mannheim (Eds.), *The dialogic emergence of culture* (pp. 1–32). Urbana: University of Illinois Press.

Markman, E. M. (1977). Realizing that you don't understand: A preliminary investigation. *Child Development, 48*, 986–999.

Martinez, M., Roser, N. L., Hoffman, J. V., & Battle, J. (1992). Fostering better book discussions through response logs and a response framework: A case of description. In C. K. Kinzer & D. J. Leu (Eds.), *Literacy research, theory, and practice: Views from many perspectives* (pp. 303–311). Chicago: National Reading Conference.

McGee, L. (1992). An exploration of meaning construction in first graders' grand conversations. In C. K. Kinzer & D. J. Leu (Eds.), *Literacy research, theory, and practice: Views from many perspectives* (pp. 177–186). Chicago: National Reading Conference.

Meece, J. L., Blumenfeld, P. C., & Hoyle, R. H. (1988). Student's goal orientations and cognitive engagement in classroom activities. *Journal of Educational Psychology, 80*, 514–523.

Mehan, H. (1979). *Learning lessons*. Cambridge, MA: Harvard University Press.

Mugny, G., & Doise, W. (1978). Socio-cognitive conflict and structure of individual and collective performances. *European Journal of Social Psychology, 8*, 181–192.

Paris, S. G., Wasik, B. A., & Turner, J. C. (1991). The development of strategic readers. In R. Barr, M. L. Kamil, P. Mosenthal, & P. D. Pearson (Eds.), *Handbook of reading research* (Vol. 2, pp. 609–640). White Plains, NY: Longman.

Pressley, M., Symons, S., Snyder, B. L., & Cariglia-Bull, T. (1989). Strategy instruction comes of age. *Learning Disability Quarterly, 12*, 1630.

Taussig, M. (1993). *Mimeses and alterity*. New York: Routledge.

Winograd, P., & Johnston, P. (1982). Comprehension monitoring and the error-detection paradigm. *Journal of Reading Behavior, 14*, 61–74.

Yorinks, A. (1986). *Hey Al*. New York: Farrar, Straus & Giroux.

Chapter Ten

Goose Bumps and Giggles

Engaging Young Readers' Critical Thinking
with Books from the Teachers' Choices
Project and Graphic Organizers

Kathy N. Headley
and Jean Keeler

Allington (2001, p. 106) has described higher levels of thinking that
go beyond recall and recitation as *thoughtful literacy:* "engaging the
ideas in texts, challenging those ideas, reflecting on them, and so
on. It is responding to a story with giggles, goose bumps, anger, or
revulsion." To encourage students' thoughtful literacy, classroom
environments must include (1) meaningful opportunities for students to read, reflect, and actively discuss text connections and
(2) instruction during which teachers model strategies and guide
students' applications. Effective comprehension strategy lessons
that incorporate both teacher demonstrations and students' repeated application to meaningful, interesting texts—not textbooks and teacher guides—take time.

To make the most of precious learning time in the classroom,
teachers can focus on a cluster of comprehension strategies that
research has shown to make a difference in student performance
(Allington, 2001). Such strategies include

- Activating students' prior knowledge
- Summarizing
- Teaching story grammar

- Using imagery
- Generating questions
- Thinking aloud

Application of effective, research-based comprehensive strategies should use teacher demonstrations and repeated student applications to a variety of meaningful, interesting texts. In these strategy lessons, teachers should guide students in making three kinds of connections: text to self (personal linkages to what the student reads), text to text (linkages between and among different readings), and text to world (linkages between what the student reads and what the student knows about the world) (Allington, 2001).

Meaningful, Interesting Texts

Matching interesting texts with strategic lessons is an ongoing challenge for teachers designing their instructional plans. Resorting to preplanned packaged materials may seem an answer to a shortage of time and a need for accountability. Instead of searching endlessly for quality books that support instruction, teachers can depend upon the advice of other teachers. Headley and Dunston (2000) recommend the International Reading Association's Teachers' Choices Project as one resource to consult for children's books that teachers have reviewed, evaluated, and selected for curriculum use (see the November issues of *The Reading Teacher* each year since 1989 for excellent recommendations). The authors of this chapter have selected primary-level books from the Teachers' Choices Project for strategy application and classroom implementation.

Graphic Organizers for Engaged Thinking

Irwin (1991) urges teachers to employ instructional methods that create active rather than passive reading. To do this, materials should support readers' meaning construction, strategy use, writing-to-learn connections, discussions about content and strategies, and interactions with other readers. Such effective comprehension processes are guided by two key principles: (1) the reader's prior knowledge affects the understanding of new and related information found in text, and (2) the way in which new information is organized affects understanding and retention (Kirylo & Millet, 2000). Teachers can use graphic organizers to meet the criteria for creating active readers and effective comprehension.

Egan (1999, p. 641) defines *graphic organizers* as "visual representation of knowledge, a way of structuring information, and of arranging essential aspects of an idea or topic into a pattern using labels." As well, practitioners may use the terms *mapping* or *webbing* to refer to graphic organizers. The use of graphic organizers, states Egan, is "widespread . . . and applauded on all levels of learning" (p. 641). It is understandable, then, that exemplary first-grade teachers frequently use graphic organizers to guide children's reading and writing (Wharton-McDonald, 2001).

For effective use of graphic organizers, Egan (1999) makes the following suggestions to teachers:

- Be authentically prepared.
- Promote interaction among students.
- Use graphic organizers with discrimination.
- Expand the use of graphic organizers.

The first suggestion nudges teachers to actually use the graphic organizer themselves before launching the lesson with students. Engagement of and interaction among students is the emphasis of the second point. Graphic organizers are excellent tools for a student's collaboration with a partner or a team. Overuse is the third suggestion's warning. Teachers, reveals Egan, should carefully reflect upon the purpose of using a particular graphic organizer in an instructional lesson. Likewise, overuse destroys interest. Egan's final suggestion, expanded use, encourages the teaming of graphic organizers with nonprint media such as discussion, film, and video.

Integrating Strategies into Instruction

Kathy Headley and Jean Keeler, authors of this chapter, have collaborated on designing and implementing instruction that engages young readers in thinking critically about quality literature. Headley is professor and coordinator of reading education at Clemson University and works extensively with preservice and inservice teachers. Keeler is the reading specialist at Mountain View

Elementary School in northeast Greenville County, South Carolina, a K–5 school nestled at the foothills of Glassy Mountain, where she works hand in hand with her principal, Tommy Hughes.

Based on mutual knowledge of Teachers' Choices primary-level books and graphic organizers as presented by Yopp and Yopp (2001), Headley and Keeler designed and implemented a series of integrated strategic lessons that purposefully engaged young readers in reading, writing, and discussing meaningful text. At Mountain View Elementary, Keeler worked with a literacy group of four third-grade students scoring 25 percent or more below level on the Metropolitan Achievement Test during the previous academic year. This chapter shows the students' responses in their authentic form, giving the students' invented spellings and sentence patterns.

To initiate the themed lessons about the use of specially trained dogs for therapeutic purposes, Keeler used a schema web to access students' prior knowledge. Although the students were familiar with Wiley, a therapy dog owned by the school's media specialist, and had met Robert Stack, an author who writes stories about his dog and visits schools accompanied by his canine friend, the students' responses revealed that they had limited background knowledge when Keeler asked them to describe what a "visiting dog" does. Danielle recalled that a visiting dog "visits nusing homes" and "goes to fire emgices"; Deanna added "schools, the park," and "people's houses." Before reading the 2000 Teachers' Choices book, *Dr. White,* by Jane Goodall (1999) and illustrated by Julie Litty, Keeler engaged the four literacy group members in predicting what the book was about based on the cover's illustration and four snippets or phrases from the text that supported meaningful content and vocabulary:

Dr. White dashed to the hospital. He was late.

Mark's face was pale. His eyes were closed and he lay motionless.

Day after day the little white dog visited the wards of the hospital.

"He's a very special dog. He has saved many lives!"

Robert wrote: "I think this story is about a boy is sike and Dr. White is goning to help hem." After all had shared their predictions, Keeler guided their reading according to Stauffer's (1976) directed listening–thinking activity (DL-TA) and a model lesson designed by Headley and Dunston (2000). Keeler posed questions at predetermined stopping points, and students composed their own questions and paired with a friend to write responses. Table 10.1 gives students' responses to prediction questions posed before and during reading.

Before the literacy group completed their predictions at the final DL-TA predetermined stopping point after reading page 17, Keeler interjected a discussion web (Alvermann, 1991) after reading page 14, where the inspector banishes the little white dog from the hospital. Keeler's decision to embed the discussion web

**Table 10.1. Directed Listening–Thinking Activity
Responses from Literacy Group: *Dr. White* (Goodall, 1999).**

	What do you think Dr. White *will be about? (prereading)*	*Why do you think the inspector is crying? (during reading prediction stop on page 17)*
Deanna	"I preduct that Dr. White is gonna go to the office and then the doctor or a child will tell the office people that Docter White helps the children."	"I think he is crying because he miss the dog and wished that he would'nt had said get the dog out and he want the dog back in and they let him back in."
Taylor	"I think that Dr. White will not be able to go back in. The hispital to treat his patients like the tail waging tretmet."	"I think he is cry because the patient are suffering sickness and no tail waging treatment from Dr. White."
Robert	"I thick that he will not be abe to go to the hospail and, stay at home."	"I think he is cring because he messes the dog."
Danielle	"I think that they will have a hospital for Dr. White and paysens."	"I think he is crying because the paycens are getting wircse."

Note: Students' responses appear as they wrote them.

followed Headley and Dunston's (2000) model linking the discussion web with the DL-TA to boost students' critical thinking and discussion. Initially, pairs of Keeler's students shared responses to the following discussion web statement: animals should be allowed inside hospitals. The final shared response involved all four students coming to consensus as to whether or not animals should be allowed inside hospitals (see Figure 10.1).

As a summarizing activity after reading *Dr. White* (Goodall, 1999), each member of the literacy group wrote in a reading response log. Deanna wrote, "I was surprised that they let Dr. White back in to the hospatal because he help children. They loved that dog. The man didn't understand. Then he understand when he saw what the dog did." Deanna's response shows her grappling explanation of the dog's banishment from the hospital and finally his permitted return. Although Deanna does not fully explain the

Figure 10.1. Discussion Web Based on *Dr. White* (Goodall, 1999) with Student Responses and Consensus Decision.

Yes ———— Animals should be allowed inside hospitals ———— No

Reasons
1. Some people may be hurt and need dogs' help.
2. Dogs help people feel better.
3. They can fetch things for people.
4. They could warn of danger.

Reasons
1. They may have germs or a disease.
2. They may get in the doctors' and nurses' way.
3. They could make a big mess.
4. Some people do not like dogs.

Consensus
Yes if they are well trained and very well washed and no diseases. They should be allowed inside hospitals.

controversy, her words show that she understands the dog's role in helping sick children.

To help the students make a text-to-world link, Mountain View Elementary's media specialist and Wiley, the therapy dog, visited the literacy group. The hands-on petting experience was also filled with information about Wiley and his purposeful work. After Wiley's visit Keeler introduced another semantic map to the group. Students' responses to the therapy dog map (Figure 10.2) engaged the literacy group in connecting their understanding of *Dr. White* to Wiley's visit.

Figure 10.2. Semantic Map of Literacy Group Responses After the Visit with Wiley, the Therapy Dog.

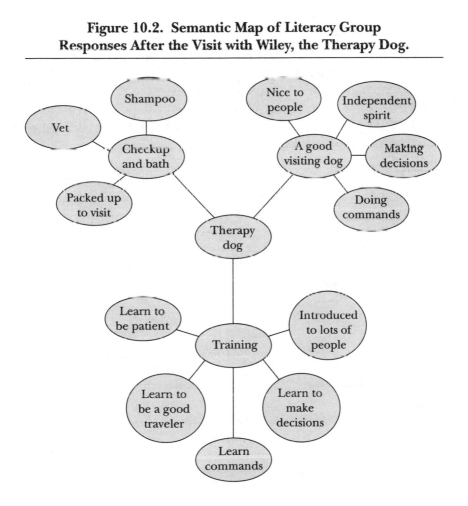

A culminating text-to-text activity linked the book *Rosie: A Visiting Dog's Story* (Calmenson, 1994) with the group's reading of *Dr. White* (Goodall, 1999). (Rosie's story is also published in level four of Houghton Mifflin's *Soar-to-Success* reading intervention program for middle school students.) In this text-to-text connection, Keeler guided the literacy group to compare and contrast elements of *Dr. White* with *Rosie*. The students recalled that while both Dr. White and Rosie helped sick children to feel better, Rosie helped older people in nursing homes, too. Likewise, Dr. White and Rosie were friendly and independent, but only Rosie received training for her work.

Three Recommendations for the Future

Thoughtful literacy (Allington, 2001) can flourish within classroom environments that include (1) meaningful opportunities for students to read, reflect, and actively discuss text connections and (2) instruction during which teachers model strategies and guide students' applications. To create such environments, teachers should take the following steps.

RECOMMENDATION 1: Focus on comprehension strategies that make a difference (Allington, 2001).

A cluster of strategies have emerged from multiple research studies as effective in improving students' comprehension: the activation of prior knowledge, the act of summarizing, story grammar lessons, imagery, and question generating. Table 10.2 outlines instructional activities and the integration of research-based strategies that connect the reader, the text, and the world.

RECOMMENDATION 2: Match strategic lessons with meaningful, interesting texts.

Application of effective, research-based comprehensive strategies should use teacher demonstrations and repeated student applications to a variety of meaningful, interesting texts. Students are motivated to read when the text matches their interests. Children's literature often provides a more authentic connection to students' interests and the world around them than do packaged curriculum materials and structured teacher guides (Allington, 2001). The International Reading Association's Teachers' Choices Project is just one resource for books of excellent quality; another resource is a list entitled "Children's Choices" published by the International Reading Association and Children's Book Council (see the October issues of *The Reading Teacher* each year for excellent recommendations).

RECOMMENDATION 3: Use graphic organizers to support students' critical thinking and text-to-self, text-to-text, and text-to-world connections.

Wharton-McDonald (2001) reported that exemplary first-grade teachers frequently use graphic organizers to guide children's reading and writing. The authors of this chapter have integrated semantic maps and a discussion web into instructional activities for visual reinforcement of students' critical thinking and engaged discussions (Table 10.2).

Summary

To engage readers in developing thoughtful literacy and to ignite those goose bumps and giggles, teachers must design instruction that challenges students to (1) activate their prior knowledge, (2) interact with their peers about ideas and issues within text, and (3) apply what they've read to the world around them. Table 10.2 summarizes the instructional activities that the chapter authors describe and the supportive links that these activities have to research-based strategies and self-text-world connections. Taking into account the concept of thoughtful literacy (Allington, 2001), the authors of this chapter have described instructional lessons that implement meaningful opportunities for students to engage in text-to-self, text-to-text, and text-to-world connections as they read, reflect, and talk about what the text means to them. For more instructional ideas to engage readers with children's books selected through the International Reading Association's Teachers' Choices Project, consult Headley and Dunston's article in the November 2000 issue of *The Reading Teacher*.

Table 10.2. Implementation of Instructional Activities.

Implement	Activity	Strategy	Connection
Prereading	Schema web about visiting dog	Prior knowledge	Self-to-text
Prereading	Prediction from cover illustration and four phrases	Prior knowledge	Text-to-self
During reading	Directed listening–thinking activity (DL-TA)	Prior knowledge Summarizing Story grammar Imagery Question generating Thinking aloud	Text-to-self
During reading	Discussion web	Prior knowledge Summarizing Question generating	Text-to-self Text-to-world
After reading	Response log	Prior knowledge Summarizing Question generating	Text-to-self
After reading	Semantic map about visit from school's media specialist and Wiley, therapy dog	Prior knowledge	Text-to-world
After reading	Semantic map about therapy dog	Summarizing	Text-to-world Text-to-self
Extended reading	Rosie the Visiting Dog	Prior knowledge Summarizing Story grammar Question generating Thinking aloud	Text-to-self Text-to-text Text-to-world

References

Allington, R. L. (2001). *What really matters for struggling readers: Designing research-based programs.* White Plains, NY: Longman.

Alvermann, D. E. (1991). The discussion web: A graphic aid for learning across the curriculum. *Reading Teacher, 45,* 92–99.

Calmenson, S. (1994). *Rosie: A visiting dog's story.* Boston: Clarion Books, Houghton Mifflin.

Egan, M. (1999). Reflections on effective use of graphic organizers. *Journal of Adolescent and Adult Literacy, 42,* 641–645.

Goodall, J. (1999). *Dr. White.* New York: North-South Books.

Headley, K. N., & Dunston, P. J. (2000). Teachers' Choices books and comprehension strategies as transaction tools. *Reading Teacher, 54,* 260–268.

Irwin, J. W. (1991). *Teaching reading comprehension processes.* Englewood Cliffs, NJ: Prentice Hall.

Kirylo, J. D., & Millet, C. P. (2000). Graphic organizers: An integral component to facilitate comprehension during basal reading instruction. *Reading Improvement, 37,* 179–186.

Stauffer, R. G. (1976). *Teaching reading as a thinking process.* New York: HarperCollins.

Wharton-McDonald, R. (2001). Teaching writing in first grade: Instruction, scaffolds, and expectations. In M. Pressley, R. L. Allington, R. Wharton-McDonald, C. C. Block, & L. M. Morrow (Eds.), *Learning to read: Lessons from exemplary first-grade classrooms* (pp. 70–91). New York: Guilford Press.

Yopp, R. H., & Yopp, H. K. (2001). *Literature-based reading activities* (3rd ed.). Needham Heights, MA: Allyn & Bacon.

Part Three

Integrating Technology and Innovative Instruction

Chapter Eleven

Using Technology to Individualize Reading Instruction

*David Rose
and Bridget Dalton*

Modern technology is radically changing the ways we can study human learning and the ways we can foster it. In this chapter we wish to examine both of these radical changes as they relate to the future of teaching reading comprehension.

Insights from New Technologies for Studying Learning in the Brain

The last decade of the twentieth century brought an explosion of knowledge in the neurosciences. Much of that explosion is due to new technologies that have revolutionized the way we can study the learning brain. In the past most of our knowledge of the human brain came from postmortem studies of individuals with brain damage. New imaging technologies (such as PET scans and MRI scans) allow us to look into active, living, learning brains without damaging them. Using computers we can view normal

Acknowledgment: We would like to express our appreciation to the teachers and students who worked with us on The Thinking Reader, the CAST Research Project at Harvard University, and to the U.S. Department of Education, Office of Special Education Programs, who funded the research project.

and abnormal patterns of activity as colorful images. Figure 11.1 contains computer images showing what we might call *hot spots* in the brain, regions that are using a lot of energy—burning a lot of glucose—and so showing up in warmer colors in the images.

Learning Is Distributed in the Brain

What have we learned from these new kinds of images? First, we have learned that processing is distributed: different regions of the brain carry out different aspects of learning (just like numerous specialists carry out different elements of movie production—"Color by Technicolor" and "Dolby Sound"). Each of these regions is specialized for a particular task, and the overall effect is rather like that of a well-organized committee or work group, where each member's special skills contribute to the group's overall success. The sum is often greater than its parts.

For example, studies have shown that when a person views an image, that person processes various features of the image—its color, shape, orientation—in different regions of the brain. Be-

**Figure 11.1. Computer Images Depicting Brain Activity:
Hearing Words and Seeing Words.**

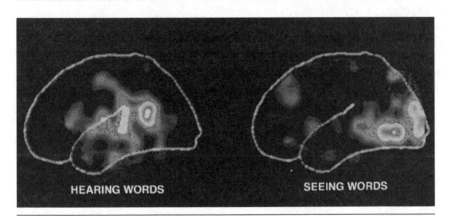

Source: Petersen, Fox, Posner, Mintun, & Raichle (1988). Reprinted with permission from *Nature*. Copyright 1988 Macmillan Magazines Limited.

Shades demarcate active brain regions: darker gray represents higher levels of activity; lighter gray indicates lower levels of activity. Thus, highly active brain regions appear as dark spots on the images.

cause each aspect of the image is processed separately but simultaneously by highly specialized regions, we can recognize images quickly and efficiently. The combined effect of these "specialists'" working is the creation of something very complex in a short amount of time.

This has some important implications for cognitive constructions—like reading comprehension and language. Cognitive constructions are composed of many component processes that are distributed throughout the brain. Although we tend to lump them together conceptually, the brain does not. All four of the images in Figure 11.2 show brain activity during the performance of language tasks, but very different regions of the brain are involved in the different instances, reflecting differences in the specific task. This suggests that the brain has no single language center but instead has many regions that contribute to normal language

Figure 11.2. Computer Images Depicting Brain Activity: Performing Four Language Tasks.

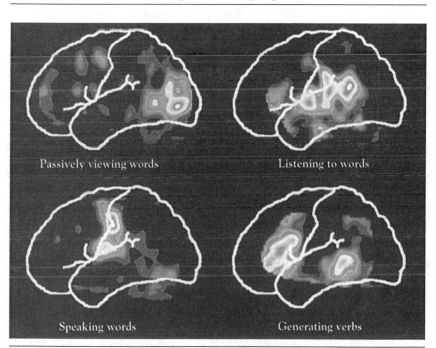

Source: Petersen, Fox, Posner, Mintun, & Raichle (1988). Reprinted with permission from *Nature.* Copyright 1988 Macmillan Magazines Limited.

facility. Different regions are recruited depending on the specific demands of the language task.

What does this say about reading comprehension? First, comprehension is likely to also be a distributed process—that is, it is likely to be made up of many component processes rather than a single process called comprehension. It is also likely that comprehending takes different forms and even that different comprehension tasks may elicit different patterns of processing. A study by Nichelli and colleagues (1995), for example, showed that reading elicits different patterns of activity in the brain depending upon the reading instructions. When researchers presented the same text (one of Aesop's fables) four times to a single individual, giving different reading instructions each time, the brain showed different patterns of activity each time the person read text. The response of the brain was not determined by the text but by the reader's purpose in comprehending the text.

Brain studies reveal that reading comprehension, like other cognitive activities, is probably a highly differentiated and distributed activity.

Individual Differences and Learning in the Brain

Brain studies reveal several other important things about how the brain operates during learning. First, brain images show that the distribution of hot spots varies among individuals: somewhat different regions of the brain become active when different individuals perform the same task. Although the overall patterns of activity across individuals exhibit some resemblance, they show consistent and compelling individual differences.

Shaywitz, Shaywitz, Pugh, and CAST Research Team (1998) performed one illustrative study of individual differences in reading. They compared brain images of reading collected from individuals with and without dyslexia-type reading disabilities. The brain patterns of these two groups turned out to be very different.

Note that in Figure 11.3 the brain activity of the dyslexic reader is heavily concentrated in the frontal regions of the brain, whereas the brain activity of the regular reader shows a much more distributed pattern of activity in posterior portions of the brain. Later in the chapter we will examine what is happening in each of

**Figure 11.3. Brain Activity of Individuals
With and Without Dyslexia Reading.**

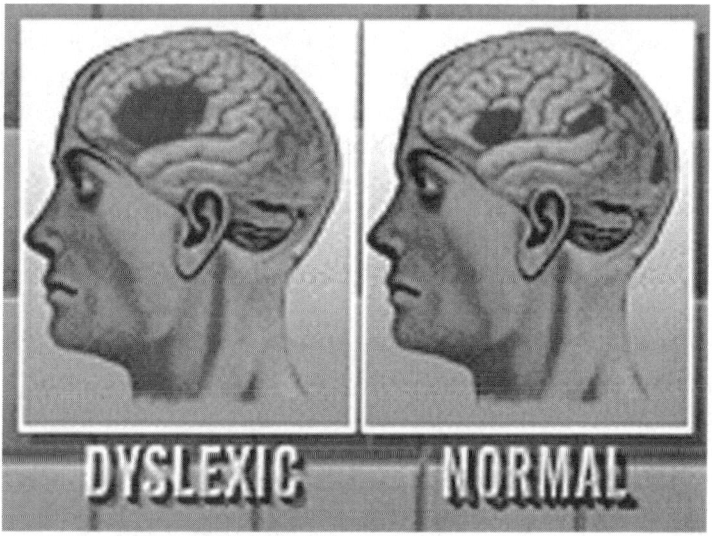

Source: Ponce (1998). Used by permission of *Online NewsHour.*

these regions. Even without this information for now, these images yield some striking insights. For one, it does not appear (as many mistakenly believe) that dyslexic individuals are "not trying." It seems more likely that they are trying quite hard but that the energy is being expended in very different ways. In this study (Shaywitz, Shaywitz, Pugh, & CAST Research team members, 1998) and in many others, individual differences are clear.

Experience and Learning in the Brain

Another source of variance in brain images is related to time and experience. One of the most remarkable and yet totally surprising findings of recent brain imaging studies is that the brain changes when it learns. The changes that brain imaging makes visible are different from those that are apparent at the anatomical and chemical level. The images show a changing distribution of activity over time.

The first two images in Figure 11.4 show brain activity recorded from a subject performing a verb generation task (the researcher presented the person with a noun and asked the person to generate a verb associated with it), either for the first time (naive) or after several iterations (practiced). The third image shows brain activity after the researcher introduced a variation of the verb generation task. Learning is accompanied by a redistribution and reduction in brain activity, and some of these learning effects carry over to a similar but somewhat novel task.

The computer images track a fairly simple language task. The researcher presented the subject with a noun and asked him or her to generate a verb in association with it. As the first image shows, this task elicits a fairly predictable pattern of brain activity—a moderate burn in the temporal region and a very large burn in the frontal region, with smatterings of activity elsewhere. What is striking is the change from the first image to the second.

**Figure 11.4.   Computer Images Depicting Brain Activity:
Changes Due to Experience.**

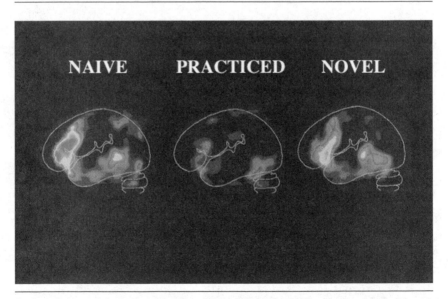

Source: Adapted from Raichle, Fiez, Videen, MacLeod, Pardo, Fox, and Petersen (1994), by permission of Oxford University Press.

The second image is of the person carrying out exactly the same task after significant learning has occurred through repeated trials. The result of the learning is a huge reduction, or savings, in activity—the brain burns less glucose once it is facile with this task.

Renewed activity is observable in the third image, the result of slight changes in the task that make the individual work again. But the activity is still less than it was to begin with—indicating a considerable savings, or transfer, of energy from the first set of trials to the last.

Many studies at the CAST Research Center have repeated this pattern of findings: the brain exhibits tremendous activity at the beginning of a task when it is unskilled. Later, as learning occurs, brain activity is redistributed or reduced. The unskilled brain shows a very different distribution of activity from the skilled one. At least one neuroscientist has described this early pattern as one of scaffolding—the brain recruiting multiple resources to assist in new and unstructured tasks (Petersen, van Mier, Fiez, & Raichle, 1998).

To summarize, any complicated activity like reading comprehension requires a highly distributed set of processors in the brain. What parts of the brain an individual actually uses can be quite variable and depend on the specific nature of the task, on the specific nature of the individual, and on what learning has already occurred. (Other factors also make a difference in what areas of the brain we use—including brain injury, sex differences, and so on, but they are beyond the scope of this chapter.)

Thus far we have described only patterns of brain activity—not their functional significance. The next section briefly probes three broad regions of the brain—which we call recognition, strategic, and affective networks—that contribute to cognitive tasks like reading comprehension.

Reading Comprehension and the Brain

Recognition Networks

The back half of the brain's cerebral hemispheres (the posterior lobes) consist of giant networks of neurons that are specialized in one way—they receive input from the various sensory organs (eyes and ears, for example) and use it to construct meaning.

These recognition networks make it possible to know that a particular pattern of input represents a cup, a dog, the sound of your grandmother's voice, or the smell of your morning coffee. In reading, these networks perform similarly to allow you to recognize the letter *A,* the word *dog,* the words of your grandmother, a paragraph about a cup of coffee, and so forth.

Damage to these posterior networks can impair the brain's ability to recognize things. At the extreme are individuals who can no longer recognize familiar people by their faces or the distinctive sounds of a classical symphony. Many aspects of reading similarly depend on intact pattern recognition: recognizing that the letters *c-a-t* are a unique pattern that stands for the word *cat,* recognizing the silent *e* pattern in spelling, identifying a particular pattern of words as a sonnet or a haiku, recognizing a particular arrangement of words as William Faulkner's style.

Strategic Networks

In the front half of the cerebral hemispheres (the frontal lobes) are networks specialized for entirely different functions. These networks construct and transmit external patterns of output for making skillful patterns of action and for knowing how to do things—like taking steps, saying words, shooting a foul shot, reading a book, driving a car, planning a vacation, and writing a narrative. All of our skills, strategies, and plans are essentially highly patterned actions.

Damage to the frontal lobes interferes with generating successful plans and actions. At one extreme are individuals who are paralyzed (unable to move voluntarily); at the other are individuals who are able to move easily but are unable to effectively plan and coordinate their various activities—they seem disorganized, impulsive, uncoordinated.

Reading comprehension requires these frontal lobe functions just as much as functions carried out in the posterior recognition cortex. Understanding is more than simply reception or perception; good readers approach text skillfully and strategically. They monitor their own performance by making and testing predictions; they scan important pieces of text for salient information; they identify the overall structure of the text and draw inferences about meaning and motive; they investigate parts of words to hypothesize their meanings; they reread puzzling sentences. All of these reading comprehension skills depend upon strategic networks.

Affective Networks

A third set of networks is localized primarily in the central core of the brain. These networks are critical for emotions—fear, desire, sadness, excitement, and hope. These networks specialize not in recognizing or generating patterns but in determining whether the patterns we perceive matter to us, thus helping us to decide which actions and strategies to pursue.

Impairments in affective networks distort the importance of various aspects of the world, thereby influencing our abilities to establish priorities, select what is valuable, focus attention, and choose actions. The ability to determine accurately the patterns that really count, to differentiate the important from the unimportant, is a third integral component to human intelligence.

Without well-functioning affective networks, the individual's reading comprehension is impaired. Readers are not able to direct and sustain attention to specific aspects of text. Nor are they able to focus appropriately on specific words or paragraphs that are important or vary their style or rate to accommodate differences in content or purpose, and so forth.

Normally, these three networks operate in concert—as a distributed system. For example, recognition networks function to identify a particular pattern of shapes, colors, and smells as a hamburger. Strategic networks create plans and actions that allow us to walk over, reach out, lift, and munch on that hamburger. And affective networks motivate us, depending on our status in Weight Watchers points, to either approach or avoid that hamburger.

Implications for Understanding Reading Comprehension

Brain research emphasizes the varied and distributed nature of comprehension—comprehension is not a single activity but many processes distributed across different functional networks that operate in parallel. We have emphasized three broad networks. All of these are essential to comprehension, and their impairment can make readers vulnerable in specific ways: students may fail because they have not learned to recognize the relevant patterns in text, because they do not have strategies for constructing meaning from text, or because they do not find reading text important enough to sustain the effort it demands.

Brain research also emphasizes that the fundamental processes underlying reading comprehension differ among individuals in important ways. Individuals do not differ in some generalized or simply quantifiable way (like a global intelligence score) but in many specific ways. Intelligence is the product of processing "committees" or networks, each element of which may be different.

Learning is marked by qualitative changes in the kinds of processors that the brain engages. Early learning activates a spatially and anatomically distinctive array of brain structures, often more expansive than those that are activated by later learning or mastery.

Do these broad generalizations about these three functional networks enlighten us as we think about comprehension? Let us close by looking again at Figure 11.3, which compares dyslexic and normal readers. It is now clear that not only is the dyslexic population displaying a pattern that is differently distributed than regular readers, the dyslexic readers are expending most of their energy within the strategic networks. What does that mean?

Certainly, more research is needed to know for sure, but this pattern is similar to that of the beginner or unskilled student in other research. The dyslexic is reading words with the front part of the brain, effortfully and strategically. Other readers are more automatic, recognizing the patterns in the words easily, with little effort. The allocation of effort to strategically sound out words must come at the cost of allocating that same effort to strategically monitoring comprehension. Thus, like the beginning reader, the dyslexic reader requires a lot of scaffolding—from either internal or external resources—in order to adequately comprehend meaning. That scaffolding can come from skillful use of the brain's internal scaffolding processes, from a willing tutor, or from a peer who is reading collaboratively.

Until now it has been difficult to find that scaffolding within the text itself. But as we shall see, that is changing.

The Engaging the Text Project

Using Technology to Transform Text into Supported Reading Environments

In this section we describe how reading instruction is evolving to offer the kinds of scaffolding that readers require to overcome weaknesses in the three networks we have discussed—each one essential to reading comprehension. We are applying recent advances in the neurosciences and reading comprehension research on strategy instruction (Palincsar & Brown, 1984; Pressley, 2000) to the design of computer-supported reading environments.

Comprehension of a particular text is the result of an interaction, or transaction, between the reader, the text, the purpose for reading, and in school, the instructional context (Lipson & Wixson, 1997). Reading is a complex cognitive process that is socially based and constructed. It is also a thinking process, and skilled readers actively construct meaning as they read. To succeed with such a multifaceted and challenging task, learners need highly effective instruction. In the Engaging the Text Project (Dalton, Pisha, Eagleton, Coyne, & Deysher, 2001), we have been working with middle school teachers to study the effects of computer-supported strategy instruction on struggling readers' comprehension. Most of the students in the study have been identified as having learning disabilities and are typically reading three to four grade levels below placement. These students struggle to decode and may never develop the automatic word recognition essential to fluent reading and text comprehension (Ehri, 1994). Many also have difficulty reading for meaning, monitoring their comprehension, and taking action when they don't understand (Lipson & Wixson, 1997).

As a result of these struggles, they find that books and other texts that constitute the general curriculum function as barriers rather than gateways for learning. Decoding difficulties block students from access to important content, and comprehension problems block them from responding to and learning from text in meaningful ways. For many students, these difficulties contribute to low self-efficacy and a feeling that applying effort will not pay off in a positive outcome (Guthrie, 2001). Some invest their energy in compensating for their difficulties, while others disengage from literacy and other academic tasks or act out. For these students, the consequences can be severe given the climate of high stakes testing in many states. Already, results show that a significant number of students are not passing basic competency exams (Massachusetts Department of Education, 2000).

How can we make reading comprehension instruction more effective? A wealth of research evidence over the last twenty years strongly supports the teaching of reading comprehension strategies (for recent reviews of this literature, see National Reading Panel, 2000; Pressley, 2000; and Rosenshine & Meister, 1994; for a review of this literature on students with learning disabilities, see Swanson, 1999). The most commonly used strategies are making predictions, questioning, summarizing, and clarifying. Visualization and graphic organizers are also often included in strategy instruction, as well as strategies for self-monitoring and evaluation. The general consensus is that "comprehension instruction can effectively motivate and teach readers to learn and to use comprehension strategies that benefit the reader" (National Reading Panel, 2000, pp. 4–6) and that multiple strategy instruction carried out in natural classroom settings is more beneficial than the teaching of individual strategies.

The Engaging the Text Project uses hypertext Web links to deliver a supported reading comprehension environment that includes interactivity and multimedia. Research on students' comprehension in hypertext is somewhat limited, but the results are promising (for a review, see Kamil, Intrator, & Kim, 2000). Studies with learning-disabled students indicate that they benefit from supports such as vocabulary definitions (MacArthur & Haynes, 1995) and anaphoric reference (Boone & Higgins, 1993), but that students do not always have access to the supports they need. The work of Anderson-Inman and her colleagues demonstrates that embedding tools and supports in hypertext can improve achievement, if the tools are pedagogically sound and an instructor teaches students to use them (Anderson-Inman, Knox-Quinn, & Horney, 1996; Anderson-Inman & Horney, 1996–1997; Anderson-Inman & Zeitz, 1993).

The Engaging the Text Project is applying research-based strategy instruction to digital text. It is grounded in universal design for learning (UDL) theory (Meyer & Rose, 1998, 2000; Rose & Meyer, in press). Universal design originates in the field of architecture. In universally designed architecture, architects design structures to accommodate the widest spectrum of users, including those with disabilities. An important benefit of designing for diversity is that all users tend to benefit from the results. For example, we all take advantage of the ramped curb cut in sidewalks that was originally designed to provide access for individuals in wheelchairs—whether we are pushing a stroller, riding a skateboard, or pulling a luggage cart.

Whereas universal design in architecture is concerned with physical access, UDL focuses on the need for instructional methods and materials that provide students a flexible system of supports for both access and learning. If we think about this in relation to what we know about how the brain learns and the processes involved in comprehending text, it means that we design reading experiences that flexibly support or scaffold students' diverse recognition, strategic, and affective networks. Scaffolding is central to this instructional approach and fits well with Vygotsky's (1978) concept of the zone of proximal development. Learning takes place within this zone, where challenge and support are in balance so that the learner is able to achieve success and increase mastery.

We designed a research prototype CD-ROM, The Thinking Reader, which embeds strategy instruction in digitized novels. From a UDL perspective, The Thinking Reader provides supports to scaffold students' diverse recognition, strategic, and affective networks of learning. Figure 11.5 presents a screen shot from The Thinking Reader, and the following classroom scenario illustrates how the tool is being used in the classroom to develop readers who not only read for understanding but are strategic and engaged readers.

Thinking Reader Scenario

Derek, a sixth-grade student who reads on the third-grade level, is seated at the computer with headphones on, reading a digital version of *Hatchet* (Paulsen,

Figure 11.5. Screen Shot from The Thinking Reader.

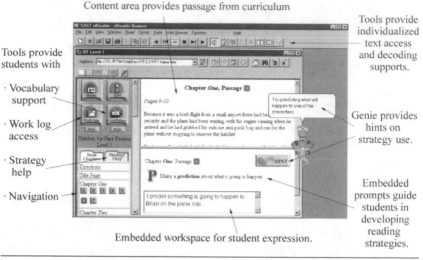

Content area provides passage from curriculum

Tools provide students with

· Vocabulary support

· Work log access

· Strategy help

· Navigation

Tools provide individualized text access and decoding supports.

Genie provides hints on strategy use.

Embedded prompts guide students in developing reading strategies.

Embedded workspace for student expression.

Currently only a prototype CD-ROM, The Thinking Reader is a computer-supported reading environment that embeds support for decoding and comprehension strategies in digital text.

1987), an award-winning novel that is required by his school district. He clicks on a read-aloud button to have the text read to him. He encounters an unknown word, *wilderness,* and clicks on it to obtain a definition from the glossary. As he continues reading, The Thinking Reader occasionally prompts him to stop and think about the story and to use one of the strategies he has learned, such as predicting, questioning, clarifying, and summarizing.

Summary writing is somewhat difficult for Derek, so he clicks on the strategy hint button. A genie appears and offers one of several hints that are based on a rubric for good summary writing, such as "A good summary captures the gist, or most important information," or "Be sure to include the character and the problem in your summary." Derek writes his summary in the response box on-screen and sends his work to be posted in his work log. He logs off and joins his class in a brief discussion of the novel. His teacher asks, "Do we need to clarify? Who can give me a summary of what just happened in the story? How do you think Brian is feeling right now? What do you predict will happen next?" As students talk, they resolve a confusion about where

Brian is flying for the summer and predict that the plane might crash or that something will happen when Brian meets his father.

The following week Derek and his teacher have a miniconference to review his work log, which includes all of his strategy responses. Derek has selected his best example of strategy use and identified a goal that he thinks he should work on for the next few weeks: using more descriptive words in his visualizations. He and his teacher decide that he is ready to move to another level of scaffolding, one that provides less structure and will help move him along toward more independent use of strategies while he is reading. Derek's teacher takes note of the fact that Derek and many other students are not clear about the distinction between questioning and clarifying, and she decides to conduct a minilesson the next day, modeling how to use these strategies and guiding students as they practice applying them while reading.

At the end of the year, Derek and his teacher reflect on how he has changed as a reader. Derek is feeling more confident about his abilities as a reader, because the read-aloud feature of the software allowed him to read the same novels that his classmates were reading, focusing on understanding rather than decoding. His growth as a reader is also demonstrated on the end-of-year standardized reading assessment, his willingness to participate in class discussions, and his new interest in adventure stories and the work of author Gary Paulsen. This has been a successful year for Derek. It has also been a successful year for his teacher, who views The Thinking Reader as an important tool for differentiating instruction and addressing the diverse needs of her students. The software does not replace her as a teacher but extends her capacity to reach all of her students and to teach more effectively.

The results of the Engaging the Text Project suggest the promise of developing computer-supported reading environments based on an understanding of recent research in the neurosciences on how the brain learns and the extensive body of research on reading comprehension, strategy instruction, and engagement.

Three Recommendations for the Future

As research in the neurosciences continues to reveal the structure of individual differences in learning, we need to continually apply those findings to understanding individual differences in reading comprehension.

As research develops new reading technologies and digital texts that allow us to individualize the teaching of reading comprehension, we need to provide teachers with those technologies.

As classrooms increasingly have access to new technologies for supporting the teaching of reading comprehension, we need to ensure that support and instruction are embedded within those technologies to assist both teachers and students in learning to use them well.

References

Anderson-Inman, L., & Horney, M. (1996–1997). Computer-based concept mapping: Enhancing literacy with tools for visual thinking. *Journal of Adolescent and Adult Literacy, 40*(4), 302–306.

Anderson-Inman, L., Knox-Quinn, C., & Horney, M. A. (1996). Computer-based study strategies for students with learning disabilities: Individual differences associated with adoption level. *Journal of Learning Disabilities, 29*, 461–484.

Anderson-Inman, L., & Zeitz, L. (1993). Computer-based concept mapping: Active studying for active learners. *Computing Teacher, 20*, 6–11.

Boone, R., & Higgins, K. (1993). Hypermedia basal readers: Three years of school-based research, *Journal of Special Education Technology, 12*, 86–106.

Dalton, B., Pisha, B., Eagleton, M., Coyne, M., & Deysher, S. (2001). *Engaging the text: Computer-supported reciprocal teaching and strategy instruction.* Final report to the U.S. Office of Special Education Programs. Peabody, MA: Cast.

Ehri, L. (1994). Development of the ability to read words: Update. In R. Ruddell, M. Ruddell, & H. Singer (Eds.), *Theoretical models and processes of reading* (4th ed., pp. 323–358). Newark, DE: International Reading Association.

Guthrie, J. T. (2001, March). Contexts for engagement and motivation in reading. *Reading Online* [On-line], *4*(8). Available: http://www.readingonline.org/articles/art_index.asp?HREF=/articles/handbook/guthrie/index.html

Kamil, M. L., Intrator, S. M., & Kim, H. S. (2000). The effects of other technologies on literacy and literacy learning. In M. L. Kamil, P. B. Mosenthal, P. D. Pearson, & R. Barr (Eds.), *Handbook of reading research* (Vol. 3, pp. 771–790). Hillsdale, NJ: Erlbaum.

Lipson, M. Y., & Wixson, K. K. (1997). *Assessment and instruction: An interactive approach.* White Plains, NY: Longman.

MacArthur, C. A., & Haynes, J. B. (1995). Student Assistant for Learning from Text (SALT): A hypermedia reading aid. *Journal of Learning Disabilities, 28*(3), 150–159.

Massachusetts Department of Education. (2000). *1999 Massachusetts Comprehensive Assessment System* (MCAS) *Technical Report.* Boston: Massachusetts Department of Education.

Meyer, A., & Rose, D. H. (2000). Universal design for individual differences. *Educational Leadership, 58*(3), 39–43.

Meyer, A., & Rose, D. H. (1998). *Learning to read in the computer age.* Cambridge, MA: Brookline Books. Available: http://www.cast.org

National Reading Panel. (2000). *Teaching children to read: An evidence-based assessment of the scientific research literature on reading and its implications for reading instruction.* Washington, DC: National Institute of Child Health and Human Development.

Nichelli, P., Grafman, A., Pietrini, P., Clark, M., Lee, J., & Miletich, R. (1995). *Brain imagery: Research report II.* Cambridge, MA: CAST—Harvard University Press.

Palincsar, A. S., & Brown, A. L. (1984). Reciprocal teaching of comprehension-fostering and comprehension-monitoring activities. *Cognition and Instruction, 1,* 117–175.

Paulsen, G. (1987). *Hatchet.* New York: Simon & Schuster.

Petersen, S. E., Fox, P. T., Posner, M. I., Mintun, M. A., & Raichle, M. E. (1988). Positron emission tomographic studies of the cortical anatomy of single word processing. *Nature, 331,* 585–589.

Petersen, S. E., van Mier, H., Ficz, J. A., & Raichle, M. E. (1998). The effects of practice on the functional anatomy of task performance. *Proceeds of the National Academy of Sciences USA, 95,* 914–921.

Ponce, P. (1998, March 11). Unscrambling dyslexia. [Interview with Sally Shaywitz and Reid Lyon]. *Online NewsHour* [On-line]. Available: http://www.pbs.org/newshour/bb/science/jan-june98/dyslexia_3-11.html

Pressley, M. (2000). What should comprehension instruction be the instruction of? In M. Kamil, P. Mosenthal, P. D. Pearson, & R. Barr (Eds.), *Handbook of reading research* (Vol. 3, pp. 545–562). Hillsdale, NJ: Erlbaum.

Raichle, M. E., Fiez, J. A., Videen, T. O., MacLeod, A. M., Pardo, J. V., Fox, P. T., & Petersen, S. E. (1994). Practice-related changes in human brain functional anatomy during nonmotor learning. *Cerebral Cortex, 4,* 8–26.

Rose, D. H., & Meyer, A. (2000). Universal design for learning. *Journal of Special Education Technology, 15*(1), 67–70.

Rose, D. H., & Meyer, A. (in press). *Teaching every student in the digital age: Universal design for learning.* Alexandria, VA: Association for Supervisors of Curriculum Development.

Rosenshine, B., & Meister, C. (1994). Reciprocal teaching: A review of the research. *Review of Educational Research, 64*(4), 479–530.

Shaywitz, S. E., Shaywitz, B. A., Pugh, K. R., & CAST Research Team. (1998). Functional disruption in the organization of the brain for reading in dyslexia. *Proceedings of the National Academy of Sciences of the United States of America, 95,* 2636–2641.

Swanson, L. (1999). Reading research for students with LD: A meta-analysis of intervention outcomes. *Journal of Learning Disabilities, 32*(6), 504–532.

Vygotsky, L. S. (1978). *Mind in society: The development of higher psychological processes.* Cambridge, MA: Harvard University Press.

Chapter Twelve

Computers, Kids, and Comprehension
Instructional Practices That Make a Difference
Linda D. Labbo

Today Ms. Smyth has focused the students' computer work on vocabulary activities that were part of a literary unit on expressing emotions. Barry, a reluctant reader who has struggled all year with reading comprehension, leaned in closer to his computer screen. A CD-ROM talking book, *Just Grandma and Me* (Mayer, 1997), brought to life a story of a young character's trip to the beach with his grandmother. Barry was thoroughly engaged with the story with its interactive text, lively sound effects, expressive music, colorful animation, and dramatic narrative. He laughed aloud as one of the main characters showed anticipation by running ahead of his grandmother. "I do that sometimes with my grandma when she takes me to the mall," he whispered confidentially to Sandra, an average second-grade reader, who sat at the computer by his side. "This is a good [scene] to show to Ms. Smyth," he added.

Sandra nodded in agreement and then turned her attention to using the KidPix2 creativity software (Hickman, 1994) to craft a screen page about vocabulary word opposites. Using multimedia tools for drawing, typing, and animating stamps, Sandra drew a line down the middle of the screen page. She then used the keyboard to type in the word *anger* on the left side of the line and the word *joy* on the right. Just a few minutes later, when the timer indicating the end of computer time rang, Ms. Smyth looked over the children's shoulders and asked them to talk briefly about what they had learned about expressing emotions. Barry clicked through several pages of the CD-ROM storybook to point out three screen animations that he thought visually and auditorially demonstrated varying emotions. Sandra talked about the contrasts in emotions she'd represented in her split-screen animated text.

Through Ms. Smyth's careful crafting of various types of computer and noncomputer-related learning activities, these children and their peers had many rich occasions throughout their unit of study for developing foundational skills of reading comprehension. Indeed, Ms. Smyth's students have had numerous occasions to interact with teacher-guided traditional storybooks, CD-ROM talking books, paper and pencils, word processing programs, multimedia creativity software, computer games, and Internet resources. It is apparent that computer-related activities are an integral component of the overall literacy curriculum for children of all ability levels in this classroom. Encountering multimedia and multisymbolic forms of meaning making provides students with unique opportunities to engage in comprehension activities that are extremely motivating and responsive to individual learning needs (Labbo, 1996). The purpose of this chapter is to explore how teachers can design computer-related multimedia instructional practices and learning activities that can make a difference for children's development of comprehension abilities.

Computers have become commonplace in most classrooms (Becker, 1991, 1993). However, teachers across the nation indicate that they do not routinely integrate available computer-related activities into their daily literacy curriculum (U.S. Department of Education, 1999; Block, Oakar, & Hirt, 2002). This is true even though many teachers in workshops, graduate courses, or at national conferences express an intense interest in learning ways to integrate the computer into their literacy curriculum (Labbo & Teale, 2001).

This interest is consistent with the research, which substantiates the critical roles that teachers perform in advancing children's abilities to benefit from assigned times at computers. These responsibilities include

- Designing effective computer-related literacy activities (Gillingham, Garner, Guthrie, & Sawyer, 1989; Labbo, Sprague, Montero, & Font, 2000)
- Providing children with adequate access to classroom computers (Labbo, Reinking, & McKenna, 1995)
- Creating social environments that allow for constructive student collaboration (Olson & Sulzby, 1991)
- Teaching through unique features of software to productively meet individual children's literacy learning needs (Eisenwine & Hunt, 2000)

Teacher's instructional styles can also affect children's attention to and completion of computer-related assignments (Clairana, 1990). Most importantly for the purposes of this chapter, carefully crafted computer activities can positively influence children's development of reading vocabulary (Higgins & Hess, 1999), story schema (Labbo & Kuhn, 2000), and story comprehension (Matthew, 1997).

Developing Effective Thematic Computer-Related Opportunities to Develop Comprehension Knowledge and Strategies

Thematic connections are carefully crafted multilayered learning activities that involve children in numerous opportunities to learn key concepts and develop literacy abilities through engagements with various symbol systems (Labbo & Teale, 2001). Over the course of a three-week unit on expressing emotions, Ms. Smyth used many well-grounded traditional approaches to help children build a conceptual understanding of emotions through whole group, small group, and individual activities such as the following.

Whole Group Activity

Ms. Smyth opened the unit by displaying a collection of storybooks that had main characters who learned to deal with and express various emotions. The children became more curious as they read the titles and predicted what the unit of study would be about

(Hoffman, Roser, Labbo, & Farest, 1992). After finishing each book, she asked the children to think about and discuss events in their own lives that connected with story situations. Children were able to make intertextual connections with other books they had read and with their own lives (Cochran-Smith, 1984).

Small Group Activity

Ms. Smyth next invited children to write scripts and engage in reader's theater (Sloyer, 1982) performances of situations that evoked strong emotions. Writing scripts reinforced students' understanding of character traits, main ideas, and supportive details. Practicing for performances allowed many struggling readers to engage in repeated readings and thus improve their fluency.

Individual Activity

Ms. Smyth asked each child to draw and label crayon pictures about how they look and feel as they experience a range of emotions (Moss, 1995). She exhibited the resulting pictures on a classroom bulletin board that she identified as the emotions portrait gallery. The activity and collective display gave children many opportunities to compare various interpretations of feeling-related words. As Ms. Smyth planned the unit, she also included computer activities as an integral learning component to help children build foundational vocabulary, knowledge, and comprehension strategies.

Designing Effective Computer-Related Vocabulary Activities

Vocabulary knowledge includes the understanding that readers have of familiar words as well as the strategies they employ in using contextual clues for figuring out the meaning of unfamiliar words they encounter while reading (Nagy & Herman, 1987). Powerful vocabulary instruction that creates in children the expectation that reading is an active meaning-making endeavor should include word-level activities that are definitional as well as contextual (Nagy & Herman, 1987; Stahl & Fairbanks, 1986). Ms. Smyth designed learning activities that capitalized upon the interactive multimedia features of computer games, CD-ROM talking books, and creativity software to provide children with contextually rich opportunities to acquire and develop vocabulary.

Vocabulary Development with Developmentally Appropriate Computer Games

Playing computer games is a cognitively engaging, motivating, and multimodal activity for children of all ages. Many game scenarios involve complex structural frameworks that require equally complex cognitive processing. When teachers make explicit the literacy-related purposes of educational computer games, children are more likely to transfer learning strategies that are supportive of their comprehension abilities, such as interpreting explicit and implicit information, inductive reasoning, metacognitive analysis, and problem solving (Pillay, Brownlee, & Wilss, 1999), word recognition, active reading, and building of word-level conceptual knowledge to other reading activities. In addition, when teachers guide children's attention to specific aspects of games that are related to vocabulary concept development, children with lower literacy ability are more likely to engage in purposeful and strategic game playing (Labbo & Teale, 2001).

Developmentally appropriate software learning games are interactive, provide logical and appropriate feedback to children's choices, have educational learning goals, and encourage children's playful engagement (Haughland, 1998). Effectively designed software programs embed opportunities for children to learn words as they complete game-related tasks. In other words, effectively designed games are not presented as drill-and-skill paper-and-pencil tests, which less effective, poorly designed games often are.

A to Zapp (1995) is a basic computer game that Ms. Smyth selected to provide her young students with general vocabulary development and word study. Children experienced embedded invitations to learn comprehension strategies and vocabulary words as soon as they entered the colorful virtual playroom (Labbo, in press). Ms. Smyth, who was familiar with the program, directed children to predict what objects might go with an alphabet letter before they clicked on an alphabet block. For example, a beach ball would appear on the screen. Simultaneously, an alphabet block with the letter *B* would appear with two other blocks showing a *D* and *F*, respectively. When the computer pronounced the name of the letter, it confirmed or denied children's predictions. The program also directed the children to use the computer mouse to click on an object to see the word in print, hear the word pronounced, and view an animation of the word (for example, a horn plays a tune, clouds produce rain). The visual multisensory representation of words in action offered children memorable and highly contextual word-learning opportunities and taught them to use the context clues provided in multimedia features.

Vocabulary Development with Carefully Crafted CD-ROM Talking Books

Well-crafted CD-ROM talking books, interactive digital versions of stories, employ multimedia features such as animation, music, sound effects, highlighted text, and modeled fluent reading. Children can click on and interact with various text or media features. Ms. Smyth invited Barry and other children in her classroom who had lower literacy ability to begin computer time with a short focused activity. She asked Barry to spend the first few minutes clicking on words he thought he recognized on the first three screen pages of *Just Grandma and Me* (Mayer, 1997) and checking to see if he was correct by clicking on the word a second time (Labbo, 2000). This brief activity helped Barry understand that CD-ROM talking books include word-level pronunciation support for words he doesn't automatically recognize. In the future when Barry attempts to read an interactive story independently, he may be more likely to use available word-recognition tools.

Barry also had occasion to view animations of story events that accompanied a highlighted, narrated reading of the text. As phrases were highlighted during the audio narration, story characters enacted events in animated scenes. Simultaneous viewing of animations that accompany text are likely to foster in children the ability to actively visualize print that they encounter in traditional print-based formats (Wittrock, 1986). In a similar vein, dramatic musical accompaniment helps create the mood of a story and enhances students' abilities to interpret characters' feelings.

It is important to note that not all CD-ROM talking books are of equal educational value. Indeed, some interactive digital books seem to focus more on edutainment than they do on education (Burrell & Trushell, 1997). Previous work suggests that CD-ROM talking books may be categorized as considerate or inconsiderate (Labbo & Kuhn, 2000). *Considerate CD-ROM talking books* are those that include multimedia effects that are integral to the story. *Inconsiderate CD-ROM talking books* are those that include multimedia special effects that are incongruent or not integrally related to the story (for example, cookies on a plate dance and sing a song, or a hot pad in the kitchen turns into a butterfly). Considerate CD-ROM talking books are likely to support children's development of traditional story schema (Mandler & Johnson, 1977).

Vocabulary Development with Creativity Software

Children have unique occasions for vocabulary development when they arc invited to study word concepts with multimedia creativity software such as KidPix2 (Hickman, 1994). Figure 12.1 illustrates how Sandra used multimedia tools of print and animation to create a split screen about vocabulary opposites. Sandra was successful in accomplishing the activity because Ms. Smyth had taken a few minutes to conduct a demonstration before the whole group.

First, she ensured that all children were able to view the activity by connecting a classroom computer to a TV monitor. Second, she discussed the purpose of the activity: to use features of the creativity program to create a multimedia vocabulary screen page that illustrated emotional opposites. Third, she used the keyboard to type in a list of emotion-related words that the children brainstormed. Fourth, after the children discussed how to sort and group the words into categories, she selected two words for demonstration purposes—curious and uninterested. Finally, after drawing a line down the middle of the screen with a drawing tool, she labeled each portion of the screen page and selected a stamp of an unopened present and a little girl who was jumping up and down to represent the word *curious*. She used drawing tools to create a picture of a little girl turning away from a winter coat under the summer sunshine to represent the word *uninterested*. She told children that she would compile their vocabulary pages in a class slide show so that they could learn from each other's ideas.

Ms. Smyth was able to create a digital innovation of vocabulary study (Haggard, 1986) that helped students generate self-selected words and allowed them to use their own interests as a springboard for learning in about ten to fifteen minutes, which is not any longer than she spent in planning activities in the past without technological support. The only extra learning needed to use the drawing program occurred during a summer in-service training session. This value-added instruction more than warranted this hour's training. The multimedia animation effects allowed students to represent and visualize words in ways that made them memorable because they were rich in context, detail, and movement. Students also had rich occasions for learning about word meanings from their peers and friends. Indeed, the children used many of the words that they had contributed to the multimedia slide show on emotions later in their creative writing stories—an apt sign that they internalized or took ownership of the words as a part of their expressive vocabularies.

Designing Effective Computer-Related Comprehension Activities

Interactive multimedia computer applications are promising avenues for effective comprehension activities. Students like Barry who are reluctant or low-ability readers are likely to embrace interactive digital reading activities that offer various types of word-level and comprehension support (for example, access to word pronunciations on demand, interactive complementary animations that are integral to telling a story in CD-ROM talking books, models of expressive fluent reading). High or average ability children like Sandra are also likely to be enthusiastic about various programs that support creative expression or inquiry.

The following checklist offers a collection of suggestions that teachers may find useful in designing effective computer-related comprehension activities with interactive multimedia applications. Some of the ideas are adapted from suggestions for effective noncomputer-related learning activities (Cambourne, in press, personal communication, May 10, 1999).

Start with a small collection of a few computer applications that you know well. The plethora of educational programs that are currently available in the marketplace can be overwhelming. Additionally, thoroughly examining and analyzing the contents of computer applications takes time. Begin by getting to know one or two CD-ROM talking books and one creativity software application. This knowledge will equip you to identify which aspects of the program lend themselves to particular comprehension activities.

Model the use of the computer applications. Although more and more children come to school with a great deal of experience with using computers at home, much of their experience may be related to playing noneducational games. Additionally, many children come from homes that have no access to computers. When children see teachers using computer applications to accomplish various communicative goals, they know that computers are of value in the classroom.

Design activities that are integrally related to unit themes. Computer activities related to thematic units of study can serve a symbiotic role in the classroom curriculum. Accessing and discussing information on-line can provide children with important up-to-date background knowledge about social studies, science, math, or literary units. For example, Ms. Smyth led the class on an on-line, virtual tour of the Plymouth Colony during a November study of pilgrim life. Before reading a basal reader selection that involved archaeology, she guided the students to a Web site about Monticello that included information about archeological digs.

Explicitly state the purpose of the activity. Children with low literacy ability in particular may not benefit from their time at the computer if they play nonstrategic games or window-shop their way through computer applications (Labbo & Teale, 2001). Some children need only a simple suggestion to look for a particular animation that represents a vocabulary concept or the theme of a CD-ROM talking book. Others may need more visual reminders of learning tasks. These reminders may take the form of a poster or think sheet placed in a classroom computer center. (See the Block & Johnson chapter for examples of such posters and think sheets.)

Select computer applications that are developmentally appropriate. Developmentally appropriate software learning games are interactive, provide logical and appropriate feedback to children's choices, have educational learning goals, and encourage children's playful engagement (Haughland, 1998). Developmentally appropriate CD-ROM talking books also include multimedia effects that are integral to the story. Such considerate CD-ROM talking books are apt to support children's development of traditional story schema (Mandler & Johnson, 1977).

Design activities that foster children's exploration of creative expression and unique individual responses. One of the more exciting aspects of multimedia computer technologies is that they lend themselves to the creative expression of ideas. Effective activities do not require children to follow a cookie-cutter recipe with identical results for each child. On the contrary, displays or computer screen slide shows should reveal each child's individual understanding and expression of concepts—as in the vocabulary opposites activity in Ms. Smyth's class.

Show interest in children's computer-related work. Perhaps nothing so devastates a child as a teacher who does not value his or her computer-related work. Although this is most likely a rare occurrence, it can occur if teachers view the computer center as a place to shuffle children through on a tightly rotating schedule. It can happen if the teacher gives little thought to what children are actually doing during their computer time or if the computer center contains activities unrelated to children's interests or the literacy curriculum. Teachers can show interest and gain valuable insights into children's literacy development by holding informal conferences about their computer engagements.

When it comes to computers, kids, and comprehension, the teacher is the key element in designing effective learning activities. Interactive features of developmentally appropriate computer applications are highly motivating and offer unique avenues for learning vocabulary, comprehension strategies, and content knowledge for children of all ability levels; however, they may be

especially important for children who are not benefiting from traditional print-based literacy instruction.

Three Recommendations for the Future

We as a profession must consider steps we might take to advance
future students' computer-related comprehension abilities. The
following three steps are in the form of questions to invite other
interested stakeholders to engage in an extended dialogue about
the role of technology in comprehension instruction. The questions are related to the areas of (1) understanding the role of computers to support the comprehension of children whose first
language is not English, (2) understanding comprehension processes required in digital environments, and (3) understanding
how to support children's development of critical literacy comprehension skills.

QUESTION 1: How can we use features of computer applications to
better serve the comprehension needs of children whose first
language is not English?

As more and more children of diverse and multiple language
backgrounds enter classrooms, educators must explore ways to
use technology to foster their students' first- and second-language
literacy development. Many CD-ROM talking books include options for children to hear or read selections in Japanese, Spanish,
French, or German. We need more research to discover the powerful role that these digital resources may have in supporting children's comprehension of passages in their native language; their
comprehension of passages that they subsequently reread in English; and opportunities for their vocabulary, language, and literacy development.

QUESTION 2: How can we support children's ability to comprehend the multiple symbol systems they encounter on the
computer?

Today's children must be prepared for more than print-based literacies if they are going to be able to enter the workplaces and

communities of the world they will encounter tomorrow (Leu, 1997). Some educational writers have posited that digital discourse forms are uniquely different from print-based genres (see for example, Garton, 1996). Digital genres consist of computer applications and Internet informational resources that use an interplay of various symbol systems that require unique comprehension processes and cognitive processing. For example, Reinking (1997) notes that hypertext formats require the reader to strategically navigate through various types of information (for example, sounds, animations, video clips, text passages, music, and narration) and make sense of the pathways the reader takes. Hypertext documents involve an associative, nonlinear web of informational modules connected by semantic links. Educators must better understand how to use various approaches to help children learn to strategically navigate through hypertext for specific purposes.

QUESTION 3: How can we support children's development of critical literacy comprehension skills for information they access on the Internet?

Information available on the Internet is freely accessible and growing exponentially; however, unlike most district-adopted educational reading materials, the Internet information has not been subject to rigorous review processes. As a result, Web content is not consistently reliable, and some Web designers frequently hide their intention to present propaganda, influence consumers, or promote political affiliations. Educators must learn how to help students critically access, analyze, navigate through, and comprehend multiple Web-based informational sources.

References

A to Zapp [Computer software]. (1995). Pleasantville, NY: Sunburst Technology.

Becker, H. J. (1991). How computers are used in the United States schools: Basic data from the I.E.A. computers in education survey. *Journal of Educational Computing Research, 7,* 385–406.

Becker, H. J. (1993). Decision making about computer acquisition and use in American schools. *Computers and Education, 20,* 341–352.

Block, C. C., Oakar, M., & Hirt, N. (2002). The expertise of literacy teachers: A continuum for preschool to grade 5. *Reading Research Quarterly, 37*(2), 150–178.

Burrell, C., & Trushell, J. (1997). "Eye-candy" in "interactive books"—a wholesome diet? *Reading, 31*(2), 3–6.

Cambourne, B. (in press). What do I do with the rest of the class?: The nature of teaching-learning activities. *Language Arts.*

Clairana, R. B. (1990). *The teacher is a variable in reading computer-based instruction.* Research Report 41. CAST—Harvard University. Cambridge, MA. (ERIC Document Reproduction Service No. ED 317 966, CS 010014)

Cochran-Smith, M. (1984). *The making of a reader.* Norwood, NJ: Ablex.

Eisenwine, M. J., & Hunt, D. A. (2000). Using a computer in literacy groups with emergent readers. *Reading Teacher, 53,* 456–458.

Garton, J. (1996). New genres and new literacies: The challenge of the virtual curriculum. *Australian Journal of Language and Literacy, 20,* 209–222.

Gillingham, M. G., Garner, R., Guthrie, J. T., & Sawyer, R. (1989). Children's control of computer-based reading assistance in answering synthesis questions. *Computers in Human Behavior, 5,* 61–75.

Haggard, M. R. (1986). The vocabulary self-collection strategy: An active approach to word learning. In E. K. Dishner, T. W. Bean, J. E. Readence, & D. W. Moore (Eds.), *Reading in the content areas: Improving classroom instruction* (2nd ed., pp. 179–183). Dubuque, IA: Kendall/Hunt.

Haughland, S. (1998). The best developmental software for young children. *Early Childhood Education Journal, 25,* 247–254.

Hickman, C. (1994). KidPix2 (version 2) [Computer software]. Novato, CA: Broderbund.

Higgins, N., & Hess, L. (1999). Using electronic books to promote vocabulary development. *Journal of Research on Computing in Education, 31,* 425–430.

Hoffman, J. V., Roser, N. L., Labbo, L. D., & Farest, C. (1992). Language charts: A record of story time talk. *Language Arts, 69*(1), 44–52.

Labbo, L. D. (1996). A semiotic analysis of young children's symbol making in a classroom computer center. *Reading Research Quarterly, 31,* 356–385.

Labbo, L. D. (2000). 12 things young children can do with a talking book in a classroom computer center. *Reading Teacher, 53,* 542–546.

Labbo, L. D. (in press). Computer-Teaching Learning Activities. Sidebar for Cambourne, B. (in press). What do I do with the rest of the class? The nature of teaching-learning activities. *Language Arts.*

Labbo, L. D., & Kuhn, M. R. (2000). Weaving chains of affect and cognition: A young child's understanding of CD-ROM talking books. *Journal of Literacy Research, 32*(2), 187–210.

Labbo, L. D., Reinking, D., & McKenna, M. (1995). Incorporating the computer into kindergarten: A case study. In A. Hinchman, D. Leu, & C. K. Kinzer (Eds.), *Perspectives on literacy research and practice: Forty-fourth Yearbook of the National Reading Conference* (pp. 459–465). Chicago: National Reading Conference.

Labbo, L. D., & Sprague, L., with Montero, K., & Font, G. (2000). Connecting a computer center to themes, literature, and kindergartners' literacy needs. *Reading Online* [On-line], *4*(1). Available: http://www.readingonline.org/default.asp

Labbo, L. D., & Teale, W. (2001). *Figuring out how computers fit in: Practical classroom applications for K–3 computer-related literacy instruction.* Paper presented at the annual conference of the International Reading Association, New Orleans, LA.

Leu, D. J. (1997). Caity's question: Literacy as deixis on the Internet. *Reading Teacher, 41,* 62–67.

Mandler, J. M., & Johnson, N. S. (1977). Remembrance of things parsed: Story structure and recall. *Cognitive Psychology, 9,* 111–151.

Matthew, K. (1997). A comparison of the influence of interactive CD-ROM storybooks and traditional print storybooks on reading comprehension. *Journal of Research on Computing in Education, 29*(1), 263–275.

Mayer, M. Just Grandma and Me [Computer software]. (1997). Living Books. Novato, CA: Broderbund.

Moss, B. (1995). Nurturing artistic images in student reading and writing. *Reading Teacher, 48,* 532–608.

Nagy, W. E., & Herman P. (1987). Breadth and depth of vocabulary knowledge: Implications for acquisition and instruction. In M. McKeown & M. Curtis (Eds.), *The nature of vocabulary acquisition* (pp. 19–35). Hillsdale, NJ: Erlbaum.

Olson, K., & Sulzby, E. (1991). The computer as a social/physical environment in emergent literacy. *National Reading Conference Yearbook, 40,* 111–118.

Pillay, H., Brownlee, J., & Wilss, L. (1999). Cognition and recreational computer games: Implications for educational technology. *Journal of Research on Computing in Education, 32*(1), 203–216.

Reinking, D. R. (1997). Me and my hypertext: A multiple digression analysis of technology and literacy. *Reading Teacher, 50,* 626–643.

Sloyer, S. (1982). *Reader's theater: Story dramatization in the classroom.* Urbana, IL: National Council of Teachers of English.

Stahl, S., & Fairbanks, M. (1986). The effects of vocabulary instruction: A model-based meta-analysis. *Review of Educational Research, 56,* 72–110.

U.S. Department of Education. (1999). *Teacher quality: A report on the preparation and qualification of public school teachers* (USDE Publication No. NCES 1999-080). Washington, DC: U.S. Government Printing Office. Available: http://nces.ed.gov/pubs00/199080.htm

Wittrock, M. C. (1986). Students' thought processes. In M. C. Wittrock (Ed.), *Handbook of research on teaching* (pp. 297–314). Old Tappan, NJ: Macmillan.

Chapter Thirteen

Out of This World

Cyberspace, Literacy, and Learning

Victoria Gentry Ridgeway,
Chris L. Peters,
and Terrell Seawell Tracy

What does it mean to be literate? At different times in U.S. history, that question has prompted different answers (Venezky, 1990). At the turn of the nineteenth century, a person who could write his or her name was considered literate. Now, however, that basic skill is not enough for one to be considered literate. As our world has changed, so have the literacy requirements to function in it. The basic skills of reading to find main ideas and details are no longer adequate to enable people to function well today.

Since 1980 we have seen the term *literacy* applied to specific fields, for example, computer literacy. To be *computer literate* means that you can operate a computer and use it and the appropriate software for productive tasks. The necessary functional literacy level has increased dramatically with the advent of technology and the information revolution. Our world has grown smaller, and we have access to a volume of information unheard of a generation ago. Recently, the entire volume of immigration records from Ellis Island became available on the Internet. One author's great-grandfather emigrated from Scotland in the late 1800s, coming through Ellis Island as so many thousands did. The Library of Congress Web site provides access to hundreds of primary source documents. We have access to the personal immigration records of our families and to documents and photographs from around the world. However, this amazing access to information is a double-edged sword. Having access to information does not guarantee that the information is accurate, credible, and current or that the user will use it appropriately. We must equip our students with a level of literacy that far exceeds levels deemed adequate in the past. Our students must be computer literate as well as critically literate. They must be able to read the words and the world (Freire, 1970).

Conceptions of Critical Literacy, Text, and Learning

Critical literacy is an ambiguous term. To some, it means higher-order thinking skills, including the ability to analyze and synthesize what one has read and transform that information in order to communicate its meaning to others. Some would argue that unless we take a stance in relation to the information available to us—unless we go beyond mere analysis, synthesis, and transformation—we are not critically literate. They call for social and political criticism that involve awareness of how and why text is constructed (Green, 2001). Gee's conception of critical literacy (2001) includes not just social and political criticism but a personal component as well: critical literacy involves not only an awareness of social and political aspects of information but of how that information influences the reader. Freire (1970) would add a component of social and political activism to that definition. In this chapter the term *critical literacy* indicates a level of literacy that involves reading between and beyond the lines, analysis and synthesis of information, an awareness of the ways that texts are constructed, and an awareness of the ways that text constructions position readers. For example, text written in the third person distances readers, causing them to read the text with less personalization than text following a second person point of view.

In addition to conceptions of literacy, our conceptions of text have changed over time. In the 1950s, text included books, periodicals, and newspapers. Now, however, text includes elements of popular culture—advertisements, music, music videos, and movies—as well as Internet resources in a conception of text. Our view of literacy includes reading books as well as reading art—visual literacy is an essential part of our current conception and standards of literacy. Our notion of what constitutes text is broadened, more inclusive.

In addition to changes in conceptions of literacy and text, our view of the learner has changed. In the 1950s, the prevailing notion of learning was one very close to the tabula rasa: learners were blank slates for the teacher to write on. Another popular metaphor was one of a sponge soaking up information or a receptacle to be filled up. Teachers who lectured and gave notes supposedly filled the heads of their students. Learners dutifully took down notes, memorized them, and regurgitated the information on tests. This produced graduates who could memorize procedures and complete repetitive jobs, such as on an assembly line. In 1950 that produced workers prepared for available jobs. In this century, however, we need workers with very different abilities. We need workers who can analyze situations, solve problems, work in teams, and think outside of the box. Educating workers with these skills and abilities dictates very different teaching methods that facilitate learners' knowledge construction, problem solving, and decision making. When learners construct their own knowledge, they own rather than rent information. And ownership of knowledge means that knowledge is uniquely personal—not exactly like everyone else's knowledge. In today's classrooms this notion of learning is embodied in constructivist thinking.

Constructivist theory views learners as actively involved in the construction of their knowledge, which includes analysis, synthesis, transformation, and evaluation of information. Learners grow by working in their zone of proximal development (Dixon-Krauss, 1996). When working in the zone, learners are to complete tasks that are too difficult for them to complete alone but that they can accomplish with a more knowledgeable other's help. In time the learner is able to do the task without help. In this way, learners grow in their ability to complete complex tasks. Assigning students to work in the zone of proximal development requires teachers to scaffold student learning: teachers must provide support and guidance so that the students can be successful learners. Scaffolding learning involves helping learners focus on essential information and make internal and external connections. It enables learners to work above their independent level to analyze, synthesize, transform, and produce information that would otherwise be too difficult for them to accomplish. With changing conceptions of literacy, text, and learning, how are teachers to help students become critically literate and improve their technology skills at the same time? One vehicle useful to accomplish these goals is the WebQuest.

The WebQuest

The *WebQuest* is an inquiry-based activity that requires the learner to think critically (Dodge, 1997). The learner obtains information from the Internet and perhaps from other sources such as the library or the community. A WebQuest requires the learner's active involvement as well as analysis, synthesis, transformation of information, decision making, and evaluation. WebQuests provide scaffolding for learners in the form of step-by-step procedures, appropriate preselected Web sites, and learning hints. In addition, WebQuests develop learners' technology skills as they facilitate development of critical literacy. In short, WebQuests are excellent vehicles through which to prepare students to be critically literate citizens. In this chapter we will describe different types of Web-Quests, discuss essential and nonessential elements that comprise them, and provide hints on how to construct successful WebQuests. We will discuss examples of WebQuests at a variety of levels.

WebQuests (Dodge, 1997) are of two types that differ chiefly in their duration and the depth at which they require students to delve into the information. Short-term WebQuests usually take one to three class periods and focus on knowledge acquisition and integration. An example of a short-term WebQuest would be one with a goal to have students acquire the skills necessary to evaluate Web sites. Such a quest would provide students with a limited number of Web sites and guidelines for evaluation, and it would require students to select the best Web sites from the list and justify their reasoning for the selection. Students focus on the acquisition of essential Internet skills, and they can complete the tasks in about three class periods.

A long-term WebQuest requires students to extend and refine their knowledge and lasts anywhere from a week to a month. Kathy Schrock (1996) created a long-term WebQuest in which she placed students in the role of museum curators who were to research specific years from the decade of the 1960s and select important events to include in a 1960s museum production. Schrock required students to create a Web page for their selected years and link it to the 1960s museum home page on the site. This WebQuest required students to consult library, community, and Internet resources; analyze the information; select and synthesize appropriate information; and finally design and create a Web page with appropriate related links.

WebQuests embody the best use of the Internet as well as off-line resources. Essential elements include the introduction, description of the task, a list of resources, procedures for completion of the task, the criteria or rubric to evaluate student learning, and the conclusion. Characteristics frequently found in WebQuests but not essential include the use of collaborative learning, different roles and audiences for students, the disciplinary nature of the quest, and classroom access to the Internet (Siwninski, 1997).

Nonessential Characteristics of a WebQuest

Although group work is not necessary, many WebQuests call for collaborative efforts. This is particularly true of WebQuests involving complex tasks. Having students assume different roles within a group focused on accomplishing a single complex task is an excellent use of the jigsaw cooperative learning structure (Johnson & Johnson, 1987) and enables a group of students to explore more information collaboratively than they could individually. Many WebQuests are interdisciplinary. Although some classes may pursue single-discipline activities in the quests, they are uniquely suited to interdisciplinary endeavors. For example, a WebQuest focused on environmental issues could involve locating, analyzing, and synthesizing data related to diversity of species as well as economic issues. Requiring students to display their results in graphs and charts would involve transformation of the data using essential mathematics skills. Decisions involved in choosing appropriate graphic displays help students learn more than just how to construct a graph. They learn how math works—and how presentation of data can influence a reader's thinking. Students might also write a letter to the editor of the local paper as a result of their research. Such a WebQuest would involve science, social studies, mathematics, and English. Dodge invented WebQuests to take advantage of the Internet and its multiple resources. However, it is possible to use a WebQuest activity in a classroom that is not connected to the Internet or in classrooms with limited access.

A teacher whose classroom does not have Internet access can print out the relevant Web pages for students and use a jigsaw structure that provides group interdependence through differentiated materials to limit the amount of duplicating required. Students share the pages. Although students may miss out on working directly with the computer, other characteristics of the learning activity will be worthwhile. Teachers in classrooms with one computer with Internet access can create WebQuests that require students to use library and community resources in addition to Internet resources. The classroom computer can become a learning station through which various student teams rotate, with one group of students using the Internet while other groups access information through library and community resources. In addition, printing selected information from the Internet can minimize the crunch for computer time. If the available classroom computers are not networked but the teacher has Internet access either at home or in the library, a program like Web Buddy or Web Whacker can provide a way to download Web pages and copy them from disk to classroom computers (March, 1998). Having Web sites available off-line also guards against students accessing inappropriate Web sites linked to target sites. In short, although WebQuests were originally designed to take advantage of the unique characteristics of the Internet, teachers can engage students in a WebQuest activity without having classroom Internet access. We now turn to a consideration of the essential components of a WebQuest.

Essential Elements of a WebQuest

All WebQuests have an introduction, task, list of resources, set of procedures, assessment rubric, and a conclusion. Although the elements may have slightly different names and some WebQuests may combine some of the elements, particularly for elementary students, every WebQuest contains information found in these elements.

Introduction

The introduction to a WebQuest is an opportunity to interest and motivate students in the focus of the quest. It includes background information to provide a context for students and may include a description of the task that students must complete in the WebQuest. First and foremost, the introduction should be interesting. Having students assume different roles, address different audiences, and communicate research findings in a variety of formats increases their interest in and motivation to pursue WebQuests. Although consideration of role, audience, format, and topic or task (RAFT) (Santa, 1988) has long been a strategy for writing to learn, we have found the RAFT structure an excellent one for WebQuests. In RAFT students take on a role other than that of student and write for an audience other than the teacher in a unique format. Taking on these roles and writing for audiences that go beyond the classroom make a WebQuest more interesting and more relevant to students. For example, they might receive this assignment: "You are a member of a special committee of *Newsweek* researchers charged with selecting the one hundred most important events of the second millennium. You must decide whether the French Revolution should be included in the list of important events and present your decision and rationale to the editorial board of *Newsweek*." This is more interesting than "in this project we will learn about the French Revolution."

The introduction should be compelling and include adequate information to structure an interesting scenario. Ways of creating compelling scenarios include personalizing contemporary world problems, evaluating history, creating products for an audience outside the classroom, dealing with life's realities, and tapping into students' imaginations (Yoder, 1999).

Task

Tasks that involve students in personalizing contemporary world problems might focus on environmental, political, or sociological issues that appear in the news. These problems often have historical roots that will require the student to consider world history as part of the WebQuest. Learning about a local water source may initiate students' investigation of local pollution, and this may lead to a consideration of pollution in the United States and the world. Should the government regulate the amount of arsenic in drinking water? Should the government require businesses to monitor and report the amount of lead released into the atmosphere? These questions have environmental, chemical, and economic aspects. A quick perusal of a recent newspaper will provide many ideas for issues to investigate.

When asking students to evaluate history, the teacher might assign them the role of a person who lived through the historical event or ask them to take a different view of the event. For example, a WebQuest focused on Christopher Columbus's first voyage to the New World might ask students to take the role of a sailor on board one of Columbus's ships or to take the view of the indigenous population and discuss the impact of the voyage from their perspective. Another type of WebQuest might prompt students to create products for an audience outside the classroom. For example, modern language students might produce a pamphlet written in Spanish giving the history of the community and summarizing available community resources for the local chamber of commerce. In an area experiencing an influx of Hispanic immigrants, this project would provide an authentic task that enhances the ability of the local community to better serve community members. Dealing with life's realities often engages students in researching information related to something they might do as an adult: finding a job, buying a car, creating a budget, or traveling to another country. These activities involve the use of on-line resources such as employment pages, airline schedules, weather information, and money-exchange schedules, as well as resources beyond the Internet, such as local newspapers. WebQuests that involve a journey back in time, a trip to outer space, or a visit to the bottom of the ocean spark students' imagination, which can increase their interest and their motivation (Yoder, 1999). The task may be one with several subtasks, may involve choosing from among several options to demonstrate learning, and may involve group work as well as individual work.

Procedures

After introducing students to the WebQuest through background information and a description of the task, the teacher should provide them with a step-by-step set of procedures. A timeline is an optional part of the procedures, but will be especially important in long-term WebQuests. Procedures should be specific rather than general. For example, rather than directing students to a Web site and asking them to read the information, the procedure should provide a purpose or specific activity like "go to http:// . . . and find three differences between concept one and concept two." Specific procedures make a WebQuest clear and manageable for students. Hints, in the form of learning advice, help to scaffold the task for students. Learning advice can include a road map for the procedures, directions and strategies for completing tasks, and models of the outcomes that students must produce. Procedures should guide the learners through the task and provide sufficient scaffolding to enable them to be successful using the resources provided.

Resources

The teacher should carefully choose the on- and off-line resources that will enable students to be successful. This includes evaluating Web sites for content, credibility, bias, and usability (Schrock, 1998–1999). Is the content on the Web site accurate? Is it written at a comprehensible level for these students? Does the site offer something other Web sites or off-line resources do not? Is the information current? When was the site created and last updated? When evaluating credibility, the Internet user must look at the author(s) of the site. Are the site's authors identifiable? What are their credentials? Do they cite sources beyond their own Web site? What is the ending on the *domain name*—the Uniform Resource Locator (URL) or Web address? Sites ending in *.com* are commercial sites. Although valuable information is available on commercial sites, the user must keep in mind the purpose for the site: to advertise or provide information for a commercial interest. For example, a tobacco company site that has information about research involving the effects of smoking could be biased. Advertising on commercial sites can be problematic as well. Web sites ending in *.gov* are government sites and provide a great deal of information including archived documents. The Library of Congress Web site (http://www.loc.gov) is an excellent source of primary documents. Educational institutions such as schools and universities maintain sites ending in *.edu*. What Web pages are linked to this site? The teacher should make sure that links are appropriate by finding all pages linked to a site. Anyone can go to the AltaVista search engine and search for links to a site; typing *link:<URL>* in the search box will bring up a list of all sites linked to that URL (Schrock, 1998–1999). The suffix [*gov., .edu, .com*] provides clues to the purpose of the site. The purpose and content of the site help the user to determine whether information presented is biased. Does the site present only one side of an argument? Are there hidden messages? Is the site trying to persuade the viewer toward one or another viewpoint? Is fact distinct from opinion? The teacher should also evaluate the usability and design of the sites under consideration for a WebQuest. Does the site take too long to download? Is the site easy to navigate and user-friendly? Does it contain spelling or grammar errors? Are the pages clean and uncluttered? Do the links on the site work? Are the links appropriate? These questions will help determine whether Web sites are appropriate for a certain group of students.

Locating appropriate sites can be made easier if the teacher uses search engines and well-documented collections of Web site links such as Kathy Schrock's (1995). In addition to hot links to many discipline-specific Web site collections, Schrock's site also offers helpful Microsoft PowerPoint presentations to teach valuable searching skills. Viewers not adept at using search engines can visit her page and consult the right-hand column for slide shows for teachers. One search tool we have used is Ask Jeeves (http://ask.com). This search engine allows the user to type a question or a phrase in the search window, and it returns a list of possible matches to the query. Not all sites on the list will be appropriate, but it is a good place to start a search. On-line searching can be very time consuming, but identifying a few good information sources such as Schrock's page or Ask Jeeves will save a great deal of time.

Off-line resources are also excellent information sources for students. These include periodicals such as *Newsweek, Time, US News and World Report, Discover, Scientific American* (which is also on-line); local, national, and international newspapers (some of which are on-line); books in the school or community library; and community-based resources such as genetics centers, hospitals, and chambers of commerce. The community itself can be an excellent source of information: interviewing community experts, family members, and experienced others can help students build bridges between generations and provide them with eyewitness accounts and different points of view about historical events. If students are to do interviews, however, they should be knowledgeable about the interview process.

Assessment Criteria

Students need to know how they will be evaluated before they complete the WebQuest. The teacher may construct assessment criteria and provide it to students at the time of the assignment or create the criteria with students.

Criteria construction should begin with the purpose of the WebQuest: What does the teacher want students to know and be able to do as a result of the WebQuest? How will the teacher know when they have successfully completed the WebQuest? What will that look like? The teacher should make a list of behavioral statements that describe the visible evidence that students have achieved the goals the quest. If it is long, the list should be broken up into categories. Each statement or category becomes a dimension on which students will be evaluated. The teacher must be sure to clearly define each dimension and be specific.

How many levels of quality will the teacher be checking for? The teacher might divide students into groups that identify those students who have successfully completed the WebQuest, those who have completed the WebQuest but have not performed as well as the first group, and those who have not completed the WebQuest successfully—a three-level rubric that identifies proficient, apprentice, and novice levels of performance. The teacher should clearly define each level of performance at the outset. In general, using scales with fewer levels of quality make it more difficult to identify small differences between students' performance, whereas scales with more levels of quality make it difficult to get scorers to agree (Chicago Public Schools, 2000). Samples of evaluation rubrics are available in on-line WebQuests; in addition, Schrock (1995) provides links to extensive resources related to assessment and rubrics.

Involving students in creating criteria helps to refine their understanding of the WebQuest tasks, and we have found that this results in better student performance. Teachers who choose to create assessment criteria with students should do so in several steps. First, the teacher might have students work for a short time on their projects, then share their work with peers. Often, asking students to choose their best work to share—their best paragraph, graphic organizer, picture, or song—can be helpful. In a discussion based on the sharing, the teacher and students could brainstorm about characteristics of their best work. This brainstormed list could become the basis for a checklist assessment or evolve into a rubric that describes several levels of competence. Helping students learn to describe exemplary, developing, and beginning achievement involves teaching them critical literacy skills associated with self-assessment. The teacher may wish to try a combination of teacher-developed rubrics for some WebQuest tasks and involve students in the creation of a few rubrics. Creating assessment rubrics with students is time consuming, but it is time well spent.

Conclusion

WebQuests are generally performance-based activities requiring students to present their products to their classmates, teacher, and other relevant audiences outside of school. Examples of performance-based conclusions might include videos, pamphlets, or PowerPoint presentations, plays, musical performances, scientific reports, and student-authored books. Sometimes the teacher's concluding questions ask students to make decisions and support them with facts based on their research. The conclusion brings closure to the WebQuest and provides an opportunity for students to share what they have learned with their peers. It can also be an occasion for reflection and self-evaluation for both students and teachers. The conclusion enables students to give feedback to the teacher and may be an occasion to promote student action.

WebQuest Examples

There are many collections of WebQuests for both elementary and secondary students. An elementary WebQuest based on the book *Stellaluna* (Cannon, 1993) provides a good example of clear procedures, great scaffolding in the form of graphic organizers for the students to annotate, and both individual and group evaluations. In this WebQuest students work in pairs to find out as much as they can about bats in order to write a letter to Stellaluna to tell her why she's so special. Because Von Feldt designed this WebQuest for elementary students, she integrated the procedures and resources, giving students very specific directions for each Web site they visit, such as, "your job is to discover how echolocation works." In addition, each Web site has a graphic organizer with a clearly described grading rubric so that students know exactly what is expected of them. Students completing this WebQuest investigate different types of bats, find out how bat mothers care for their babies, discover how echolocation works, learn about unique bat characteristics, and explore why bats are important to the world.

Another example of a WebQuest is one focused on Vietnam created by McMullin (2001). This WebQuest is a good example of the combination of RAFT and jigsaw. The context for the WebQuest involves citizens in a town in which the mayor wants to commission a mural commemorating the Vietnam War. Students assume one of four roles: historian, Vietnamese immigrant, Vietnam veteran, and protestor. Groups research the positions of the role based on Web sites provided on McMullin's site. The tasks involve creating a group HyperStudio presentation and an individual newspaper article about the town meeting in which the students play the roles and make the presentations. The town meeting provides closure for the WebQuest in the form of group presentations, which provide the basis for individually produced newspaper articles, and a final town vote. Such a WebQuest enables students to consider a large amount of information from a variety of perspectives.

Hints for Success with WebQuests

A successful WebQuest requires careful planning. We have compiled this list of directions to help teachers organize their work.

Look at existing WebQuests for ideas on topics, tasks, and evaluation rubrics. Two good places to begin your search for existing WebQuests are Bernie Dodge's WebQuest site (1993) and Kathy Schrock's Web site (1995).

Decide on a main idea or general theme for your WebQuest first. Next, research your resources, both on- and off-line. Only after determining the most appropriate resources that can be made available to your student do you decide on a task or tasks for the WebQuest (Peters, 2000). This saves time and energy, as nothing is more frustrating than trying to find specific information on the Internet to support a task you want students to complete.

Use the RAFT format. Offer students different roles and authentic tasks created for audiences beyond the classroom. Combining the jigsaw cooperative learning structure with a RAFT format results in interesting and relevant WebQuests. The McMullin's Vietnam WebQuest (2001) is an excellent example of the RAFT and jigsaw combination.

Use a WebQuest template, available at several Web sites (http://www.ga.k12.pa.us/curtech/WEBQPRE/tempques.htm and http://itcenter.clemson.edu/quest). A template will enable you to quickly and easily set up your WebQuest without having to know a great deal about designing Web pages. Simply follow the directions associated with the template, save your work as a hypertext markup language (HTML) file, and post it on your school's Web site or print out the final product to display on a class bulletin board. WebQuests are excellent vehicles for the development of critical literacy skills. They also provide technology experiences to increase students' computer literacy. A wide variety of WebQuests already exists, and many resources are available to help minimize the task of creating custom WebQuests for your students.

Three Recommendations for the Future

In order to implement WebQuests in the classroom, the teacher will need access to the Internet for initial explorations; some skill in using word processing programs and Web page authoring tools; experience in navigating the World Wide Web; and knowledge of the technology available for students. Fortunately, none of these resources is hard to acquire.

RECOMMENDATION 1: The teacher must have access to the Internet.

Without such access, the teacher will find the WebQuest project daunting but not impossible. Most school libraries offer Internet services. If the teacher has neither a computer nor Internet access, he or she might look for help from the business sector or in grants. Some businesses donate used computers to schools when they update their hardware. Good resources are computer stores, colleges or universities, foundations, companies, and district or county offices that might fund a project. Someone somewhere is giving money away! Although teachers are not traditionally good at asking for money (our salaries are a case in point), we can usually provide excellent reasons for our needs.

Any computer that is capable of Internet connection is capable of supporting work with WebQuests; however, a computer with a fast processor and good amount of random access memory will affect the ease and speed of on-line work. The abundance of multimedia components on Web pages requires more and more memory. A local computer store would be helpful in explaining hardware specifications. If a school is connected to the Internet but a particular classroom is not, the teacher may want to explore the possibilities of using wireless connections to tie into the school network.

RECOMMENDATION 2: The teacher should develop the necessary skills to explore the World Wide Web and work with documents in a variety of formats.

The teacher who is a novice at computers should not fear! First-graders can master computers and the Internet, and so can adults.

The help feature of most word processing programs will be useful for learning about saving files in different formats such as HTML for Web documents. The novice user should ask a computer-savvy student about how to log on to the Web and visit Schrock's Web site (1995), which lists teacher resources in the far right-hand column. The PowerPoint presentations and articles available there will enable the novice to learn how to navigate the Internet, use a search engine and a directory, differentiate among the various kinds of Web sites, and use Web page authoring tools.

Keeping a learning log while first working with word processing programs and navigating the Internet can be useful. The novice user can jot down any actions he or she takes in the word processing program; keep track of the URLs of interesting Web sites visited; or note the results of Internet explorations. Above all, the user should relax and not worry about breaking the computer by pressing the wrong key.

RECOMMENDATION 3: The teacher should investigate the technology available to his or her students in context.

The teacher must know how many computers would be available to students at any one time as well as how many of these are capable of accessing the Internet. Although computers in the classroom are more convenient, a central computer lab is a viable alternative as long as the teacher prepares students for specific tasks when they go to the lab. Even if computers available to students are not all on-line, the teacher can use software (March, 1998) to copy Web sites for off-line use. Use of Web sites off-line will minimize the risk of student access to inappropriate Web sites. The teacher will need to keep the availability of computers in mind when designing the WebQuest tasks. If at least four or five computers are available, the teacher can organize cooperative learning groups to limit the number of computers necessary to complete the WebQuest. If only one or two are available, the teacher will need to plan for some off-line resources to minimize the number of computers students will need.

WebQuests are excellent vehicles for the development of students' critical literacy skills. At the same time, they provide technology experiences to increase students' computer literacy. A wide variety of WebQuests already exist, and many resources are available to help minimize the task of creating custom WebQuests for students.

References

Cannon, J. (1993). *Stellaluna.* San Diego, CA: Harcourt.

Chicago Public Schools (2000). *Elements of a scoring rubric* [On-line]. Available http://intranet.cps.k12.il.us/Assessments/Ideas_and_Rubrics/Intro_Scoring/Scoring_Rubrics/scoring_rubrics.html

Dixon-Krauss, L. (1996). *Vygotsky in the classroom: Mediated literacy instruction and assessment.* White Plains, NY: Longman.

Dodge, B. (1997). *Some thoughts about WebQuests* [On-line]. Available: http://edweb.sdsu.edu/courses/edtec596/about_webquests.html

Dodge, B. (1993). *WebQuests.* Available: http://edweb.sdsu.edu/web quest/webquest.html

Freire, P. (1970). *Pedagogy of the oppressed.* New York: Herder and Herder.

Gee, J. P. (2001). Critical literacy/socially perceptive literacy: A study of language in action. In H. Fehring & P. Green (Eds.), *Critical literacy: A collection of articles from the Australian Literacy Educators' Association* (pp. 15–39). Newark, DE: International Reading Association.

Green, P. (2001). Critical literacy revisited. In H. Fehring & P. Green (Eds.), *Critical literacy: A collection of articles from the Australian Literacy Educators' Association* (pp. 7–14). Newark, DE: International Reading Association.

Johnson, D., & Johnson, R. (1987). *The achieving student in the heterogeneous cooperative learning groups.* Paper developed for a workshop at the University of Minnesota.

March, T. (1998). WebQuests for learning. *Ozline.com* [On-line]. Available: http://www.ozline.com/webquests/intro.html

McMullin, G. (2001). *Vietnam WebQuest.* Available: http://students.itec.sfsu.edu/itec815/mcmullin/

Peters, C. (2000, Spring). Assignment 8: WebQuest. SC Center of Excellence for Instructional Technology Training. Clemson University.

Santa, C. (1988). *Content reading including study systems.* Dubuque, IA: Kendall/Hunt.

Schrock, K. (1995). *Kathy Schrock's Guide for Educators* [On-line]. Available: http://school.discovery.com/schrockguide/

Schrock, K. (1996). WebQuest: The 1960s Museum. *Kathy Schrock's Guide for Educators* [On-line]. Available: http://school.discovery.com/schrockguide/museum/webquest.html

Schrock, K. (1998–1999, December–January). The ABCs of web site evaluation. *Classroom Connect,* 4–6. Available: http://school.discovery.com/schrockguide/pdf/weval.pdf

Siwninski, C. (1997). WebQuest attributes. In *Workshop for Germantown Academy Staff Development Summer Workshop* [On-line]. Available: http://www.ga.k12.pa.us/curtech/WEBQPRE/temques.htm

Venezky, R. L. (1990). Definitions of literacy. In R. L. Venezky, D. A. Wagner, & B. S. Ciliberti (Eds.), *Toward defining literacy* (pp. 2–16). Newark, DE: International Reading Association.

Von Feldt, D. (1999). *Example of a student-generated WebQuest* [On-line]. Available:

http://projects.edtech.sandi.net/chavez/batquest/batquest.html

Yoder, M. B. (1999). The student WebQuest: A productive and thought-provoking use of the Internet. *Learning and Leading with Technology, 26*(7), 6–9, 52–53.

Chapter Fourteen

Reading in the Digital Era
Strategies for Building Critical Literacy
Lisa Patel Stevens
and Thomas W. Bean

Since 1995, abundant literacy policy in the United States has been written and implemented to have all students reading by the end of the third grade. This policy reflects a nostalgic view of childhood that denies the realities of an e-business globalized economy (Luke & Luke, 2001). This emphasis on students' becoming skilled at decoding the text alone ignores other important issues: Whose agenda do various texts serve? Whose voices do stories, media, textbooks, and other print forms represent? Striving for these national goals in K–3, under the assumption that fast decoding access will free the students' attention for comprehension, negates the highly complex and deliberate explicit attention that dynamic comprehension at factual, affective, and critical levels requires.

The oft-touted goal of K–3 oral reading fluency contains within it some faulty assumptions about literacy. First, the sole conversation about reading, versus a more inclusive discussion of literacy, negates the intertextual nature of reading the world through words. Second, if reading is a skill that can be accomplished by the end of the third grade, then logic dictates that there would be little need to continue literacy instruction. However, substantive evidence stands to the contrary; Bean (2001) found, for example, through an almost century-old inquiry into content-area literacy and also treated cogently in the International Reading Association's Adolescent Literacy Position Statement (Moore, Bean,

Birdyshaw, & Rycik, 1999). Further, the policy goal of having students reading by the end of the third grade typically values only those studies that have researched reading in experimental settings and emphasizes, even overemphasizes, the role of decoding, phonemic awareness, and phonics, subjugating the ultimate goal of literacy—comprehension—to a foregone conclusion (Strauss, 2001). A focus on these studies denies the vast array of studies and treatises on the social and political aspects of literacy, discourse, and reading. Concurrent with this emphasis on code-based definitions of reading, schoolwide programs that rely on repeated readings, choral responses, and timed oral reading exercises have grown in popularity. These trends are alarming for a number of reasons; one of the most basic areas of concern is how these policies define reading.

If reading is defined as an ability to read that children can acquire by the end of third grade, it follows that this performance objective is a rather static process based on mastery and rote skill—one in which students gain input from text without engaging in critical stances. This places students, especially those who struggle with school-sanctioned literacies, at a particular disadvantage in a world that is increasingly driven by digital technologies, media saturation, and worldwide marketplaces that rely upon economies of attention (New London Group, 1999; Gee, 1996). Such a definition of reading also erroneously sequences the parallel functions that proficient readers use concurrently to create meaning and critique texts. It is our contention that we can no longer regard critical literacy as a higher-order thinking skill, reserved for those students whom we deem proficient at decoding, and only then if time allows. Instead, aspects of critical literacy must become part and parcel of the definition of comprehension.

Defining Critical Literacy

Freebody and Luke (1990) define critical literacy as one of four roles that readers should employ when encountering text. Along with the more familiar processes of code breaker (coding competence), meaning maker (semantic competence), and text user (pragmatic competence), we need to consider the practices of reader as text critic. This fourth dimension forces us to explicitly discuss the ways in which text is mediated as a tool of institutional shaping of discourses and social practices. This positioning is quite different from the traditional stance that text occupies in U.S. political discourse. Typically, texts, namely, print-based books, are glorified as gateways to other worlds, keepers of stores of knowledge, and inanimate confidants and friends. In this way, texts are innocuous sources of information and wisdom. And although we can all think of certain texts that have performed those functions for us, to treat reading education in this manner belies the highly dialogic nature of classrooms, in which interactions shape knowledge, power, and discourse (Fairclough, 1989). Narrowly defined views of reading also deny the pervasive role that text, both print and visual, plays in shaping our identities, resources, and opportunities (Luke & Freebody, 1999). All four processes (Freebody & Luke, 1990) work in conjunction, but the role of critically analyzing and transforming texts is one that is rarely sanctioned in school settings. Helping students to assume critical stances toward texts means supporting them in questioning the voices behind texts, whom texts represent and whom they do not, and what positions texts are assuming.

It is important to note that when we are talking about critical literacy we make a distinction between its philosophical orientation and that of critical reading. Critical reading, arising from the liberal-humanist philosophical tradition emphasizes such skill-based tasks as distinguishing fact from opinion and, at a more advanced level, recognizing propaganda in texts (Cervetti, Damico, & Pardeles, 2001). At that more advanced level, critical reading begins to edge in the direction of critical literacy, but it is still rooted in a rationalist view of the world (Cervetti et al.). That is, critical reading rests on the fundamental view expressed by Descartes and others that "knowledge of the world can be attained through reason, that this knowledge is universal and deductive in character, and that everything is fundamentally explainable by this universal system" (Cervetti et al., p. 4). In essence, meaning resides in texts to be deduced through careful, thoughtful exegesis.

In contrast, critical literacy views textual meaning making as a process of construction with a particularly critical eye toward elements of context, historical, social and political dimensions of power relations. Thus, the reader is always looking behind the text to identify its hidden agendas, power groups with an interest in its message, and a recognition that all texts are ideological (Cervetti et al., 2001). When readers take this stance, they develop a critical consciousness, fostering a search for justice and equity by reading the meanings behind the text. Questions about whose version of history the text sanctions, whose energy policy it supports, or how an author positions the reader or characters in a novel fall within the realm of critical literacy. Indeed, these questions go well beyond a technorational critical reading stance. In an era of mass consumerism and fast capitalism (New London Group, 1999), critical literacy offers a balance point to counter hegemonic forces and simple solutions to complex issues. Most important, it places students and teachers in a questioning frame of mind that moves beyond didactic, factual learning.

Several U.S. studies in the past few years explore potential uses of critical literacy in classrooms (Alvermann, Moon, & Hagood, 1999; Tobin, 2000; Stevens, 2001). Typically, these studies have drawn from popular culture texts to engage students' interests in exploring critical literacy roles. For example, Hagood (1999) explored children's discussions as they explained why they shaped their self-created superheroes in certain ways and what visual images they used to depict traits such as gender, power, and personality. In another classroom students shared examples of popular culture and explored questions of who the culture did and did not represent, what aspects of U.S. society it reflected, and who stood to benefit from or be hurt by the images (Stevens, 2001).

Although this handful of studies sheds light on the great potential for critical literacy practices to create space for children's complex interpretations of media texts, few studies have explored this potentiality with the texts more typically sanctioned in school settings. In the next section, we explore a scenario in which a teacher and students pose the same types of questions with a more commonly used text. We base this fictional scenario on our experiences with a few science teachers who have used critical literacy activities in their classrooms.

Mrs. Cutter's Class

As the students filter into Mrs. Cutter's fifth-grade classroom, they notice the large, unwieldy science textbooks on their desks. A few students groan as they suspect another session of round-robin reading, a common practice when working with textbooks. Although this textbook, *Scott Foresman Science* (Cooney et al., 2000) features the bright colors, bold headings, and graphics suggested by content-area literacy researchers (for example, Alvermann & Phelps, 1997), the students do not seem to be any more enraptured by its content. To set the stage for today's lesson and topic, Mrs. Cutter asks students to spend a few minutes freewriting about the recent energy crises that have been occupying the nation's headlines. During a class sharing session, several students offer what they recall of the news items.

Jeremy begins, "The news shows are all talking like we're going to run out soon."

Kirsten adds, "I heard from my cousin in California that her lights went out last week. They do it to save electricity for later."

After a few more students share some of their thoughts, Mrs. Cutter asks them to open their books to pages B134 and B135, which contain information about how electricity reaches consumers. She asks Justin to read aloud the first paragraph. He reads the following section: "Different sources of energy can be used to turn a generator's drive shaft and produce electricity. Notice in each of the pictures below that the generator's drive shaft attaches to a turbine. Like a pinwheel that spins when air rushes past it, each turbine below spins as steam or water moves through it. This spins the drive shaft. The drive shaft turns a magnet inside a coil of wire in the generator. Electricity is produced" (Cooney et al., p. B134).

After Justin has finished reading, Mrs. Cutter asks Jacwelin to read the next paragraph: "A few power plants use tides or waves as their energy source. Modern windmills, such as those to the right, use wind energy to spin built-in generators. Altogether, generators produce almost all the electricity people use. Some devices produce electricity without a generator. Batteries change chemical energy directly into electrical energy. Special solar panels change light energy directly into electrical energy" (Cooney et al., p. B135).

Mrs. Cutter then asks students to use the reading to answer the following questions displayed on the overhead projector:

- Who runs the power plants?
- Who receives the electricity?
- Is the electricity distributed in equal quantities?

- How much does the electricity cost?
- What are all the possible alternative sources of energy?

After the students struggle with the questions for a few moments, Eric raises his hand and tells Mrs. Cutter that it doesn't seem like the answers to the questions can be found in the book.

"Great point, Eric. I knew that when I gave you guys the questions. Do you think that these are still good questions to pursue?" she asks. Mrs. Cutter leads the students in a discussion of the gap between the book's representation of electricity production and consumption and the realities of the current energy crisis. Mrs. Cutter then gives them the assignment for the day: to research how the information about electricity and energy should be written and to rewrite the passages in the textbook. Students work individually, in pairs, and in small groups and use the textbook, trade books, and current periodicals on the Internet to investigate issues related to electricity.

At one point during the day, a group of students approaches Mrs. Cutter to ask if they can change the focus of their project to nuclear energy. When Mrs. Cutter inquires about the need to switch, the students point out that the textbook's authors only devoted three to four paragraphs to nuclear energy, whereas they had given other energy sources three to four pages' worth of explanation and diagrams. Mrs. Cutter compliments the group on their critical reading of the text and encourages them in their newly defined project.

By the end of the day, most students are ready to share their writings. Before sharing their paragraph, Justin and his peers explain that they tried to rewrite the sentences so that the reader could tell who the active agents were. For example, they have changed the sentence that read "Electricity is produced" to "Public and private companies produce electricity and sell it to people for a profit."

Another group has constructed a list of pros and cons of using windmills as a power source. They cite the role of climate and the dominance of generators as obstacles to increased use of alternative sources of producing electricity.

At the end of the sharing session, Mrs. Cutter asks the students if they like their versions better than the textbook's. Most students nod to indicate that they like the revised versions better. Mrs. Cutter then asks the students if these versions could appear in a textbook. The students are not quite as sure about this question. Some of the students maintain that the versions could be used, while others state that textbooks should stick to the facts. Mrs. Cutter asks the students to consider whether any of their versions used anything other than facts.

"No," Chelsea clarifies, "it's just that you could tell what we thought."

"And you couldn't tell what the textbook authors thought from their writing?" Mrs. Cutter asks.

"No, I don't think so," Chelsea concludes.

"Maybe they just think that electricity is given equally to everyone," suggests Justin.

"Maybe," Mrs. Cutter says. "Is that the opinion that they'd like you to form?"

The class continues to discuss the intentions of the textbook's authors.

This scenario highlights a possible situation in which students read for a purpose, construct meaning, and also assume critical stances toward a seemingly innocuous text. Conducting lessons that foster critical literacy requires that teachers explicitly confront their own beliefs and assumptions about the role of activities, discourse, and power within classrooms. Teachers must also be prepared to provide space for students to express the complex ways in which we respond to texts (Tobin, 2000). To assume that students are innocent dupes at the mercy of print and media texts is to effectively silence their voices. The issues raised by critical literacy as a component of literacy pedagogy are complex, to say the least. They are also, however, apropos in today's fast-paced, text-saturated, media-driven world.

Problematizing Classroom Applications of Critical Literacy

In this scenario Mrs. Cutter provides guidance by acting as a sort of mediator between the text and her students as they construct comprehension and assume critical stances. This role is a common classroom application of critical literacy (Gilbert, 1993), as is providing multiple texts and using questions to raise issues of power and agency. However, this role is far from problematic. As many authors have discussed, teachers who employ critical literacy questions and discussions with their students must wrestle with the complexities of opening the possibilities to alternative readings and meanings (for example, Gilbert, 1993; Comber, 1993). Teachers may find themselves replacing the hegemonic positioning of traditional readings with their preferred reading. For example, would a feminist teacher be open to a student's masculine reading of a popular culture advertisement? On what bases could the teacher decide that the construction of his critical comprehension was critical enough?

Another key aspect of critical literacy in the classroom is the question of which texts to use. As Gilbert posed it (1993, p. 76), "How, for instance, can students learn about the social context of language, unless they are able to experience the impact of actual language practices in contexts that are of interest and concern to them?" Questions such as these underscore the need for educators to reformulate critical literacy practices and adapt them according to specific contexts, purposes, and participants. And although the endeavor of using critical literacy in the classroom is not without complication, its very complexities are the reason that educators should pursue it. Texts are used for various purposes and to varying degrees of success in today's fast, text-saturated economy. It is no longer appropriate for classroom discussions of text to assume that all literacy forms are innocuous and equal in their use of power and agency. In a democratic society, it is imperative that we critique texts with the rigor that will empower our students to be proficient, purposeful, and savvy consumers and producers of text.

Critical Literacy in the Classroom

For teachers who are embarking on the use of critical literacy in the classroom, a logical segue is through questioning, one of the most powerful scaffolding and modeling tools that teachers can employ. As a starting point to building critical literacy into comprehension activities, here are some examples of questions and inquiry points:

- Who or what does the text represent?
- Who or what is absent or does the text not represent?

- What is the author trying to accomplish with this text?
- For whom did the author write this text?
- Who stands to benefit from or be hurt by this text?
- How does the author use language in specific ways to convey ideas in this text?
- How do other texts and authors represent this idea?
- How might we rewrite this text to convey a different idea or representation?

Three Recommendations for the Future

1. Problematize and consider the use of texts in the classroom, including traditionally classroom, bureaucratic, and popular culture texts.
2. Help students to become researchers and analysts of language.
3. Convey respect for student resistance and configurations of nondominant cultures' literacy and language uses (adapted from Comber, 1993).

References

Alvermann, D. E., Moon, J. S., & Hagood, M. C. (1999). *Popular culture in the classroom: Teaching and researching critical media literacy.* Newark, DE: International Reading Association.

Alvermann, D. E., & Phelps, S. F. (1997). *Content reading and literacy: Succeeding in today's diverse classrooms.* Needham Heights, MA: Allyn & Bacon.

Bean, T. W. (2001). An update on Reading in the Content Areas. *Reading Online* [On-line]. Available: www.reading.org.

Cervetti, G., Damico, J. S., & Pardeles, M. J. (2001). A tale of differences: Comparing the traditions, perspectives, and educational goals of critical reading and critical literacy. *Reading Online* [On-line]. Available: http://www.reading.org

Comber, B. (1993). Classroom expectations in critical literacy. *Australian Journal of Language and Literacy, 16*(1), 90–102.

Cooney, DiSpezio, Foots, Matamoros, Nyquist, & Ostlund (2000). *Scott Foresman science.* Reading, MA: Addison-Wesley.

Fairclough, N. (1989). *Language and power.* White Plains, NY: Longman.

Freebody, P., & Luke, A. (1990). Literacies programs: Debates and demands in cultural context. *Prospect: Australian Journal of TESOL 5*(7), 7–16.

Gee, J. P. (1996). *Social linguistics and literacies: Ideology in discourses* (2nd ed.). Bristol, PA: Taylor & Francis.

Gilbert, P. (1993). (Sub)versions: Using sexist language practices to explore critical literacy. *Australian Journal of Language and Literacy, 16*(4), 75–83.

Lankshear, C., & Knobel, M. (2001, January). *Do we have your attention: Attention economies and multiliteracies.* Paper presented at the Symposium on Digital Technologies and Adolescents' Multiple Literacies, Athens, GA.

Lewis, C., & Fabos, B. (2000). But will it work in the heartland? A response and illustration. *Journal of Adolescent and Adult Literacy, 43,* 462–469.

Luke, A., & Freebody, P. (1999). Further notes on the four resources model. *Reading Online* [On-line]. Available: http://www.reading online.org/research/lukefreebody.htm.

Luke, A., & Luke, C. (2001). Adolescence lost/childhood regained: On early intervention and the emergence of the techno-subject. *Journal of Early Childhood Literacy, 1*(2), 91–120.

Moore, D. W., Bean, T. W., Birdyshaw, D., & Rycik, J. A. (1999, September). Adolescent literacy: A position statement. *Journal of Adolescent and Adult Literacy, 43,* 97–112.

New London Group (1999). A pedagogy of multiliteracies: Designing social futures. *Harvard Educational Review, 66*(1), 60–92.

Stevens, L. P. (2001). *South Park* and society: Instructional and curricular implications of popular culture in the classroom. *Journal of Adolescent and Adult Literacy, 44,* 548–555.

Strauss, S. L. (2001). Research news and comment: An open letter to Reid Lyon. *Educational Researcher, 30*(5), 26–33.

Tobin, J. (2000). *"Good guys don't wear hats": Children's talk about the media.* New York: Teachers College Press.

Part Four

Overcoming Comprehension Challenges

Chapter Fifteen

Hitting the Wall
Helping Struggling Readers Comprehend

D. Ray Reutzel,
Kay Camperell,
and John A. Smith

> *It's hard for me to sound it out, and then I don't know*
> *what it means.*
> CANDACE, GRADE 2, STRUGGLING READER

In this chapter we describe reasons why some students seem to hit a wall with reading comprehension. We begin by reviewing theory that stimulated comprehension research beginning in the late 1970s. Next, we highlight research related to comprehension problems that struggling readers face. We follow this with a discussion about some of the difficulties associated with preparing teachers to teach comprehension. We end with a summary of the instructional research on comprehension, focusing on three strategies teachers can use to help students who struggle with comprehending and learning from text.

Overview of Comprehension Theory and Research

Schema theories during the late 1970s and early 1980s (Anderson & Pearson, 1984) dominated comprehension theory and research. A *schema* refers to the knowledge readers have about a topic, event, or situation; and *schema theories* were efforts to show how prior knowledge provides a conceptual framework for comprehending texts. This research alerted teachers to the active and idiosyncratic nature of comprehension. Researchers demonstrated that the same text may be processed, interpreted, and remembered differently depending on readers' background knowledge and experience. Schema-based research and emerging theories of text-based processing at that time focused on the products of reading—how information is represented in memory and how that representation influences what readers remember after reading (Kintsch & van Dijk, 1978; van den Broek, Young, Tzeng, & Linderholm, 1999).

In the 1990s theory and research shifted to investigations about the cognitive processes that emerge during reading as a result of reader-text interactions. These theories present a dynamic view of comprehension in which readers actively use information from the text and from prior knowledge at multiple cognitive levels to build and maintain a coherent representation of meaning (Goldman & Rakestraw, 2000; Graesser, Millis, & Zwann, 1997; Kintsch, 1998). Text-driven processes operate on words, clauses, sentences, and paragraphs; knowledge-driven processes interact with text processes to transform ideas into meaning. Multiple schemas are involved in processing text information, each of which waxes and wanes as needed to help readers maintain a coherent representation (van den Broek et al., 1999; van den Broek & Kremer, 2000).

Sometimes comprehension processes are automatic, fluid, and unconscious; sometimes they are effortful, intentional, and conscious. This automaticity varies depending on textual density (for example, syntactic complexity) and on a reader's purpose(s) and knowledge. Due to the complexity of comprehension, there are many reasons why a reader may encounter difficulties. In this section we will briefly review three of them: (1) the influence of oral language and vocabulary development; (2) prior knowledge effects; and (3) the interactions among strategy development, motivation, and self-regulation.

Oral Language and Vocabulary Development

Comprehension processes emerge early in life as children learn to talk about their experiences, listen to stories, and experience the world. These early experiences provide the foundation for comprehension instruction. In most children, the cognitive and linguistic processes that foster success in learning to read are in place long before they enter school (Paris & Cunningham, 1996). Shared book reading with adult guidance has helped them acquire (1) concepts about the conventions of print, (2) phonemic awareness, (3) expressive and receptive language for talking about stories, (4) awareness of differences between spoken and written language, and (5) extensive vocabularies. These children live in print-rich homes where they learn the purposes and uses of literacy. They also learn ways of behaving and talking that are valued by and reflected in schools. Most children who struggle with comprehension have not had these experiences, and therefore, they have not acquired the expressive and receptive language skills that undergird comprehension. For these children, oral language deficits predict later reading comprehension difficulties (Scarborough, 2001).

Limited vocabulary knowledge is a major contributor to the oral language deficits that diminish young children's comprehension. For instance, researchers have reported differences of more than two thousand words between the vocabulary size of struggling young readers and their more successful peers. They have found similar differences in the vocabulary size of students attending schools in low-socioeconomic neighborhoods compared to those attending middle-class schools (Baker, Simmons, & Kameenui, 1998). Part of this problem is instructional. Teachers in low-socioeconomic schools focus more on word-level tasks and worksheet activities than do teachers in middle-class schools (Duke, 2001). Such practices compound the problems for struggling comprehenders.

Many researchers are now convinced that vocabulary growth comes from extensive experience reading and being read to (Nagy & Scott, 2000; Stahl, 1998). Some even argue that exposure to print influences vocabulary growth more than everyday oral language experiences (Stanovich, 2000). Print exposes students to more complex linguistic registers, new concepts for known words, new words, and ideas and experiences that are beyond the child's localized geographic, personal, and cultural context. Although many struggling readers eventually master decoding processes, their language deficits can reappear if (1) they do not know what words mean when they say or hear them, (2) they cannot parse syntactic structures or establish semantic (meaning) relationships among words, and (3) they lack inferential skills or have gaps in background knowledge. As these children leave the primary grades, negotiating the more complex syntax and abstract ideas in content-area textbooks presents new obstacles for them (Baker et al., 1998).

Background Knowledge Effects

Readers differ in the kinds of knowledge they have as well as in the depth and breadth of knowledge they bring to texts. Research in the 1980s revealed that what adults recalled was influenced by their knowledge about the topic of the texts they read (Voss, Vesonder, & Spilich, 1980), and similar research contrasting the recall of high- and low-knowledge students soon appeared. This research shows that prior knowledge influences what students attend to, what inferences they make, and what they remember after reading. Students with low topic knowledge answer fewer inferential questions and recall less information after reading compared to students with high topic knowledge (Lipson, 1983; Pearson, Hansen, & Gordon, 1979; Recht & Leslie, 1988). Students whose knowledge is simply different from that of most middle-class Americans also experience comprehension failures when teachers do not recognize how background knowledge affects comprehension.

Bransford and his colleagues were among the first to show that less successful readers with knowledge equivalent to that of successful peers often adopt a passive approach to learning and do not try to use what they already know to elaborate and connect ideas so that they make sense (Bransford et al., 1982; Pressley & Wharton-McDonald, 1997). Successful comprehenders, on the other hand, actively strive to use background knowledge to establish connections among ideas as they read (van den Broek & Kremer, 2000). They reread when they encounter confusion and elaborate on text information by drawing inferences, generating images, creating analogies, or asking and answering questions (Cote & Goldman, 1999; Pressley, 2000).

Finally, researchers also have found at least two circumstances in which prior knowledge can interfere with comprehension. First, when information is inconsistent with what young and poor comprehenders know or believe, they fail to detect inconsistencies. They distort the information to make it conform to what they already know, or they simply ignore it (Paris, Wasik, & Turner, 1991; Beck & McKeown, 2001). This causes students to misinterpret what they read, and it is a particular concern when the goal of instruction is for students to learn new information. Alvermann, Smith, and Readence (1985), for example, found that inaccurate prior knowledge (misconceptions) interfered with learning in science. Second, some poor readers overrely on background knowledge (Pressley, 2000). Good readers tend to make knowledge-based inferences that are directly related to what they are reading. In contrast, poor comprehenders frequently draw on unrelated prior knowledge, leading to unwarranted and unnecessary inferences and comprehension failures.

One of the major implications of this line of research is that teachers can improve the comprehension of struggling readers by helping them develop or activate prior knowledge before they read. Dole, Brown, and Trathen (1996) caution, however, that overreliance on such teacher-directed activities decreases student motivation and fails to help students acquire strategies that help them become independent, self-regulated readers.

Interactions Among Strategies, Motivation, and Self-Regulation

Pressley and Afflerbach (1995) found that skilled readers use a wide array of strategies suited to meeting their purposes for reading. One of the most frequently noted is use of text structure. Successful readers are aware of differences between narrative structures and expository structures, and they use this knowledge to guide and monitor their comprehension. Narratives or stories are assumed to be more easily understood because children are familiar with both their structure and content. Stories are organized into sequences of events in which the main characters pursue goals and overcome obstacles (Graesser, Golding, & Long, 1991; Mandler & Johnson, 1977). Comprehending stories involves understanding characters' motives and identifying a theme that relates to recurring experiences in people's lives. Many struggling comprehenders have problems following the structure of stories, understanding characters' motives, and identifying themes (Dole et al., 1996; Mastropieri & Scruggs, 1997; Williams, 1998). These difficulties have been demonstrated to frequently arise from limited experiences in hearing and talking about stories before children enter school. Similarly, children with learning disabilities may have problems following story sequences because they have less well-developed knowledge about human intentions and interactions (Dickson, Simmons, & Kameenui, 1998a). For example, Williams (1998) suggests that learning disabled students have particular problems learning in literature-based classrooms that emphasize personal interpretations and involve student-centered approaches to instruction. She argues that students with learning disabilities are not prepared to take advantage of such instruction. Because of this, they fail to develop important knowledge about recurring plots and themes in stories that they will encounter in more complex literature in later grades.

Expository texts present additional comprehension obstacles for struggling comprehenders. Expository genres are written to inform readers about new ideas and information, and the patterns in which authors organize their ideas (for example, cause and effect, comparison and contrast) differ depending on their purpose and content domain (Alexander & Jetton, 2000). As such, expository texts are presumed to be more difficult than narratives because both their structure and content are less familiar to students. Many young and poor readers fail to identify and follow the organizational structure and the explicit expository cues so that the tasks of identifying main ideas, distinguishing important from less important ideas, noting inconsistencies, recalling and summarizing information, and monitoring comprehension become extremely difficult. Because expository texts are the primary means for acquiring academic and schooled knowledge, students' failure to understand and learn from these texts can create a cumulative knowledge deficit as children progress through schools.

Pressley (2000) lists numerous strategies that skilled comprehenders use flexibly and efficiently. One, self-questioning, has received less attention than others in the instructional research but has been shown to distinguish effective readers and learners from less accomplished peers (Bransford et al., 1982; Cote & Goldman,

1999). Self-questioning stimulates students' use of prior knowledge to make facts and difficult text more comprehensible and memorable. Given the goal of learning new ideas through reading, good comprehenders also use self-questioning to draw on knowledge gained from other texts, generate explanations, and monitor comprehension. Another problem is that poor comprehenders' standards for maintaining connections among ideas are lower than those of good readers. Although they may ask themselves questions about something that they do not understand in a text, they do not employ strategies to help themselves find the answers to their own questions (Dickson, Simmons, & Kameenui, 1998a and 1998b; van den Broek & Kremer, 2000).

During the 1980s researchers discovered that students could be taught strategies but generally did not use them once instruction ended. Many researchers attributed this neglect to metacognitive deficits (Brown, Armbruster, & Baker, 1986). *Metacognition* refers to an awareness of and knowledge about strategies for planning, monitoring, and controlling one's own learning. Researchers designed comprehension instruction to develop struggling readers' abilities to monitor and evaluate their own performance (see Block & Pressley, 2002, for a review of these programs). The passivity of poor readers, however, still did not seem to be altered by instruction (Block, 2001). During the 1990s researchers turned to motivational constructs as another tool to expand struggling readers' metacognition.

A general consensus has emerged among psychologists and reading researchers that low-achieving students' beliefs about themselves as learners and their low expectations for success undermine their willingness to employ strategies, limit their desires to control their own meaning-making processes, and diminish their persistence when facing comprehension challenges (Paris & Cunningham, 1996; Paris & Paris, 2001; Paris et al., 1991). Attribution theory suggests that struggling comprehenders begin to perceive that their lack of success is due to innate ability, which they cannot change. Once they attribute their performance differences to ability, these students stop investing effort, believing that effort won't pay off. These attributions are perceptions shaped by classroom practices that emphasize performance outcomes instead of learning outcomes, competition instead of collaboration, and teacher control instead of student choice (Pressley & Mc-Cormick, 1995). These findings led to the increased emphasis we now see in comprehension research that encourages developing instruction that promotes engagement in learning and students' regulation of their own efforts (Guthrie et al., 1998).

Clearly, research has generated considerable knowledge of reading comprehension processes and instructional strategies in recent decades. But how effectively is this information being shared with preservice and inservice teachers? Does this information actually contribute to higher levels of student comprehension? The two introductory quotes in the next section come from research decades apart. They suggest that, to borrow an agricultural metaphor, "the water wasn't and still isn't getting to the end of the row."

How Well Are Teachers Prepared to Teach Comprehension to Struggling Readers?

Although the research we reviewed previously points to clear understandings about how educators can help struggling comprehenders, serious questions abound about teachers' knowledge of how to teach comprehension to struggling readers. These concerns are as current in 2000 as they were twenty years before; as the following quotes demonstrate: "Many of the procedures likely to improve comprehension and that are mentioned in all the reading methodology textbooks (and probably in all the reading methods courses) were never seen" in classroom observations (Durkin, 1978–1979, p. 526). "There is a need for greater emphasis in teacher education on the teaching of reading comprehension. Such instruction should begin at the preservice level, and it should be extensive, especially with respect to teaching teachers how to teach comprehension strategies" (National Reading Panel [NRP], 2000, pp. 29–41).

The recent emphasis on the need for increased accountability in education and particularly in reading achievement (Bush, 2000) has focused attention on teacher quality and especially on teacher education. Many voices in the popular media vilify the effectiveness of teacher education (Learning First Alliance/American Federation of Teachers, 1999; Finn & Petrilli, 2000), sometimes to serve a political agenda (Berliner & Biddle, 1995). As members of the National Reading Panel met with educators and interested citizens around the country, they found that preservice and inservice teacher education emerged as two of the most frequently mentioned areas of concern (NRP, 2000). Fortunately, recent research suggests that teacher education at both these levels does make a difference in teacher quality and student achievement. Darling-Hammond (2000) found that even after controlling for student socioeconomic status and language factors, teacher quality variables including teacher training had the largest effect on student achievement.

What About Teacher Education in Reading?

The knowledge base about preservice and inservice teacher education in reading is growing (Anders, Hoffman, & Duffy, 2000; International Reading Association [IRA], 1998; Lyons & Pinnell, 2001; NRP, 2000; Pearson, 2001; Roller, 2001; Snow, Burns, & Griffin, 1998) though more research is needed (Hoffman & Roller, 2001). This knowledge base provides direction for teacher preparation and inservice programs. For example, teachers need to know the psychology of reading and be able to teach the functions and uses of language. In addition, teachers must be familiar with the many pedagogies of reading including teaching about letter-sound associations, building students' word identification automaticity, exposing students to a variety of text structures, developing students' comprehension and metacognition strategies, cultivating students' interests in literacy, assessing students' instructional needs, providing interventions for children in need, and enlisting the cooperation of families and school and community resources (Snow et al., 1998). Anders, Hoffman, and Duffy (2000) provide a history of reading education research at both the preservice and inservice levels. They note that the best teachers are thoughtfully adaptive, and they wonder how teacher education can foster competent creative responsiveness rather than technical compliance. They conclude that reading teacher educators should be trying to develop teachers who can analyze reading instructional situations and thoughtfully construct appropriate responses.

The IRA publication *Standards for Reading Professionals* (1998) outlines what reading teachers should know and be able to do. The first part of the document, "Knowledge and Beliefs About Reading," points out the importance of teachers' familiarity with reading research, components of reading, influences of diversity, and the nature and causes of reading difficulty. The section titled "Instruction and Assessment" lists reading teacher competencies including using instructional technologies; creating a literate environment; involving parents as partners; teaching word identification, comprehension, writing skills, and strategies; and using multiple forms of assessment to monitor students' progress. The final section of the IRA standards document, "Organizing and Enhancing a Reading Program," focuses on teachers' planning and implementing instruction, communicating with parents and colleagues, and understanding the ethical responsibilities of teaching.

The NRP (2000) paid particular attention to the important connection between teacher education and reading comprehension instruction. In discussing the comprehension instruction research, the panel recommended against adopting instructional packages. Rather, the panel favored the use of flexible comprehension instruction using multiple strategies. Such instruction allows teachers to select which combinations of comprehension strategies they will teach based on the readers' instructional needs. Such instruction allows students to learn both comprehension strategies and content through focused but naturally flowing discussions. More specifically, the panel recommended reading comprehension instruction in which "Teachers help students by explaining fully what it is they are teaching: what to do, why, how, and when; by modeling their own thinking processes; by encouraging students to ask questions and discuss possible answers among themselves; and by keeping students engaged in their reading via providing tasks that demand active involvement" (NRP, 2000, pp. 29–41).

Just as research has demonstrated that teacher education positively influences student learning (Darling-Hammond, 2000), it is also showing that reading teacher education can be effective. The NRP (2000, pp. 29–41) reviewed studies on reading teacher education and found "overwhelmingly" that when comprehension strategies are effectively taught in teacher education settings, such instruction can have a direct positive effect on student learning.

What Problems Do We Face?

In spite of our growing research base, a number of obstacles delay its integration into instructional practice. Some of these have to do with the lingering lack of consensus on effective practices. Some have to do with the research base. Others have to do with problems inherent in teacher education.

Stanovich (2000), describing the fractious nature of the reading profession, argues that reading teacher educators are not using the research database to find common ground or unify the field. The reading wars continue despite increasing scientific knowledge about reading and increased calls for instructional balance. Stanovich points out that some prominent reading educators continue to promote views of the reading process that directly contradict research findings.

More specific to reading comprehension, a lack of consensus on what should constitute the canon of reading comprehension skills or strategies may be affecting the quality of reading comprehension instruction. Each reading methods textbook, teacher education course, and basal teacher's manual offers its own version of comprehension skills and strategies. Are predicting, clarifying, questioning, and summarizing (Palincsar & Brown, 1984) the most important comprehension skills? How about connections, inferences, and imagery (Keene & Zimmermann, 1997)? What about text structure, vocabulary, background knowledge, and metacognition (Block & Mangieri, 1996)? Is there an instructional sequence to these skills and strategies? Once researchers identify a scope of comprehension skills and strategies, how should teachers teach these? Is a direct explanation approach the best or should students learn reading comprehension interactively from each other during discussion groups? Clearly, practitioners need more focus. The NRP (2000) argues that although reading comprehension research has moved the field along in meaningful ways, we still lack a coherent or satisfactory model for effective comprehension instruction.

Another obstacle to effective teacher education in reading comprehension is the lack of a research base at the preservice level. Anders, Hoffman, and Duffy (2000) reviewed 140 studies of varying quality published between 1970 and 2000 and found that although teacher education research has not been a high priority historically, researchers are conducting an increasing number of studies employing diverse research methodologies. However, they concluded that we don't yet have a coherent research base for preservice teacher education programs. Similarly, the NRP found that there is not sufficient research to associate preservice teacher preparation and student reading achievement. The panel concluded that although inservice research linked improved teacher outcomes to greater student achievement, there is no such evidence for preservice programs.

Snow, Burns, and Griffin (1998) discussed a number of structural constraints to effective teacher education in reading. For example, teachers are generally tied to their classrooms and spend on average only three days per year in the formal study of curriculum and content. The average school district spends less than one-half of one percent of its budget on staff development (Darling-Hammond, 1996). Staff development activities are often one-shot presentations with little consistency of content or attention to the qualifications of the presenters. Other obstacles to effective teacher education include inadequate amounts of coursework devoted to reading instruction, lack of subject-matter integration across courses, programmatic inconsistencies across teacher education institutions, and the lack of teacher induction programs.

Finally, too many teachers are not being adequately prepared for the complexities of teaching reading comprehension effectively. Reading comprehension instruction has been neglected (Durkin, 1978–1979, 1981), and this has not changed in twenty years (Pressley, 1998). Teachers need to understand the reading comprehension research base and associated instructional models. They must be able to show students how to use multiple comprehension strategies flexibly and purposefully. This requires that teachers understand the comprehension strategies they are teaching the children and also the instructional methods that they can employ to achieve their goal. However, the NRP (2000) suggests that many teachers find this type of teaching to be challenging, probably because they have not been adequately prepared.

Recommendations

How can teacher education be structured to better facilitate teachers learning and providing effective reading comprehension instruction? The NRP (2000) suggests that we need more complete and coherent models of teacher education. Based on the obstacles that teacher educators face and the requirements of effective reading comprehension instruction, we would like to suggest that teacher educators need to develop clearer consensus on two points:

- The pedagogy of reading comprehension instruction
- How preservice and inservice teachers are to learn and implement this pedagogy

The content of teacher education in reading comprehension instruction must reflect comprehension's complexities. Rather than predisposing teachers to follow a manual or a rigid set of guidelines, teacher education must acquaint teachers with multiple comprehension strategies and then enable them to teach these strategies in combination, thoughtfully, selectively, and effectively based on students' needs. The NRP (2000, p. 4–47) suggests that the art of instruction involves "knowing *when* to apply *what* strategy with *which* particular student(s)."

Snow, Burns, and Griffin (1998) provide an important list of competencies for teachers who work specifically with struggling readers. These teachers must possess the instructional knowledge and skills of classroom teachers but also apply the specialized research and effective practices that address the specific population of students they teach. More specifically, Snow, Burns, and Griffin suggest that teachers of struggling readers need

- Ways to access and evaluate research pertaining to reading difficulties
- Knowledge of techniques for helping other educators prevent and treat reading difficulties
- Knowledge of techniques for helping parents promote literacy at home

The structure of both preservice and inservice teacher education programs also needs to be carefully considered. Teacher education coursework at both preservice and inservice levels must be closely tied to clinical experience. For example, preservice teachers may learn about reciprocal teaching (Palincsar & Brown, 1984) in a methods course, implement it in a practicum or student teaching classroom, and receive quick formative feedback. Snow, Burns, and Griffin (1998) argue that the most important component of preservice reading teacher preparation is a supervised clinical experience that provides ongoing guidance and feedback.

Teacher educators should also consider making greater use of case-based instruction (Snow et al., 1998). This instruction incorporates background information, lesson plans, students' reading scores and records, descriptions of interventions, and recordings of student participation into lessons that are provided for discussion and analysis in teacher education programs. The emphasis is on thoughtful observation, analysis, and intervention. Teachers who have experienced case-based education tend to be better at recognizing and solving instructional problems (Risko, 1996).

Finally, reading teacher education should resist the political pressures for quick-fix wide-scale instructional reform. Pearson (2001) suggests that the most effective teacher learning takes place in local school-based communities. Successful teacher education requires extensive support for an extended period of time (Lyons & Pinnell, 2001; NRP, 2000). Teachers who share instructional goals and methods and who collaboratively study and refine their practice demonstrate more substantial and continuous professional growth. We strongly encourage teachers to study and work together to develop appropriate solutions to instructional challenges.

We cannot overemphasize the importance of high quality comprehension teaching when it comes to helping struggling readers who have hit the wall in reading comprehension. Teachers must understand the theoretical underpinnings of comprehension processes, know the research on comprehension strategy instruction, and teach a variety of effective comprehension strategies in order to succeed in meeting the needs of readers who struggle with comprehending text. To this end, we next discuss recent research on comprehension instructional strategies and provide an in-depth treatment of three comprehension instructional strategies to help struggling readers get over the wall of comprehension.

Strategies for Helping Struggling Readers Comprehend

Comprehension instructional research has evolved through several generations of development and refinement since the 1970s. During the early 1970s, comprehension instruction was based primarily on asking children to answer teachers' questions at various levels of thinking, particularly higher levels of thinking: analysis, synthesis, and evaluation. In the early 1980s, comprehension research turned its focus on the development and validation of effective singular comprehension strategies intended to help students represent their understandings and react to text in ways that would result in improved long-term memory for text content. A substantial collection of singular comprehension strategies proved their worth during the early 1980s including these nine: (1) activating prior knowledge, (2) identifying main ideas, (3) identifying the source of information for answering questions, (4) constructing mental images, (5) analyzing the components of story structure and text structures, (6) questioning in a structured manner, (7) self-monitoring comprehension, (8) fixing up broken comprehension processes, and (9) summarizing.

From the mid- to late 1980s, comprehension instruction research focused on developing and validating the effectiveness of combinations of singular comprehension strategies woven together into comprehension instructional frameworks or repertoires; examples are K-W-L (Ogle, 1986), reciprocal teaching (Palincsar & Brown, 1984), and context-text-application (Wong & Au, 1985). Concurrent with the development and validation of comprehension instructional frameworks or repertoires of effective singular comprehension strategies, psychological and sociocultural theories of the comprehension process resulted in two major directions that greatly influenced the nature of comprehension instruction: (1) direct explanation approaches à la Roehler and Duffy (1984) and (2) conversation and literary response approaches à la Peterson and Eeds (1990) and book clubs à la Raphael and McMahon (1994).

During the past decade of the 1990s, Pressley and his colleagues carefully studied the nature of comprehension instruction in schools and classrooms where there was evidence of effective comprehension instruction (El-Dinary, Pressley, & Schuder, 1992; Gaskins, Anderson, Pressley, Cunicelli, & Satlow, 1993; Pressley, Gaskins, Wile, Cunicelli, & Sheridan, 1991). Across their several observations of effective classroom comprehension instruction, the researchers identified a limited repertoire of individual comprehension strategies. This limited repertoire or collection of individual comprehension strategies included (1) making predictions based on prior-knowledge activation, (2) generating questions, (3) seeking clarification when confused, (4) constructing mental images, (5) relating prior knowledge to text content, and (6) summarizing. According to Pressley and Wharton-McDonald (1997), these singular comprehension strategies when taught one at a time or together were often used as vehicles for directing talk about texts. As such, individual comprehension strategies were explicitly taught and then applied in various forms of response groups.

The combination of effective, individual comprehension instructional strategies into a comprehension instructional framework was to become known as transactional strategies instruction because students transacted with texts and with others about texts in discussion and dialogue. Studies of the effectiveness of this method across varying ages and abilities have demonstrated strikingly positive effects on students' comprehension (Anderson & Roit, 1993; Collins, 1991; Brown, Pressley, Van Meter, & Schuder, 1996). The NRP (2000) recommended two effective comprehension instructional types from their extensive review of the research literature: (1) direct explanation and (2) transactional strategies instruction.

In more recent reviews of comprehension instruction, Block and Pressley (2002) and Pressley (2000) indicate that comprehension is developed through several lower-order or word-level processes including decoding and vocabulary development. Above the word level, students need to relate text content to their prior knowledge and background experiences and learn to self-regulate the application of a collection of effective comprehension strategies such as those embodied in the transactional strategies instruction framework.

From these reviews, it appears that teachers must first determine the level at which students are struggling to comprehend text (Pressley, 2000; Simmons & Kameenui, 1998). If students are struggling with comprehension at the word level or below, then instructional interventions should focus on developing smooth, automatic decoding abilities along with an elaborated web of vocabulary concepts. However, if these lower-order comprehension processes are in place, then it appears that students who struggle with comprehension at levels above the word can benefit by (1) activating personal experience and background knowledge and connecting these to text content, (2) understanding how text is structured to facilitate remembering text ideas, and (3) self-regulating the selection and use of strategies for comprehending text.

To help struggling readers improve their comprehension, we describe three validated comprehension strategies appropriately taught in the context of real text discussions (that is, grand conversations, book clubs, and literature circles) that fit the general specifications associated with transactional strategies instruction: (1) elaborative interrogation (Menke & Pressley, 1994); (2) text organization instruction (Dickson et al., 1998a and 1998b); and (3) social and self-regulatory process instruction (Schunk & Zimmerman, 1997). Our focus here is on teaching struggling readers to comprehend expository text because many of them prefer information texts and view the act of reading as one of "work" to learn information rather than one of recreation to "enjoy" a story (Reutzel & Gali, 1998).

Strategy 1: Elaborative Interrogation

Elaborative interrogation is a questioning intervention using why questions to promote active processing of factual reading materials (Wood, Pressley, & Winne, 1990). Students are encouraged to activate their prior knowledge and experiences and use these to create relationships linking facts together from text. Facts linked together into a network of relationships improve students' understanding and memory for text information.

It is important to frame why questions so that students are oriented to activate prior knowledge supporting the facts they need to learn—otherwise such questions will not enhance comprehension and memory for text. We describe the elaborative interrogation strategy using a trade book titled *My Book of the Planets* (Krulik, 1991) in the following model lesson.

Lesson Using Elaborative Interrogation

PURPOSE FOR LEARNING THE STRATEGY

"This strategy will help you relate your own experiences and knowledge to the facts you read in books and other texts. By using this strategy, you will improve your understanding of and memory for the text."

OBJECTIVE

"Learn to respond to statements in text as if they were stated as why questions."

TEACHER EXPLANATION AND MODELING

"This strategy begins by reading a section of text. For example, in the book *My Book of the Planets* (Krulik, 1991) I begin by reading the title. I might ask myself, 'Why would someone write a book about the planets?' My answer might include such ideas as the author wanted to teach others and me about planets as compared with stars, or I might wonder if other planets can support life like on Earth, etc. Next, I read about the first planet, Mercury, in the book. 'Mercury is the planet closest to the sun. It is very hot and dry' (Krulik, 1991, p. 20). I might ask myself the why question "Why is Mercury so hot?" I read on, 'Because it is so close to the sun, Mercury takes the shortest amount of time of any of the planets to circle the sun.' I ask myself, 'Why is closeness to the sun related to a shorter time needed to circle the sun?'"

GUIDED APPLICATION

"Now let's try this strategy together. Mariann, come read this statement aloud for the class. After she has read this statement, I will make a why question from the statement. OK, read this statement."

Mariann reads, "Mercury is gray and covered with craters."

"My question is, 'Why would Mercury be gray and covered with craters?'" Teacher invites students to use their knowledge and background to answer this why question.

"Now let's reverse the roles. I will read aloud the next statement, and you make this statement into a why question. 'Some of Mercury's craters are bigger than the whole state of Texas!'"

Children raise their hands. Benji asks, "Why are the craters on Mercury so big?" Other children ask questions. A discussion ensues to potentially answer these why questions.

INDIVIDUAL APPLICATION

"Now I want you to read the rest of this book. When you get to the end of each page, pick one statement to write a why question about in your notebooks. Next see if you can answer the question from your own knowledge or experiences. If not, try using the book to answer your question. If neither source can answer your question, save it for our discussion of the book when we are all finished reading. Now go ahead and read. If you forget what I want you to do, look at this poster for step-by-step directions." The teacher displays the following poster at the front of the room:

USING THE ELABORATIVE INTERROGATION STRATEGY

- Read each page carefully.

- Stop at the end of each page and pick a statement.

- Write a why question in your reading notebook for the statement you pick.

- Think about an answer to the why question using your own knowledge and experiences.

- If you can, write an answer to your why question.

- Read the page again looking for an answer. Read on to another page to look for the answer.

- If you can, write an answer to your why question.

- If you can't write an answer to your why question, save it for our group discussion after reading.

ASSESSMENT

After the children read, the teacher leads a discussion in which children share their why questions and answers. The children hand in their reading notebooks with their why questions and answers. The teacher examines these notebooks to determine the success of using this strategy. Unanswered why questions can be placed into a question web (see Figure 15.1) for further reading and research. Children may use other trade books, reference books, and textbooks to answer the questions in this why question web.

PLANNED REVIEW

In about one week, the teacher should review the use of the elaborative interrogation strategy by using trade books or textbooks with other curricular subjects such as health, social studies, or math word problems.

Menke and Pressley (1994, p. 644) assert that "Answering why questions is as good as constructing images to boost memory for facts, providing the questions are well focused." The elaborative interrogation strategy has been validated to improve readers' comprehension of factual material among students ranging from elementary school ages to adult (Menke and Pressley, 1994). It is recommended that teachers use elaborative interrogation when they train struggling students to access relevant prior knowledge in situations where they typically do not do so spontaneously.

Strategy 2: Text Organization Instruction

Instruction in higher-level text organization not only enhances struggling readers' retention of major ideas in text but also improves their retention of lower-level story or text details (Williams,

Figure 15.1. Question Web for Elaborative Interrogation Lesson About Planets.

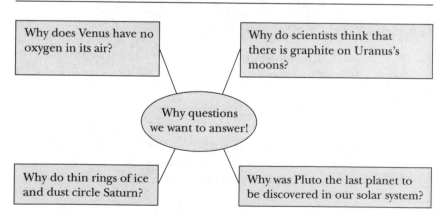

Brown, Silverstein, & deCani, 1994). This finding was true only for students with learning disabilities but was not true for students without learning disabilities.

Dickson et al. (1998a and 1998b) describe a six-principle instructional framework for effective text structure strategy instruction:

1. Big ideas: teaching features of text structure and presentation styles of print
2. Conspicuous strategies: teaching comprehension strategies explicitly
3. Mediated scaffolding: teaching content and comprehension tasks with support
4. Strategic integration: pulling together a collection of related strategies and applying these in natural and novel settings
5. Primed background knowledge: activating prior knowledge of content and text features
6. Judicious review cycles: closely spaced and shorter reviews

Lesson on Text Structure Using Graphic Organizers

PURPOSE FOR LEARNING THE STRATEGY

"This strategy will help you recognize the pattern(s) authors use to organize their ideas when they write stories, books, or other printed materials."

OBJECTIVE

"Learn to use the knowledge of text structures to organize study, note taking, and memory for reading a variety of texts."

TEACHER EXPLANATION AND MODELING

"When I read, I try to think about how the author has organized the information so that I can remember it better. In the book *My Book of the Planets* (Krulik, 1991), the author presents a list of planets in the solar system from the planet nearest the sun to the planet farthest from the sun. I also notice that the author writes a description of each planet with several interesting facts. So I have drawn a graphic organizer to show how this author has written the book. Look at what I have drawn up here on the board." The teacher indicates Figure 15.2. "By using this graphic organizer strategy for the text, I can read, take notes, and remember how this book works much better."

Figure 15.2. Using a Graphic Organizer to Determine Text Structure.

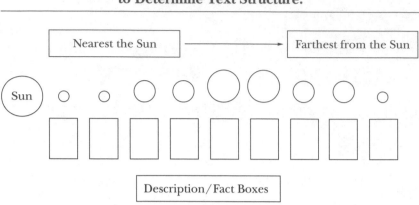

GUIDED APPLICATION

Ms. J.: "Let's look through our copies of the book to see if the graphic organizer on the board properly shows the order of the book's organization. What is the first planet that is closest to the sun?"

Chad: "Mercury."

Ms. J.: "Is that the planet shown first in the graphic organizer?"

Chad: "Yes."

Ms. J.: "Good. What is the second planet in the graphic organizer at the board?"

Chad: "Venus."

Ms. J.: "Is that the second planet in the book?"

Chad: "Yes."

Ms. J.: "Good. Now look through the rest of the book and check to see if the graphic organizer properly shows the author's organization."

INDIVIDUAL APPLICATION

"I am giving each of you a copy of the graphic organizer for *My Book of the Planets.* As you read about each planet, write down two to three facts about it in the descriptive box underneath each planet in the graphic organizer to help

you remember what you have read. Please notice that the author has organized the book to be a collection or list of descriptions about each planet."

ASSESSMENT

The teacher asks students to turn in their completed graphic organizers,
checking to see what they have done and how they have used the organizer.
The teacher may want to give students a blank organizer to fill in after the discussion of the book. This will help them to see how this strategy creates a mental organizer for the book's structure and the facts about each planet.

PLANNED REVIEW

About one week after this lesson, the teacher should plan to review the use of
the text structure – graphic organizer strategy by using trade books or textbooks with other curricular subjects such as health, social studies, or math.

Strategy 3: Promoting Self-Efficacy and Self-Regulation

A sense of personal or self-efficacy in learning and using comprehension strategies plays a key role in struggling readers' development of competence and confidence. *Self-efficacy* denotes one's
beliefs about his or her own capabilities to learn or to perform a
given task at specified or designated levels of proficiency (Bandura,
1986; Paris & Winograd, 2001; Schunk & Zimmerman, 1997).
Previous research has clearly demonstrated links among learners' sense of self-efficacy, motivation, and self-regulatory processes
(Schunk, 1996). Self-efficacy has been shown to influence task
choice, effort, persistence, and ultimate achievement. Effective
comprehension strategy instruction requires that students develop
a sense of self-efficacy as well as self-regulating behaviors and dispositions. Typically, a student's development of self-efficacy moves
from socially regulated processes to self-regulated processes.

To facilitate this shift from socially controlled processes in comprehending text to self-regulated text comprehension processes,
Schunk and Zimmerman (1997) describe a three-phase instructional sequence: (1) observing social models, (2) participating in
goal setting, and (3) engaging in self-evaluation. Modeling serves
the functions of facilitating comprehension strategy use and provides opportunities for observational learning. Schunk & Zimmerman assert that the more alike models are to observers, the greater

the likelihood that observers will see the actions modeled as possible and appropriate, leading to the desired results.

Goals motivate students to persist in a task, focus on learning the features of a task, and exert extra effort to learn strategies that will help them (Meece, 1991). Meece found that those goals, which are achieved in the short term typically, result in greater motivation and a heightened sense of self-efficacy. Goals that focus on moderately difficult tasks increase motivation by conveying a clear sense of progress coupled with a genuine sense of achievement. The focus of goals, learning versus performance, may affect the goal attainment (Meece, 1991). And feedback on goal progress is also important for students to develop self-regulating behaviors.

Self-evaluation is critical in developing a sense of self-efficacy and promoting self-regulated behaviors. Positive self-evaluations help students feel efficacious in their efforts and promote increased motivation and commitment to learning. Negative self-evaluations do not diminish the feelings of efficacy for students if they believe they are capable of achieving the goal but that their current approach is ineffective. Negative self-evaluations often lead students to work harder, persist longer, modify their strategy selection and use, or seek needed assistance from peers or teachers. We depict in Figure 15.3 a five-step process that incorporates the three instructional components we have discussed to help struggling readers shift their comprehension behaviors from the socially controlled to the self-regulated.

Three Recommendations for the Future

In conclusion, we propose the following three steps to improve comprehension instruction for those students who have hit the wall of reading comprehension.

RECOMMENDATION 1: We need more research concerning the development of comprehension abilities in young children because this maturity predicts later comprehension achievement.

One useful line of research has been developed by Duke (2000) that provides information about kindergartners' ability to differ-

**Figure 15.3. Five-Step Instructional Process
to Promote Self-Efficacy and Self-Regulation.**

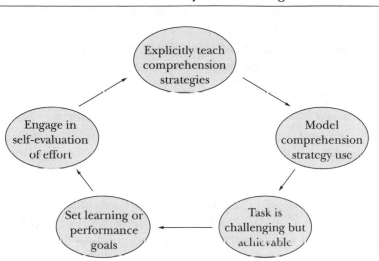

entiate between features of spoken and written language and between different types of text genres (Duke & Kays, 1998). Duke's
research has shown that young children can comprehend expository texts. Reading these types of books to young children with
oral language deficits is one way we can enhance their vocabulary
knowledge, familiarity with more complex syntactic structures,
and background knowledge. Another innovative line of research
by van den Broek (2001) suggests that preschoolers' comprehension of television programs is a better predictor of later comprehension ability than are their basic word analysis skills. He suggests
that explicit comprehension instruction using a variety of media
may help young children with language deficits and that we need
to find ways to help parents foster the comprehension abilities of
their young children.

RECOMMENDATION 2: The teacher education community needs to
    pursue a more aggressive reading teacher education research
    agenda.

We need to identify the most effective models of conveying to teachers the complex content and pedagogy associated with comprehension instruction. Hoffman and Roller (2001) argue that reading educators have been professionally negligent because they have not been systematically collecting data on the effectiveness of their efforts. Without such data, they have no basis for deciding how to make improvements in education programs for reading teachers.

Reading educators face the challenge of developing consistent research-based reading comprehension and teacher education pedagogies while simultaneously preparing teachers to thoughtfully adapt pedagogy to meet the instructional needs of a wide variety of readers. Strengthening the link between classroom learning and supervised implementation and increasing the use of reading instruction case studies in teacher education will prepare knowledgeable strategic teachers who will help develop successful strategic readers.

Recommendation 3: We need to develop comprehension instruction that provides greater depth and breadth than presently occurs in elementary schools.

Attention to word-level processes in the early years is a necessary but insufficient precondition to promote well-articulated comprehension strategy selection and use in the later school years. Pressley (2000) asserts that if comprehension instruction were to be transformed so that children were taught the skills and knowledge associated with transactional strategies instruction in addition to word-level comprehension process instruction, children's comprehension would be better. We agree with Pressley that this is truly "a hypothesis worth testing" (p. 557).

References

Alexander, P. A., & Jetton, T. L. (2000). Learning from text: A multidimensional perspective. In M. L. Kamil, P. B. Mosenthal, P. D. Pearson, & R. Barr (Eds.), *Handbook of reading research* (Vol. 3, pp. 285–310). Hillsdale, NJ: Erlbaum.

Alvermann, D., Smith., L., & Readence, J. (1985). Prior knowledge activation and the comprehension of compatible and incompatible text. *Reading Research Quarterly, 20,* 430–436.

Anders, P. L., Hoffman, J. V., & Duffy, G. G. (2000). Teaching teachers to teach reading: Paradigm shifts, persistent problems, and challenges. In M. L. Kamil, P. B. Mosenthal, P. D. Pearson, & R. Barr (Eds.), *Handbook of reading research* (Vol. 3, pp. 719–742). Hillsdale, NJ: Erlbaum.

Anderson, R. C., & Pearson, P. D. (1984). A schema-theoretic view of basic processes in reading. In P. D. Pearson (Ed.), *Handbook of reading research* (pp. 255–292). Hillsdale, NJ: Erlbaum.

Anderson, V., & Roit, M. (1993). Planning and implementing collaborative strategy instruction for delayed readers in grades 6–10. *Elementary School Journal, 94,* 121–137.

Baker, S., Simmons, D., & Kameenui, E. J. (1998). Vocabulary acquisition: Instructional and curricular basics and implications. In D. C. Simmons & E. J. Kameenui (Eds.), *What reading research tells us about children with diverse learning needs: Bases and basics* (pp. 219–238). Hillsdale, NJ: Erlbaum.

Bandura, A. (1986). *Social foundations of thought and action: A social cognitive theory.* Englewood Cliffs, NJ: Prentice Hall.

Beck, I. L., & McKeown, M. G. (2001). Text talk: Capturing the benefits of read-aloud experiences for young children. *Reading Teacher, 55,* 10–20.

Berliner, D., & Biddle, B. (1995). *The manufactured crisis: Myths, fraud, and the attack on America's public schools.* Reading, MA: Addison-Wesley.

Block, C. C. (1993). Strategy instruction in a literature based program. *The Elementary School Journal, 92,* 123–132.

Block, C. C. (2001). A case of exemplary classroom instruction: especially for students who come to school without the precursors for literary success. *National Reading Conference Yearbook, 49,* 421–439.

Block, C. C., & Mangieri, J. (1995–1996). *Reason to read volumes 1 & 2.* Boston: Addison-Wesley.

Block, C. C., & Mangieri, J. (1996). *Reason to read volume 3.* Boston: Addison-Wesley.

Block, C. C., & Pressley, M. (2002). *Comprehension instruction: Research based best practices.* New York: Guilford Press.

Bransford, J., Stein, B., Vye, N., Franks, J., Auble, P., Mezynski, K., & Pefetto, G. (1982). Differences in approaches to learning: An overview. *Journal of Experimental Psychology, 111,* 390–398.

Brown, A. L., Armbruster, B. B., & Baker, L. (1986). The role of metacognition in reading and studying. In J. Oransanu (Ed.), *Reading*

   comprehension: From research to practice (pp. 49–76). Hillsdale, NJ:
   Erlbaum.

Brown, R., Pressley, M., Van Meter, P., & Schuder, T. (1996). A quasi-
   experimental validation of transactional strategies instruction with
   low-achieving second-grade readers. Journal of Educational Psychology, 88, 18–37.

Bush, G. W. (2000). No child left behind [On-line]. Available: edworkforce
   .house.gov/press/press107/NoChildLeftBehind.pdf

Collins, C. (1991). Reading instruction that increases thinking abilities.
   Journal of Reading, 34, 510–516.

Cote, N., & Goldman, S. (1999). Building representations of informational text: Evidence from children's think-aloud protocols. In
   H. Van Oostendorp & S. Goldman (Eds.), The construction of mental
   representations during reading (pp. 169–193). Hillsdale, NJ: Erlbaum.

Darling-Hammond, L. (1996). The quiet revolution: Rethinking teacher
   development. Educational Leadership, 53(6), 4–10.

Darling-Hammond, L. (2000). Solving the dilemmas of teacher supply, demand, and standards: How can we ensure a competent, caring, and quali-
   fied teacher for every child? National Commission on Teaching and
   America's Future. New York: Teachers College Press.

Dickson, S. V., Simmons, D. C., & Kameenui, E. J. (1998a). Text organization: Instructional and curricular basics and implications. In
   D. C. Simmons & E. J. Kameenui (Eds.), What reading research tells us
   about children with diverse learning needs: Bases and basics. Hillsdale,
   NJ: Erlbaum.

Dickson, S. V., Simmons, D. C., & Kameenui, E. J. (1998b). Text organi-
   zation: Research bases. In D. C. Simmons & E. J. Kameenui (Eds.),
   What reading research tells us about children with diverse learning needs:
   Bases and basics (pp. 239–278). Hillsdale, NJ: Erlbaum.

Dole, J. A., Brown, K. J., & Trathen, W. (1996). The effects of strategy instruction on the comprehension performance of at-risk students.
   Reading Research Quarterly, 31, 62–88.

Duke, N. K., & Kays, J. (1998). "Can I say 'Once upon a time'?": Kindergarten children developing knowledge of information book language. Early Childhood Research Quarterly, 13, 295–318.

Durkin, D. (1978–1979). What classroom observations reveal about reading comprehension. Reading Research Quarterly, 15, 481–533.

Durkin, D. (1981). Reading comprehension instruction in five basal
   reading series. Reading Research Quarterly, 16, 515–544.

El-Dinary, P. B., Pressley, M., & Schuder, T. (1992). Becoming a strategies
   teacher: An observational and interview study of three teachers
   learning transactional strategies instruction. In C. Kinzer & D. Leu

(Eds.), *Cognitive strategy research: Educational applications* (pp. 133–156). New York: Springer-Verlag.

Finn, C. E., & Petrilli, M. J. (2000). *The state of state standards, 2000: English, history, mathematics, science* [On-line]. Available: www.ed excellence.net/library/soss2000/2000soss.html

Gaskins, I. W., Anderson, R. C., Pressley, M., Cunicelli, E. A., & Satlow, E. (1993). Six teachers' dialogue during cognitive process instruction. *Elementary School Journal, 93,* 277–304.

Goldman, S., & Rakestraw, J. (2000). Structural aspects of constructing meaning from text. In M. L. Kamil, P. B. Mosenthal, P. D. Pearson, & R. Barr (Eds.), *Handbook of reading research* (Vol. 3, pp. 311–335). Hillsdale, NJ: Erlbaum.

Graesser, A., Golding, J., & Long, D. (1991). Narrative representation and comprehension. In R. Barr, M. L. Kamil, P. Mosenthal, and P. D. Pearson (Eds.), *Handbook of reading research* (Vol. 2, pp. 171–205). New York: Longman.

Graesser, A. C., Millis, K. K., & Zwaan, R. A. (1997). Discourse comprehension. *Annual Review of Psychology, 48,* 163–189.

Guthrie, J., Van Meter, P., Hancock, G., Alao, S., Anderson, E., & McCann, A. (1998). Does concept-oriented reading instruction increase strategy use and conceptual learning from text? *Journal of Educational Psychology, 90,* 261–278.

Hoffman, J. V., & Roller, C. M. (2001). The IRA Excellence in Reading Teacher Preparation Commission's report: Current practices in reading teacher education at the undergraduate level in the United States. In C. M. Roller (Ed.), *Learning to teach reading.* Newark, DE: International Reading Association.

International Reading Association (IRA). (1998). *Standards for reading professionals, revised.* Newark, DE: Author.

Keene, E. O., & Zimmermann, S. (1997). *Mosaic of thought: Teaching comprehension in a reader's workshop.* Portsmouth, NH: Heinemann.

Kintsch, W. (1998). *Comprehension: A paradigm for cognition.* Cambridge: Cambridge University Press.

Kintsch, W., & van Dijk, T. (1978). Toward a model of discourse comprehension and production. *Psychological Review, 85,* 363–394.

Krulik, S. (1991). *My Book of the Planets.* New York: Simon & Schuster.

Learning First Alliance/American Federation of Teachers. (1999). *Teaching reading is rocket science: What expert teachers of reading should know and be able to do.* Washington, DC: Learning First Alliance.

Lipson, M. Y. (1983). Learning new information from text: The role of prior knowledge and reading ability. *Journal of Reading Behavior, 14,* 243–261.

350   IMPROVING COMPREHENSION INSTRUCTION

Lyons, C. A., & Pinnell, G. S. (2001). *Systems for change in literacy education: A guide to professional development.* Portsmouth, NH: Heinemann.

Mandler, J. M., & Johnson, N. S. (1977). Remembrance of things parsed: Story structure and recall. *Cognitive Psychology, 9,* 111–151.

Mastropieri, M., & Scruggs, T. (1997). Best practices in promoting reading comprehension in students with learning disabilities: 1976 to 1996. *Remedial and Special Education, 18,* 197–213.

Meece, J. L. (1991). The classroom context and students' motivational goals. In M. L. Maehr & P. R. Pintrich (Eds.), *Advances in motivation and achievement* (Vol. 7, pp. 261–285). Greenwich, CT: JAI Press.

Menke, D. J., & Pressley, M. (1994). Elaborative interrogation: Using "why" questions to enhance learning from text. *Journal of Reading, 37,* 642–645.

Nagy, W., & Scott, J. (2000). Vocabulary processes. In M. L. Kamil, P. B. Mosenthal, P. D. Pearson, & R. Barr (Eds.), *Handbook of reading research* (Vol. 3, pp. 269–284). Hillsdale, NJ: Erlbaum.

National Reading Panel (NRP). (2000). *Teaching children to read: An evidence-based assessment of the scientific research literature on reading and its implications for reading instruction.* Washington, DC: National Institute of Child Health and Human Development and U.S. Department of Education.

Ogle, D. M. (1986). K-W-L: A teaching model that develops active reading of expository text. *Reading Teacher, 39,* 564–570.

Palincsar, A. M., & Brown, A. L. (1984). Reciprocal teaching of comprehension-fostering and monitoring activities. *Cognition and Instruction, 1,* 117–175.

Paris, S. G., & Cunningham, A. (1996). Children becoming students. In D. C. Berliner & R. C. Calfee (Eds.), *Handbook of educational psychology* (pp. 117–147). Old Tappan, NJ: Macmillan.

Paris, S. G., & Paris, A. H. (2001). Classroom applications of research on self-regulated learning. *Educational Psychologist, 36,* 89–101.

Paris, S. G., Wasik, B., & Turner, J. C. (1991). The development of strategic readers. In R. Barr, M. L. Kamil, P. Mosenthal, & P. D. Pearson (Eds.), *Handbook of reading research* (Vol. 2, pp. 641–668). White Plains, NY: Longman.

Paris, S. G., & Winograd, P. (2001). *The role of self-regulated learning in contextual teaching: Principles and practices for teacher preparation.* Ann Arbor, MI: Center for the Improvement of Early Reading Achievement.

Pearson, P. D. (2001). Learning to teach reading: The status of the knowledge base. In C. M. Roller (Ed.), *Learning to teach reading.* Newark, DE: International Reading Association.

Pearson, P. D., Hansen, J., & Gordon, C. (1979). The effect of background knowledge on young children's comprehension of explicit and implicit information. *Journal of Reading Behavior, 11,* 201–209

Peterson, R., & Eeds, M. (1990). Grand conversations: Literature groups in action. New York: Scholastic.

Pressley, M. (1998). *Reading instruction that works: The case for balanced teaching.* New York: Guilford Press.

Pressley, M. (2000). What should comprehension instruction be the instruction of? In M. Kamil, P. Mosenthal, P. D. Pearson, & R. Barr (Eds.), *Handbook of reading research* (Vol. 3, pp. 545–562). Hillsdale, NJ: Erlbaum.

Pressley, M., & Afflerbach, P. (1995). *Verbal protocols of reading: The nature of constructively responsive reading.* Hillsdale, NJ: Erlbaum.

Pressley, M., Gaskins, I. W., Wile, D., Cunicelli, E. A., & Sheridan, J. (1991). Teaching literacy strategies across the curriculum: A case study at Benchmark School. In J. Zutell & S. McCormick (Eds.), *Learner factors/teacher factors: Issues in literacy research and instruction: Fortieth yearbook of the National Reading Conference* (pp. 219–228). Chicago: National Reading Conference.

Pressley, M., & McCormick, C. (1995). *Advanced educational psychology for educators, researchers, and policymakers.* New York: HarperCollins.

Pressley, M., & Wharton-McDonald, R. (1997). Skilled comprehension and its development through instruction. *School Psychology Review, 26*(3), 448–66.

Raphael, T. E., & McMahon, S. I. (1994). Book club: An alternative framework for reading instruction. *Reading Teacher, 48,* 102–116.

Recht, D. R., & Leslie, D. (1988). Effects of prior knowledge of good and poor readers' memory of text. *Journal of Educational Psychology, 80,* 16–20.

Reutzel, D. R., & Gali, K. (1998). The art of children's book selection: A labyrinth unexplored. *Reading Psychology, 19*(1), 3–50.

Risko, V. (1996). Creating a community of thinkers within a pre-service literacy education methods course. In K. Camperell, B. Hayes, & R. Telfer (Eds.), *Literacy: The Information Superhighway to Success* (pp. 3–15). Logan: Utah State University Press.

Roehler, L. R., & Duffy, G. G. (1984). Direct explanation of comprehension processes. In G. G. Duffy, L. R. Roehler, & J. Mason (Eds.), *Comprehension instruction: Perspectives and suggestions* (pp. 265–280). White Plains, NY: Longman.

Roller, C. M. (2001). *Learning to teach reading.* Newark, DE: International Reading Association.

Scarborough, H. (2001). Connecting early language and literacy to later reading (dis)abilities: Evidence, theory, and practice. In S. B. Neuman & D. K. Dickinson (Eds.), *Handbook of early literacy research* (pp. 97–110). New York: Guilford Press.

Schunk, D. H. (1996). Goal and self-evaluative influences during children's cognitive skill learning. *American Educational Research Journal, 33*, 359–82.

Schunk, D. H., & Zimmerman, B. J. (1997). Developing self-efficacious readers and writers: The role of social and self-regulatory processes. In J. T. Guthrie & A. Wigfield (Eds.), *Reading engagement: Motivating readers through integrated instruction* (pp. 34–50). Newark, DE: International Reading Association.

Simmons, D. C., & Kameenui, E. J. (Eds.). (1998). *What reading research tells us about children with diverse learning needs: Bases and basics.* Hillsdale, NJ: Erlbaum.

Snow, C. E., Burns, M. N., & Griffin, P. (1998). *Preventing reading difficulties in young children.* Washington, DC: National Academy Press.

Stahl, S. (1998). Four questions about vocabulary knowledge and reading and some answers. In C. Hynd, S. Stahl, M. Carr, & S. Glynn (Eds.), *Learning from text across conceptual domains* (pp. 73–94). Hillsdale, NJ: Erlbaum.

Stanovich, K. (2000). *Progress in understanding reading: Scientific foundations and new frontiers.* New York: Guilford Press.

van den Broek, P. (2001). *Fostering comprehension skills in preschool children* [On-line]. Available: http://www.ciera.org/ciera/information/presentations

van den Broek, P., & Kremer, K. E. (2000). The mind in action: What it means to comprehend during reading. In B. M. Taylor, M. F. Graves, & P. van den Broek (Eds.), *Reading for meaning: Fostering comprehension in the middle grades* (pp. 1–31). New York: Teachers College Press.

van den Broek, P., Young, M., Tzeng, Y., & Linderholm, T. (1999). The landscape model of reading: Inferences and online construction of memory representation. In H. Van Oostendorp & S. Goldman (Eds.), *The construction of mental representations during reading* (pp. 99–122). Hillsdale, NJ: Erlbaum.

Voss, J. F., Vesonder, G., & Spilich, G. (1980). Generation and recall by high knowledge and low knowledge individuals. *Journal of Verbal Learning and Verbal Behavior, 19*, 619–667.

Williams, J. P. (1998). Improving the comprehension of disabled readers. *Annals of Dyslexia, 48*, 213–238.

Williams, J. P., Brown, L. G., Silverstein, A. K., & deCani, J. S. (1994). An instructional program in comprehension of narrative themes for adolescents with learning disabilities. *Learning Disability Quarterly, 17,* 205–221.

Wong, J. W., & Au, K. H. (1985). The concept-text-application approach: Helping elementary students comprehend expository text. *Reading Teacher, 38,* 612–618.

Wood, E., Pressley, M., & Winne, P. H. (1990). Elaborative interrogation effects on children's learning of factual content. *Journal of Educational Psychology, 82,* 741–748.

Chapter Sixteen

At-Risk Students

Learning to Break Through Comprehension Barriers

Lynn Romeo

"Comprehension instruction can be enhanced by long-term instruction that fosters development of the skills and knowledge articulated by very good readers as they read" (Pressley, 2000, p. 557). However, although teachers have reported that they teach comprehension strategies (Rankin-Erickson & Pressley, 2000), very little comprehension instruction goes on (Wendler, Samuels, & Moore, 1989; Lloyd, 1995). Sometimes teachers tell students to use strategies but do not encourage their self-regulated use (Pressley, Wharton-McDonald, Hampston, & Echevarria, 1998). Not much has changed since Durkin's study (1978–1979). The lack of strategy instruction has implications for the comprehension development of all students but especially for those that are identified as being at risk. The purpose of this chapter is to address the special comprehension needs of this population.

This chapter is divided into three sections. The first section provides a brief review of the research on reading strategy instruction. The second describes a new comprehension strategy designed especially for students who are experiencing difficulties in reading. The third gives suggestions about the direction that teacher educators and teachers should take in the future in regards to the comprehension instruction of at-risk students.

Review of Research

Teaching Individual Strategies

Since the 1980s comprehension instruction has evolved. Initially, researchers studied individual strategies such as identifying the elements of a story (Beck, Omanson, & McKeown, 1982; Idol & Croll, 1987; Nolte & Singer, 1985; Short & Ryan, 1984).

Beck and colleagues (1982) revised basal stories to make salient the basic story elements. Both skilled and nonskilled readers' comprehension improved when they did so. These readers recalled more information from the stories and were able to respond to more questions. Very shortly after that study, researchers were evaluating much more complex interventions.

For example, researchers asked fourth-grade students to ask themselves questions about story grammar as they read (Short & Ryan, 1984): who, where, when, what, and how. The questions were: Who was the main character? Where and when did the story take place? What did the main characters do? How did the story end, and how did the main characters feel? Students trained in story grammar recalled more information from the stories than the control group of students. Further, as in the Beck study (1982), the poorer readers in the experimental groups performed as well as the skilled readers in the control groups. Similar results were produced by Carnine and Kinder (1985) in elementary special education classrooms.

Nolte and Singer (1985) asked teachers of students ages nine and ten to discuss story elements and the importance of asking appropriate questions. After teacher modeling and guided practice, students read silently and asked themselves questions. The teacher continued scaffolding until the students were able to generate their own questions while working in groups and independently. Students trained in self-questioning outperformed the control students both during the training and on a new passage given after the training.

In Idol and Croll (1987), the comprehension of both regular education students and students with learning disabilities ages nine to twelve improved when they were directly taught to develop a story map, including story grammar elements. Students taking part in the experiment were better able to answer questions and analyze narrative text setting, characters, problems, events, and resolutions of problems.

Gurney, Gersten, Dimino, and Carnine (1990), investigated the use of story grammar with high school students who had learning disabilities. The scaffolded instruction included modeling, guided, and independent practice. The students were asked questions following the lessons. Similar to other studies cited, the learning disabled students' comprehension improved when their teacher directly taught them the components of story grammar. Teaching weak readers to attend to story grammar elements is very defensible based on research.

Imagery, another individual strategy that has been effectively used to increase comprehension (Gambrell & Bales, 1986; Gambrell & Javitz, 1993; Pressley, 1976; Sadowski & Paivio, 1994) is grounded in the work of cognitive psychologist Paivio (1971). Pressley (1976), for example, gave eight-year-olds practice at forming images and then provided feedback using examples of good images. Both the treatment group and the controls then read a story. The children trained in imagery performed significantly better on questions about the story than did the controls.

In Gambrell and Bales (1986), fourth- and fifth-grade poor readers were tested after reading two passages, both of which included inconsistent statements. The experimental subjects had received a thirty-minute training session the previous day during which they were instructed to make pictures in their minds as they read. These imagery condition participants did not outperform control subjects in detecting inconsistencies in text.

In Gambrell and Javitz (1993), fourth-grade students, after reading a story silently, were asked to write a story for a friend who had never read the text. The stories were rated for story elements and number of propositions. In addition to this control group, another group of students was instructed to attend to the text illustrations and make images. A third group, who read a text without illustrations, was asked to construct images representing what happened in the story. A fourth group was asked to look at the illustrations while reading. The imagery-illustration group's comprehension was significantly superior to that of the other groups.

In addition, the recall of story elements was higher for those in the imagery-only group than for those in either the illustration-only or the control group.

Williams, Konopak, Wood, and Avett (1992) used direct instruction and guided practice to teach imagery techniques to sixth-grade students who then read content texts over a two-day period. The experimental students outperformed the controls on a social studies posttest recall of ideas, but there was no significant difference in groups when tested in science. Mental imagery can help less skilled readers enhance reading comprehension.

Teaching Repertoires of Strategies

Current comprehension instruction is grounded in the work of Roehler and Duffy (1984), who developed a model that centered on teacher modeling and elaboration of strategies, with constant scaffolding by way of prompts during guided, peer, and independent practice. Duffy and colleagues (1987) conducted a yearlong study with twenty third-grade teachers and their students in a midwestern urban district. The teachers in the treatment group were taught how to make appropriate decisions about how and when to use strategies in their reading and to model such reasoning for their students. Treatment group teachers learned how to teach students to be strategic. In particular, weaker readers taught by these teachers learned how to self-regulate their reading and scored better in reading achievement.

Pressley and his colleagues (1992) then developed transactional strategy instruction, which was grounded in the Roehler and Duffy model (1984). In addition to the teacher modeling, explanation, coaching, and scaffolding, the transactional approach emphasizes engaging students in interpretive discussions about texts (Pressley, 2000; Van den Branden, 2000) rather than teacher-led questioning and assessment. During these discussions students made predictions and related ideas in the story to background knowledge as they self-questioned, imaged, clarified, summarized, and interpreted (Pressley, 2002). Transactional strategy instruction takes place over months to years of teaching (Pressley, 2000). For example, Brown, Pressley, Van Meter, and Schuder (1996) spent a year studying the use of transactional strategy instruction in five second-grade classrooms. At the end of the treatment, weak readers in the experimental classrooms outperformed the control classroom's weak readers in reading comprehension, made better interpretations of what they read, and learned more content information during their daily lessons.

Collins (1991) taught sixth- and seventh-grade middle school students to use reading strategies three days per week over a three-month period. Her approach was consistent with both the direct explanation model and transactional strategies instruction. She taught students to clarify information, recognize patterns, use backward reasoning and visualization, employ metacognitive skills by comparing themselves to famous people born on their birthdays, summarize information by reordering parts of the text, and work in groups and alone to reason about and interpret text. Students in the experimental group scored significantly higher than control subjects in comprehension.

Anderson (1992) studied small group instruction of students in sixth- to tenth-grade classrooms. The students' reading levels were grade four and below. Teachers implemented transactional strategy instruction using informational texts. The experimental subjects made greater gains in reading achievement than did the control groups and learned to discuss effectively the use of strategies to comprehend content information as well as to self-evaluate their learning.

A New Method of Strategy Instruction for At-Risk Students

Sensory Imaging Strategy (SIS)

Sensory imaging strategy (SIS), a multisensory comprehension strategy that combines imagery with story elements, is directly inspired by the work of Gambrell and Block (2001) as well as by transactional strategies instruction.

Gambrell and Koskinen (2001) recommended that teachers can assist students to develop the ability to form images as a component of a model that promotes active, self-regulated learning (Pressley, 2000). Teacher explanation, modeling, scaffolding, and student self-regulation are emphasized, especially for students who are experiencing difficulty with learning to read. Gambrell and Koskinen, (2001) suggested the use of texts that evoke images during the read alouds of both narrative and expository texts. Teachers should stop during read alouds and guided reading to ask students to share their images about story events. With practice, students can learn to use imaging as an independent listening and reading strategy.

Block (in press) teaches students to paint pictures in their minds by first reading nouns that can evoke images and describing them to a peer. Then the students read a paragraph and compare and contrast the images that they formed. She also developed the read, cover, and close technique in which students are taught to look away from the text toward the ceiling when developing images.

The sensory imaging strategy employs a mnemonic picture, SIS (see Figure 16.1), to aid students in using their senses to evoke images. Modeling, teacher elaboration, scaffolding, and student self-regulation are elements of the strategy (Romco, 2001). Student

Figure 16.1. Sensory Imaging Strategy (SIS).

choice and the use of challenging materials are frequently emphasized to increase student engagement and motivation.

Prior to beginning to use SIS, the teacher should be certain that the students have had some training in making images. For visual images, this can be accomplished by introducing the students to imaging by using vivid nouns and verbs or simple objects (Gambrell & Koskinen, 2001; Block, in press). The teacher should initiate similar lessons to introduce the other sensory images, using common sounds, smells, and tastes. To teach about touching images, the teacher can place objects in a bag for students to feel and describe (Romeo, 2002). As part of this, teachers can use Walker's guided imagery experience (1999). The teacher has students close their eyes as she prompts them to focus on the sound and visual images present in the classroom and compare them to other familiar sights, sounds, tastes, and smells. The students then meet in pairs to share their imagery experiences.

Introducing SIS

Teacher Explanation

Mrs. Deluca, a third-grade teacher, began a lesson on SIS by saying, "Today we are going to learn a new strategy called SIS that will help you with your comprehension. SIS is an acronym for sensory imaging strategy, just as DEAR is an acronym for drop everything and read. SIS will help you to use your senses." Mrs. Deluca asked for volunteers to identify the five senses. As the students volunteered, she wrote the names of the senses on chart paper. Mrs. Deluca said, "SIS will help you to use these five senses when you are reading about characters, settings, and events in stories." She then showed the picture of SIS to the class and explained that SIS would always be in the literacy center to help them remember to use their senses to make images. She also said that SIS was an important strategy because it would help them to remember more about the stories that they would be reading both in school and at home. "But for today, we're going to hang SIS up on the chalkboard."

Mrs. Deluca said, "While I was reading during DEAR time earlier in the day, I used SIS to help me to make pictures in my head about what the main character in my novel looked like and where her house was. I also used SIS yesterday when I tasted the sauce I was making for dinner. From the way it smelled and tasted, I could visualize the delicious stuffed shells I was going to have for dinner." Mrs. Deluca then asked, "Can anyone tell me what SIS is and why it can help you?" As the students volunteered the information about SIS, Mrs. Deluca wrote the information on chart paper.

TEACHER MODELING

Mrs. Deluca modeled the strategy by saying, "Today we are going to read the book *Sweet Dream Pie* by Audrey Wood and Mark Teague." She asked the class to predict what the story was about and linked the predictions to background knowledge. After introducing the book and making predictions, Mrs. Deluca read the first two pages and stopped. She said to the class "Oh, I wonder what is in the big trunk. Maybe it is a piece of sweet dream pie. I bet the sweet dream pie is large with a lot of pink icing and tastes like strawberry shortcake. I can just hear the wind creeping through the rusty attic. When you are reading, you would say to yourself, 'How could I use my senses to make images about the story?' Sometimes you can use both the pictures and the images you make to help you get information about the story. At other times you'll be thinking about the sounds in the book or how something smells, tastes, or feels."

Mrs. Deluca then read the next two pages and said, "I can hear the small meows of all the cats as they opened their eyes as the big trunk creaked open. I can hear and see the large utensils bumping on the attic steps on the way to the kitchen. How funny it looked when I pictured all the people on Willobee Street rolling out of their beds and landing with a bang. I wonder why that happened to them?" She then stopped and said, "Using my senses of hearing, smelling, seeing, tasting, and touching was really helping me get images of what was happening in the story. Now you will have a chance to use your senses and SIS to make images."

Mrs. Deluca then continued to read the story, stopping every few pages to think aloud and ask the students to use their senses. One child said, "I can smell all of the yummy treats hitting all over the kitchen floor with a bang. What a mess I see, but it would be worth tasting the sweet cookies."

At the end of the story, Mrs. Deluca asked the students, "Who can tell me what strategy we've been using?" The students raised their hands to volunteer the name of the strategy.

"Why is SIS an important strategy to know and use?" asked Mrs. Deluca.

Jennifer replied, "SIS is a strategy that helped me to make pictures and think about sounds while I'm reading."

Tom said, "It helped me to picture the gooey yummy pie with its sweet smell."

Mrs. Deluca concluded the modeling part of the lesson by saying, "Think about SIS tonight while you're reading and then tomorrow we'll spend more time using SIS to help us with our reading."

When assessing the lesson, Mrs. Deluca decided that the class was ready to begin guided practice of SIS. She was aware, however, that she might have to provide much more modeling and elaboration as she and the students continued to work with SIS.

GUIDED PRACTICE

Mrs. Deluca begins each guided practice session by referring to the picture of SIS (Figure 16.1) and asking for volunteers to explain the strategy and its importance. She provided more teacher modeling and elaboration as necessary. Mrs. Deluca and the students worked together with various types of genres, discussing the images that they evoked about setting, characters, and events. She explicitly encouraged the students to pay attention to important story grammar elements as they made sensory images representing the text. She pointed out, asked about, or clarified other appropriate strategies that students should use while reading the text.

Each guided practice session concluded with a discussion about what the students learned about the strategy and the setting of goals for the next lesson. Mrs. Deluca reminded students to use SIS on their own, both at home and at school. She told them that they would share their experiences the following day.

COOPERATIVE AND INDEPENDENT PRACTICE

After Mrs. Deluca had given the students three different experiences in using SIS (see Block, in press), she felt that the students were ready to use SIS in groups, pairs, and then independently. In addition to text reading, the students engaged in lively discussions as they read. Students wrote about, drew, and acted out the images that they made representing the elements in stories that they read. During this type of practice, the teacher provided pivotal point scaffolding (Block, Schaller, Joy, & Gaine, 2001): as students were reading, they raised their hands when they experienced difficulty with a text. The teacher met with the student, provided praise for what the student had accomplished, questioned him or her about what the student might need to have in order to be able to continue reading, and then modeled what the student required for continued success. The teacher recorded information about the pivotal point scaffolding session on a form designed for forming decisions about future instruction (Block et al., 2001).

During independent practice the teacher held discovery discussions (Block, 1999; Block et al., 2001), which were designed for students to discuss their reading abilities with the teacher or other trained adult. Both the student and teacher asked each other questions, such as "What is bothering you about your imaging abilities?" All sessions culminated with a discussion about what the students had learned, how they could use the strategy in their lives, and what goals they should develop for the next session.

The SIS Framework

Step 1: Explain

The teacher explains the strategy and why it is important: "Today we are going to learn a strategy called SIS. SIS is an acronym for sensory imaging strategy. It helps you to use your senses—seeing, hearing, smelling, tasting, and feeling when you're reading about characters, settings, and events. Here is a picture of SIS [teacher indicates Figure 16.1] to help you remember the name of the strategy. It is an important strategy because it will help you to remember more about the stories that you'll be reading both at school and at home."

The teacher personalizes the use of the strategy: "I use SIS in my own reading to help me create images in my mind." The teacher also should give a personal example of how the strategy can be used (shopping, cooking, and eating).

The teacher questions the students: "Who can tell me what SIS stands for and why it is an important strategy?"

Step 2: Model

Reading from a text that evokes images, the teacher models the SIS strategy, pausing to think aloud and describe the images that the text and the pictures evoke. The teacher explicitly informs the students what they would say to themselves when using SIS to help them with their comprehension. At the conclusion of the modeling, the teacher asks the students to identify the strategy that the teacher has been using and why this strategy is an important one to know and use.

Step 3: Guided Practice

The teacher begins the lesson by showing the picture of SIS and asking the students to recall the strategy and its use. If necessary, the teacher models the strategy once more, explaining that it is a tool to help them comprehend what they are reading. The teacher informs the students that they will be reading a story together and talking about the images they make.

As the teacher reads the text, he or she stops at spots in the texts that evoke images and asks for students to volunteer to describe a sensory image as well as to share the name of the sense (sight, hearing, smell, taste, touch) with the class.

After finishing the book or piece of text, the teacher displays Table 16.1, encouraging students to give examples of the images that help give information about the setting, characters, and events.

The teacher asks the students to recall what they have learned about the strategy and its use. The teacher then reminds the students to use SIS on their own as they read that evening and the

Table 16.1. SIS: Sensory Images for Comprehension.

	Seeing	Hearing	Smelling	Tasting	Touching
Setting					
Character 1					
Character 2					
Event 1					
Event 2					
Event 3					

next day. "I'll be asking you tomorrow to tell us about when you used SIS to help you comprehend."

Step 4: Cooperative Practice

Students work in pairs or small groups to discuss, write about, draw, and act out images that they find in texts that help them to gain meaning about setting, characters, and major events of a story. The pairs and groups can compare and contrast the images that they've made. Each group or pair session concludes with a discussion about what the students have learned about SIS and what goals they will try to develop the next time they read. The goals should include how they can use SIS to help them with their reading.

Step 5: Independent Practice

When the students are able to use SIS independently, the teacher provides individual practice experiences, first with easy texts and then with more challenging books. Each independent practice session ends with student self-regulation and future goal setting.

Three Recommendations for the Future

Recommendation 1: We need to validate the use of SIS in third- and fifth-grade classrooms over a period of one school year. SIS is embedded in transactional strategy instruction, with explicit modeling and explanation of a variety of strategies, a high level of scaffolding, thought-provoking discussions, and emphasis on students self-regulating their reading (Anderson, 1992; Collins, 1991; Pressley et al., 1992). Students are being taught to use SIS in conjunction with making predictions, relating the information to background knowledge, self-questioning, clarifying, summarizing, and interpreting. The classroom teachers are trained in the use of transactional strategy instruction and are given opportunities to dialogue about the lessons regularly. We are especially interested in the achievement, motivation, and self-regulation of at-risk and culturally diverse students. Because this population frequently has the compounded problems of difficulties at the word level (Metsala & Ehri, 1998; Pressley, 2000; Tan & Nicholson, 1997) and often does not possess adequate or relevant background knowledge (Pressley, 2000), it is imperative that they receive excellent, long-term instruction. This work addresses three essential needs:

Recommendation 2: We need to conduct longitudinal research study in which at-risk students are explicitly taught to choose, use, and self-regulate multiple strategies, including SIS. Over the course of the year, I hope to gain some understanding of how students internalize the SIS approach.

As part of the treatment, I provide professional development opportunities for the practicing teachers. This is a first step in developing explicit, comprehensive staff development opportunities for classroom and remedial teachers as well as administrators. The professional development must center on why and how to use the transactional strategy instruction model with all types of learners.

Recommendation 3: We need to provide preservice and inservice degrees. I feel a need to shift emphasis to performance-based programs. As part of that, I am emphasizing inquiry, reflection, and classroom research (Houston & Warner, 2000) as well as the dispositions needed to embrace the concept of lifelong professional learning.

References

Anderson, V. (1992). A teacher development project in transactional strategy instruction for teachers of severely reading-disabled adolescents. *Teaching and Teacher Education, 8*(4), 391–403.

Beck, I. L., Omanson, R. C., & McKeown, M. G. (1982). An instructional redesign of reading lessons: Effects on comprehension. *Reading Research Quarterly, 17,* 462–481.

Block, C. C. (1999). Comprehension: Crafting understanding. In L. B. Gambrell, L. M. Morrow, S. B. Neuman, & M. Pressley (Eds.), *Best practices in literacy instruction* (pp. 98–118). New York: Guilford Press.

Block, C. C. (in press). *Comprehension instruction: The process approach.* Needham Heights, MA: Allyn & Bacon.

Block, C. C., Schaller, J. L., Joy, J. A., & Gaine, P. (2001). Process-based comprehension instruction. In M. Pressley & C. Block (Eds.), *Reading comprehension* (pp. 42–61). New York: Guilford Press.

Brown, R., Pressley, M., Van Meter, P., & Schuder, T. (1996). A quasi-experimental validation of transactional strategies instruction with low-achieving second-grade readers. *Journal of Educational Psychology, 88,* 18–37.

Carnine, D., & Kinder, B. D. (1985). Teaching low-performing students to apply generative and schema strategies to narrative and expository material. *Remedial and Special Education, 6*(1), 20–30.

Collins, C. (1991). Reading instruction that increases thinking abilities. *Journal of Reading, 34,* 510–516.

Duffy, G. G., Roehler, L. R., Sivan, E., Rackliffe, G., Bood, C., Meloth, M., Vavrus, L. G., Wesselman, R., Putnam, J., & Bassiri, D. (1987). Effects of explaining the reasoning associated with using reading strategies. *Reading Research Quarterly, 22,* 347–368.

Durkin, D. (1078 1070). What classroom observations reveal about reading comprehension instruction. *Reading Research Quarterly, 15,* 481–533.

Gambrell, L. B., & Bales, R. J. (1986). Mental imagery and the comprehension-monitoring performance of fourth- and fifth-grade poor readers. *Reading Research Quarterly, 21,* 454–464.

Gambrell, L. B., & Javitz, P. B. (1993). Mental imagery, text illustrations, and children's story comprehension and recall. *Reading Research Quarterly, 21,* 264–273.

Gambrell, L. B., Koskinen, P. S. (2001). Imagery: A strategy for enhancing comprehension. In M. Pressley & C. Block (Eds.), *Reading comprehension* (pp. 305–318). New York: Guilford Press.

Gurney, D., Gersten, R., Dimino, J., & Carmine, D. (1990). Story grammar: Effective literature instruction for high school students with learning disabilities. *Journal of Learning Disabilities, 23*(6), 335–342.

Houston, W. R., & Warner, A. R. (2000). Twin needs for improved teacher education. In D. J. McIntyre & D. M. Byrd (Eds.), *Research on effective models for teacher education* (pp. 72–77). Thousand Oaks, CA: Corwin Press.

Idol, L., & Croll, V. J. (1987). Story-mapping training as a means of improving reading comprehension. *Learning Disability Quarterly, 10,* 214–229.

Lloyd, C. V. (1995). How teachers teach reading comprehension: An examination of four categories of reading comprehension instruction. *Reading Research and Instruction, 35*(2), 171–185.

Metsala, J., & Ehri, L. (Eds.). (1998). *Word recognition in beginning reading.* Hillsdale, NJ: Erlbaum.

Nolte, R. Y., & Singer, H. (1985). Active comprehension: Teaching a process of reading comprehension and its effects on reading achievement. *Reading Teacher, 30,* 24–31.

Paivio, A. (1971). *Imagery and verbal processes.* Austin, TX: Holt, Rinehart and Winston.

Pressley, G. M. (1976). Mental imagery helps eight-year-olds remember what they read. *Journal of Educational Psychology, 68,* 355–359.

Pressley, M. (1996). Concluding reflections. In E, McIntyre & M. Pressley (Eds.), *Balanced instruction: Strategies and skills in whole language* (pp. 277–286). Norwood, MA: Christopher-Gordon.

Pressley, M. (2000). What should comprehension instruction be the instruction of? In M. Kamil, P. Mosenthal, P. D. Pearson, & R. Barr (Eds.), *Handbook of reading research* (Vol. 3, pp. 545–562). Hillsdale, NJ: Erlbaum.

Pressley, M. (2002). *Reading instruction that works: The case for balanced teaching.* (2nd ed.). New York: Guilford Press.

Pressley, M., El-Dinary, P. B., Gaskins, I., Schuder, T., Bergman, J., Almasi, L., & Brown, R. (1992). Beyond direct explanation: Transactional instruction of reading comprehension strategies. *Elementary School Journal, 92,* 511–554.

Pressley, M., Wharton-McDonald, R., Hampston, J. M., & Echevarria, M. (1998). The nature of literacy instruction in ten grade-4 and grade-5 classrooms in upstate New York. *Scientific Studies of Reading, 2,* 159–191.

Rankin-Erickson, J. L., & Pressley, M. (2000). A survey of instructional practices of special education teachers nominated as effective teachers of literacy. *Learning Disabilities Research and Practice, 15*(4), 206–225.

Roehler, L., & Duffy, G. G. (1984). Direct explanation of comprehension processes. In G. G. Duffy, L. R. Roehler, & J. Mason (Eds.), *Comprehension instruction: Perspectives and suggestions* (pp. 265–280). White Plains, NY: Longman.

Romeo, L. (2001). *Developing and extending comprehension in the middle school.* Paper presented at the annual meeting of the International Reading Association, New Orleans, LA.

Romeo, L. (2002). *At-risk students: Learning to break through comprehension barriers.* Paper presented at the annual meeting of the International Reading Association, San Francisco, CA.

Sadowski, M., & Paivio, A. (1994). A dual coding view of imagery and verbal processes in reading comprehension. In R. B. Ruddell, M. R.

Ruddell, & H. Singer (Eds.), *Theoretical models and processes of reading* (4th ed.). Newark, DE: International Reading Association.

Short, E. J., & Ryan, E. B. (1984). Metacognitive differences between skilled and less skilled readers: Remediating deficits through story grammar and attributions training. *Journal of Educational Psychology, 76,* 225–235.

Tan, A., & Nicholson, T. (1997). Flashcards revisited: Training poor readers to read words faster improves their comprehension of text. *Journal of Educational Psychology, 89,* 276–288.

Van den Branden, K. (2000). Does negotiation of meaning promote reading comprehension? A study of multilingual primary school classes. *Reading Research Quarterly, 35,* 426–443.

Walker, B. J. (1999). Guided imagery as language experience. In O. G. Nelson & W. M. Linek (Eds.), *Practical classroom applications of language experience: Looking back, looking forward* (pp. 68–72). Needham Heights, MA: Allyn & Bacon.

Wendler, D., Samuels, S. J., & Moore, V. K. (1989). The comprehension instruction of award-winning teachers, teachers with master's degrees, and other teachers. *Reading Research Quarterly, 24,* 382–401.

Williams, N. L., Konopak, B. C., Wood, K. D., & Avett, K. D. (1992). Middle school students' use of imagery in developing meaning in expository text. In C. K. Kinzer & D. J. Leu (Eds.), *Literacy research, theory, and practice: Views from many perspectives* (pp. 261–267). Chicago: National Reading Conference.

Wood, A., and Teague, M. (1998). *Sweet Dream Pie.* New York: Blue Sky Press.

Chapter Seventeen

Helping Struggling Readers Make Sense of Reading

Irene W. Gaskins,
Sally R. Laird,
Colleen O'Hara,
Theresa Scott,
and Cheryl A. Cress

Students who struggle in learning to read do not need different curriculum, different goals, or different standards. In fact, they can and do learn to read using the same materials and programs found in regular classrooms. What they do need is instruction that differs in intensity from the instruction usually provided in U.S. classrooms (Allington, 2001). This intensity is achieved by low student-teacher ratios, ample time devoted to teaching students how to decode and comprehend, and the professional expertise of those providing the instruction (Pearson, 1999).

Increased intensity means well-trained teachers devoting lots of time to explicitly teaching small groups of students how to use strategies to make sense of what they read. One model of such an approach is the explicit instruction found in transactional strategies instruction (Gaskins, Anderson, Pressley, Cunicelli, & Satlow, 1993; Pressley et al., 1992). Despite a strong research base that supports explicit instruction of reading comprehension strategies (National Reading Panel, 2000), researchers continue to report that there is little explicit instruction of comprehension strategies in primary classrooms and that very, very few elementary teachers teach children to use a repertoire of comprehension strategies (for example, Pressley, in press).

In addition to being intense, instruction for struggling readers must be long-term (Pressley, 1998, 2002) because the impact of short-term reading interventions typically fades over time (Hiebert & Taylor, 2000; Shanahan & Barr, 1995). Short-term interventions can get students on track, but struggling readers need something more in order to stay on track (Gaskins, 1998; Pressley, in press). This chapter tells how teachers in grades one through six of a school for struggling readers (Benchmark School) provide intense long-term strategy instruction to help students think about what they read. The result of at least four years of intense strategy instruction across the curriculum is that elementary school struggling readers become successful middle school and high school students.

Background About Our Struggling Readers

Most children enter Benchmark School as second-, third-, or fourth-graders reading on a first-grade reading level. Many, in fact, are virtual nonreaders. Most have average or better intelligence, an understanding of word meanings that is at least typical for their grade level, and an adequate background of knowledge. The initial stumbling block for these struggling readers is often the fact that they lack the most rudimentary understanding of the alphabetic principle and how it works. We have developed a multidimensional decoding program (word detectives) that guides students in discovering how our language works at a pace and level that meets each student where she or he is along the developmental continuum of acquiring and using alphabetic knowledge (Gaskins, Ehri, Cress, O'Hara, & Donnelly, 1996–1997). Fluency is also emphasized and practiced during word detectives lessons, reading group instruction, and a books-in-bags program. Like Pearson (1999, p. 244), we believe that instruction in decoding and fluency needs to be "accompanied by an equally strong, maybe even stronger, emphasis on meaning." We do not believe that decoding instruction should dominate beginning reading instruction, with a comprehension emphasis being introduced later. Decoding, fluency, and comprehension instruction must proceed together.

Getting Started

A focus on meaning begins the first day a struggling reader attends Benchmark. After students read a short passage, the teacher may say, "So what did you think of the story?" The reply is often similar to what one of our new-to-Benchmark students said: "The story didn't make sense." The teacher then asked, "What do you do when stories don't make sense?" The child's response was, "The stories I read in school don't have to make sense—they are just used to teach us how to read."

The belief that stories read in school do not have to make sense is a belief that Benchmark teachers try to change from their very first moments with a new class. The first objective with students who are new to Benchmark is to guide them to believe that reading must make sense.

Benchmark teachers often begin their instruction of first-level readers by thinking aloud about their own miscues as they read to students a simple passage from a preprimer story. After making a miscue, the teacher thinks aloud about the phrase or sentence that, because of the miscue, does not make sense. She might say: "I just read that Bing and Sandy ran up the help. That doesn't make sense. Animals don't run up a help. I had better read that sentence again and see if I read all the words correctly." The teacher reads the sentence again, stopping on the word *hill*. The teacher writes *hill* on the chalkboard and asks students if there are any clues as to whether *help* is the correct word. The teacher scaffolds the discussion so that students conclude that looking at just one or two letters in a word is not sufficient to correctly identify a word; instead they must look at every letter in the word.

To reinforce the concept that reading must make sense and to provide virtual nonreaders with a successful reading experience, teachers engage beginning readers in echo and choral reading as an integral part of both word detectives lessons and directed reading lessons. The teacher provides each student with a copy of a simple and often predictable book, including those that accompany the word detectives program and those published by Wright Group and Rigby. They instruct the children to survey the pictures in the book and, as they survey, to make predictions about what they think will happen. Once they have completed gathering information through surveying, students discuss their predictions and generate purposes for reading. Next the teacher reads the story to the group. A brief discussion focuses on understanding the story, then the class reads the story sentence by sentence, employing the technique of echo reading. The teacher reads a sentence while students point to each word; then students read the same sentence in unison with the teacher, as they again point to each word. The emphasis is always on, Does what we are reading make sense? Then the class completes several pages of the book in this fashion. Next the group reads the book chorally, and finally each student takes the book home to read chorally with a parent with a dual emphasis on accurate reading and the story making sense.

Strategy Instruction as Part of Reading Group Instruction

During daily forty-minute directed reading lessons in small groups, students in grades one through six learn and practice strategies for monitoring and constructing meaning. The classroom teacher meets with a small reading group (3 to 5 students) around a table, while other students in the class read and write responses about text from a variety of genres written at their independent levels.

Identifying Story Elements

Once the new students have a beginning understanding that reading must make sense and that each one of them must monitor for sense and take action when reading does not make sense (reread, read on, or ask for help), the next strategy the teacher introduces is often identifying story elements. In introducing the strategy, the teacher might say something like the following:

TEACHER: Boys and girls, today we are going to learn a new strategy that will help us understand what we read. One way this new strategy helps us understand what we read is by keeping us actively involved in thinking about the story. What does it mean to be actively involved?

STUDENT A: We are doing something.

TEACHER: Any other ideas?

STUDENT B: We are thinking about the story.

STUDENT C: There is something going on in our head. We aren't daydreaming.

TEACHER: Yes, if you are actively involved, you are thinking about what you are reading, trying to make sense of the story. You may even be constructing a TV version of the story in your head. The new strategy we are going to learn today is called identifying story elements. Does anyone know what *elements* are?

STUDENT A: Things in a story?

STUDENT B: Parts of a story?

TEACHER: You are on the right track. An *element* is a part. We are going to talk about parts of a story. I have the elements of a story written on these four cards with pictures to help you remember the words. I will put the cards with names of the four elements on the chalkboard with a magnet. In a few minutes, we will discuss what each means. *(The teacher places cards on the chalkboard with the words and pictures that cue what the word is: characters, setting, problem, solution.)* We are going to identify story elements. What does *identify* mean?

STUDENT C: Find or name.

STUDENT A: It's like if you identify someone, you know who the person is.

TEACHER: We are going to identify, or point out, four different parts of a story. I wonder why this is a good strategy for grown-ups and kids to use? I will tell you why I think it is a good strategy. Then, when I finish, I will ask someone to tell me why identifying story elements might be a helpful strategy for you.

There are at least three reasons why I identify story elements when I read. One is that it helps me focus on the most important information in the story. A second is that the strategy helps me check my understanding. If I can provide information about the four story elements, I probably understand what I read. Third, the strategy keeps me actively involved in thinking about what I am reading. If I am searching for story elements, I can't be daydreaming about what I am going to cook for dinner. Did you know that our brains do not automatically remember everything we see or read? We have to do something with the information we read or we won't remember what we read—not even long enough to discuss the story with one another. Who can tell me a reason why identifying story elements will be helpful to you? *(Teacher listens to and comments on student responses.)*

The strategy we are going to learn today is one that we can use any time we read a made-up or fiction story.

This is how I do the strategy. I ask myself questions about the different elements of the story. I have those questions written on sentence strips that I will put on the chalkboard next to one of the story element words that are already on the chalkboard.

The first sentence says: Who are the important people or animals in the story? Is that question about the characters, setting, problem, or solution? *(Teacher reads the story element words; students respond.*

Yes, I will put this sentence behind the word *characters*. Characters are the important people or animals in a story. Yesterday I read you the story of *Three Billy Goats Gruff* (Carpenter, 1998). Who are the important characters in *Three Billy Goats Gruff? (Students respond.)*

Yes, the three goats and the troll. I bet you noticed that I have a picture of goats and a troll on the card that says characters.

The second sentence says: Where and when does the story take place? Is that question about the setting, problem, or solution? Put up your hand if you think it is about our second word, *setting. (Students put up hands.)*

Yes, the setting tells where and when a story takes place. For example, *Three Billy Goats Gruff* takes place in a mountainous country near a stream with a bridge over it, and it takes place in the morning. Did you notice the sun coming up behind the mountains on the card that says setting?

The next sentence strip contains two sentences. It says: What does the main character want, need, think, or feel? What is getting in the way? In the story about the three billy goats, what do the goats want? *(Students respond.)*

Yes, the three goats want to cross the bridge to get to the other side of the stream so they can eat the grass. What is getting in their way? *(Students respond.)*

Yes, the troll. On the problem card, you see three goats waiting to go over the bridge and a troll standing in the middle of the bridge, blocking them from crossing the bridge.

The next sentence strip says: How is the problem solved? Who knows how the problem is solved in the story about the three billy goats? *(Students respond.)*

Yes, the largest goat pushed the troll into the stream, then crossed the bridge to the green grass on the other side. His younger two brothers had already solved their problem by telling the troll that he should let them cross the bridge and wait for their brother who was larger and would make a more tasty meal. On the solution card, you see the big goat pushing the troll off the bridge and two little goats eating grass on the hill.

Next I am going to read a short story to you and model my thinking as I read and answer the questions on the chalkboard about characters, setting, problem, and solution. Answering these questions will be one way I can check my understanding. I will certainly have to be actively involved in thinking about what I am reading to be able to answer the questions.

After the teacher reads a story and models her thinking in applying the strategy, she guides students page by page as they silently read a story at their instructional level. As each page is read, students share the information they have found related to characters, setting, problem, and solution. Later in the school year, the teacher teaches students to summarize fiction by collecting clues about characters, setting, problem, solution, and key events as they read, identifying the most important information among those clues and putting the clues together into several sentences that tell about what they read.

The outline used at Benchmark for introducing a new strategy is to tell students

- What strategy the teacher will teach or review
- Why the strategy is important
- When they can use the strategy
- How to implement the strategy

The discussion of the what, why, when, and how of the strategy is followed by teacher modeling, with personal examples of strategy use, then guided practice using the strategy while reading a text at the group's instructional level. At Benchmark teachers usually focus on one strategy for approximately six weeks of daily instruction. After a few days of instruction on a new strategy, teachers begin to gradually release responsibility for discussing and applying the strategy to the students. For example, the teacher might begin reading group by asking questions about the strategy, such as: What strategy are we practicing as we read? Why is this strategy important? When can we use this strategy? How do you use this strategy? (See Gaskins & Elliot, 1991, for more information about explicit strategy instruction at Benchmark.)

Survey-Predict—Set a Purpose

Another strategy that we teach to our struggling readers early in the program for fiction (and in modified form for nonfiction) is that of surveying, predicting, and setting a purpose for reading. In fact, some teachers prefer to teach this strategy before teaching students to identify story elements. Once the survey, predict, and set a purpose strategy is introduced, we ask students to apply some form of the strategy across the curriculum for the duration of their stay at Benchmark. The outline for teaching and daily review of the strategy is this:

What strategy are we learning?	To survey, predict, and set a purpose for reading.
Why is the strategy important?	It helps us get actively involved in our reading. Getting involved in our reading helps us understand what we read.
When can we use the strategy?	Whenever we read fiction or nonfiction.
How do we do the strategy?	When we are reading fiction:

- We read the title and the author's name and look at the pictures to get a sense of what the story is about.
- We ask ourselves: Who are the characters? What is the setting? What might the problem be?
- We make a prediction about what will happen in the story.
- We think about what we want to find out in the story.

As with all strategies, the discussion of what, why, when, and how of the strategy is followed by teacher modeling, with personal examples of strategy use, then guided practice using the strategy while reading a text at the group's instructional level.

We also teach students explicit strategies for reading nonfiction. In Benchmark classrooms about half of what students read, during directed reading lessons and free reading, is nonfiction. This is the outline teachers use in teaching students to summarize nonfiction:

What strategy are we learning?	To summarize nonfiction.
Why is the strategy important?	Summarizing nonfiction helps us

- Focus on important information.
- Monitor our understanding.

	• Remember what we have read.
	• Share what we have learned with others.
When can we use this strategy?	Whenever we read nonfiction.
How do we do the strategy?	• We survey the text and predict what we think the text will be about.
	• We activate our background knowledge.
	• We set a purpose for reading.
	• We read and retell in our own words.
	• We collect notes on the important ideas.
	• We read the notes and identify the most important information to include in our summary.
	• We put the important notes together into sentences that tell about what we have read.

Categories of Strategies

The strategies that we teach at Benchmark fall into three categories: monitor for sense, look for patterns, and make inferences (Pearson, 1993). Monitor-for-sense strategies help students check to be sure that what they hear or read makes sense and to use fix-up strategies as needed. Some strategies we teach in the monitor-for-sense category include taking action when reading doesn't make sense, surveying, predicting, setting a purpose, identifying story elements, making and describing mental pictures, self-questioning about story elements or key events, and summarizing story elements. Look-for-patterns strategies encourage students to look for story elements, genre and text-structure characteristics, and major concepts or themes. Some strategies we teach in this category include identifying story elements, identifying elements of a genre, gathering clues about theme and author's message, identifying key events, identifying how character traits influence events, identifying topics and main ideas in nonfiction, identifying text structure in nonfiction, and categorizing information. Make-inferences strategies guide students to connect clues (from the author or speaker) with background knowledge. Some strategies we teach in this category include supporting statements, inferences, and conclusions with evidence in the text; identifying character traits based on what characters do or say; identifying the author's message, lesson, or universal truth based on genre or text clues; and identifying point of view or bias based on clues in the text.

Analyze the Task

As students become comfortable with individual strategies, teachers cue them to orchestrate an array of strategies to accomplish specific tasks. Instruction in how to orchestrate strategies begins with analyzing the task. What follows are the five steps a teacher guides students through when giving an assignment. We call the strategy "to analyze the task," signaling in the strategy's name that we want students to stop and think about the job to be accomplished.

1. What do I need to do?	Students are to write in their own words their interpretation of the assignment.
2. How will I do it?	Students are to break the task into manageable parts and make a plan. Again, we usually ask for this in writing, particularly if the task to be completed is one that will take several days or weeks.
3. What could help me succeed? What could get in my way?	We ask students to discuss with us the situation, text, task, and personalized variables that will influence their satisfactory completion of the task.
4. What can I do about those things	Under the teacher's guidance, students are asked to make a

that could get in my way?	plan for taking charge of the situation, text, task, and person variables that could get in the way of successful completion of the task.
5. How am I doing?	Students are asked to complete daily self-assessments regarding the quality of the job they are doing and factors that are influencing how well they are doing. If necessary, they are asked to revise their plans.

Sharing the Big Picture About Reading Comprehension

As a general focus of comprehension instruction throughout the school, we share with students that meaning is not in the text; rather, readers actively construct meaning based on what is in the text and what is in their background of knowledge. We help our students become aware that reading is also an interactive process that involves four variables: the reader, the text, the task, and the situation or context. Their job as readers is to take charge of these variables. In addition, we want our students to view reading comprehension as both an individual and a social process. Thus it is to their advantage to discuss with others what they read and alter their understandings, as appropriate, based on others' input. We share with students our belief that cultural forces within a community or a society shape our values and behavior, as well as shape the interpretation of what we read.

Three Recommendations for the Future

We believe that improved comprehension among struggling readers is the result of an intense program provided over many years. Some researchers call it *academic press*, an approach to instruction that is well supported in the research literature (Lee & Smith, 1999). The program that we envision requires well-trained teachers explicitly teaching small groups of students how to use strategies to make sense of what they read. Students must receive this instruction daily, in all areas of the curriculum, and for the long term, lasting no less than four years.

RECOMMENDATION 1: Universities and elementary schools must provide in-depth professional development for preservice and inservice teachers regarding how to implement strategy instruction in a directed reading lesson, as well as across the curriculum.

RECOMMENDATION 2: School administrators must put in place policies that ensure long uninterrupted periods of time each day for teachers to teach reading comprehension strategies and for students to apply comprehension strategies to reading texts at their appropriate reading levels, both in small reading groups and in whole-class, content-area instruction.

RECOMMENDATION 3: Curriculum directors in school districts should provide a plan for coordinating strategy instruction throughout a school or district so that strategy instruction begun at one grade level will be reinforced and practiced throughout the grades.

References

Allington, R. L. (2001). Teaching children to read: What really matters. In B. Sornson (Ed.), *Preventing early learning failure* (pp. 5–14). Alexandria, VA: Association for Supervision and Curriculum Development.

Carpenter, S. (1998). *Three Billy Goats Gruff*. New York: HarperCollins.

Gaskins, I. W. (1998). There's more to teaching at-risk and delayed readers than good reading instruction. *Reading Teacher, 51,* 534–547.

Gaskins, I. W., Anderson, R. C., Pressley, M., Cunicelli, E. A., & Satlow, E. (1993). Six teachers' dialogue during cognitive process instruction. *Elementary School Journal, 93,* 277–304.

Gaskins, I. W., Ehri, L. C., Cress, C., O'Hara, C., & Donnelly, K. (1996–1997). Procedures for word learning: Making discoveries about words. *Reading Teacher, 50,* 312–327.

Gaskins, I. W., & Elliot, T. T. (1991). *Implementing cognitive strategy instruction across the school: The Benchmark manual for teachers*. Cambridge, MA: Brookline Books.

Hiebert, E. H., & Taylor, B. M. (2000). Beginning reading instruction: Research on early interventions. In M. L. Kamil, P. B. Mosenthal,

P. D. Pearson, & R. Barr (Eds.), *Handbook of reading research* (Vol. 3, pp. 455–482). Hillsdale, NJ: Erlbaum.

Lee, V. E., & Smith, J. B. (1999). Social support and achievement for young adolescents in Chicago: The role of school academic press. *American Education Research Journal, 36,* 907–945.

National Reading Panel. (2000). *Teaching children to read: An evidence-based assessment of the scientific research literature on reading and its implications for reading instruction: Reports of the subgroups.* Washington, DC: National Institute of Child Health and Human Development.

Pearson, P. D. (1993). Teaching and learning reading: A research perspective. *Language Arts, 70,* 502–511.

Pearson, P. D. (1999). A historically based review of *Preventing Reading Difficulties in Young Children. Reading Research Quarterly, 34,* 231–246.

Pressley, M. (2002). *Reading instruction that works: The case for balanced teaching.* New York: Guilford Press.

Pressley, M. (in press). Effective beginning reading instruction: A paper commissioned by the National Reading Panel. *Journal of Literacy Research.*

Pressley, M., El-Dinary, P. B., Gaskins, I. W., Schuder, T., Bergman, J. L., Almasi, J., & Brown, R. (1992). Beyond direct explanation: Transactional instruction of reading comprehension strategies. *Elementary School Journal, 92,* 511–554.

Shanahan, T., & Barr, R. (1995). Reading Recovery: An independent evaluation of the effects of an early instructional intervention for at-risk learners. *Reading Research Quarterly, 30,* 958–996.

Conclusion

Improving Comprehension Instruction: A Path for the Future

Michael Pressley

My first year of graduate school, I came to an insight that changed my life: children probably could be taught cognitive strategies that would improve their understanding and memory of text. I was particularly interested in dual coding theory then. Thus, I developed instruction to stimulate children to construct mental images representing what they read, which did, in fact, improve their comprehension of concrete stories (Pressley, 1976). Although I have not continuously conducted research on comprehension since that early start in graduate school, I have thought about comprehension and comprehension instruction in particular at least a little bit every day of my professional life. I brought that history with comprehension instruction as a problem to my reading of this book, concluding that the book is filled with insights about what comprehension instruction is (and is not) and what it could be (and should be) from my perspective.

What Comprehension Instruction Is

When I began my work on comprehension instruction, there was much more faith then than now that the messages of texts are more or less fixed, with the reader's task to find the ideas the author put in the text. Publication of Louise Rosenblatt's book (1978) *The Reader, The Text, The Poem* brought a heightened awareness that understanding is jointly determined by ideas in the text and the mind of the reader, what the reader knows and believes. During the same era, cognitive psychologists would make the same point, with Anderson and Pearson (1984) the most prominent reading instructional researchers who were concerned with the role of reader knowledge in comprehension. The central tenet of their schema theory was that prior knowledge very much affects the understanding that the reader constructs from a text. For example, readers who know the realities of Dickens's life and times find very different meanings in Dickens's *Christmas Carol* (2000) than do readers who do not.

Having knowledge is one thing, using it to comprehend text quite another. Whitehead (1929) coined the term *inert knowledge* to describe information that we have acquired but do not know so well that we can actually use it. Much that students learn in school for recall on tests is inert knowledge. Sometimes we have knowledge that we could use to understand text but do not use. I think my most underappreciated finding as a scientist is about this phenomenon. In a series of studies, my colleagues and I showed that the learning of factual material can be improved dramatically simply by asking learners to think about why the factual ideas (for example, as expressed in an expository text) make sense. Thus, when Canadian college students were asked to learn texts containing information like, "The first Canadian baseball teams were in Ontario," their memory of the facts was much greater if they tried to figure out why that was so. This work was sufficiently analytical to make clear that this why-questioning effect (also known as an elaborative interrogation effect) was because the why questions prompted the reader to relate facts in text to relevant prior knowledge, something that did not happen in the absence of why questions. One of the ways good readers can be strategic, active, and effective comprehenders is to ask themselves why the relationships specified in text occur. The why-questioning strategy encourages the reader to make the most of prior knowledge, to use it to make the most sense of text. Such self-questioning, however, is just one of many strategies that have been validated in the past three decades.

Since I began my work on comprehension instruction, researchers have identified many strategies that readers can be taught to increase their understanding and memory of texts they read. This book is filled with the fruits of those researchers' labors.

Based on their work alone, a case could be made that readers should be taught many, many comprehension strategies. This position might also make sense by reflecting on the many verbal protocols of reading that are now available (Pressley & Afflerbach, 1995): when good readers think aloud as they read text, they report many processes, including making predictions based on prior knowledge, constructing inferences and updating knowledge based on ideas in text, relating new ideas in text to prior knowledge, constructing mental images of ideas represented in text, self-questioning, rereading for clarification, summarizing, reviewing ideas in text as a reading nears completion, and planning on how to use ideas in text in the future (for example, to use ideas just encountered in writing an article). In fact, when researchers have taught readers, including children, repertoires of comprehension strategies (such as prediction, imagery, self-questioning, rereading for clarification, and summarization), they have succeeded in creating more active readers who are better comprehenders (Anderson, 1992; Brown, Pressley, Van Meter, & Schuder, 1996; Collins, 1991).

Finally, since I began my work on comprehension, awareness has increased enormously that comprehension largely takes place in consciousness, which is in short supply. That is, human short-term memories only permit a very little to be held in mind at a time. In order to comprehend various parts of a sentence, the reader has to hold them all in mind simultaneously. That is easier if the reader has no problem reading the words, for unproblematic word recognition takes up little of the precious consciousness, leaving much for comprehension itself. In contrast, if word recognition is difficult, then much consciousness is consumed by it, reducing the amount of capacity available for comprehension and thus reducing comprehension. Throughout the discussion that follows, I will consider the criticality of limited consciousness in reading comprehension at several different places.

Comprehension Instruction That Is Not Occurring

Despite all that we have learned about comprehension instruction, relatively little of it is occurring (Pressley, Wharton-McDonald, Hampston, & Echevarria, 1998). Rather, in recent years, reading education has focused on word-level processes, in particular, the development of word recognition skills. Sometimes the result is a word caller, as described in Flood, Lapp, and Fisher's chapter (Chapter Seven). At best, such instruction is premised on a simple view of reading comprehension (Gough, 1984), although one that has thrived in the past decade: to understand a text, read the words and listen to yourself read! Humans are hardwired to understand connected words, and thus we need do nothing except let the hard wiring operate. As it turns out, the comprehension assessments that predominate in the marketplace are ones that are well matched to this simple view of reading. Before turning to more explicit discussion of those assessments, however, I point out that even if teachers wanted to teach comprehension more, there is no good reason to expect they could do it. Keene's chapter (Chapter Three) in particular dealt with attempts to develop teachers who know how to teach students to be better comprehenders. In her book (Keene & Zimmermann, 1997), Keene made the point that one critical problem is that many teachers do not know how to comprehend text at a high level themselves. By teaching teachers to comprehend texts better, Keene and Zimmermann believe that they will come to understand comprehension and the importance of teaching it to children. That is, the teaching will be driven by teachers' conceptual understanding, rather than the realities of the assessments that children face. For the moment, however, those assessments are a huge force in determining what teachers cover during reading instruction.

Comprehension Assessments

How do we know whether a person has comprehended a text? Sadly, more often than not, at least in school, the answer is that the person can complete short-answer questions about the text that he or she has read. It was true before the last three decades of research (see Durkin 1978–1979), and it remains true today (Pressley et al., 1998): comprehension gets tested more than students get taught how to comprehend! That is, even though we know that students comprehend better if we teach them comprehension strategies, we do not routinely teach such strategies in school. Rather, we test comprehension with short-answer questions that are somehow supposed to stimulate students to become better comprehenders. This is consistent with the current belief of many policymakers that the curriculum can be shaped through assessments: if assessments test for it, educators will teach it.

How do educators respond to such testing pressures if they do not teach comprehension strategies? In fact, the answer is summarized on a poster found in many elementary and secondary classrooms, one that reads, "Read, Read, Read." This is one of the most enduring legacies of the whole language movement, that comprehension develops simply from reading a lot. In fact, there is probably some truth to it. With increased reading, fluency in word recognition should increase, which would promote comprehension. So should prior knowledge, assuming the reader is reading quality books. With greater prior knowledge, the reader has more to relate to ideas encountered in new texts. That is, today's newly acquired knowledge from reading is tomorrow's prior knowledge. However much comprehension improves from extensive reading, it could improve more if readers were taught to use the comprehension strategies that skilled readers use. I have my doubts whether the current accountability system offers much incentive to increase teaching of comprehension strategies, but I want to try to offer some: we are now in an era of exceptionally heavy testing, and standardized testing in the most traditional sense of the term. Comprehension strategies instruction has a big impact on standardized test performance, at least in the elementary years (Anderson, 1992; Brown et al., 1996; Collins, 1991). Those living in high stakes testing educational worlds should be doing all possible to encourage much more comprehension strategies instruction in their schools. Why won't they, however? It is because doing little more than having students practice reading will produce improvement from one testing time to the next (for example, from the beginning to end of the school year). That is, by practicing reading, fluency does increase, which increases comprehension. As reading the individual words becomes easier, that frees up cognitive capacity to listen to oneself read and thus makes it easier to understand what one hears as one reads.

Multifaceted Development of Comprehension

The authors of this book make clear that development of competent comprehension is much more than comprehension strategies instruction. Fluent word recognition is critical for high comprehension. Thus, effective word recognition instruction is important in developing comprehension skill, followed by the extensive practice of reading that results in fluent reading of individual words. If comprehension is to occur, readers must not only read words but also understand them. Thus, extensive vocabulary knowledge is required, which also can be developed through instruction (Beck & McKeown, 1991). The rich prior knowledge possessed by skilled readers can be developed through instruction (for example, high quality science and social studies curricula), reading, viewing of informative television, and generally rich experiences in the world (such as visits to museums and landmarks, concerts, talks, and so on). Comprehension strategies instruction, especially instruction emphasizing the articulation of prior knowledge and comprehension processes, that occurs in the context of reading excellent texts permits the development of even more complete world knowledge and awareness.

Developing skilled comprehenders requires that comprehension instruction occur over a very long period of time. Indeed, comprehension instruction probably should occur from kindergarten through the twelfth grade, even continuing into adulthood. It takes several years to develop word recognition skills and additional years to become fluent word readers. The skilled reader does not acquire a fifteen-thousand to twenty-thousand word vocabulary overnight! We spend our lifetimes developing prior knowledge as we visit new places and learn new things. As someone who teaches advanced courses in education and psychology, I know that students often need to be taught how to get the most out of the complicated texts of psychology articles, that they can be taught new comprehension strategies (for example, read the abstract of the article carefully, read the methods section next) and variations on already known comprehension strategies (such as writing summaries of key points in the margin of the article).

Comprehension instruction is decidedly about teaching people how to construct meaning from text rather than simply finding the meaning put there by the author. Thus, the teacher who teaches vocabulary in advance of a reading is providing a preview of ideas that the student will encounter in the reading, a preview that the reader can build upon while reading. When readers are taught to construct images and summaries, they are constructing personal images and reducing the ideas in text to the ones they consider important. Individual readers construct their understandings as they read; when several readers discuss a text they have been going through, they also engage in knowledge-constructive processes. Any given text can have a variety of meanings depending on the fluency of the reader's word recognition skills, the extent of the reader's vocabulary and prior knowledge, and the particular comprehension processes he or she applies to the text in reading it. Comprehension is multifaceted and never the same for any two readers. It is probably never the same for any one reader going through a text more than one time.

This constructivist vision of comprehension fared well in this volume. I am particularly heartened that it fared well in the RAND report summarized in Snow and Sweet's chapter (Chapter One), for that report promises to go far in shaping the research agenda on comprehension instruction for the next decade or so. I have heard criticisms that the report is too conservative, reflecting too much the perspectives of the past thirty years. That is fine to me, for I come back to a point made earlier: we are not making the most of what we know about comprehension instruction. That is, even though we know comprehension is facilitated by extensive word recognition instruction and development of word recognition skills to the point of fluency, some continue in their reluctance to teach word recognition skills systematically and completely. Even though it is known that vocabulary instruction increases comprehension, some believe that natural acquisition of vocabulary words is the way to go, with no hope of teaching students nearly enough vocabulary given the large number of words that an educated English-speaking person knows. And of course, despite the demonstrations of clear gains in comprehension when comprehension strategies are taught, teachers rarely teach them. I am hopeful that the RAND report and information in Snow and Sweet's chapter will serve as a reminder that there is much we know how to do, a stimulus to many to begin doing those things that do increase comprehension.

Vygotsky and Bruner

Vygotskian and Brunerian thinking about the development of mind fill this volume (Bruner, 1986; Vygotsky, 1962). The Vygotskian position is that much of cognitive competence is learned in interaction with others, in particular with skilled adults who pass on cognitive skills and concepts. Thus, when teachers model comprehension processes for children, children begin to learn the tactics, with learning continuing as the children try to do as the adults do. This is particularly important in Chapter Two by Block and Johnson, who report new approaches to modeling comprehensive processes. One of Bruner's most important contributions was in making the point that adults do not just model and then expect children to be able to perform cognitive skills, but rather they provide supports of various sorts including new types of higher-level discussion of texts (as demonstrated by Almasi in Chapter Nine) and encroached text (as reported by Headley and Keeler in Chapter Ten). Thus, if a child tries predicting what might be in text but makes predictions that make little sense, the supportive parent might give the child a hint to think about how the story situation is like something the child knows. Such support is known as scaffolding, and like the scaffolding of a building that increasingly can support itself, the adult withdraws support as the child needs less and less help.

When I began my work on comprehension instruction, the thinking very much was that comprehension strategies would be passed directly to children. The Vygotskian and Brunerian positions are much more constructivist, with adults and children working together as the child tries out approaches and develops an understanding of comprehension processes and how to use and adapt them. The prominence of Vygotskian and Brunerian positions in this book make very clear that comprehension instruction is a completely constructivist perspective at the beginning of the twenty-first century.

What Comprehension Instruction Could Be

There have been great accomplishments in research on comprehension instruction. This is far from a finished research story, however. In fact, as great as the accomplishments are, I think we are closer to the beginning of the hunt for widely deployed comprehension instruction than we are near the end of the hunt.

Adding Comprehension Instruction to Existing Instruction

In Chapter Four, Pinnell made the point well that comprehension instruction can be added to existing instructional approaches, for example, teaching comprehension as part of guided reading lessons. In Chapter Five Dunston offered a very nice analysis about how to incorporate comprehension instruction into dialogical thinking. We need much, much more reflection on how comprehension teaching can be moved into instruction already occurring in school. As I have argued elsewhere (Pressley, 2002), comprehension instruction should be part of the balance of skills and higher-order teaching that occurs in every elementary classroom. Getting teachers to think about comprehension instruction as absolutely essential every day, as something that can be fit into the school day, will be no small accomplishment, however.

Developing Comprehension Instruction for All Readers

Since the 1970s researchers have focused on how to improve the reading of struggling readers, largely neglecting average and gifted readers. Fortunately, there are more than just weak readers in school. Unfortunately, we are operating under the assumption that the comprehension teaching that works with the weakest readers will also serve other children well. The strategies discussed in this text need to be evaluated fully with respect to all abilities.

It also cannot be missed that most cultural minorities are not well represented in the comprehension instruction literature. Wood's chapter (Chapter Six) reminded us that the type of instruction reviewed in this volume can probably be adapted in ways that will be powerfully appealing to different cultural groups. Studies evaluating how this can be done should be a high priority.

Teaching Comprehension for Different Purposes

We know a great deal about how people comprehend text in anticipation of a short-answer test. Unfortunately, this is a task that matters only in school. For the most part, our purposes for reading in the real world are very different, from reading for pleasure to reading to perform a particular task (for example, to assemble a bicycle) to reading to find important information (such as the best time of year to vacation in Toronto) to reading to teach something to a child (perhaps reviewing the Bill of Rights to help a fifth-grader understand them). Several authors in this volume correctly pointed out the need for much more understanding of the effects of different purposes on comprehension.

One of the most important purposes for reading is to do so in anticipation of writing something. The Hefflin and Hartman chapter (Chapter Eight) was a reminder that we know little about the connections between comprehension and writing in children. This is a huge gap, one that definitely needs filling with high quality research that is designed to inform instruction immediately. For example, we do want children to learn how to read as part of researching topics, with writing an obvious way to summarize the results of such research. How students find texts to read, what they do to locate relevant information in the texts read, and how they combine information across texts to write new texts are all mysteries for the most part. That is despite the fact that these are skills that every high school and college student is expected to exhibit. Perhaps if we learned how to develop these processes in young children, there would be greater competence in the student writing observed in secondary and postsecondary settings. Of course, there is also the possibility that learning to do such writing will also affect reading, perhaps developing a more critical understanding of information that is central and important in readings versus information that is less likely to prove useful later.

Instruction to Develop Critical Comprehenders

There was plenty in this volume about the development of critical thinking skills and critical comprehension skills (for example, see Block and Johnson in Chapter Two, Stevens and Bean in Chapter Fourteen, and Ridgeway, Peters, and Tracy in Chapter Thirteen). All that said, I think we are far from being certain about how to promote intelligent understanding of text, understanding that includes sifting the ideas in a text that are wheat from ideas that are chaff. We are far from knowing how to educate readers who will think hard about what they can do with ideas in text, when they apply and when they do not. There needs to be a great deal of thinking about how students can be taught to be comprehenders who use what they read for intelligent decision making. We know more about comprehension strategies that promote simple memory of text than we do comprehension strategies that promote critical understanding of ideas in text.

Instruction to Develop Fluent Comprehension

Although developing fluent word recognition is a clear goal of many reading educators, Reutzel, Camperell, and Smith (Chapter Fifteen) offered an equally important idea: they threw out the possibility of attempting to develop fluency in comprehension. Pressley and Afflerbach (1995) reported on fluent comprehension in their book *Verbal Protocols of Reading*. Good readers automatically use and report a variety of processes to make sense of text they read, from previewing and predicting based on world knowledge to summarizing and reviewing at the end of a reading. The fluent comprehender relates newly encountered ideas in text to prior knowledge, making appropriate inferences in doing so. The fluent comprehender jumps around in text, sometimes looking ahead for information that addresses a particular purpose and sometimes looking back to seek clarification for points that are confusing.

What does it take to develop such fluent comprehenders? We do not know, but I think it should be a high priority to find out. Presumably, it begins with instruction: word recognition instruction, teaching of vocabulary, and comprehension strategies instruction. Presumably as well, it depends on much practice reading, in particular of texts that permit expansive development of world knowledge that the reader can use to understand ever more demanding texts. The real question is how much reading—how many years of active reading—does it take for active comprehension processes to be automatic and all they can be. My guess is that the answer is "a while." My other sense is that fluent comprehension is not an all-or-nothing proposition, with it occurring earliest with familiar texts and expanding to more challenging and less familiar texts.

Why is fluency in comprehension processes important? If you have never used comprehension strategies, executing even one of them can be burdensome and difficult. Thus, the child first learning a summarization strategy struggles to construct summaries while reading. So much effort to execute the strategy takes a toll on the capacity available to understand what has been read. Thus, a child might struggle to construct summaries, construct them, and then not remember them a few minutes later. As strategies are more practiced, less capacity is taken up in their execution, more capacity is left over for actual understanding, and comprehension increases as a result. Presumably, the fluent comprehender is using relatively little capacity to execute strategies, permitting much capacity for understanding of text. The result can be that the fluent comprehender can take on difficult texts, ones requiring quite a bit of comprehension processing to understand, processing that occurs automatically and effortlessly, permitting the reader to get a great deal of understanding out of the predictions made, the images generated, the questions considered, the rereadings undertaken, and the summaries summarized.

Development of Comprehension of a Text over Readings and Time

Some of the most important texts in our lives are ones we read over and over. As this is being written, the first film in the *Lord of the Rings* trilogy is being released. The news is filled with comments from people who have been rereading Tolkien's classic for decades and writing about how their understanding of the text has increased over readings and time. We know nothing about how comprehension expands and elaborates over rereading and reflecting again on important texts. Rather, we know much about how people comprehend texts they read one time, texts they would never want to read a second time.

Comprehension Instruction for Many Text Types

A major criticism of elementary literacy instruction is that it is much too filled with narratives. The obvious omission is expository text, with many calls for increased teaching of expository comprehension. Of course, that makes sense, for so much of high school reading and beyond is of expository material. But even a healthy dose of expository reading will not prepare young readers for the variety of texts they may face, as contributors to this volume recognized. Kids are more and more interacting with books on CD-ROMs, hypertexts, and WebQuests, which have comprehension demands that are not yet understood, with a major challenge in the years ahead to discover how students can be taught to get the most out of such texts. The contributions of Rose and Dalton (Chapter Eleven), Labbo (Chapter Twelve), and Ridgeway, Peters, and Tracy (Chapter Thirteen) make the point that the scientific community is at least starting to think about comprehension with these new types of texts.

Need for More Existence Proofs

Benchmark School is the best existence proof that I know that comprehension instruction can be done well as part of an overall excellent program of instruction, even for greatly challenged learners (see Chapter Seventeen by Gaskins, Laird, O'Hara, Scott, & Cress). The problem is that there is only one Benchmark School. It is the best research-based educational institution I have ever encountered. I wish I could think of a few close runners-up. We need them. We need schools that emphatically make the point that excellence is possible.

What difference has Benchmark made? My own work on comprehension strategies instruction would not have been as rich or persuasive if I had not been able to spend time at Benchmark and watch its teachers do comprehension instruction across grades and the curriculum. Those who have found inspiration in my work to introduce comprehension strategies instruction in their schools were really inspired by Benchmark. We need that kind of inspiration in our world. I hope there are some aspiring radical educationalists who will do what Gaskins did: start a school, one that you will make simply excellent by doing all possible to translate the state-of-the-science knowledge of instruction into instructional reality for real kids. If this book inspires just one or two who will start such inspirational institutions, it will have been an amazing success.

Final Comment

What happened in the past thirty years was that many educational scientists and educators became determined to identify comprehension instruction that can really improve children's understanding of text. I've known many of the contributors in this volume as we have participated in this adventure together, with newcomers all the time (for example, Romeo). The search for comprehension strategies that worked was a great adventure, with great accomplishments as I summarized in the first part of this chapter. Great adventures still lie ahead, however, as summarized in the second half of the chapter, with plenty for the contributors to do during the second half of their illustrious careers. We now have to move what we know about improving comprehension into the larger world—into many more classrooms and schools, with sophisticated comprehension processing applied to many more types of texts by many more learners, and with strategies becoming habits of mind for young readers, teachers of readers, and lifetime readers who both explore new texts and return again and again to their favorites. What the researchers in this volume now know is going to be known by many others soon and will be much more apparent in the world than it is now.

References

Anderson, V. (1992). A teacher development project in transactional strategy instruction for teachers of severely reading-disabled adolescents. *Teaching and Teacher Education, 8,* 391–403.

Anderson, R. C., & Pearson, P. D. (1984). A schema-theoretic view of basic processes in reading. In P. D. Pearson (Ed.), *Handbook of reading research* (pp. 255–291). New York: Longman.

Beck, I. L., & McKeown, M. (1991). Conditions of vocabulary acquisition. In R. Barr, M. L. Kamil, P. Mosenthal, & P. D. Pearson (Eds.), *Handbook of reading research* (Vol. 2, pp. 789–814). White Plains, NY: Longman.

Brown, R., Pressley, M., Van Meter, P., & Schuder, T. (1996). A quasi-experimental validation of transactional strategies instruction with low-achieving second-grade readers. *Journal of Educational Psychology, 88,* 18–37.

Bruner, J. (1986). *Actual minds, possible worlds.* Cambridge, MA: Harvard University Press.

Collins, C. (1991). Reading instruction that increases thinking abilities. *Journal of Reading, 34,* 510–516.

Dickens, C. (2000). *A Christmas Carol.* New York: North-South Books.

Durkin, D. (1978–1979). What classroom observations reveal about reading comprehension instruction. *Reading Research Quarterly, 35,* 202–224.

Gough, P. B. (1984). Word Recognition. In P. D. Pearson (Ed.) *Handbook of Reading Research* (pp. 225–254). New York: Longman.

Keene, E. O., & Zimmermann, S. (1997). *Mosaic of thought: Teaching comprehension in a reader's workshop.* Portsmouth, NH: Heinemann.

Pressley, M. (1976). Mental imagery helps eight-year-olds remember what they read. *Journal of Educational Psychology, 68,* 355–359.

Pressley, M. (2002). *Reading instruction that works: The case for balanced teaching* (2nd ed.). New York: Guilford Press.

Pressley, M., & Afflerbach, P. (1995). *Verbal protocols of reading: The nature of constructively responsive reading.* Hillsdale, NJ: Erlbaum.

Pressley, M., Wharton-McDonald, R., Hampston, J. M., & Echevarria, M. (1998). The nature of literacy instruction in ten grade 4 and 5 classrooms in upstate New York. *Scientific Studies of Reading, 2,* 159–191.

Rosenblatt, L. M. (1978). *The reader, the text, the poem: The Transactional theory of the literary work.* Carbondale: Southern Illinois University Press.

Vygotski, L. (1962). *Thought and language.* Cambridge, MA: MIT Press.

Whitehead, A. N. (1929). *The aims of education.* Old Tappan, NJ: Macmillan.

Name Index

Subject Index

A

A to Zapp (computer game), 279–280

Abbreviated writing-to-reading practice: K-W-L strategy for, 205, 335; language experience approach to, 209–210; list-group-label approach to, 203–204; prereading plan for, 204; probable passages for, 206–207; reading recovery approach to, 210–211; scheme for, 202*t*; semantic mapping for, 205–206

Academic press approach, 381–382

AltaVista search engine, 299

American Library Association, 140

Analyze the task strategy, 380–381

Ask Jeeves (search tool), 299

At-risk students: teaching individual strategies to, 355–357; teaching repertoires of strategies for, 357–358. *See also* Struggling readers; Students with disabilities

Attribution theory, 327–328

Authoring cycle approach, 212–213

B

Babysitter's Club series, 183

Beach Music (Conroy), 112

Benchmark School: analyze the task strategy used at, 380–381; background information on, 371; beginning comprehension instruction at, 372–373; focus of comprehension instruction at, 381; instruction on identifying story elements, 373–377; as proof of good comprehension instruction, 397; recommendations on academic press approach for, 381–382; survey-predict–set a purpose strategy used at, 377–379; three categories of strategies used at, 379–380

Bilingual programs, 22–29

Boys: in peer discussions, 143–144; written communication by, 141–142

Brain: activity when performing language tasks, 259*fig*; activity with/without dyslexia reading, 261*fig*; affective networks of the, 265; computer images depicting activity in, 258*fig*; experience and learning in the, 261–263; how learning is distributed in, 258–260; individual differences/learning in the, 260–261; reading comprehension implications from research on, 265–266; reading comprehension and the, 263–265; strategic networks of the, 264–265; studying learning in the, 257–258*fig*

Bunker Elementary (California), 80

C

Cam Jansen and the Mystery of the Circus Clown (Adler), 107, 111, 115, 118, 121, 122, 125*e*

CAST Research Center, 260, 261, 263

Literacy learning (*continued*)
teacher understanding of, 99–
101. *See also* Learning
Literature-Based Activities (Yopp &
Yopp), 146
Lon Po Po IEPC lesson, 164*t*–165*t*,
166
Lord of the Rings (film), 396
Lunch (Pinnell), 118–120, 121, 122,
123, 126

M
McMullin's Vietnam WebQuest, 302,
303
Macropatterns, 215–216
Major Point Interview for Readers
(Keene, Goudvis, & Schwartz), 83
Meaning: critical literacy view on
textual, 310–311; monitoring of,
91*t*; strategies for expanding,
109*t*–110*t*, 123–124, 125*e*, 129*t*
Metacognition: comprehension
strategies using, 84–85; defining,
327
Microquestions, 216–217
"Misplaced concreteness" fallacy,
215
"Misplaced confidence" fallacy, 215
"The Monkey's Paw" (Jacobs), 189,
191, 193*e*–194*e*
Mosaic of Thought (Keene & Zimmerman), 81, 87
Motivation: using goals for student,
344; interactions among strategies, self-regulation and, 325–
328; link between instruction
and, 43; provided for comprehension instruction, 7–8; requiring application of knowledge,
137
Mountain View Elementary (South
Carolina), 245–246
Multiple Outcomes (Lesson Four),
72*fig*
Mumble reading, 158

My Book of the Planets (Krulik),
338–340*fig*

N
NAEP (National Assessment of Educational Progress): described, 3;
on good reader characteristics, 4;
on peer discussion benefits, 232;
suggestions regarding reading instruction by, 6–7
Narrative text structure, 325–326
National Research Council, 18
Nonprint medium: CD-ROM talking
books as, 275, 276, 280–285;
proliferation of visual/audio/
Internet, 140–141, 145–146;
promoting student interest using,
161–168. *See also* Computers
"Notable Children's Books" (American Library Association), 140
NRP (National Reading Panel), 18,
36, 39, 156, 168, 329, 331, 332,
333, 336

O
On-line resources, 298–300
Oral reading approaches, 157*t*–159
"Organizing and Enhancing a Read-
ing Program" (*Standards for Read-
ing Professionals*), 330

P
Paired/assisted reading, 158
Partner Reading and Retelling
Exercise, 160*e*
Peer discussion: based on *Dr. White*
(Goodall), 248*fig*; comprehension facilitated by, 230–232;
creating classroom context for,
237; DL-TA (directed listening–
thinking activity) used for, 247–
248; IRE participation structure
of, 229–230; monitoring of
comprehension to prepare for,
237–340; new directions in re-